Praise for *God and Ronald Reagan*

"What an outstanding and thoroughly documented demonstration of the role faith in God and Christ played in the life and leadership of President Reagan! Those who read Paul Kengor's excellent and readable book will better understand why even today those who wish to expunge all references to God from public life are determined to try to besmirch Reagan and his reputation which, thanks to this book, will be harder than ever to do."
        —Don Hodel, Secretary of the Interior, Reagan Administration

"An informed writer has presented clearly the spirituality of Ronald Reagan. Why has such a review taken so long? Part of the answer lies in President Reagan's quiet humility and selflessness. Both media and biographies have for the most part bypassed the President's total faith and trust in God. Paul Kengor now reveals the inner heart and soul of this great man, and the results."   —Judge William P. Clark, National Security Advisor, Reagan Administration

"Paul Kengor takes the reader to depths where no other writer has yet been— Ronald Reagan's very soul. He gives both historians and layman a vital and enlightening look at one of the most important leaders in American history."
        —Peter Schweizer, author of *Reagan's War*

"Ronald Reagan's deep religious faith has been overlooked because, in his typical modest way, Reagan kept it hidden in plain sight. Paul Kengor has performed a masterful service by shining a light on this underappreciated but central aspect of Reagan's life and statecraft."
        —Steven F. Hayward, author of *The Age of Reagan*

"An important volume about one of the most significant figures of the twentieth century. Ronald Reagan's spiritual beliefs were central to who he was, and this aspect of Reagan's life has been neglected by far too many historians and political scientists. Paul Kengor has filled the void with this superb book—no interpretation of Ronald Reagan will be complete without reference to this vital work."

     —Stephen Knott, Ronald Reagan Oral History Project,
     University of Virginia

"A penetrating history of the President's evolving religious faith."

     —Kenneth W. Thompson, University of Virginia

"Meticulously researched and insightful."

  —Andrew E. Busch, author of *Ronald Reagan and the Politics of Freedom*

"Throughout the Cold War, sophisticated people—conservatives and liberals alike—supposed that communism could possibly be contained, but not defeated. Ronald Reagan believed otherwise, and acted on that belief. Why did Reagan believe it could be done? In his fine new book, Paul Kengor argues that it was a matter of faith. In the vast body of Reagan scholarship, what has been missing is a spiritual biography. Kengor has admirably supplied our need."   —Robert P. George, Princeton University

GOD

a n d

RONALD REAGAN

a spiritual life

PAUL KENGOR, Ph.D.

HARPER  PERENNIAL

NEW YORK • LONDON • TORONTO • SYDNEY

To Nelle Reagan

HARPER ● PERENNIAL

A hardcover edition of this book was published in 2004 by ReganBooks, an imprint of HarperCollins Publishers.

GOD AND RONALD REAGAN. Copyright © 2004 by Paul Kengor. All rights reserved. Printed in the United States of America. No part of this book may be used or reproduced in any manner whatsoever without written permission except in the case of brief quotations embodied in critical articles and reviews. For information address HarperCollins Publishers Inc., 10 East 53rd Street, New York, NY 10022.

HarperCollins books may be purchased for educational, business, or sales promotional use. For information please write: Special Markets Department, HarperCollins Publishers Inc., 10 East 53rd Street, New York, NY 10022.

First paperback edition published 2005.
Reprinted in Harper perennial 2011.

Designed by Kris Tobiassen

The Library of Congress has cataloged the hardcover edition as follows:

Kengor, Paul, 1966–
    God and Ronald Reagan : a spiritual life / Paul Kengor—1st ed.
      p. cm.
    ISBN 978-0-06-057141-2 (alk. paper)
    1. Reagan, Ronald—Religion.   2. Religion and politics—United States—History—20th century.   3. United States—Politics and government—1945–1989.   4. Presidents—United States—Biography.   5. Governors—California—Biography.   I. Title.

E877.2.K46 2004
973.927'092—dc22
[B]
                                                2003069454

ISBN 978-0-06-057142-9 (pbk.)

11   12   13   WB/RRD   10 9 8 7 6 5 4 3 2

CONTENTS

PREFACE

"Whenever Mr. Reagan delivers a speech, he always mentions his religious feelings."

—*Soviet news analyst Anatoly Krasikov, November 22, 1986*[1]

"My own prayer is that I can . . . perform the duties of this position so as to serve God."

—*Ronald Reagan, letter to Bernard Cardinal Law, Archbishop of Boston, March 11, 1987*[2]

My rendezvous with the religious Ronald Reagan started with a close reading of his Evil Empire speech when I was an undergraduate. Those two words he used to describe the Soviet Union may have been critiqued by the media as strident political rhetoric, but within them I perceived something else, something more surprising: a striking and cohesive religious declaration.

A decade and a half later I had a deeper encounter with the same speech, this time as a professor sitting silently at a table in the Reagan Library. As I huddled in a remote research room perched high upon a hillside overlooking a balmy, picturesque landscape in Simi Valley, California, an archivist brought over a cart of materials from the Presidential Handwriting File, a large collection of Reagan Administration documents marked by Reagan's personal handwriting. In Box 9, Folder 150, I met the real Evil Empire speech—and the real Reagan.

That inked-up speech copy was an awakening. Reagan's hand was all over it—deleting a word here, inserting whole new pages there. I read slowly and carefully. Here was the elusive, behind-the-scenes Reagan few had seen or known. And in that seventeen-page anticommunist manifesto, I had stumbled upon yet more evidence of Reagan's intense religious thinking, which had already unexpectedly snowballed into an avalanche as I perused his public presidential papers.[3]

Prior to that moment in the library, I'd been engaged in writing a relatively straightforward book on Reagan's personal role in his administration's effort to undermine the Soviet empire. Not long into that book, I realized that I'd be including a unique chapter on his spiritual views and motivations. That chapter grew into three chapters. In the months to come, as I accumulated further evidence from other sources concerning Reagan's religious beliefs, the story of the former president's faith overtook the rest of the book.

It was odd: Reagan was said to be private about his faith, not sharing it with those around him. To a significant extent, that was true.[4] Yet there it was—an endless trail of religious remarks that coursed unmistakably through his papers and letters. Almost everywhere I seemed to look, there he was: the religious Reagan, motivated in every aspect of his life and career by his spiritual convictions.

That moment was a turning point in the life of this book. My re-search on Reagan's religious beliefs would give rise to a new work al-together.

THIS IS A SPIRITUAL BIOGRAPHY OF RONALD REAGAN. IT begins where his religious life began, in his earliest childhood. At least at the outset, Reagan's was a typical religious life for a man of his time and place; it began as he confronted the typical questions that believers in most historical ages have dealt with. Once Ronald Rea-gan left his hometown, however, his life became anything but typical. His religious sensibility was soon accompanied by a political sensibil-ity, each complementing and informing the other. And by the time he was a young man, Reagan was aware of an international move-ment that ran in direct, violent opposition to everything he stood for: the atheistic strain of communism that precipitated the Russian Revolution of 1917.

Reagan's life and political career coincided almost exactly with the rise and fall of communism in Russia. He was born on February 6, 1911, in Tampico, Illinois; when the Bolsheviks launched their bloody coup in St. Petersburg in October 1917, he was an innocent six-year-old. Only days after that revolutionary fire broke out in Russia—with Vladimir Lenin emerging from the flames—the Uni-versalist church in Dixon, Illinois, burned to the ground.[5] Five years later the First Christian Church emerged from the ashes on that same spot; that sanctuary, at 123 S. Hennepin Avenue, would shape young Ronald Reagan as surely as the coals of the Russian Revolution forged Lenin.

As Lenin was nearing death in the first month of 1924, Reagan was approaching his teen years. When Joseph Stalin at last seized absolute power, Reagan was heading to the friendly confines of Eureka College. As Stalin murdered tens of millions, Reagan was looking for a job. As the Soviet communists pursued the expansion of Marxism-Leninism and their brutal campaign against religion, the mature Reagan watched with pity, disgust, and a commitment not to be silent. By the time he became president in January 1981, he was not only ready to take action against Lenin's empire, he was committed to doing so by every means necessary.

Only in that moment, perhaps, does it become clear how deep, and how atypical, the man's faith actually was. When faced with what he saw as a dark force of history—Soviet communism—Reagan met it with not only his political but his spiritual beliefs. The Cold War is recognized by historians as the great ideological struggle of the twentieth century, but to many—including those jailed in the USSR for religious reasons—it also represented the great struggle for faith in the twentieth century. Reagan shared that view.

Thus, this spiritual biography, like Reagan's own pilgrimage, will culminate in President Reagan's personal "crusade"—a word both he and Soviet commentators used to describe his actions—to undermine Soviet communism.

That is the journey explored by this book. We'll trace Reagan's journey from the baptismal tank of the First Christian Church on S. Hennepin in Dixon in 1922 to the podium at a tense, packed Moscow State University in 1988. And we'll examine Reagan's vision of America as both a divinely ordained beacon of freedom—a "shining city upon a hill"—and a nation chosen, in his view, to place a stake in the future of communism.

While Reagan's religious belief system was distinctively Christian, the goal of this exploration is not to prove his faith, to debate whether he was a good Christian, or to assess the sophistication of his religious views. Nor is the goal to categorize his theology or where he best fit denominationally.[6] My concern is with Reagan's spiritual beliefs: how they mattered, and how they strongly affected his thinking and actions. Most important, my intention is to underscore that it's impossible to understand Ronald Reagan fully—and especially his Cold War actions—without grasping the influence of religion on his thought.

Alzheimer's disease felled Reagan only a few short years after the USSR fell onto that ash heap of history he foresaw. Mercifully, his mind lasted long enough to recognize what had happened. Soviet communism had met an end he had pursued for more than forty years.[7] In part, as he himself said, his campaign was motivated by his belief that as a Christian he was "enjoined by Scripture" to resist and attack evil wherever it lurks. As he told a Joint Session of the Irish National Parliament on June 4, 1984, he believed the "struggle between freedom and totalitarianism today" was ultimately not a test of arms or missiles "but a test of faith and spirit." It was, he said, a "spiritual struggle."[8]

This, then, is not simply a story of an influential man in a powerful position who came to believe that God had chosen him for a special purpose. Reagan's religious faith was a critical factor in one of the most important events of the twentieth century. It had an immense impact on his thinking and action toward Soviet communism and the Cold War. As the Soviets themselves recognized in a formal statement from TASS, the official Soviet news agency, "President Reagan uses religion with particular zeal to back his anti-Soviet policy."[9]

Obviously, it would be too strong to claim that Ronald Reagan's faith alone brought about the downfall of communism. But it was in-

tricately tied to that event. For as with most individuals highly influenced by their religious beliefs, Reagan's faith had a profound affect
on how he lived, on what he did, and on those around him. It just so
happened that what Reagan did involved one of the supreme contests
of the twentieth century.

1.

Jack and Nelle

"You can be too big for God to use, but you cannot be too small."

—*an annotation in Nelle Reagan's Bible[1]*

January 20, 1924, was a blustery cold, wind-swept Sunday across
the plains of Illinois. According to the *Dixon Evening Telegraph*,
tiny Alton, Illinois, had been hit the night before with "the heaviest
and most spectacular" snowstorm of the winter. Rail, streetcar, and
automobile traffic was plunging valiantly through the storm, but by
ten o'clock all were losing the fight. The weather was so cold near
Chicago, where the temperature dipped to eighteen degrees below
zero, that many of the entries in the International Tournament of the
Norge Ski Club failed to jump. And if that weren't enough, the Associated Press was reporting that "a new cold wave" was on its way from
Alaska, threatening to exceed already-record lows.

Suffering through the freeze, in the northwest corner of the state,
was idyllic little Dixon, home to Jack and Nelle Reagan and their two

sons. Dixon sits some one hundred miles west of Chicago, and less than an hour's drive to the Mississippi River and the Iowa border. The town is geographically unusual by Illinois standards: the terrain of Illinois is largely flat, but Dixon is nestled among woods and rolling hills. Most of the state was dusted by a fine snow blowing across naked fields, the kind of cutting snow that hurts when it assaults uncovered faces. Dixon, however, enjoyed some protection on that frigid day.

Long before Ronald Reagan, the town already had its run-ins with presidential history. On May 12, 1832, Captain Abraham Lincoln and his company of mounted volunteers arrived at Fort Dixon on the Rock River to serve in the Blackhawk War. Lt. Col. Zachary Taylor was in command, and Lt. Jefferson Davis swore in recruits. At that moment, three future presidents saluted together in obscure Dixon: Taylor became U.S. president in 1848, Lincoln in 1860, and Jefferson Davis became president of the Confederacy shortly thereafter. (A colorful painting of the encounter by local artist Fran Swarbrick resides today in the building where Ronald Reagan attended school.)

A continent away on that January day in 1924, fifty-three-year-old Vladimir Ilyich Lenin lay near death in an even colder—in many ways—Bolshevik Russia. He had few hours remaining. As Lenin clung to life, twelve-year-old Dutch Reagan clung to his hymnal in the comfort of a pew near the front of the First Christian Church in Dixon, beside his beaming mother, Nelle. Filled with the spirit, Nelle had just finished her closing prayer with her True Blue Sunday school class.

Though no one in that contented congregation could know it, this was the start of a spiritual pilgrimage that would lead that boy in the front pew to a spot in front of a bust of a grim Lenin at Moscow State University sixty-four years later, inspired with a religious drive very much like what he and his mother had felt that Sunday in 1924.

As Reagan would recognize, Lenin too had been moved by a kind of religious zeal, though very different from his own. It was the clash of their belief systems that would make possible their rendezvous on May 31, 1988.

And it was Nelle Reagan who would inculcate her innocent boy with a set of beliefs that helped convince him of the need to defeat the Soviet Union. She and the faith she imparted were the central forces in his life. Without them it is difficult to imagine Ronald Reagan becoming president, let alone mounting a crusade against "godless Soviet communism."

FROM ALL EVIDENCE, IT APPEARS THAT RONALD Reagan's faith peaked in intensity at the bookends of his life—during his youth in Dixon, and again in his mature years as president and former president of the United States.

The origins of Reagan's faith were forged in the 1910s, his first decade of life, and the ideas he formed there persisted in his belief system through the 1990s. They predated by far his key political beliefs, which weren't set in stone until the late 1940s—and, by some measure, until his Republican conversion in the 1960s. The historical record demonstrates abundantly that Reagan was driven by those core political convictions. What has gone overlooked is how deeply, and for how much longer, his core *religious* convictions moved him.

How did he come by his spiritual beliefs? There were a number of key influences.

NELLE AND JACK

Ronald Reagan's parents were John Edward and Nelle Clyde Wilson Reagan, called simply Jack and Nelle by their friends (and by their children, at their own request). Jack was a first-generation Irishman, Nelle from Irish-English-Scottish stock. Both hailed from the town of Fulton, in Whiteside County, Illinois, where they were born within eleven days of each other in July 1883. A couple of decades later they were married, on a crisp fall day in November 1904 at the Catholic Church of the Immaculate Conception in Fulton.[2]

Though Nelle grew up as the youngest of seven, she and Jack had only two children: Ronald and his older brother Neil, who was given the nickname "Moon" by his parents. The young couple seemed carefree in their early years. Each was good-looking, with an attractive personality; they were a fun pair. But that began to change, slowly at first, with the arrival of the boys. Though theirs seemed largely a happy home, with normal problems, there was a split in the Reagan household over religion. It was not a major rift that created bickering, but a difference nonetheless: Jack was Catholic; Nelle a Protestant.

One overriding concern both parents shared was that their boys should believe in God and go to church. Nelle, however, was much more earnest in her faith than Jack, who was apparently more apathetic. (Certainly he was no Bible thumper.)[3] By Dutch's own account, his father left the boys' religious rearing to Nelle.[4]

Nelle's stronger commitment drew Dutch toward her faith. She made her life a model of Christian virtue, and her example begged emulation. At ease with herself and in helping others, Nelle Reagan proved herself a woman of genuine faith, warmly expressed.[5]

Jack's influence did make its mark on Dutch's faith—though in other, less flattering ways. Whereas Nelle apparently thought about God not just daily but constantly, her husband was consumed with something else: making a living. Money dominated his thoughts. The Reagans had little or no savings, and Jack's obsession with money seemed less a matter of greed than of survival. He scraped and scrapped so that he and his family could get by. And before long, drinking—a lot of drinking—was helping him cope with his ever-present financial struggles.

"They were awful poor," said the Reagans' neighbor Cenie Straw. Another neighbor, Helen Lawton, recalled that her family frequently sent plates of food to the Reagan house. Lawton's father even built a hinge onto the Reagan kitchen window, so food could be easily set inside. "It wasn't that we had so much," said Lawton, "but we had a garden. And they only had an electric plate to cook on."[6]

Jack was a shoe salesman with a habit of chasing rainbows. He uprooted the family at every turn. Throughout young Dutch Reagan's childhood, his family never owned a home; they were always on the hunt for an affordable rental.

From February to May 1911, the family lived in a second-floor apartment above the bank in Tampico, where Dutch was born. Baby Ronald lived in his first home only four months before the family moved to 104 W. Glassman Street, a house opposite the rail depot outside of town; they stayed there until December 1914. The family's next Christmas was spent in the big city, near the University of Chicago, where the Reagans rented two apartments. Jack sized up patrons in the shoe section of Marshall Field's department store. It was not an easy stay for young Dutch, who almost died from a bout with bronchial pneumonia.[7]

The Reagans left Chicago for Jack's job selling shoes at O.T. Johnson in Galesburg, Illinois, where they lived in a pair of houses a block apart on N. Kellogg. It was as a five-year-old in Galesburg that Reagan had a kind of epiphany.[8] Wrestling with the loneliness of a little boy who had just moved to a third new town in five years, young Dutch ventured alone to the attic of his latest home. There he found a large collection of bird's eggs and butterflies enclosed in glass, left behind by the previous tenant. In the weeks to follow, the curious first-grader escaped into the attic for hours at a time, "marveling at the rich colors of the eggs and the intricate and fragile wings of the butterflies." To him these collected wonderments were like "gateways." "The experience," Reagan remembered, "left me with a reverence for the handiwork of God that never left me."[9] The notion of a Creator was etched into the boy's consciousness.

This event took place several years before he was baptized. He later thanked that previous tenant as "an anonymous benefactor to whom I owe much."[10] Jack's never-ending moves may have brought his family desolation, yet in retrospect his son Ronald might have reflected (as he generally did) that even his family's trials seemed to be part of God's plan.[11]

From Galesburg, the Reagans hit the road again. As American doughboys fought the Kaiser in Europe, the Reagan family occupied no less than three different residences in Monmouth between early 1917 and August 1919. The stay in Monmouth was hardly uneventful. The family moved there when Dutch was in second grade. Shortly after, the jubilant Illinois town celebrated the end of WWI; that was followed by the influenza epidemic of 1918–19. Dutch was alarmed by the sight of townspeople donning masks, of the wreaths with black ribbons that adorned local doorways. Affected areas were quarantined, and schools, libraries, dance halls, even churches closed, though ministers were busier than ever tending to the dying. The mounting toll was chronicled in a death column in the daily paper.[12]

The flu hit Nelle as well. Though it wiped her out, and she nearly perished, ultimately Reagan's mother escaped the early death that came to millions of young mothers around the world. Nelle had been a healthy middle-aged Midwestern woman before the epidemic, but at her worst Dutch, Moon, and Jack thought she was a goner. The experience brought the idea of mortality close to home for all of them.

The Reagans were back in Tampico through December 1920, in an apartment on Main Street above Pitney's Shoestore, where Jack was shop manager. Though his return to Tampico was brief, Reagan, ever the optimist, would have nothing but fond memories of his second stay, which he called his "Huck Finn years."[13] But happiness was halted again shortly thereafter, as the Reagans reloaded the Model T.

The family finally "settled" in Dixon shortly thereafter, though they would live in five different rented houses—portions of which they subleased to pay their own rent—before Dutch left for his first job at WOC radio in Davenport, Iowa, in 1932.[14]

Moving, of course, is never easy for children, and young Ronald lived in five different towns and twelve rented apartments before he reached his teen years. At any given spot, he could have easily forgotten his address. This took a toll on the boy, making him lonely and introverted. Dutch Reagan walked by himself to each new school, day after day. The perpetual new kid, he was regularly exposed to the mean-spirited, uncaring glares, taunts, and whispers of other kids. At the end of the school day, he strolled "home" alone to the latest residence, often with a handful of bullies dogging his step. As an adult, he frequently remembered the day they chased him all the way to his front door. A stern Nelle barred the entrance, forcing her son to fend for his dignity, which he did with flailing fists and some success.[15]

Dutch spent many of his days without playmates in these years, entertaining himself in the yard, on the porch, in the parlor, in the attic. Then, just as he was finally settling in and beginning to make friends—his natural good looks always helped—Jack packed the bags and the whole miserable process would repeat itself. As a young man, then, Ronald Reagan came to see a danger in making friends—the risk that any new friend would sooner or later disappear from his life forever. Decades later, he acknowledged that his nomadic life as a child had probably made him "a little slow in making friends. In some ways I think this reluctance to get close to people never left me entirely."[16]

This created a void in the young Reagan—a hole that religion came to fill. In need of a rock of reliability, he looked to where his mother, his heart, and his desolation pointed him—upward. And in God he found what he perceived as a permanent friend. No matter how often Jack Reagan should relocate his family, his son saw that he could get close to God without any fear of abandonment. God the Father was always in his place, constant, always with the boy, and always in his perfect heaven. Dutch Reagan may have been a stranger to all those peering kids, but he was never foreign to God, who knew him wherever he went.

God also provided a reliable paternal figure for young Reagan, whose own father was less than a steadying force in the family. Reagan loved his father and knew he had the family's best interests at heart, but Jack Reagan didn't offer the unwavering stability his son needed. "He couldn't really *rely* on his father," his daughter Patti has said.[17]

Years later, in remarking on Reagan's apparent aloofness, his good friend Paul Laxalt said that the president was a "loner" even in his relationship with God.[18] Perhaps this is no surprise, considering that he first sought and connected to God as a lonely boy.

This is not to suggest that Ronald Reagan's spirituality was purely emotional—a "crutch," as skeptics often characterize religious faith. At a relatively young age Reagan's became an intellectual Christianity, and it would remain so. But his religious beliefs were always marked by a degree of emotionality, and there's no doubt that the emotional appeal of religion was a key factor in his boyhood.

Intriguingly, another failing of Jack's may have contributed further to Dutch's turn to God. It came to a head on a brisk February evening in Dixon in 1922, shortly after young Reagan's eleventh birthday. He had just strolled up the 800 block of South Hennepin, returning from a basketball game at the YMCA. He knew that Nelle was out on a sewing job, trying to scare up a few dollars, and he was expecting to come home to an empty house. Instead, he was shaken by the sight of Jack sprawled out in the snow on the front porch, passed out, flat on his back, freezing, too inebriated to make it to the door. "He was drunk," his son later remembered. "Dead to the world." The boy leaned over and smelled the whiskey escaping through his dad's long snores. His hair was soaked with melted snow, matted unevenly against the side of his reddened face.[19]

Jack's arms were stretched out, recalled his son, "as if he were crucified—as indeed he was." He had been taken by the "dark demon in the bottle." Dutch stood over his father for a minute or two, not sure how to react. He wanted to simply let himself in the door, go to bed, and pretend his dad wasn't there.

Dutch grabbed a fistful of the old man's overcoat and heaved him toward the door. He dragged him into the house and to the bedroom, out of the way of the weather's harm and the neighbors' fixed attention. It was a sad moment for father and son. Dutch felt no anger, no resentment, just grief. This was the man who until that point had always carried *him*. Surely, to see his father so out of control must have frightened him. His world was in chaos—again, just when it seemed to have stopped spinning, when Dixon appeared to be the last stop on the Reagan family train.

The event occurred at a crucial time in young Reagan's spiritual development. Four months later he would be baptized, starting life over as a child of God; the thought of his father sprawled spread-eagle in the snow might have lingered in Reagan's mind that day, as it would for the rest of his life.

NELLE AND THE CHURCH

Jack Reagan's role in his son's faith may have been unintentional. Nelle's, on the other hand, was very deliberate. She became the formative figure in making Ronald Reagan a Christian.

Nelle chose the Disciples of Christ denomination, also known today as the Christian Church. Founded as separate entities in Western Pennsylvania, Ohio, and Kentucky, the Christian Church and Disciples of Christ were unified at a meeting in Lexington, Kentucky, on New Year's Day 1832 before moving westward.[20] By the 1830s, Illinois was proving ripe territory for the spread of the Disciples.[21] One historian described the farmer-preacher pioneers of the Disciple movement in Illinois as "the voice of democracy, of individualism in the religious sphere."[22] There, in the early 1900s, the Disciples eventually reached Nelle Reagan.

Biographers usually begin the story of Nelle's own faith in Dixon, but her role in the church in Tampico deserves attention. In the last months before Jack moved the family yet again, Nelle was very active in the church on 201 Fremont Street. Drawn by a 1910 revival held there, one source claims that Nelle ran the pastorless church virtually single-handed, writing bulletins, preparing Sunday programs, prodding the congregation to better support the struggling church, and even possibly doing a fair amount of preaching. The preaching itself is difficult to confirm, though not out of the realm of possibility.[23] Even after moving to Dixon, Nelle made frequent trips back to Tampico to help her old church, with Dutch in tow.

Settled in Dixon, Nelle joined a local Disciples congregation led by Reverend Harvey Waggoner. The group first met in the basement of the town's YMCA until it could raise funds for a building. The new church opened at 123 S. Hennepin on June 18, 1922.

Nelle became a leader, eventually a pillar, in the local church. Aside from the minister, she was perhaps its most visible face. Among the congregation's fourteen officers she was the only one who wore two hats—and often more, whether directing the choir, missionary society, the "Cradle Roll" nursery, or some other function. The vigorous congregation boasted fourteen Sunday school classes each week. Among these, Nelle's True Blue class was the largest. The church directory for 1922 registered thirty-one students in her class; the pastor's class had only five, his wife's nine.[24]

It was said that if Nelle had had the education she would have taken the pulpit herself; no doubt today she would have been ordained.[25]

Nelle gave religious readings, both outside the church and within—a service for which she was in great demand. Blessed with an engaging voice and the confidence of a natural performer—qualities she passed on to her son—she also acted in many plays. She was the only performer to hold two roles in a May 1924 drama called *The Pill Bottle*, described in the town paper as "a delightful portrayal of missionary work." In June 1926, she brought the house down at the Baptist church with a reading titled "The Ship of Faith." "Mrs. Reagan is one of Dixon's favorite readers," the *Telegraph* informed, "and has appeared before many audiences, always greatly pleasing them."[26]

Nelle was renowned in Dixon for her recitations, self-written stories and poems that were frequently published locally. Some of these focused not just on God but also democracy. Eight years after the WWI armistice, Nelle published an "Armistice Day Poem" in the November 11, 1926, *Telegraph*, in which she urged that "God forbid that we forget" those soldiers who gave their lives. Those brave men, wrote Nelle, "have won for the world democracy, and doomed forever and always the cruel autocracy." One Wednesday afternoon in 1927, Nelle appeared at the American Legion to give what was described as a "splendid talk" on the boyhood of George Washington—surely a story that must have made an impression on young Dutch.[27]

Typically, however, Nelle's thoughts and works were fixed heavenward. A firm believer in the power of prayer, she led prayer meetings at church. When the minister vacationed in Missouri, she was put in charge of Mid-week Prayers, and she led discussions on prayer outside the sanctuary. Along with four other women, Nelle acted as a "leader," providing "home prayer services." In a January 1926 prayer discussion held at the home of Mrs. James Kindig, described by the *Telegraph* as "most interesting," Nelle said: "We cannot expect to get much out of prayer, unless we put much in it. . . . Draw nigh to God, and He will draw nigh to you."[28]

Nelle's commitment to the Disciples was never restricted to the Dixon town lines. She also offered a hand to other churches in the area. When the Disciples congregation in Grand Detour underwent reorganization in 1928, Nelle endured the snowy drive each Thursday in February to help the church's Young People's Choir.[29]

It would almost trivialize Nelle Reagan to characterize her as an occasional "faith healer," given the image the term conjures up today. Nonetheless, she developed a reputation as someone whose prayers were powerful, even to the extent that they might cure the sick. As Mildred Neer, a fellow church member, recalled:

When our little daughter was about four years old, she developed what seemed to be tonsillitis. The doctor said it was that and prescribed medicine. . . . We returned to him several times for a couple of weeks, and he prescribed other medicines, but they did no good. Finally, an abscess developed on her neck, which swelled to twice . . . normal size. She become so ill she could neither eat nor sleep. . . . On Sunday morning my husband said to me, "Why don't you go to church? It will do you good." . . . [The pastor] spoke on how we as Christians should accept death. I could hardly take the sermon because we did not know whether our daughter was going to live. When the service was dismissed, I couldn't leave my seat. At last, everybody had left except Mrs. Reagan who was on the platform gathering up the music that the choir members had left.

I thought, "If only I could talk to Mrs. Reagan," and went up to her. . . . I told her about our daughter, and she said, "Let's go into the back room." . . . We did. Then Mrs. Reagan said, "Let's get down on our knees and pray about it." She made a wonderful prayer and when [we stood] I felt the prayer was answered. . . . I went home. . . . Pretty soon there was a knock on the door. It was Mrs. Reagan. . . . She spent the whole afternoon [in prayer] with us. . . . She left about six o'clock. . . . Moments later the abscess burst. . . . The next morning the doctor said, "I don't need to lance this." . . . God had heard Nelle Reagan's prayer and answered it.[30]

Another member of the congregation recalled:

Many of us believed Nelle Reagan had the gift to heal. She never laid on the hands or anything like that. It was the way she prayed, down on her knees, eyes raised up and speaking like she knew God personally, like she had had lots of dealings with him before. If someone had real troubles or was sick, Nelle would come to their house and kneel and pray. Maybe she didn't always pray herself a miracle, but folks could bear things a lot better after she left.[31]

Given such stories, which quickly became common knowledge in the Reagans' congregation, it is hardly surprising that even as an adult Nelle's son believed so strongly in the power of prayer.

"Lemme tell you," one Dixon resident later commented, "Nelle was a saint." That was not a rare sentiment. "If there is such a thing as a saint on earth, it is Nelle Reagan," said Mildred Neer. Cenie Straw agreed: "Nelle was too good for this world."[32] One member of the congregation called Nelle a leader "everybody loved."[33]

NELLE'S WORK

Nelle Reagan dedicated her life quite earnestly to the "poor and help-less." It was a promise she is said to have made to her own mother on her mother's deathbed. Nelle extended her ministry to hospitals and mental institutions, to the tuberculosis (TB) sanitarium every Thursday, and in her weekly visits to the local jail, where she came equipped with apples, cookies, and her Bible. By all accounts, neither the prisoners nor the contagious TB gave her a moment's pause.[34]

She gave special attention to those behind bars. After a modest lunch of crackers at the dress shop, where she worked as a seamstress, she headed faithfully to the jail to read the Bible to the incarcer-ated.[35] One contemporary said that Nelle's flair as an "elocutionist"—notably in her "dramatic readings" of Scripture—made her a favorite among prisoners.

There are even accounts of criminals allegedly changing their be-havior as a direct result of her ministry—one actually in the midst of a criminal act. According to Cenie Straw, who was active in the church, the "kid" in question had been released from jail. Having hitched a ride to nearby Sterling, he was planning on pulling out his concealed gun and holding up the driver. As he sat in the car contemplating his dirty deed, he thought of what Nelle had told him about Jesus during one of her jail visits, and had a change of heart. "Goodbye, thanks for the ride," he reportedly told the driver, stepping out of the car. "You'll find a gun in the back of the seat. I was going to use it, but I was talking to a woman at the jail. . . ."[36]

Three women who grew up with the Reagans tell stories of Nelle picking up hitchhikers on long drives, with no fear of being harmed. Some prisoners—mostly in jail for theft or drunk-and-disorderly citations—were released to Nelle's custody and ended up sleeping in the family's sewing room until they found another situation.[37] "She had faith God would protect her for doing the right thing," said one Reagan neighbor.[38]

Some of those men released and welcomed into the Reagan house were African Americans—"coloreds," in the language of the time. Here was one of many ways that Dutch learned racial tolerance. And prisoners weren't the only ones to whom she extended hospitality: on one occasion two visiting basketball players, both black, had no place to stay in town. Young Ronald brought them home to spend the night and have breakfast. The two visitors stood hesitantly at the door, fearing their friendly host's mom would change her mind when she saw their skin color. When Nelle saw the three of them she smiled and said "Come in, boys."[39]

Among Nelle's chief concerns at church was the Missionary Society, which she served as president. In March 1921, she assembled a group of sixty at a local home where a collection was taken for the poverty-stricken of Europe.[40] She even did some work on behalf of Russian believers. In the summer of 1924, she helped raise money to erect a chapel for the Russian church in New York City, a symbolic act that showed solidarity with Russian Christians.[41]

Nelle was a prodigious newspaper reader, who followed international events closely out of personal interest and a sense of Christian obligation. It was another interest that found its way into her itinerary: in April 1927, at the home of the Fellows family on 723 Peoria Avenue, for example, she held a talk on Japan and the status of Christianity there.[42]

A few months later, at her own home, Nelle hosted the Woman's Missionary Society; the topic was "The Large World—My Neighborhood." The theme of the discussion was that the world was slow in applying the spirit of Christ to nations and relationships; such broader fellowship, the ladies all agreed, would provide "the great cure for war, crime, and sin of every kind."[43] Such confidence in the power of the Holy Spirit was not unlike the thinking of Ronald Wilson Reagan sixty years later.

NELLE REAGAN HAD A HEART FOR GOD, AND SHE DID her best to impart that faith to her son Ronald. It was *her* aspiration that he should one day take that faith to the world. And she began his training with a particular book that would make a major impression on her young son.

2.

That Printer of Udell's

"I want to be like that man, and I want to be baptized."

—*Dutch Reagan, age eleven, after reading*
That Printer of Udell's[1]

Nelle was not the only Reagan to play a role in the Dixon church. On July 21, 1922, three days after the church opened on S. Hennepin, Dutch, his brother, Neil, and twenty-three others were the first to be baptized in the new church.[2]

The Disciples consider baptism a holy sacrament, and practice it by immersion. Most Disciples baptisms occur between the ages of twelve to fifteen; Dutch was immersed at age eleven. When he arose from the water and heard the minister command him, "Arise and walk in newness of faith," he said he felt "called"—and that in that moment he had had "a personal experience when I invited Christ into my life."[3]

As an adult, Ronald Reagan would refer to the Bible as his fa-

vorite book, and as "the greatest message ever written." That its
words were of divine origin and inspiration he said he "never had any
doubt."[4] Yet the Bible was not the only book that played a role in
Dutch's arrival at the immersion tank in 1922. The other book is far
less well-known, a page-turning novel that changed the direction of
his life.

Fifty years later, Reagan would recall that moment when asked
which books he had read as a young person. Most of the books he
named were the sort one might expect a boy in the heartland to read
in the early 1900s. But there was one exception. The book that had
"made a lasting impression on me at about the age of 11 or 12, mainly
because of the goodness of the principal character," he said, was one
"I'm sure you never heard of."[5] The book was *That Printer of Udell's: A
Story of the Middle West*, written by Harold Bell Wright and published
in 1903.[6] Wright, himself a child of the Midwest whose drunkard father constantly moved the family from town to town, eventually became a Disciples minister and moved to California. The plainspoken
minister-author with a knack for communication preached that God
had a plan for everyone.

Reagan mentioned *Udell's* again in his memoirs, when speaking
of his "heroes." He described the work as a "wonderful book about a
devout itinerant Christian," which "made such an impact on me that
I decided to join my mother's church."[7] And in a letter he wrote from
the White House to author Harold Bell Wright's daughter-in-law, he
added:

> It is true that your father-in-law's book, indeed books, played a def-
> inite part in my growing-up years. *When I was only ten or eleven years
> old, I picked up Harold Bell Wright's book, That Printer of Udell's. . . .*
> and read it from cover to cover. . . .

That book . . . had an impact I shall always remember. After reading it and thinking about it for a few days, I went to my mother and told her I wanted to declare my faith and be baptized. We attended the Christian Church in Dixon, and I was baptized several days after finishing the book.

The term, "role model," was not a familiar term in that time and place. But I realize I found a role model in that traveling printer whom Harold Bell Wright had brought to life. *He set me on a course I've tried to follow even unto this day. I shall always be grateful.* [Reagan's emphasis][8]

DICK AND MOM, DUTCH AND MOM

The first words of *That Printer of Udell's* are "O God, take ker o' Dick!" This was the final plea of the broken-hearted, dying mother of the novel's protagonist, Dick Walker. Little Dickie's mother was a committed Christian who suffered at the hands of a horrible creature—an alcoholic, abusive spouse. In the opening scene, Dick's mom succumbs as his father lies passed out on the floor in a drunken stupor.

Young Dick escapes. He immediately runs away from home, and eventually becomes a tramp in Boyd City. No one will hire him, including the Christians he appeals to in a brave, moving moment when he wanders into a church, attracted by the music, words, and warmth his late mother had described to him. The young vagabond goes inside for inspiration and guidance, knowing from what his mother has taught him that this is a good place, a place of refuge and stability he can count on. Like Nelle Reagan, Dick's mother conditioned him to find comfort in God. Dick had no home of his own, always moving, always surrounded by strangers, often isolated. At church, with God, he found an anchor.

This church scene is a pivotal part of the book. Here Dick Walker learns about the church, himself, and the difference between phony and real, or "practical," Christianity. A practical Christian, the book makes clear, is one who would give Dick a job.[9]

Fortunately, a man named George Udell hires him as a printer, setting young Dick off on a Horatio Alger–style path to personal and spiritual improvement and fulfillment. He becomes a prominent player in the church and community—a man of action.

That Printer of Udell's is an evangelical novel, the kind of thing that might only find a spot today in the fiction section of a Christian bookstore. It features chapters with titles like "Philippians 4:8," a section of the New Testament that emphasizes the importance of prayer for "everything" and, in Christ's words, exhorts Christians: "Whatever you have learned or received or heard from me, or seen in me—put it into practice."[10]

Reagan later said that he picked up the book after seeing his mother reading it.[11] Accounts of how the book ended up in his hands differ: either he picked it up on his own, or Nelle handed it to him. Either way, the book entered his life through his mother—just another step in the religious instruction she'd pursued with her sons practically since birth.

Dutch was already living in a Christian environment, where important decisions and daily behavior alike were guided by Christian precepts. The story of *Udell's* offered an instructive parable, grounded in a world Reagan could relate to and learn from. Little Dickie Walker's world was one of constant reflection and consideration of the Deity and His plan for peoples' lives. But it was also a real world of Sunday school, populated by memorable characters (the cute girl with a big pink bow in her hair in the next pew, a shy parishioner nervously addressing the congregation) and full of Christian good works (raising funds for a new building, regular and earnest prayer, preaching to the unsaved). Ensconced as he already was in a Christian environment—and ready to take another step forward—a boy like Dutch Reagan was ideally placed to take inspiration from such a story.

To that end, official Reagan biographer Edmund Morris says that reading *Udell's* "was a religious experience for Dutch." "He once told me, shyly," recalled Morris, "that the novel made him 'a practical Christian.' "[12]

Udell's is a lengthy novel for a young person (my edition spans 346 pages; another covers 468), and would overwhelm most eleven-year-olds. It probably averages at least one reference to "God" or "Christ" or "Christianity" every page or two. It is also theologically advanced, especially for a youngster.

This sophistication is evident in the scenes where Dick, now an adult flirting with Christianity, is considering joining the congregation. One day, a church member tells him that he has the benefit of being "free from ecclesiastical chains," and that he is fortunate to be a "follower of no creed but Christ." The member adds that Dick is a "Christian so far as he is a believer in the truths that Christ teaches; but not in the generally accepted use of that word, which is, that a man can't be a Christian without hitching himself up in some denominational harness." (The adult Reagan never found himself harnessed into a specific denomination.) "If you believe that, why do you wear the badge?" asked Dick in response. "Because," replied the church member, "I believe that while the man who takes the initiative must owe allegiance to no particular congregation, the work must be carried on by the church; . . . and I hope you will some day see that the church with all its shortcomings and mistakes, is of divine origin; and that she needs just such men as yourself to lead her back to the simplicity of Christ's life and teaching."[13]

These were not simple issues for a boy not yet twelve years old. Yet somehow Nelle must have figured her boy could handle the text, and that he would internalize and be enriched by it.

One of the book's most powerful messages for young Dutch Reagan must have been its embrace of speaking frankly in behalf of truth. In one sermon, the pastor fires away at dishonesty and falsehood in the church, not afraid of offending anyone. One of the few characters who approve of the words, one Mr. Lindsey, calls the sermon "fearless," "just the kind of sermon we need." He vows he'll be back next week for sure. The novel abounds with plainspoken accusations: "Tom Wharton, you're a liar and a cheat," one character charges at a critical moment. (Nearly sixty years later, in his first presidential press conference, Reagan would complain of the Soviet leadership's willingness "to lie, to cheat," he said.)[14]

The novel's battle between right and wrong had a profound impact on young Reagan. More than fifty years after reading *Udell's*, he reminisced that it and other books from his youth left him with "an abiding belief in the triumph of good over evil." These books, he said, contained "heroes who lived by standards of morality and fair play."[15] This was a world not of moral equivalency, but of good guys and bad guys.

A PLAN OF ACTION FOR A "PRACTICAL CHRISTIAN"

The moral of the story takes shape as the new, improved Dick, now on his way to becoming a "practical" Christian, conceives a plan to help save the wretched city. Believing himself to be moved by God, he makes a plan to do "Christ's work in the city"—Boyd City, with its "low standard of morality."[16]

The plan Dick envisioned was a form of social welfare for the poor—but one that stressed the need (in Dick's words) to distinguish between the "deserving and undeserving." Any plan that failed to do this, said Dick, would "prove a failure because it would encourage the idle in their idleness, and so prove a curse instead of a blessing."[17] For the words of a fictional young man at the turn of the century, Dick's warnings about welfare largesse sound surprisingly contemporary: "The present spasmodic, haphazard, sentimental way of giving does [encourage idleness]. It takes away a man's self-respect; it encourages him to be shiftless and idle; . . . it kills the man."[18] Students of Reagan's political career will recognize in those sentiments a virtual blueprint for his thinking on welfare.

Sounding like both Reagan and his 1990s Gingrich-era conservative descendants, Dick called for the added touch of decentralizing (today we'd call it block granting) welfare to local levels—a plan that echoes the 1994 GOP welfare reform bill signed by President Bill Clinton. "Different localities would require different plans," lectured Dick, rejecting the one-size-fits-all approach to attacking poverty, "but the purpose must always be the same: To make it possible for those in want to receive aid without compromising their self respect."[19]

Dick prefers and champions localized, private-sector solutions—reminiscent of today's faith-based initiatives—to social problems and poverty. Dick subscribed to biblical notions of helping the poor, such as the idea that it is better to teach a man to fish than simply to give a man a fish. In essence, this welfare plan was a form of "applied" or "practical" Christianity.

Significantly, it is this sense of practical Christianity that seems to have had the biggest effect on Reagan's later thinking. As the rube in the story, Uncle Bobbie, puts it: "Christianity's all right, but it ain't a goin' to do no good 'less people live it."[20] Dick lamented that the problem with the teaching of Christ was not His teaching but that the teaching "don't seem to go very far."[21] Dick wanted those Christian teachings to go somewhere—to have a practical effect.

Dick needed a "plan," and he devised one. He also needed to sell the plan to the people. That required presence, leadership, and rhetorical skills—the attributes and talents, in other words, of a politician.

On that score, Wright offers a memorable description of the presence Dick possessed as he entered church to make his case—a description that sounds remarkably like Edmund Morris in one of his more effusive meditations on Reagan:

> Even the most careless observer would know that [Dick] would be both swift and sure in action, while a closer student would say, "Here is one who rules himself, as he leads others; who is strong in spirit as well as body; who is as kind as he is powerful; as loving as he is ambitious; this is indeed a man whom one would love as a friend and be forced to respect as an enemy." . . . Charlie Bowen, one of the ushers, came hurrying up and caught the stranger by the hand: ". . . Folks will think you're a congressman sure."[22]

Dick's big moment, when he unveils his plan, is Reaganesque in its appeal to simplicity. After a brief preface, Dick makes his plain-spoken appeal:

> [L]et me add simply this: What I have to say to you is in no way new or startling. I claim no originality, for I have simply gathered from the works of better men that which seems to me best fitted for the needs of this particular city. . . . As I understand it, the problem

that we have to consider is, briefly, how to apply Christ's teachings in our own city.[23]

Dick's speaking debut proved both sparkling and wondrously effective, though the young man himself seemed initially unaware of his rhetorical talents. "Both Charlie and Cameron [two fellow churchgoers] wondered at his ease of manner," the narrator mused, "and the strange power of his simple, but well-chosen words."[24] Dick's words put the crowd at ease. He won them with his charm.

Like Reagan, also then years away from thoughts of public service, Dick was learning to speak in a chapel. The budding rhetorician was discovered as he honed his craft—in church. Dick gained the support of local officials for his plan because he was recognized as a leader. He initiated the effort, prompted the changes, and devised the plan, carrying the day with his can-do, confident optimism.

Dick's plan goes on to make a real difference. The city's bums, burglars, and prostitutes find good work; bars are supplanted by reputable businesses, concerts replace burlesque shows. Churches grow, naturally, as does attendance at colleges and high schools. Boyd City becomes a model of how applied Christianity and basic, common-sense solutions can make a difference. At one point, a traveling salesman peering out the window of a passing train is struck by the improvement; "I'm sure of one thing," he mutters, "they were struck by good, common-sense business Christianity."

Young Ronald Reagan learned from Dick Walker the benefits of being motivated by Christian faith to do God's work.

Ultimately, of course, Dick becomes a committed Christian, practicing "real" Christianity. After joining the Disciples of Christ, he is instantly smitten with a brown-eyed girl named Amy Goodrich, and marries her. Then he is sent off to Washington, D.C.—a "field of wider usefulness at the National Capitol"—as a polished elected representative from Boyd City. The last image we get of Dick is one that would have moistened Reagan's eyes: we witness him kneeling in prayer before heading to Washington to change the world, the admiring Amy at his side.

THE LESSON OF *UDELL'S* IS THAT A CHRISTIAN MUST honestly stand by his convictions, actively helping those in need. He must boldly follow God's will, and not be silent or cowardly in attacking evil. He must proselytize and evangelize, making no excuses. Parking one's Christianity at the door is simply not what Jesus wants; it is not an option. This, *Udell's* conveyed, is the only true recipe for betterment—for changing the world.

Upon finishing the book, Reagan later recalled, he walked over to his mother. "I want to be like that man," he exclaimed, referring to Dick, "and I want to be baptized." His fervor to "declare my faith" and be baptized was so strong that he persuaded his brother, Neil, an indifferent Catholic, to leave Jack's church and join him in total immersion under the waters at 123 S. Hennepin.[25] By his own account, this one book—which he had encountered just a few months after lifting his drunken father out of the snow—had single-handedly changed his life.

3.

Inheritance

"One thing I do know, all the hours in the old church in Dixon (which I didn't appreciate at the time) and all of Nelle's faith have come together in a kind of inheritance without which I'd be lost and helpless."

—Governor Ronald Reagan in a letter to his childhood pastor, Ben Cleaver, 1973[1]

After reading *Udell's* and being baptized, Dutch Reagan became an especially active member of the local Disciples congregation. He had already been a churchgoer and participant, but now his faith ascended to a higher level. That added commitment brought him into contact with a group of individuals who nurtured his faith and molded him into the person he became. These people provided him with a special kind of "inheritance." Of course, among those influences, Nelle remained central.

* * *

EACH SUNDAY THROUGHOUT THE 1920s, NELLE AND Dutch walked the seven blocks to the doors of the church. On especially cold days, they might take the Model T. The church was just two blocks from the Rock River, where in the 1890s the Disciples had performed baptisms; nowadays Dutch lifeguarded a few miles upstream during the summer.[2]

In Nelle Reagan's house Sundays were strictly about God, and she and the boys had a full church agenda. Moon later detailed the schedule: "Sunday school Sunday mornings, church Sunday morning, Christian Endeavor Sunday evening, church after Christian Endeavor, and prayer meeting on Wednesdays."[3]

Growing up in Dixon, Dutch was caught up in the fervor of his mother's faith. Nelle included him in Bible readings held at their home and took him to conferences to hear religious lectures, such as the local Chautauqua and Rock River Bible conferences. Active in the congregation, he was also a dedicated participant in Sunday school; one source remembered him as "a live wire." He raised money to plaster and paint his Sunday school classroom by doing janitorial work in a nearby building, and personally took the initiative in seeing the project through.[4]

While still a young boy, Reagan even performed recitations at the church. The local paper for May 6, 1920, reports that nine-year-old Ronald Reagan had recited "About Mother" at the church. The June 3 edition reports that his recitation of "The Sad Dollar and the Glad Dollar" immediately preceded his mother's reading "How the Artist Forgot Four Colors." As part of the church ministry, he and Nelle performed for patients at hospitals. At Dixon State Hospital in 1922, according to the local paper, Dutch and Nelle "entertained the patients with a short and enjoyable program," she with a banjo and he with "two entertaining readings." This outreach worked so well that it became a monthly church program for patients.[5]

Soon he was taking solo turns as well. In December 1924 he embraced the role of Jimmie in the church Christmas play, *The King's
Birthday*.[6] He enjoyed it so much that he was back on the First Christian Church stage three weeks later for a program at the congregation's annual meeting, open to the community at large. Most
performers sang or played an instrument, but Dutch chose to perform
alone. The reviewer for the *Dixon Telegraph* was impressed, writing of
the thirteen-year-old: "Ronald Reagan convulsed the audience by his
one-act dramatic reading."[7]

Together again, mom and son took the show on the road to other
churches. In July 1925, a large audience in Tampico greeted the
Dixonites at their old church. A reporter from the *Telegraph* made the
trip as well, and recorded that "Each number Mrs. Reagan gave was
enthusiastically encored; Ronald Reagan was encored several times."[8]

But church was about much more than performance. In his earliest years in Dixon, Reagan had been influenced by his Sunday school
teacher Lloyd W. "Brownie" Emmert, who is remembered for in-
structing his students that God took a guiding hand in daily events
and chose individuals for spiritual missions. "My father and mother
loved those Reagan boys—both Dutch and Neil," recalls Emmert's
daughter, Marion Emmert Foster. In a June 1977 letter from his Los
Angeles office, Reagan remembered Emmert as "my Sunday school
teacher and a wonderful man."

At fifteen, Dutch began teaching his own Sunday school class to
a group of boys, lecturing in the same furnace room he had plastered
and painted a few years earlier. He cherished the class, and the boys
responded. "He became a leader among those boys," said childhood
friend Savila Palmer. "They looked up to him."[9] Lucille Patterson,
who taught the girls' class while Reagan taught the boys, recalled: "I
can still see the row of upturned faces as he sat on a table and held

them all spellbound. There were no discipline problems."[10] The future president's knack for communication clearly surfaced early in life.

These boys, many of who were older than Reagan, later described Dutch as "their supremely self-assured teacher." Interviewing Reagan's pupils sixty years later, biographer Norman Wymbs was startled to find that they remembered specific lessons Dutch taught. They recalled his using testimonies of faith from contemporary Christian sports figures. And they remembered his zeal at incorporating Christ's parables into his instruction; he early recognized how effective stories could be in illustrating his points.[11]

Dutch taught his first Sunday school class on July 4, 1926. The school register for the day shows that four "scholars" attended; the total collection was twenty-eight cents. Also teaching that day were Reverend Ben Cleaver and his wife, and Reagan's own former Sunday school teacher Lloyd Emmert. (As Emmert's star pupil, Dutch had shown enough promise to splinter off and get his own class.) This was a thriving day for Sunday school; it netted a full two dollars in collections.

Reagan didn't stop teaching until September 1928, when he moved on to Eureka College. Even then, church records show that he came home from college—a hundred-mile drive that must have taken more than two hours back then—for the remaining three Sundays that September to teach his class. (That last class netted a grand twelve cents in collections.) In the two-and-a-quarter years he taught the class, Dutch didn't miss a single Sunday.[12]

The young Reagan also led several prayer meetings before the church. "The congregation was much taken with his voice and delivery, which they believed owed a great deal to the private elocution lessons Nelle gave him," biographer Anne Edwards found. "Parishioners of the church like to recount how Dutch could make the Bible seem personal, like a 'phrase might just have been written.' "[13]

Records of the time demonstrate that Reagan participated actively in a broad array of church activities. The bulletin for Easter Day and Week services for 1926 lists fifteen-year-old Dutch and one Frances Smice as the "leaders" starting Easter Day services, kicking off the Annual Sunrise Prayer Meeting at 7:00 A.M.[14] Reverend Cleaver counted on Reagan for activities and prayer meetings, and on Sunday-evening Christian Endeavor—a youth group whose members endeavored to become "true Christians"—he led discussions on topics such as "What Would Happen If All Church Members Were Really Christians?" and "What Difference Does It Make What We Do on Sundays?" This group often took its show on the road to larger Christian gatherings, where Reagan gave talks with titles like "We Must Make God."[15]

Years later, older members of the congregation were "genuinely surprised" when Norman Wymbs told them how young Dutch had been at the time.[16] By the time he was a teenager young Reagan was already so advanced in his faith, and so serious about his church role, that congregation members thought he might become a minister. Wymbs claims that "all of the officials" in the congregation, as well as close family friends like Ward Hall, saw in Dutch a "stirring evangelical zeal they interpreted as guiding him toward a church pulpit."[17] Ron Marlow, the local historian at the First Christian Church, confirms: "The general opinion was that Neil would be the actor and Ronald was the minister type. So, by the early 1940s, people were surprised it was turning out the way it was." Though the congregation members had also witnessed Reagan's acting skills, they were still convinced his real calling was the ministry.[18]

Through church activities, he also continued to hone his oratorical talent. As a high-school senior he became a toastmaster, emceeing a number of large church-affiliated events. In April 1928, for example, he presided over a Saturday evening Citizenship Banquet at the annual convention of the First Congregational Church in nearby Moline for several Christian Endeavor Union groups from Northwest Illinois, introducing speakers and opening and closing the event.[19]

In Dutch's final public act as a Dixon adolescent, he spoke at his high-school commencement ceremony. Beginning a habit he would resume decades later as governor and president, he mixed church and state, quoting the words of Jesus Christ in John 10:10: "I have come in order that they all have life in all its abundance."[20]

BEN CLEAVER

Among other Dixonites who became central in forming Dutch Reagan's faith, one who made a sharp impact was Reverend Ben Cleaver, who preached his first sermon at the Dixon church on September 17, 1922. Cleaver recognized the spiritual maturity of certain younger members of his church, and he and the eleven-year-old Reagan hit it off right away.

Their bond was only strengthened when Reagan began dating Cleaver's daughter, Margaret, known by her nickname "Mugs." The couple swiftly grew serious; even into the 1930s, Reagan was convinced he would marry her. In his teenage years, young Reagan practically lived at the Cleaver house. "Naturally, he was *often* in our home," remembered Mugs's sister Helen, "and felt the influence of father's guidance during those formative years."[21] Cleaver taught Dutch how to drive, and eventually helped get him into college. As one biographer has observed, Reagan was as close to being a preacher's kid as one could be without moving into the manse.[22]

Ben Cleaver was a father figure to young Reagan. He saw mentoring as a God-given duty, and one he thoroughly enjoyed, particularly in Ronald's case. He asked his congregation to pray for him in providing inspiration and enthusiasm to the church youth.[23]

Cleaver's records from his First Christian Church years—especially the annual reports he filed from 1923 to 1930—reveal him as an energetic, highly ambitious, productive steward. He grew the church extremely well, averaging thirty new members or more each year. At the same time he was temporarily lent out to other churches in the area for a few months each year, and grew attendance in those congregations at comparable rates. The current pastor of the church on 123 S. Hennepin, who has studied Cleaver's writings and relationship with Reagan, observes that Cleaver's example may have "rubbed off" on the younger man, sparking not only his spirituality but also his ambition: the adult Reagan's remarkable can-do attitude reflects Cleaver's.[24]

Though he preferred rural settings, Cleaver was no backwoods preacher. According to Stephen Vaughn, he was well-read and curious; a former student at the University of Chicago who read Hebrew and classical Greek, Cleaver was inclined to exploring the derivation of words like "baptism" with parishioners. He encouraged free thinking; indeed, some in the congregation seem to have considered him too intellectual. One of his daughters recalled: "We were absolutely free to say anything that came into our heads."[25]

Politically and theologically, Cleaver was probably what we would consider conservative. He was patriotic, with a passionate faith in the American founders. In February 1927, he delivered a speech on Washington and Lincoln to the local American Legion. He spoke of the very different upbringings of the two presidents, emphasizing that neither man's background, whether rich or poor, stopped him from making his mark on history.[26]

In his patriotism as well as his faith, Cleaver was influenced by the writings of Disciples of Christ father Alexander Campbell, as well as other church leaders. For nineteenth-century Disciples, America's destiny was often prophetically interpreted. Church leaders expressed a deep patriotism and confidence in the providence of God, and the early Disciples identified their faith in the American nation closely with their Christian faith. Moreover, many shared a view that America had a democratic mission to save the world from autocrats. Campbell in particular encouraged the belief that the world's fate rested with America—that it was a land prepared by God to restore the Gospel and carry it to the world. In July 1830, Campbell declared that the world "must look" to America "for its emancipation from the most heartless spiritual despotism ever." "This is our special mission in the world as a nation and a people," said Campbell, "and for this purpose the Ruler of nations has raised us up and made us the wonder and the admiration of the world."[27]

Campbell confidently predicted the "speedy overthrow" of "false religion [and] oppressive governments." He spoke of America as a "beacon," a "light unto the nations," and predicted that when the "light which shines from our political institutions" penetrates "the dungeons of European despots," the millennium would begin. Other nineteenth-century Disciples leaders, including David S. Burnet, James Shannon, and Walter Scott, shared Campbell's vision of a "divinely chosen" America with a duty to spread Christianity globally. That strong missionary zeal would continue as part of church tradition into the twentieth century.[28]

Ben Cleaver had read Campbell, and it's quite likely he passed on such views to the young Reagan.[29] In almost every report he filed as pastor in the 1920s, Cleaver promoted missionary work as a top priority. "[Y]our minister wishes the church more and more to become a center to radiate Gospel effort," he wrote to his congregation at the end of 1924. "I note with joy the increase in missionary giving, but it is not yet large enough for us to be proud."[30] He encouraged "soul-winning," and urged vigilance among his parishioners in spreading the Gospel: "Mediocre or passable service for Christ," he admonished, "is almost a crime."[31]

The lasting effects of Reverend Cleaver's outreach are evident in the little church in Dixon to this day. As one enters the First Christian Church's side entrance and approaches the Reagan Room at the top of the stairs, the first item visible through the doors is a colorful painting by Fran Swarbrick of Dutch and four other boys painting their Sunday school classroom. Directly to the left of the painting is a picture of Campbell and a bookcase with a Bible opened to the start of the Gospel of Matthew.[32] To the right of the painting is a picture of Barton W. Stone (another Disciple with a global outlook) and a bookshelf with volumes donated by local parishioners, including 1912 and 1913 titles on the Disciples outreach to Asia, the Congo, and more—volumes that were likely present when Dutch grew up in the church.

And then there was Russia. Cleaver's congregation was aware quite early of the religious persecution in Bolshevik Russia. On November 11, 1928, the church hosted a Russian Jew named B. E. Kertchman, whose Sunday evening speech offered a modern history of Jews and their relations with other people and nations. Though the Dixon church was active in missions, it seldom brought in speakers from outside; Kertchman was recruited by an enthusiastic Cleaver. Reagan had left for Eureka College two months earlier, but he often returned home on weekends, and may well have attended.[33]

Cleaver was highly troubled by communism and its atheistic foundations. Cleaver once related his father's story of traveling thirty miles on horseback to hear Alexander Campbell debate Robert Owen, "the British-Welsh Atheist Philanthropist," in a crowded courtroom in New London, Missouri. According to Cleaver, Owen was the founder of "a sort of communist colony" in New Harmony, Indiana, that "opposed all religions"; Cleaver's father remembered the talk "as one of the best he ever heard."[34] Ben took the lesson to heart, as Stephen Vaughn has written, and recognized the link between the New Harmony experiment and twentieth-century Bolshevism.[35]

It's hard to imagine that the young Reagan could not have heard from Cleaver about Soviet communism, with its atheistic doctrines, in the 1920s. We do know that the two shared serious discussion on matters of faith. Five decades later, in May 1971, Governor Reagan wrote Cleaver, then retired in Cape Girardeau, Missouri, and told him that he was "very grateful today for a faith in which you played a part in instilling within me." In particular, he said he was grateful for how that faith had helped him through his current job.[36] After Ben's death in 1975, Reagan wrote to Cleaver's daughter Helen, "You were all so much a part of my life and had so much to do with charting my course."[37] Shortly after exiting the presidency, he remembered Ben as a "wonderful man" who had "a great influence" on him.[38]

As an adult, Reagan often expressed a belief that God had carefully planned the course of his life, placing the right people in his path when they were needed. As fate would have it, Ben Cleaver came to the Dixon church in 1922, the same year as Dutch Reagan.[39] Cleaver played an integral role in Reagan's adolescence—the formative years when the young man's lifelong devotion to Christian principles was crystallized.

Mugs and the Waggoners

Ben Cleaver's daughter Mugs also had an effect on Reagan's youthful spiritual life. She and Dutch connected in many ways, and the church was at the center of their romance.

Reagan and Mugs Cleaver both enjoyed drama. They acted in plays together, inside and outside the church. On one of many occasions, the pair, along with Nelle and Ben, performed what the *Dixon Telegraph* called a "delightful program" at the church on a Thursday afternoon in February 1926. "Each took their part in a most pleasing manner," raved the *Telegraph*, "especially the young folks, who seemed to be right at home in the naturalness of their acting."[40] The performance, hosted by the Missionary Society, was part of "Guest Day," intended to attract new church members.

Mugs Cleaver was active in the church. She sometimes led prayer meetings, attended the "Willing Workers" girls' Bible study class, and was an officer in the Mission Triangle Club, reporting on world mission situations as the club's correspondent.[41] Her romance with Reagan was no Jazz Age fantasy of dancing at speakeasies; gifted and intelligent, the girl Dutch hoped to marry was also a promising orator, an ambitious and serious young woman both academically and spiritually.

Along with the Cleavers, another family who would hold a strong influence over young Ronald Reagan was that of Reverend Harvey Garland Waggoner.[42]

It was Harvey Waggoner who had attracted Nelle and her boys to the First Christian Church. A Eureka College graduate, Waggoner had ministry in his blood. His father had been a well-known pastor in Illinois for fifty years. A brother of his became a minister, attending Yale Divinity School after Eureka; a sister married a minister, and both were missionaries for fourteen years in Cuba. Harvey himself served as secretary for state missionary conventions. A forceful orator and indefatigable worker, he was also unwaveringly patriotic. He headed the local Red Cross during WWI; for years thereafter, his children chuckled at the memory of him celebrating what turned out to be a premature report of an armistice in late 1917.

Soon after the Reagans arrived in Dixon, the families forged a bond: Harvey's wife, Jenny, grew close with Nelle Reagan; the two prayed together and held Bible discussions together. But the Reagans' relationship with Harvey was short-lived: on May 31, 1922, he succumbed to "pernicious anemia" at the age of forty-seven. Ironically, at the time of his death researchers in Boston were already working toward a cure for the disease; they would later receive the Nobel Prize in Medicine for their work, but the cure came too late for Harvey. "If only dad's disease would have come a bit later, he wouldn't have died," laments his ninety-three-year-old daughter Phyllis Waggoner Cole today from her home in Morrison, Illinois.

Harvey's death rocked the town. "A shadow of gloom passed over the city," reported the *Telegraph*. Two days later, his son John—a football star known by his middle name, Garland—graduated from high school, in a ceremony at which Harvey had been scheduled to perform the baccalaureate service.

Waggoner's funeral service, attended by all of Dixon's ministers, was held in the barely completed auditorium of the new church at 123 S. Hennepin, a building Harvey had labored to finish. He would miss the First Christian Church's grand opening a couple of weeks later, on June 18, as well as the baptism of his youngest daughter, Phyllis, on June 21. Young Dutch Reagan was also baptized that day.

In one of those twists in the road that made sense only later, it was Reverend Waggoner's tragic early death that brought Ben Cleaver and his family to town. Still, the Waggoners' influence in Dutch Reagan's life continued in the person of Garland, the minister's son, who became one of Reagan's earliest role models.

Like Mugs Cleaver, Garland Waggoner was ambitious; he was also successful and optimistic. He was a town celebrity, and from an early age Dutch came to idolize him, referring to him as his "hero."[43] Like Mugs, he was a nonrebellious preacher's kid, and his seriousness was evident around church. As an upperclassman in high school, he taught Dutch at Sunday school, in the class Reagan himself would eventually inherit. He and Reagan spent hours together after school punting and passing the pigskin; they also spent time talking about God—and football.[44] According to his sister Phyllis, Garland— "Wag," as Dutch called him—was the main reason that a teenage Reagan chose to attend Eureka.

Wag returned to Dixon often after leaving for Eureka in 1922. One November Sunday in 1924, thirteen-year-old Dutch observed as Waggoner, now captain of the Eureka College football team, addressed the Bible school at the church his father had built. Garland also stayed involved with the boys' Sunday school class, which he helped reorganize in 1926.[45]

Garland graduated from Eureka in 1926, along with his fiancée Neva Maude Reichel—the daughter of a minister and missionary who himself had graduated from Eureka. After graduation, Waggoner followed in his father's ministerial footsteps, attending the University of Chicago and Yale Divinity School before graduating from Hartford Seminary in Connecticut. For forty-two years he served as pastor of the Storrs, Connecticut, Congregational Church of the United Church of Christ. Reagan and Garland stayed in touch through the years, and just as Dutch had once followed Wag's path from Dixon to Eureka, in later life Waggoner followed Reagan as he shifted from movies to politics. Garland lived just long enough to see Dutch become president, and Reagan ensured he had a ticket to his inauguration. "One of my dad's last happy memories was to attend that inauguration," says Garland's daughter, Sarah DeMont. On May 23, 1981, two days after his seventy-eighth birthday, the former football star died of congestive heart failure. Recording that he was "deeply saddened" by the news, the fortieth president sent a letter to Wag's wife, Neva:

> [A]t moments like this we must believe and trust in God's infinite wisdom and mercy. Time will bring healing. . . . Those of us who care can only stand by, share some measure of your sorrow, and pray for that healing to come.
>
> My heartfelt condolences and prayers are with you.
>
> Sincerely, Dutch

THROUGHOUT HIS YOUTH AND TEENAGE YEARS, THEN, Reagan was surrounded by—and drawn to—seriously religious figures, committed to their faith. These fellow Disciples were his roots—his "inheritance," as he put it. Many years later, he wrote of his adolescence in Dixon: "There was the life that has shaped my body and mind for all the years to come after." The town, said Reagan, was "a small universe where I learned standards and values that would guide me for the rest of my life."[46] And the people in that town, as he later told the Cleaver family, provided him with an "unshakable" faith that gave him "a peace beyond description."[47]

The most lasting effect of these years was how surely they instilled in Reagan the conviction that God had a special plan for everyone, and for America as a whole. To Reagan that conviction became a charge for himself, his country, and his world.

4.

From Eureka to Hollywood

"He was a deeply religious man. . . . Whatever he accomplished was God's will."

—*a Reagan radio colleague from the early 1930s[1]*

Reagan left Dixon for Eureka College in the fall of 1928. For him, the 1930s and 1940s would be a time of enormous change. He began the period in Eureka—yet another northern Illinois spiritual haven.

Eureka College was established by the Disciples of Christ in the 1850s.[2] From the outset, Eureka provided its students with a decidedly Christian education. As the school's 1871 catalogue stated, "The Bible is a regular textbook, and every student may prepare and recite a lesson in it at least once a week." The college's mission was "designed to enforce the sublime morality of the Divine Volume." That aim did not change during the years Reagan attended. As the 1936 catalogue informed prospective students: "Religious values shall be found in courses of study, in the work plan and in recreational activities. The development of religious attitudes . . . is essential."[3]

Eureka held a place in young Reagan's imagination from early on. The church on S. Hennepin was constantly involved in its fundraising and endowment campaigns, and the college's glee club even performed there.[4] Many of those closest to him attended the rural Illinois school; he heard about it from the Cleavers, the Waggoners, even Nelle.

In retrospect, it's hard to imagine Dutch attending another institution. "If I had to do it all over again," he would say decades later in an appearance at Eureka, "I'd come right back here and start where I was before. . . . Everything good that has happened to me . . . started here on this campus in those four years."[5] The college was "such an important part" of his life, providing him and his classmates with "a sound foundation on which to build our lives."[6]

Though his family had little money to spare, Reagan dreamed of joining the small student body, only two hundred and fifty strong. "I fell head over heels in love with Eureka," he recalled years later. "It seemed to me then, as I walked up the path, to be another home. I wanted to get into that school so badly that it hurt." Through sheer persuasion, he received a football scholarship that covered half of his $180 tuition, without which he would have been unable to afford the school.[7]

Money was tight. The Great Depression descended during Reagan's time at Eureka, and his family's earnings were lowered further by Nelle's commitment to tithing, even during the worst of times. While at Eureka her son followed the practice earnestly, giving 10 percent of his income back to the church. (His father, Jack, was considerably less enthusiastic, but Nelle dismissed his grumbling: "The Lord [will] make your 90 percent twice as big if you [make] sure He [gets] his tenth." Her son's eventual success vindicated her prediction many times over.)

Reagan first hit it "big" when he landed a job broadcasting football games at WOC radio in Davenport, Iowa. The job paid a hundred dollars a month. After all costs were considered—from rent to his weekly meal ticket at the Palmer Chiropractic School—not much was left. By this time Moon was also at Eureka, and he needed his brother's help to stay there. Concerned about making ends meet, Dutch consulted a minister at the local Disciples church. "Would the Lord consider His share as being His," he asked, "if I gave the ten percent to Moon to help him through school?" The pastor told him it would be acceptable. Moon got $2.50 per week from his brother's labors; Dutch kept $5.00.[8]

Reagan's rise through the 1930s, when so many other Americans suffered miserably, can only be described as meteoric. He did very well in radio. When WOC consolidated with its parent station, the 50,000-watt WHO in Des Moines (an NBC affiliate), his profile grew overnight: re-creating Chicago Cubs baseball games from the WHO studio, his voice rang into households throughout the Midwest. It was his first national exposure.

And he kept the faith. A friend who worked with Reagan in radio in the early 1930s remembered him as "a deeply religious man." Though "not the kid who went to church every Sunday," Reagan was "a man with a strong inner faith. Whatever he accomplished was God's will—God gave it to him and God could take it away."[9]

His success in radio was just the beginning. In the late 1930s he moved to Hollywood, where he would go on to earn a pile of money making movies, at one point becoming one of the largest box-office

draws in the industry. In a span of just five years after college graduation, Dutch Reagan had made it in radio and on the silver screen—in
the heyday of each medium. Happily ensconced in California, he was
living the American dream.

BACK IN DIXON, MEANWHILE, JACK GRAPPLED WITH A
bad heart. He suffered more than one heart attack in his later years,
and eventually became physically unemployable. He refused to take
public assistance, only exacerbating his family's financial straits. Reagan began sending his parents monthly checks from Iowa during his
first radio job.[10] Jack's son's big break in Hollywood came none too soon.

In 1938, after Dutch signed with Warner Brothers, he bought his
parents a brick house near him in Hollywood—their own home at
last. Dutch gave his father a job answering his fan mail—easy work
for the long-toiling shoe salesman, now ailing badly. Jack enjoyed
only a few short years of California sun and financial security before
he died on May 18, 1941, at the age of fifty-seven. The funeral service was held in a small church off Sunset Boulevard. Feeling "deso-
late and empty" at the funeral, Dutch heard his father call out to
comfort him, "I'm okay and where I am it's very nice. Please don't be
unhappy." Dutch turned to Nelle and said: "Jack is okay, and where
he is he's very happy." He felt the desolation disappear.[11]

Such stories of connecting with the dead would later elicit snick-
ers from some quarters during Reagan's presidency. But Reagan
seemed to harbor a faith in the ability of heavenly spirits to commune
from the afterlife. In the 1949 film *Night Unto Night*, Reagan played a
terminally ill, agnostic biochemist from Chicago who believed only
in the observable. The scientist falls in love with a widow who is
haunted by the voice of her dead husband, but he dismisses her talk
of ghosts as imagination and "self-hypnosis" brought on by stress and

the death of a loved one. "Science teaches us that life is a mechanical phenomenon," Reagan's character lectures her. "You stop the brain, consciousness stops."

Reagan's character may be the skeptic in the film, but his character's resistance is challenged by believers around him, particularly Shawn, an artist played by Broderick Crawford. Shawn is inspired by the Nineteenth Psalm, which gives the film its title: "The heavens declare the glory of God; the firmaments show his handwork. Day unto day, utter his speech, night unto night, show his knowledge." The scientist eventually softens his views on the supernatural, sensing that there may be another reality that cannot be measured by test tubes. During the film's climax, the widow reminds Reagan's character that he'd once told her "there's a reason for everything," that "behind every action" there's a "logic" that only makes sense later—sentiments Reagan himself shared. At one point Reagan even penciled a line for the widow into the script: "It was almost as if in death he had tried to come back to me." Reagan was proud of the line, which he said provided a basis for the story's central theme—the persistence of souls, even in ghostly form, after death.[12]

THOUGH NOW WIDOWED HERSELF, NELLE REAGAN WAS hardly separated from God. She also maintained her connection to the Dixon church. Ten years after moving to California, there was a split in the old church, with one faction refusing to support the mission society. When word reached Nelle, she fired off a letter meant for the whole congregation:

> Those who have turned against Missions have turned against every thing Christ taught—and the very words he uttered, "Go ye into all the world and *preach* the Gospel, to every creature." . . .

I even wish you'd see that this letter was read to every one, for those who don't believe in the Missionary work of the church have surely turned against Christ—and again[st] his words—"Love thy neighbor as thyself." Please, God, I wish they'd all come back together again.[13]

Still, Nelle found new work in Southern California, working at a TB sanitarium in the area and in at least three other medical treatment centers. She joined her son at the Hollywood Beverly Christian Church, where she worshiped until her death. She persuaded her fellow church members to wrap Christmas gifts for sick residents, something she had done for years. At Christmastime she wrapped to the point of exhaustion, leaving a pile of gifts covering her dining room, ready for shipping.[14]

She also continued her work with prisoners. In an impressive display of faith and commitment, late in life the ailing widow picked up a personal prison ministry. Letters she wrote to the president of her son's fan club provide a portrait of her conviction. In one sent a week after her seventy-fourth birthday in July 1957, she described her frail condition, reporting that her physician had warned that her heart could give at any moment. Nonetheless, she wrote, "don't mourn for me for I really want God to call me home I'm so tired." She signed the letter "Lovingly[,] old Nelle Reagan." In another, sent in December 1955, she apologized for her negligence in writing; in addition to being too busy visiting Olive View sanitarium, she explained that she had also "taken on the jails and prisons. . . . So I'm pretty worn out when I get home in the evening."[15]

Her physical health was only part of the problem. In those final years, Nelle's mind wore out as well. Her "senility," however, did not deter her from the drive from her home near West Hollywood to Olive View in Sylmar. The drive worried her son; Reagan feared that Nelle might get lost and have trouble remembering how to get home, or even who she was. One day he drove Nelle's route by himself and stopped at every gas station along the way, leaving a picture of his mom with her name and contact information.[16]

Nelle's health never seemed to get in the way of her ministry. As she wrote to a pen pal after recovering from a bout with pneumonia in 1953, she had found a way to cope with sickness: "I just kept my mind on God."[17]

Olive View later expressed its gratitude for Nelle's fifteen years of devotion by creating a Nelle Reagan Award for Distinguished Community Service, a program that still continues. Today, the presidential library and museum dedicated to Nelle's son sits in Simi Valley, a short drive from Olive View.

Nelle died on July 25, 1962, in Santa Monica, a day after her seventy-ninth birthday. Back in Dixon, Cenie Straw, a member of the True Blue class, dusted off a poem published by Nelle decades earlier in the *Telegraph*:

> *When I consider how my life is spent*
> *The most that I can do will be to prove*
> *'Tis by His side, each day, I seek to move.*
> *To higher, nobler things my mind is bent*
> *Thus giving of my strength, which God has lent,*
> *I strive some needy souls' unrest to soothe*
> *Lest they the path of righteousness shall lose*
> *Through fault of mine, my Maker to present.*
> *If I should fail to show them of their need*

How could I hope to meet Him, face to face,
Or give a just account of all my ways
In thought of mind, in word, and in each deed
My life must prove the power of His grace
By every action through my living days.[18]

The poem, entitled "My Sonnet," is probably an adaptation of a well-known poem by John Milton, which shares its opening words.[19] Certainly its sentiments were Nelle's; as another annotation in her personal Bible reads, "You can be too big for God to use, but you cannot be too small."[20]

Decades later, Dutch spoke of Nelle's spiritual influence. "I know now that she planted that faith very deeply in me," he told a Christian women's group.[21] As governor, he recalled: "Just seeing my mother's faith under trying circumstances over long periods of time has enabled me to realize that when Jesus said, 'wherever two or three are gathered in My name, there am I also,' He meant He is with us in every situation and circumstance."[22] From his mother he learned about "the God who will guide us through life," as the then-president told the nation in a Mother's Day radio address in 1983. In a tribute Nelle would have loved, he used a passage from the Book of Proverbs to describe her.[23] As president, Reagan once told a private citizen that he liked to think that "maybe she's [Nelle] still giving me a hand now and then."[24]

Nelle was the most important person in the first half of Reagan's life, and her influence carried on even after she passed away. Had she not presented him with an example of committed Christian faith and good works, his own life may have proven quite different.

FINDING GOD IN HOLLYWOOD

As an adult in Hollywood, the kid from the First Christian Church was no longer surrounded by people who deliberately nurtured his faith; indeed, it was probably difficult for him to find many who cared much about it. Yet Ronald Reagan's own spiritual beliefs, and observances, remained constant.

Reagan joined the Hollywood Beverly Christian Church, a Disciples church, upon arriving in Hollywood in the 1930s, and though he wouldn't always attend Disciples churches, he listed himself as a member of the denomination.[25] His first wife, Jane Wyman, taught Sunday school at Beverly Christian, and their children attended Sunday school. Remarkably, over four decades later, long after Reagan had ceased attending the church and joined another congregation, the current pastor reported that Reagan was still technically a member and contributed financially to the church.[26] Even today, into the twenty-first century, Nancy Reagan still sends a monthly check to Beverly Christian in their names, almost five decades after Reagan left the church.[27]

The evidence of Reagan's continued faith during this period is scattered but intriguing. In a letter he wrote to the president of the Pittsburgh chapter of his Hollywood fan club in the 1940s—a long and personal letter to someone he barely knew—he requested prayer for his marriage to Wyman.[28] In June 1950, he published a piece called "My Faith" in a Hollywood magazine. In that article, he noted that though he attended the Beverly Christian Church, he did not go "as regularly as I should. I suppose it's true that a man can be religious without going to church." Yet even as his public observance declined, his private commitment abided: "There hasn't been a serious crisis in my life when I haven't prayed, and when prayer hasn't helped me."

He concluded the article with the words "God's in His Heaven, All's right with the world"—a familiar expression that nonetheless captured Reagan's essential optimism.[29]

One witness to Reagan's faith in this period is his son Michael. Born in 1945, Michael was adopted by Reagan and Wyman four years after the birth of their daughter Maureen. Michael remembers his father as "always religious." He recalls his dad pointing out the wondrous California trees and landscape during their walks together, and commenting on how they revealed God's handiwork.[30]

Reagan and Jane Wyman divorced in 1948, and four years later Reagan married Nancy Davis; the couple would have two children, Patti and Ron. In the late 1950s, when fourteen-year-old Michael came to live with the Reagans, his father left him at home while the rest of the family went to church. When Michael later complained about this, his father explained, "I didn't want to upset your mother." Jane Wyman had converted to Catholicism in 1953, and she and her two children were all baptized into the Catholic faith. Reagan was careful to respect his ex-wife's wishes: He had long ago learned to respect the beliefs of a Catholic parent.[31]

STARTED IN A CHURCH

The years Ronald Reagan spent in Hollywood were also an intensely political period, for the actor and for the world around him. It was a time of cataclysmic world events. The late 1930s and first half of the 1940s marked the rise of fascism in Europe and the world war that followed. The latter 1940s saw the launch of the Cold War between the United States and USSR. Reagan did not escape this glare; to the contrary, he eagerly walked toward the heat. By the time he left Hollywood, he would be a full-fledged anticommunist, a Cold Warrior ready to fight atheistic Soviet communism.

The momentum for Reagan's Cold War crusade took form in a church—not the Dixon church of the 1920s, but the Beverly Christian Church in Hollywood, where Reagan worshiped in the early years of the conflict. By this time Reagan had become a popular after-dinner speaker in Hollywood, and he often received raucous applause for his comments condemning fascism, the totalitarian monster of the recent past.[32] But it was a figure from Reagan's religious life who refocused his attention on the growing threat of communism in the postwar world.

One night, after addressing the men's club at the Hollywood Beverly Christian Church, Reagan was approached by Reverend Cleveland Kleihauer. Dr. Kleihauer was known as a straight shooter, less a partisan ideologue or jingoist than a commonsense thinker; for four decades, he was also one of the most influential pastors in the city.[33] He commended Reagan for warning the audience about rising neo-fascism. However, he told Reagan, an even more disturbing cloud on the geopolitical horizon was the prospect of Soviet communism. "I think your speech would be even better if you also mentioned that if communism ever looked like a threat, you'd be just as opposed to it as you are to fascism."

Reagan told his minister that he hadn't given much thought to the threat of communism. Nonetheless, he accepted Kleihauer's advice. Speaking to a "local citizens' organization" in Hollywood soon thereafter, he defended American values against the fascist threat abroad, and was applauded after nearly every paragraph. By his own description, he was a smash. Then he added a new line at the end: "I've talked about the continuing threat of fascism in the postwar world, but there's another 'ism,' communism, and if I ever find evidence that communism represents a threat to all that we believe in and stand for, I'll speak out just as harshly against communism as I have fascism." You could hear a pin drop. Something wasn't quite right. *What's happening?* he wondered, and awkwardly left the stage—to dead silence.

Reagan had failed to anticipate the cool reception his challenge to communism would elicit from the predominantly left-wing show business audiences he commonly addressed. With that slight tweak to his talk, he had not only flopped—he had stumbled upon the fault line between Hollywood's opposition to fascism and its naïveté to communism. Bulbs began flickering. He never forgot the experience. Over five decades later, after his presidency, he thanked Kleihauer for the "wake up" call.

In that one moment, prompted by a man of God in a house of God, Reagan's crusade against communism had begun.

Finding Politics and Communism in Hollywood

As the 1940s began, Ronald Reagan's own politics were liberal: like Jack Reagan, he was an FDR Democrat. But by the end of the decade his politics were changing—so swiftly, in fact, that his party affiliation took more than a decade to catch up. A Truman Democrat in the late 1940s, he was an Eisenhower Democrat by 1952, and a Nixon Republican by the early 1960s. "I didn't leave the Democratic Party," Reagan later said repeatedly. "The Democratic Party left me." And his concerns were as much domestic as foreign: once a New Dealer, Reagan eventually became the leading free-market conservative of his time.

It was during his Hollywood years that Reagan first became fed up with the high tax rates, intrusive regulations, and burgeoning welfare state he associated with the Democratic Party. The upper income tax rate had mushroomed to over 90 percent, a rate he felt was so punitive that it discouraged work—including his own. He also decried what he perceived as the growing permanency of the welfare state. He came to believe that many of the relief programs that FDR instituted during the Great Depression were "necessary measures during an emergency," but in the years since had unfortunately "trapped families forever on a treadmill of dependency."[34]

Yet Reverend Kleihauer's early warning about communism had become a permanent political motivation for the actor, and by the early 1950s he was a committed anti-communist—at a time when the question of communist sympathy was tearing Hollywood apart—and the leader of the Soviet Union itself was facing his own day of reckoning.

In March 1953, a gasping Joseph Stalin lay on his deathbed in unbearable pain, after a severe stroke that had left his right side paralyzed. His final hours were a slow strangulation: his daughter Svetlana later reported that he choked to death as they watched.

In those final hellish moments, Stalin appeared to be fighting not only death but the God he denied. Though apparently semiconscious at best, he suddenly opened his eyes and cast a quick terrified glance upon everyone in the room. Then, as his daughter put it, "something incomprehensible and awesome happened that to this day I can't forget and don't understand." The Soviet leader suddenly lifted himself halfway up in bed, clenched his fist toward the heavens, shook it in defiance as if at the God he had forsaken, and with one unintelligible murmur dropped motionless onto his pillow.[35]

Stalin could not escape the great equalizer. "My father died a difficult and terrible death," his daughter reflected. "God grants an easy death only to the just."

HALFWAY AROUND THE WORLD, RONALD REAGAN WAS encountering his own personal changes. Just as Reagan's movie career was waning in the late 1940s, his anti-communist passions were evident in his first quasi-political role, as president of the Screen Actors Guild (SAG) during the Hollywood blacklist period.[36] And in another of the many ironic twists in his life, it was communism that brought him into contact with Nancy Davis, the actress he first encountered when she came to him for help in clearing her name from a blacklist.

Reagan's tenure as SAG leader gave the actor his first personal exposure to Marxist ideology—one that never left him. Indeed, when aide Lyn Nofziger four decades later warned the American president that his conservative allies were afraid he'd give away the store to the Soviets at Reykjavik, Reagan told him not to worry, saying he still had scars on his back from fighting communists in Hollywood. To Reagan, few passages in his life had been as grueling as those years: he faced physical intimidation, including a threat he would be splashed with acid, ruining the big-screen face he depended on for income. He began packing a .32 Smith & Wesson pistol, holstering the gun on every morning for months and wearing it until he stepped into bed at night.[37] He later wrote: "Thank heaven for those hide-toughening experiences . . . the arrows were coming in volleys."[38]

There were upwards of three hundred party members in Hollywood during the period Reagan spent battling what was then known as the Red Menace.[39] He was especially concerned at the prospect of certain actors groups turning communist, among them the American

Veterans Committee (AVC) and the Hollywood Independent Citizens Committee of the Arts, Sciences, and Professions (HICCASP). In a later letter, he described the seven months he spent in daily negotiations across a table from communists and "communist influenced people" while picketers rioted in front of studio gates, homes were bombed, and the "great industry" of moviemaking was, in his estimation, almost ground to a halt. He complained of the difficulty of sitting down with communists in "countless hours of meetings," in "honest attempts at compromise," only to find that his attempts were met by "dishonesty, lies, and cheating."[40]

Reagan's SAG years also marked his first introduction to the atheistic side of communism, which he feared was looking to sliver its way into Hollywood. In a later letter to a friend, he described his wrangles with communists on the producing staff of a show at his studio. One scene featured a little girl saying her prayers. "Two individuals including the director wanted to cut the whole scene about the little girl," wrote Reagan; "they literally resorted to sabotage to pull the punch out of the show." "Finally," he said, "in a near knock down drag out—they admitted their objection was because they were Atheists."[41]

By the time of Stalin's death, Reagan's own career as a Hollywood film actor was on the wane; the film world itself was being rocked by the onset of television, and Reagan looked to the new medium as a potential escape hatch. He was recently married, and characteristically optimistic. In just a year he would become a traveling spokesman for General Electric—a job that would find him crisscrossing the country by train to speak to thousands from Oklahoma to Ohio. His job with GE offered him his first national political platform. And Soviet communism was his primary target.

*   *   *

YEARS LATER, RONALD REAGAN WAS ASKED HOW BEING an actor qualified him to be president. With a smile, he replied that there were times he couldn't imagine being president without having been an actor. It was a good-natured quip, but the line contained quite a bit of truth. In Reagan's unique case, it wasn't merely being an actor that had trained him for the presidency. Rather, it was his experience in the ideological struggle over communism that helped inform, and galvanize, Reagan's already strong political beliefs. No one can fairly assess Reagan's later political career without appreciating how his Hollywood experience tested his mettle in the real-life battle against communism.

5.

War and Evil in Moscow

"All worship of a divinity is a necrophilia."

—*Vladimir Lenin*[1]

"Lenin was Jesus. . . . They wanted you to worship Lenin."

—*Ukrainian Olena Doviskaya*[2]

Driving Ronald Reagan's fears during this period were events across the globe in the USSR. Communism in Hollywood concerned him, but far worse was the specter of any connection between American communists and the cruel tyranny of the Soviet state. Throughout Reagan's long march from Dixon to the White House, a very different set of circumstances was evolving in Moscow—

circumstances that would bring about the split between East and West that remained throughout most of the twentieth century.

From the time of his childhood, when he enjoyed his own father's yarns, Ronald Reagan always loved stories, and recognized their power in communication. His presidential papers feature speech drafts bearing his handwritten note: "insert a story here." Whether teaching the Bible or acting in Hollywood productions, he spent much of his life collecting and sharing tales of good versus evil. And he knew that the best stories had an antagonist—a bad guy. In the narrative of his political and spiritual life, the most profound and persistent villain was no black-hatted poker player in a Dodge City saloon; rather, he carried a red flag, robbed the individual in the name of the state, and dismissed religion as the opiate of the masses.

As Dutch Reagan was being raised in the serene church off the banks of the Rock River, Lenin's Bolsheviks were closing and dynamiting some of the most beautiful chapels ever built. As the Eureka grad took his radio job in Davenport, Stalin ruthlessly administered the gulag with the enthusiasm of an executioner, earmarking innumerable religious believers for Siberia. As the actor made movies and hosted television shows in Hollywood, Nikita Khrushchev offered no peaceful coexistence to people of faith.

Moscow's war on religion was prosecuted by all the hard-line Soviet leaders, from Lenin to Brezhnev. Around the world, like-minded communists carried their cause beyond the USSR in a decades-long bid to spread the sphere of Soviet oppression. From the 1940s onward, Ronald Reagan observed all this with indignation. The malevolency of atheistic Soviet communism stoked his passions; it fueled him. And without it America and the world might never have seen Reagan ascend to the presidency.

* * *

FROM CALIFORNIA, CITIZEN REAGAN BECAME PAIN-
fully aware of the Soviet war on religion. Christianity was a Soviet
focal point, but persecution of Jews was long a craft in this part of the
world, and Muslims also experienced repression under the regime: the
Soviet leadership was an equal opportunity oppressor. Reagan followed stories of Soviet persecution of every denomination, and in
later life he would speak in support or defense of Russian Jews almost
as often as he did for Russian Pentecostals. Nonetheless, due to their
sheer numbers Christians were perceived as the primary religious
threat to the Soviet state, and bore the brunt of the religious persecution under the Bolsheviks.

In order to understand Reagan's lifelong enmity toward communism, it is crucial to review the role of atheism in Soviet philosophy.
As observers today, it's impossible to assess Reagan's visceral reaction
to the Soviet regime without grasping its concerted and violent hostility toward the practice of religion.

THE SOVIET WAR ON RELIGION

The USSR did in fact orchestrate a war on religion. As librarian of
Congress and leading historian James Billington has observed, Lenin
and his cohorts aimed for nothing less than the extermination of religious belief.[3] Malachi Martin, a biographer of Pope John Paul II, has
likewise called the USSR the only self-professed, officially anti-
religious empire the world has known.[4] Soviet historian Eduard
Radzinsky concurs from the inside, describing the Bolsheviks' creation as an "atheistic empire."[5]

In calling the Bolshevik assault on religious practice a "war," Reagan had another ally in his onetime adversary Mikhail Gorbachev. "Just like religious orders who zealously convert 'heretics' to their own faith," Gorbachev wrote in his memoirs, "our [communist] ideologues carried out a wholesale war on religion."[6] He complained that the Bolsheviks, even during a time of "peace" after the civil war ended, had "continued to tear down churches, arrest clergymen, and destroy them. This was no longer understandable or justifiable. Atheism took rather savage forms in our country at that time."[7]

The Soviet Union was openly hostile to religion—not irreligious or unreligious, but officially atheist. The state actively held that there was no God. And it was this state-mandated rejection of religion that undergirded the Soviet leaders' systematic campaign to eliminate belief, which began with the Revolution and continued until the 1980s.

This officially sanctioned intolerance of religion was an essential element of communist thought. As a totalitarian ideology, communism represented an attempt to transform human nature itself. Within such a framework, religion was viewed as a powerful, dangerous rival belief system. It was Marxism-Leninism's chief competitor for the Russian mind. Alexander Donskiy, a Ukrainian man who once served as a soldier in the Red Army, offered this brief explanation when asked why the USSR saw religion (and Christianity in particular) as a threat that had to be purged: "Because Christian faith gives people freedom, and this can create a belief in something other than the government."[8]

The Soviet leadership wanted Marxism and the state to be central to citizens' lives. The words of Karl Marx's 1848 *Communist Manifesto* were to be read and learned, drilled and memorized— internalized as surely as the words of the Bible had been to centuries of Jews and Christians. Any challenging text, especially an influential one like the Bible, was unwelcome. Religion was perceived as a ubiquitous enemy, not to be taken lightly.

It was Marx, a passionate, baptized Christian as a teenager, who had dubbed religion the "opiate of the masses." The phrase became a slogan in the Communist Party: Soviet political prisoner Anatoly Sharansky, jailed from 1977 throughout the 1980s, recalled being advised by one of his interrogators that "according to Marx, religion is the opiate of the masses. We won't permit anyone to poison our children."[9]

Marx was also a utopian, who believed that the path to utopia could be found in a classless society. "Crime would disappear" under such circumstances, he wrote; "the span of life would increase, brotherhood and cooperation would inculcate a new morality, scientific progress would grow by leaps and bounds. Above all, with socialism spreading throughout the world, the greatest blight of humankind, war, and its twin brother, nationalism, would have no place. International brotherhood would follow." The "classless society"—a "workers' paradise," as he envisioned it—would make its "own history! It is a leap from slavery into freedom; from darkness into light."[10]

Lenin, who internalized Marx's ideas about this new morality, was another atheist, and an implacable enemy of religion. The future revolutionary had separated from religion as a teen. "I broke sharply with all questions of religion," he fondly recalled. "I took off my cross and threw it in the rubbish bin."[11] Lenin helped create groups with names like the Society of the Godless, also known as the League of the Militant Godless, which was responsible for the dissemination of anti-religious propaganda.[12] In a 1913 letter, he wrote that "any religious idea, any idea of any God at all, any flirtation even with a God is the most inexpressible foulness . . . the most dangerous foulness, the most shameful 'infection' "; the specific phrase he used has been identified by historian James Thrower as a reference to venereal disease.[13] Never one to shy away from provocative imagery, Lenin went so far as to insist that "all worship of a divinity is a necrophilia."[14]

"There can be nothing more abominable than religion," Lenin wrote to Maxim Gorky in January 1913.[15] After the 1917 revolution, he professed his atheism on behalf of the Bolsheviks in a famous address on October 2, 1920: "We . . . do not believe in God."[16] Organized religion was an enemy of the state, and Lenin concluded that such an enemy must be dealt with by force, which he used viciously and effectively. He personally ordered the shooting of as many clergy as possible. As biographer Dmitri Volkogonov writes, the Russian Church never recovered from the "massive blow Lenin had dealt it."[17]

Lenin's partner Leon Trotsky also combated the forces of religious belief. A leader of the Society of the Godless, Trotsky was a stalwart atheist and moral relativist who found gods of his own in Karl Marx and Charles Darwin. "Darwin destroyed the last of my ideological prejudices," he exclaimed. For him, the "facts" about the world and the origins of life were established via the "certain system" of evolutionary theory. "The idea of evolution and determinism," he wrote, "took possession of me completely. Darwin stood for me like a mighty doorkeeper at the entrance to the temple of the universe. I was intoxicated with his . . . thought." Barry Lee Woolley, author of a history of Trotsky and his Fourth International, observed wryly that when "Trotsky took up the faith of Marx and Darwin. . . . the conversion experience was genuine and thorough." Accounts of Trotsky's life and of his atheist followers are filled with such language, attesting both to Trotsky's nearly religious faith in Darwinism and to the devotion of his followers, who "adored him as a god."[18]

The Bolshevik war on religion was far more than theoretical. By the end of 1918, Lenin had set in motion a host of assaults on religious liberty:

– All land and buildings were confiscated from the Russian Orthodox Church

– All schools were taken from the church and handed over to the state

– Marriage was transformed into a strictly civil, secular ceremony

– Weddings, baptisms, and funerals were replaced by bizarre communist ceremonies[19]

– The church's long-standing prohibition against divorce was lifted

– Churches were destroyed or transformed into clubs, workshops, and storage houses[20]

This is a short list. After destroying hundreds of churches, the Bolsheviks wised up and learned that their gleeful demolitions were a waste of precious material. Rather than obliterating fully functional buildings, the churches could be used for secular and even atheistic purposes. They were transformed into warehouses, metal and wood shops, schools, workers' clubs, factories, offices, and more. Some churches even found incarnation as antireligious museums.[21] The Church of the Archangel Michael, a beautiful redbrick edifice crowned with five cupolas built in 1740 on the southwest edge of Moscow, was used to store grain. The Church of Christ the Savior, on the banks of the Moscow River near the Kremlin, once described as the most ornate church in the city, was dynamited in the early 1930s at Stalin's orders to make room for a skyscraper; when the ground was discovered to be too soft, a decidedly less majestic municipal swimming pool was put in its place.[22]

Of the 657 churches that existed in Moscow on the eve of the 1917 revolution, only 100 to 150 remained by 1976, according to official Soviet statistics. Of those, the Moscow Russian Orthodox Patriarchy said only 46 (less than 10 percent) still held services by the mid 1970s.[23] The challenge of the Soviet war on religion was immense. The USSR spanned twelve time zones; within the Orthodox Church alone, there were over 40,000 churches and some 150,000 priests, monks, deans, and nuns.[24] Nuns were housed in special sections of the gulag with prostitutes, effectively labeled whores to Christ. Tons of holy church relics, gems, and precious stones were confiscated and/or liquidated; the resulting fierce battles with the church culminated in the tragic Moscow and Petrograd church trials of 1921–22.[25] According to Gerhard Simon, the Catholic church in the USSR was completely destroyed by the 1930s, and unlike some other churches, Catholicism was not permitted to reestablish a central apparatus after WWII. Writing in the mid 1970s, Simon reported that there was not a single Catholic monastery, convent, school, or welfare institution in the entire Soviet Union.[26]

A defiant Russian poet Tanya Khodkevich bravely captured the despair of believers:

> *You can pray freely*
> *But just so God alone can hear.*[27]

She received a ten-year prison sentence in the gulag for those two lines of verse.[28]

The state hostility begun by Lenin festered under the rule of Joseph Stalin, especially in the 1930s. At one time outsiders believed that things got better under Khrushchev, who denounced the "crimes of Stalin" in 1956 after coming to power. Yet in reality, WWII and the years immediately thereafter had seen a surprising relaxation of state hostility toward religion under Stalin, as the dictator tried to unite and rally the nation against the Nazis. After Stalin's death, a new wave of persecution was unleashed by Khrushchev.[29] One missionary during the Khrushchev era sentenced to twenty-five years in prison, where he was routinely tortured, contended that even as Khrushchev disowned Stalin, he "continued to do the same thing" in regard to religion. After 1959, he claimed, half of the Soviet churches that then remained open were closed.[30]

"PROTECTING" SOVIET YOUTH AND ANTI-CHRISTIAN INSTRUCTION

Throughout the history of the Soviet Union, religious instruction of children was a special concern to its rulers. By 1918, Lenin and his disciples forbade religious instruction to anyone under eighteen years of age.[31] Some parents were even jailed for sharing their faith with their children. It was a practice that continued at least through the Brezhnev period: children were encouraged to turn in their parents if they taught them about God.[32] The baptism of a child was likely to take place at the expense of an approved church official's career.[33]

The Soviet public school system used cruel gimmicks to indoctrinate young children and turn them against religion. A teacher would ask a room of hungry students if they'd like a loaf of bread, then lead the class in prayer for the bread. After their prayers the students would wait and wait, but no bread would come. They would then pray to the state and its current rulers—and the bread would be walked miraculously into the room.[34]

Another tactic was to have the teacher stand in front of the class and use a powder that turned water into a winelike color to persuade the children that Christ used "hocus pocus," not miracles, when he turned water into wine. A classroom of six-year-olds was not advanced enough to ask the teacher to sample the concoction; they merely absorbed the point, further damaging any faith they might have had in Christian teachings.

This "protection" of Soviet youth from the devilish influence of religion continued for decades—until Gorbachev's changes in the late 1980s. Olena Doviskaya, born in 1959, was a teacher in the Ukraine during the 1980s. She relayed the following anecdote:

> I was a teacher and at my school I was sent by the principal to watch worship [services] at the church—as an observer—and make [a] list of children and their parents at the church. There was only one church. I never read the Bible, but I watched and saw all these people saying these things and singing beautiful songs and I wondered what was wrong with this. . . . Sometimes children would attend the worship at Easter time. [As their teacher], I had to go to make notes of which children attended worship, which went with grandma and grandfather, who the parents were, who ate the bread. And we should write it down.[35]

Doviskaya was writing not of the 1930s but of the 1980s, by which time Reagan had become president of the United States. And Reagan was aware of precisely such surveillance. He spoke of how the KGB looked for those who attended church: "When you see the little old ladies going to church, as they do . . . they're watched; the KGB watches to see who goes to church."[36]

Unappreciated and surprising was a hidden weapon in the Soviet war arsenal: the state actually invented alternative Christian texts to undermine the practice of true Christianity. In 1998, a former student told me of her family's travels throughout the USSR as missionaries in the late 1980s. She enrolled in a Soviet public school, and shared her Christian beliefs with fellow students. She was surprised to watch them nod their heads and add details to her description of the life of Christ. But nods became shakes when she got to the part about Christ rising from the dead—the defining moment in the Christian gospel. "No, no, no," the young Soviets responded, "that's where you are wrong. Christ did not rise from the dead. He did not walk from his tomb. His body was removed from the tomb by wild dogs. The dogs ate his flesh and took and buried his bones."

Such instruction was calibrated to appeal to the masses. Universities had professors of atheism who traveled around the country giving mandatory state-sponsored lectures to groups of factory workers, for instance. These lectures not only provided atheistic arguments but ridiculed religious faith, chiding Christians as "stupid" and condemning Christ as a charlatan.

In colleges and public schools, courses on atheism were often mandatory. In 1964, the Central Committee made it a formal requirement that all college students take the course Fundamentals of Scientific Atheism. The classroom instruction for this course was accompanied by "practical work": students partook in various "antireligious activities" under guidance from atheism faculty and the Soviet Komsomol (the Soviet communist youth league). The Komsomol assigned students to deliver atheism and antireligion lectures to the public and to perform "agitation" duties at nearby farm collectives. Students often made their presentations on Sundays and during vacation breaks, receiving intensive training for the task. These athe-ist missionaries were expected to pass their faith to potential future specialists; many eventually made it their life's work.[37]

REVERSING AND UNDOING BELIEF

The USSR did not try merely to block or halt religious faith but to re-verse it altogether. This was also true for many communist bloc states, particularly Romania, which even before the Ceausescu era was among the most world's most bigoted empires.[38] This meant not just forbidding religious practice and jailing priests and believers, but em-ploying torture to force them to renounce their faith. It was not enough to contain, silence, even punish believers in prison; it was de-cided they must be tortured harshly to *undo* their religious faith alto-gether.

One of the best sources on the communists' efforts to reverse be-lief is Richard Wurmbrand, a pastor who endured fourteen years of earthly hell in a Romanian prison. He detailed some of the unspeak-able cruelty he witnessed in congressional testimony and in his cele-brated memoir *Tortured for Christ*, which sold millions of copies after it was first published in 1967 and is still in circulation today.[39] In its pages Wurmbrand refers to communism as "a force of evil" that could only be countered by a greater force, "the Spirit of God"—language that must have struck a chord with Reagan.

In a shocking May 1966 appearance to testify before the Internal Security Subcommittee of the U.S. Senate, Wurmbrand described his actual crucifixion by his Romanian torturers. Wurmbrand and other Christians were tied to crosses for four days and nights, and many seem to have suffered greater humiliation than Christ himself:

The crosses were placed on the floor and hundreds of prisoners had to fulfill their bodily necessities over the faces and bodies of the crucified ones. Then the crosses were erected again and the Communists jeered and mocked: "Look at your Christ! How beautiful he is! What fragrance he brings from heaven!" . . . [A]fter being driven nearly insane with tortures, a priest was forced to consecrate human excrement and urine and give Holy Communion to Christians in this form. . . . All the biblical descriptions of hell and the pains of Dante's Inferno are nothing in comparison with the tortures in Communist prisons.

This is only a very small part of what happened on one Sunday and on many other Sundays in the prison of Pitesti. Other things simply cannot be told. My heart would fail if I should tell them again and again. They are too terrible and obscene to put in writing. . . .

If I were to continue to tell all the horrors of Communist tortures and all the self-sacrifices of Christians, I would never finish.

Wurmbrand corresponded with Reagan during his governorship and again during his presidency, and though the two men never met Wurmbrand's stories could hardly have failed to move the American.[40] As a leader himself, Reagan was especially sensitive to the fact that this mass effort against religion demanded not only the complicity of individuals but a massive allocation of state resources. Such a systematic campaign drained the energy and preciously limited resources of the Soviet state for decades; Reagan called it the USSR's "uncompromising Marxian denial of God."[41]

POLITICAL RELIGION IN THE SOVIET UNION

Ironically, the Soviet leadership violated its rejection of religious worship by treating Marxism-Leninism as a religion.[42] In the years ahead, Reagan frequently highlighted this hypocrisy. The Bolshevik leadership had no God in the sense that most organized religions envision God—rather, Marxism-Leninism served that purpose throughout the lifespan of the Soviet state.

More than a century before the Bolshevik Revolution, Jean-Jacques Rousseau observed that no state had ever been founded without a religious basis—and the advent of Soviet communism did little to disprove his point. Rousseau concluded that no state could survive without appealing to its citizens through some form of religion, but he foresaw that such efforts might include some form of "civil religion," which he saw as necessary for the continuing survival of a state.[43] Citizens needed a transcendent cause, something larger to believe in.

For most typical states, civil religion is understood as a sort of fusion of sacred principles drawn from a nation's own civil traditions and from those of a conventional, organized religion—a blend of political allegiance and religious sentiment. Americans, for example, have assembled a collection of beliefs, rituals, and symbols that reach back before the Revolution to stories of the first British settlement of the continent. Many of these have a biblical basis, and have in turn been accepted by many Americans as part of the American experience. As historian Robert Bellah notes, among these are the view of Americans as a chosen people, America as a promised land and new Jerusalem, America as a light to all the nations—the shining city upon a hill of Winthrop's and Reagan's vision.[44] Indeed, much of Reagan's most memorable political imagery could be categorized as civil religion.

The Soviet civil religion was a far different matter, due largely to its flat rejection of conventional religious beliefs. Soviet civil religion was utopian, geared toward a perfect society, a workers' paradise. It drew little or none of its imagery from the traditional biblical sources that enriched American civil religion, such as the adaptation of language and imagery from the Old and New Testaments. Christel Lane argues that the Soviet system should actually be categorized as a sort of *political*, rather than civil, religion. In political religion, Lane writes, the religious element is seen in the "sacralization of the existing political order"—in the Soviet case, the Bolshevik founders and leadership, and the life and writings of Marx himself.[45]

Nevertheless, Karl Popper has called Marxism a faith, in which the religious element was "unmistakable." The Marxist movement in Central Europe, Popper wrote, could be called a religious movement.[46] Another renowned thinker, Joseph Schumpeter, in his classic *Capitalism, Socialism, and Democracy*, said flatly: "Marxism is a religion. To the believer, it presents, first, a system of ultimate ends that embody the meaning of life and absolute standards to judge events and actions." It offered a "plan of salvation" to its disciples, for which a "chosen section of mankind" could be "saved."[47] Soviets themselves said much the same: the early Bolshevik A. V. Lunacharsky, a close observer of the October revolution, asserted that "Marxism is the most religious of all religions and the Marxist the most deeply religious of men."[48]

Indeed, the veneration of Marxism in the USSR is filled with echoes of traditional Judeo-Christian religious imagery. Brian Lowe of the University of Virginia notes that in the Soviet system Marx was the Messiah, the Party was the Church, the Proletariat was the Elect, the Revolution was the Second Coming, and more.[49] The *Communist Manifesto* reached a level of sacredness approaching Holy

Scripture; Marx and Engels, Lenin and Stalin were all but canonized, their statues distributed throughout the nation. Lenin's body was embalmed and preserved in a shrinelike tomb in Red Square as if it were a holy relic, an inscription in the marble reading "Lenin: The Savior of the World."[50] Yuri Gagarin, the first Soviet cosmonaut, visited Lenin's mausoleum immediately before his flight to draw strength for his mission; after his return he revisited the sacred site to report to Lenin on his mission.[51]

The "Leninization" of the nation's spiritual life, which began immediately upon the man's death, derived directly from Lenin's ideas, according to Dmitri Volkogonov, who lived through it all. Lenin's rule demanded an "unquestioning obedience" comparable only to the faith of the most fanatical fundamentalists. Throughout the USSR, "Lenin Corners" were established and thrived, modeled on the Icon Corners of the Russian Orthodox Church. These mini-shrines included iconlike paintings of Lenin along with his immortal words and writings. Aphorisms from the sage adorned these corners.[52] Ukrainian citizen Olena Doviskaya despaired: "Everywhere you went, there were statues everywhere of Lenin. They wanted you to worship Lenin."[53] So certain was the Party of Lenin's infallibility that in 1925, as early as one year after his death, the Politburo established a special laboratory to study his inactive brain. The purpose, said Volkogonov, was to show the world that the ruler's ideas had been hatched from an almost supernatural mind.[54]

Ronald Reagan recognized communism as a sort of perversion of religious faith. As early as 1951, he told a reporter: "Scratch a Hollywood Communist—especially the 'intellectual'—and you'll find a person afflicted with some kind of neurosis. These people might otherwise have gone in for some kind of phony religion to ease their personal pressures. For them, communism filled that need."[55]

A decade later, he told this story:

I had an occasion to see a page of a letter written by a young American Communist to a friend. In the letter he was explaining his belief and he said of his faith in Communism, "It is my life, my business, my religion, my hobby, my sweetheart, my wife, my bread and I have already been in jail because of my ideas, and if necessary I am ready to go before a firing squad. We have a cause to fight for, a finite purpose in life. We have a morale, an esprit de corps such as no Capitalist army ever had, a devotion to our cause that no religious order can touch."[56]

Throughout his career, Reagan would lodge this complaint against communists. In the 1960s, he regularly assailed the "false god of Marx and his false prophet Lenin."[57]

DESPITE HIS ETERNAL OPTIMISM, REAGAN SEEMED TO believe that man had fallen, that he had a dark side. He saw the danger in handing too much power to leaders in a pernicious system that might further perpetuate iniquity. A communist system that suppressed God needed to be feared, rejected, and denounced. Long before he arrived in Washington, he recognized the Soviet Union's war against religion, where he saw unbounded evil. And he resolved to do something about it.

6.

Two Witnesses

"I see in communism the focus of the concentrated evil of our time. . . . Communism is absolutely evil."

—Whittaker Chambers, Witness[1]

"The Communist vision is the vision of Man without God."

—Whittaker Chambers, Witness[2]

The intensity of the Cold War reached a fever pitch by the early 1950s. Fear of Soviet communism and nuclear conflict absorbed Americans, as did reports of Soviet espionage in the U.S. government.

During this period, Ronald Reagan read widely in his effort to comprehend the Soviet situation. Though his views on communism were colored indelibly by his own personal experience, a handful of thinkers were especially influential as he refined his thinking about the Soviet Union during these years. Many of those to whom he paid closest attention wrote not simply on communism or the USSR, but particularly on the relationship between Soviet communism and atheism—who brought God into the mix. They included Malcolm Muggeridge (whom Reagan described as "brilliant"), Aleksandr Solzhenitsyn, whom he greatly admired; Wilhelm Roepke, and Frank Meyer.[3] He was also strongly influenced by the lesser-known historian Laurence W. Beilenson, who wrote *The Treaty Trap: A History of the Performance of Political Treaties by the United States & European Nations*. While Beilenson focused on breaches in Soviet treaties, he also wrote scathingly on Soviet atheism.[4] He and Reagan carried on a longtime relationship, exchanging ideas in numerous letters.[5]

However, of all the writers who had an impact on Reagan, the most influential was the former KGB operative turned anti-communist crusader Whittaker Chambers.[6] No serious attempt to craft a spiritual biography of Reagan can fail to draw upon the spiritual autobiography that Chambers published in 1952—a volume that dwelt particularly on the author's firsthand account of the conflict between God and communism. Indeed, among the most unappreciated aspects of Reagan's intellectual evolution is the place that Chambers's memoir, *Witness*, held in Reagan's estimation. Four decades after it was published, Reagan kept copies of *Witness* on his bookshelves at both Rancho del Cielo and his home in Los Angeles. Also on a bookshelf at the ranch is a copy of *Odyssey of a Friend*, a collection of letters from Chambers to William F. Buckley, Jr.[7]

Published at a critical time in the development of Reagan's thinking about the Cold War and communism, *Witness* was to Reagan a mesmerizing source of information and affirmation.[8] Though Reagan had been a staunch anti-communist for roughly five years by the time it was published, Chambers's account offered a wealth of insight that Reagan would draw upon for decades. Just as *That Printer of*

Udell's was the most important book of Reagan's childhood years, *Witness* was the one book that most profoundly shaped his political consciousness as an adult. Countless Reagan associates interviewed for this book confirm that Reagan could recite passages from *Witness* verbatim, and he drew upon it in speeches throughout his public life— sometimes crossing out lines and inserting long quotations from Chambers's narrative from memory.[9]

FINDING HIS CHURCH

Whittaker Chambers was born in Philadelphia on April 1, 1901. An awkward boy and equally awkward man, he possessed a keen mind and searching political curiosity. In the course of his life, he would find himself present at the unfolding of some of the most important historical events of his time, though often inadvertently. As one observer noted, Chambers "seemed at once to enjoy and to resent the burdens of history."[10]

Chambers joined the communist cause in the mid-1920s. In his 1997 biography, Sam Tanenhaus noted that in communism Chambers "had at last found his church"—an image Reagan would have appreciated. From 1932 to 1938, Chambers spied for the KGB; though he lost the faith in the late 1930s, he was still a leftist when Henry Luce hired him at *Time* magazine at that time.[11] By the end of his life he was a diehard anti-communist and devout Christian who joined Buckley's *National Review* as a senior editor in 1957.

Chambers's most lasting contribution to history was his role in exposing Alger Hiss, a State Department official whom Chambers named as a Soviet spy. Hiss was everything Chambers was not: charming, smooth, socially connected. He was a darling of the eastern liberal elite, with solid credentials among the foreign-policy establishment, at one point heading up the prestigious Carnegie Endowment for International Peace in Washington. Early in his career he had clerked for Oliver Wendell Holmes; while at State he attended Yalta with FDR's delegation, and was present at the creation of the United Nations. Yet, as Chambers would charge in 1948, Hiss had been a member of his own communist cell throughout the 1930s.

The Hiss affair gripped the nation from 1948 through 1950. It was the case that first brought California congressman Richard Nixon to national prominence. When the smoke cleared, Alger Hiss had been unanimously convicted of perjury by a jury of twelve. He spent forty-four months of a five-year sentence in federal prison in Lewisburg, Pennsylvania; Hiss quipped that his nearly four years in prison was a good corrective to his four years at Harvard.[12] Until the day he died Hiss claimed innocence, but Chambers's testimony and extensive corroborative evidence established his guilt beyond doubt.[13] Among the earliest such works is the opening chapter of Nixon's first memoir, Six Crises, a copy of which occupied Reagan's office bookshelf in California in the mid-1960s.[14] Harry S. Truman's administration would be embarrassed after Secretary of State Dean Acheson and other members expressed support for Hiss; Truman himself had once called the charges a "red herring," but by 1950 even he was converted, exclaiming, "That SOB Hiss is guilty as hell!"[15]

The outcome of the case was not lost on the then-president of the Screen Actors Guild: in a private letter, Reagan emphatically scorned Hiss as "a convicted perjurer and spy."[16]

CHAMBERS'S *WITNESS*

Published only a few years after the Hiss case erupted, *Witness* reflects the literary talent that must have attracted Luce to hire Chambers at

Time. From his childhood on, Chambers was evidently an atypical child: his one major problem seems to have been an overheated imagination. Readers might be forgiven for wondering whether any seven-year-old has ever really been that complex.

T. S. Matthews, who worked with Chambers at *Time*, remarked that Chambers carried "a suppressed air of melodrama about him."[17] But as *Witness* makes clear, his problems had their basis in real family dysfunction: everyone in his immediate family was carrying a fair share of emotional baggage, and Chambers's mother was genuinely disturbed. Throughout his life Chambers himself was unhealthy in both physical and emotional terms. He seemed a man dealing with years of scars.

The Whittaker Chambers of *Witness* seems as preoccupied with God as Wright's Dick Walker was in *Udell's*. The book's title was a nod to the author's place as a witness to history, yet fellow Christians would have understood its reference to another kind of witness—to faith and to Christ. The Greek word for witness is "martyr," which Chambers knew; in the New Testament, martyrdom is directly linked with bearing witness to religious faith.[18] He ultimately saw himself as both a martyr to the cause of anti-communism, and a witness in the religious manner. "I only knew that I had promised God my life, even, if it were His will, to death," he wrote solemnly. "This is my ultimate witness."[19]

Chambers's pilgrimage to Christianity is a thread that runs throughout his autobiography. It was the negative example of Communism in particular—specifically its faith in man and rejection of God—that drove him to Christianity. And the terms in which he described his journey had a long-term influence on Ronald Reagan.

In publishing *Witness*, Chambers included an unusual introductory essay entitled "Foreword in the Form of a Letter to My Children." For conservatives, this foreword is the most critical part of the book, the moment that best captures the author's sense of his own journey; to this day it is often reprinted in anthologies of classic conservative writings.[20] A few pages into the foreword, Chambers writes that it was his "fate" to be a "witness" to each of the "two great faiths of our time." In a passage that presages Reagan's "Time for Choosing" speech a decade later, he continues: "For in this century, within the next decades, will be decided for generations whether all mankind is to become Communist, whether the whole world is to become free, or whether, in the struggle, civilization as we know is to be completely destroyed or completely changed." And Chambers challenged his readers to take the cause personally: "It is our fate to live upon that turning point in history."[21] If there was any real difference between Chambers and Reagan on this score, it was that Reagan found a way to lead the political push toward that turning point in history—to go beyond mere testimony and take action.

As president, Reagan would quote this Chambers passage verbatim in a February 26, 1982, speech to a conservative group. And he would dramatize the distinction with a characteristically dramatic call to arms: "We've already come a long way together. Thank you for all that you've done for me, for the common values we cherish. Join me in a new effort, a new crusade."[22]

COMMUNISM AS AN "EVIL"

But it may have been in his characterization of the nature of communism that Chambers contributed most directly to Reagan's thinking. In his foreword Chambers writes candidly: "I see in communism the focus of the concentrated evil of our time."[23] It was an image that would make its way almost verbatim into one of Reagan's most controversial and lasting presidential addresses, the Evil Empire speech of 1983 in which Reagan called the USSR "the focus of evil in the modern world." Chambers was referring to communism in general, whereas Reagan directed his comment specifically toward the USSR; in every meaningful respect, though, their points were one and the same.

Throughout *Witness*, Chambers used the word "evil" frequently to describe Soviet communism.[24] "Communism is absolutely evil," he wrote. "It was communism that was evil, and the more truly a man acted in its spirit and interest, the more certainly he perpetuated evil."[25] As a communist, he was forced to come to grips with his own complicity in the matter: "This is evil," he wrote, "absolute evil. Of this evil I am a part."[26] He left the Communist Party when he "became convinced it was evil and a threat to Western civilization."[27]

In 1880, Dostoyevsky wrote in *The Brothers Karamazov* that "If God does not exist, everything is permissible." The words were an eerie harbinger of the Bolshevik revolution. Chambers cherished Dostoyevsky; Arthur M. Schlesinger, Jr. noted insightfully that Chambers seemed to see himself as a character out of one of the Russian novelist's epics.[28] Among Chambers's favorite quotations was Dostoyevsky's observation that "The problem of Communism is not an economic problem. The problem of Communism is the problem of atheism."[29] Chambers himself was certain that man needed God, citing as an axiom that "man cannot organize the world for himself without God; without God man can only organize the world *against* man."[30]

On page nine of *Witness*, a passage appears that was later featured in Reagan's Evil Empire speech, as well as in a lesser-known March 1981 address by Reagan to a Conservative Political Action Conference (CPAC) dinner. Speaking of communism, Chambers wrote, "It is not new. It is, in fact, man's second oldest faith. Its promise was whispered in the first days of the Creation under the Tree of the Knowledge of Good and Evil: 'Ye shall be as gods.' " He continued: "They [other ages past] have always been different versions of the same vision: The vision of God and man's relationship to God. The Communist vision is the vision of Man without God. It is the vision of man's displacing God as the creative intelligence of the world."[31] Chambers continued the thought, which Reagan would later reiterate:[32]

> Communism restores man to his sovereignty by the simple method of denying God. . . .
>
> Hence the Communist Party is quite justified in calling itself the most revolutionary party in history. It has posed in practical form the most revolutionary question in history: God or Man? It has taken the logical next step which three hundred years of rationalism hesitated to take, and said what millions of modern minds think, but do not dare or care to say: If man's mind is the decisive force in the world, what need is there for God? Henceforth man's mind is man's fate. . . .
>
> [T]o the challenge: *God or Man?*, they [communists] continue to give the answer: Man.[33]

Chambers also wrote of the infallibility of Communist Party leadership in Moscow. "And the party will be right." Any member who committed heresy against the infallible judgment of the Party had "betrayed that which alone justifies its faith—the vision of Almighty man."[34]

Witness borrows liberally from classic literature and biblical imagery, often melodramatically, and in a way that reflects Chambers's tormented soul. He ends the foreword to *Witness* by evoking Golgo-tha, the "place of skulls." However, he then goes on to start the book by evoking Lazarus, citing his own "impossible return" from the soul-crushing bottomless depths of the communist philosophy. "In 1937," Chambers dates it, "I began, like Lazarus, the impossible return."[35]

Chambers pinpoints 1938 as the year of his break from commu-nism and toward God and freedom. He "freely made the choice—the decision to die, if necessary, rather than live under communism."[36] In one of the memoir's most mystical passages, he describes being struck one day by a physical awareness, which seemed like words spoken to him, presumably from above: "If you will fight for freedom, all will be well with you." He himself said he wasn't sure whether he had actu-ally heard the words, but he felt them. "What was there," recalled Chambers, "was the sense that, like me, time and the world stood still, an awareness of God as an envelopment, holding me in silent as-surance and untroubled peace." He made his commitment: "There was a sense that in that moment I gave my promise, not with the mind, but with my whole being, and that this was a covenant that I might not break."[37]

"Henceforth," he wrote, "in the depth of my being there was a peace and a strength that nothing could shake. It was the strength that nothing could shake. It was the strength that carried me out of the Communist Party, that carried me back into the life of men." The strength, he said, carried him through the ordeal of the Hiss case. "It never left me because I no longer groped for God; I felt God. The ex-perience was absolute."[38]

Chambers went on to sound a note about God's will that sounds strikingly Reaganesque. "I did not seek to know God's will," he writes. "I did not suppose that anyone could know God's will. I only sought prayerfully to know and to do God's purpose with me."[39] Such sentiments were like second nature to Reagan, who believed whole-heartedly not only in God's will but that one could not know God's will ahead of time, and could only seek counsel through prayer. "[W]hatever the outcome, it will be His doing," Reagan would say in 1976 and many other times throughout his life. "I will pray for under-standing of what it is He would have me do."[40]

CHAMBERS, REAGAN, AND THE FINGER OF GOD

Among the many passages from *Witness* that Reagan enjoyed citing off the top of his head, perhaps the most inherently moving was the one in which Chambers described his final disaffection with commu-nism.[41] It was a simple moment, which captured Reagan's own per-ception of the chasm between Christianity and communism. Here is the original passage:

> I date my break [from communism] from a very casual happening. I was sitting in our apartment on St. Paul Street in Baltimore. . . . My daughter was in her high chair. I was watching her eat. She was the most miraculous thing that had ever happened in my life. I liked to watch her even when she smeared porridge on her face or dropped it meditatively on the floor. My eye came to rest on the delicate convolutions of her ear—those intricate, perfect ears. The thought passed through my mind: "No, those ears were not created by any chance coming together of atoms in nature (the Communist view). They could have been created only by immense design." The thought was involuntary and unwanted. I crowded it out of my mind. But I never wholly forgot it or the occasion. I had to crowd it out of my mind. If I had completed it, I should have had to say: De-

sign presupposes God. I did not then know that, at that moment, the finger of God was first laid upon my forehead.[42]

Here is the passage as Reagan retold it in his own words:

Chambers marked the beginning of his personal journey away from communism on the day that he was suddenly struck by the sight of his infant daughter's ear as she sat there having breakfast. And then, he said, he realized that such intricacy, such precision could be no accident, no freak of nature. He said that while he didn't know it at the time, in that moment, God—the finger of God had touched his forehead.[43]

Deep in the Presidential Handwriting File at the Reagan Library is a Speech Department draft of an address that Ronald Reagan was to give to CPAC in February 1982. A speeechwriter who knew of Reagan's affinity for Chambers had included a passage quoting him; Reagan scratched it out and inserted the ear passage instead.[44]

God, Communism, and Freedom

In terms indistinguishable from later Reagan remarks, Chambers wrote apocalyptically that the triumph of communism would mean "slavery to men" and "spiritual night to the human mind and soul."[45] He took note of the relationship between God and freedom, and described his break with communism as an effort to be free. In fact, claimed Chambers, one thing most ex-communists agreed upon was that "they broke because they wanted to be free." Not everyone, he wrote, mean[s] the same thing by "free." Freedom is a need of the soul, and nothing else. It is in striving toward God that the soul strives continually after a condition of freedom. God alone is the inciter and guarantor of freedom. He is the only guarantor. . . . Political freedom, as the Western world has known it, is only a political reading of the Bible. . . . Hence every sincere break with Communism is a religious experience. . . . A communist breaks because he must choose at last between irreconcilable opposites—God or Man, Soul or Mind, Freedom or Communism.

Communism is what happens when, in the name of Mind, men free themselves from God. There has never been a society of a nation without God. But history is cluttered with the wreckage of nations that became indifferent to God, and died.[46]

Those last two sentences in the passage rang true to Reagan as well. He would speak frequently of nations and empires that had "turned their back on God" and paid consequences as great powers.

Chambers followed this section with another passage that became a Reagan favorite. "The crisis of Communism exists to the degree in which it has failed to free the peoples that it rules from God," wrote Chambers. "Nobody knows this better than the Communist Party of the Soviet Union. The crisis of the Western world exists to the degree in which it is indifferent to God." He asserted: "The Western world does not know it, but it already possesses the answer to this problem—but only provided that its faith in God and the freedom He enjoins is as great as Communism's faith in Man."[47]

Once president, Reagan quoted these sentences in a number of speeches, including the Evil Empire speech. In a February 1984 speech at his alma mater in Eureka, Reagan said that Chambers recognized "that faith, not economics, is the central problem of our age and that 'the crisis of the western world exists to the degree in which it is indifferent to God.' "[48]

Quoting the same passage on March 20, 1981, just days before he was almost assassinated, Reagan said that in Chambers's words Americans could find "the real task" before them. That task, he said, was to reassert their commitment as a nation to a "law higher than our own, to renew our spiritual strength." "Only by building such a wall of spiritual resolve," said Reagan, "can we, as a free people, hope to protect our own heritage and make it someday the birthright of all men."[49]

Despite all the resonances between Whittaker Chambers and Ronald Reagan, there is nevertheless one consistent difference that would color everything they said and did: where Chambers was a lifelong pessimist, Reagan was the quintessential optimist. Each man brought his respective mind-set to bear on his attitude toward the Cold War.

Chambers famously described his fear that by rejecting communism, he was leaving "the winning side for the losing side." His full assessment was this:

I said: "You know, we are leaving the winning world for the losing world." I meant that, in the revolutionary conflict of the twentieth century, I knowingly chose the side of probable defeat. Almost nothing that I have observed, or that has happened to me since, has made me think that I was wrong about that forecast.[50]

Ronald Reagan felt quite the opposite. Every step he took in the political battle against the Soviet Union seemed predicated on an intrinsic faith that the United States would win the battle against communism. He trusted that communism was not the future, and vowed that his nation could defeat the USSR and win the Cold War. And in aspiring to the presidency, he seemed bent on finding a way to help the United States pursue a deliberate course to achieve that goal.

In a letter written on April 6, 1954, Chambers noted that his remark about "the losing side" had aroused more concern among "good folk" than almost anything else in *Witness*. However, he complained, nobody noticed another passage in which he added that the right side "was so powerless to help itself that even God had given up."[51] It would take Reagan another quarter century to reach the White House, but before the end of the 1980s he would set out to prove Chambers wrong.

7.

That Shining City: America as a Chosen Land

"I believe that God in shedding his grace on this
country has always in this divine scheme of
things kept an eye on our land and guided it as a
promised land."

—*Ronald Reagan, June 1952*[1]

In contrast to the bleak and godless system of Soviet communism,
Reagan recognized in his own country both a special quality and a
special duty in checking Bolshevik ambitions. By the 1950s, Ronald
Reagan was publicly speaking of America as a nation chosen by God.

In any number of speeches through the years, Reagan said generally that God had "blessed our land."[2] Borrowing from song, he re-

ferred to "America the beautiful" and concurred that God had "shed His grace on thee." For Reagan this was more than a politician's simple rhetoric. From his days in the Disciples Church forward, Ronald Reagan had believed that God had chosen America for a special purpose—that He had a "divine plan" for this select nation, a "Shining City Upon a Hill." Specifically, Reagan believed that the American people were preordained to play a crucial role in history, beginning with the trials of the nation's earliest settlers and continuing into his time in the Oval Office.

Reagan's evocation of America as "A Shining City Upon a Hill" has become one of the phrases most memorably associated with his presidency.[3] Yet the sheer religiousness of this image is often overlooked—and it's impossible to grasp the full scope of Reagan's vision without knowing its origins. Here is the image in his own words:

> Standing on the deck of the Arabella in 1630 off the Massachusetts coast, John Winthrop said "we shall be as a city upon a hill. The eyes of all people are upon us, so that if we deal falsely with our God in this work we have undertaken and cause him to withdraw His present help from us, we shall be made a story and a byword throughout the world."[4]

"We shall be as a City upon a Hill," Winthrop wrote; "the eyes of all people are upon us."[5] Reagan knew the lines to the exact word. He frequently invoked the memory of America's earliest settlers—of their religious pilgrimage and of the faith that sustained them.[6] "We've come a long way since those first settlers reached these shores, asking nothing more than the freedom to worship God," he said fondly. "They asked that He would work His will in our daily lives, so America would be a land of fairness, morality, justice, and compassion."[7]

"A City on a Hill Cannot Be Hidden"

The image of the Shining City was appropriately attributed to Winthrop, but its origins were biblical—perhaps most prominently in the words of Matthew 5:14–16. The first book of the New Testament, Matthew underscores the news that the long-awaited Messiah has come to save all people, both Jews and Gentiles. Matthew, one of the twelve disciples, devoted his writing to arguing that Jesus Christ was the promised Messiah of the Old Testament. His Gospel was probably written sometime before the Romans destroyed the temple in Jerusalem in A.D. 70.

Chapters 5–7 of the Gospel contain the Sermon on the Mount (5:1–7:27), which Christ preached from a mountainside in Galilee. Christ began the sermon by spelling out what are called the Beatitudes—a group of statements fundamental to Christianity, containing a sacredness approaching the Ten Commandments of the Old Testament. These are essentially nine statements that begin "Blessed are . . . ," running from verses 5:3 to 5:11. For instance, 5:9 is the line "Blessed are the peacemakers . . ." Almost immediately thereafter, in verses 5:14–16, come the lines Reagan so loved and internalized:

> You are the light of the world. A city on a hill cannot be hidden. Neither do people light a lamp and put it under a bowl. Instead they put it on its stand, and it gives light to everyone in the house. In the same way, let your light shine before men, that they may praise your good deeds and praise your Father in heaven.[8]

Drawn from Christ's own words, the passage calls on Christians to reflect God's light, not simply absorb it. The role of the Christian, according to Christ himself, is to shine that light where it is needed—to cast it on the darkness.[9] In short, these words constitute a call to practical Christianity, of a kind Ronald Reagan had responded to since his childhood exposure to the teachings of Campbell and the Disciples, Lloyd Emmert, Ben Cleaver, and *That Printer of Udell's*.

Throughout his political career, Reagan would display an inclination to nationalize the individualized message of Wright's novel. In his vision, it was the destiny not only of each private citizen but of America as a whole to share God's light, to serve as a beacon and a model for all other nations. It was Reagan who added the word "shining" to the image of the city, in a gesture that may have recalled his mother's weekly message to her Sunday school students: "Jesus said that the Christian is like a light set where it cannot be hid; come out to Sunday School next Lord's day at ten o'clock. Let us all be shining lights."[10] To the adult Reagan, who would refer to the Soviet Union as "the heart of darkness,"[11] it was an irresistible image.

In a gesture that would have amused President Reagan, the official Soviet news agency, TASS, would later attack his city-on-a-hill remarks as "particularly sacrilegious."[12] Sacrilege, after all, was communism's stock in trade. For Ronald Reagan, however, celebrating America as a beacon of hope was not only a natural extension of his personal philosophy, it was a message he had been promoting since his earliest days as a political voice.

WILLIAM WOODS COLLEGE

In the spring of 1952, Dutch Reagan got a call from an old college buddy, Raymond McCallister. "Mac," as Reagan called him, had become a pastor, and for over thirty years was a mainstay at Webster Groves Christian Church, a Disciples of Christ denomination in St. Louis, Missouri. He was also a member of the board of William

Woods College, a tiny women's college in Fulton, Missouri—a couple of hours from the neighborhood of Cold War architect Harry Truman, and the same town where, six years earlier, Winston Churchill had issued his warning that an "iron curtain" was closing across the European continent.[13]

Mac and Dutch had kept in contact over the years, and McCallister had followed Reagan's career from Des Moines to Hollywood.[14] By the late 1940s, when Reagan headed to Washington to testify on communist infiltration in the film industry, McCallister recognized his old friend's evolving interest in politics as serious and committed.

With that in mind, he convinced Dr. T. T. Swearingen, then the president of William Woods, to invite Reagan to Fulton to deliver the commencement address to the graduating seniors on June 2. "I remember I got a lot of flak for inviting him to give the commencement address because they had never had an actor before," recalled Swearingen almost thirty years later. "They thought we were going out of the realm of where you go to get speakers."[15]

Nonetheless the invitation was accepted, and on the day before the ceremony Reagan and his pregnant wife, Nancy, arrived in Fulton after a long train ride (Reagan refused to fly in those days). The McCallisters picked up the newlyweds at the station. On the way back to the McCallister home, Nancy peered out the car window and was thrilled to see that the local movie theater was showing a double feature—one of her movies and one of her husband's.[16]

Raymond McCallister, Jr., then a high-school senior, enthusiastically went along for the ride. "You could tell the guy was a leader," he says of Reagan today. He particularly remembers being struck by Reagan's religious conviction. "He was a very strong Christian and a man of faith," says the younger McCallister, who followed his father's footsteps and likewise became a minister in Fulton.[17]

The next morning, Dr. Swearingen drove the Californian to the college for Reagan's address. After a rendition of "America the Beautiful"—surely at Reagan's request; he had assigned his talk the same title—the tall, tanned movie star took the stage for a speech that offers a fascinating early window into his lifelong beliefs about America's place in the world.[18]

Reagan began his remarks by affirming that America is "less of a place than an idea." Using language he would restate on innumerable later occasions, he told the students that this idea had been carried deep in the souls of men "ever since man started his long trail from the swamps." He continued:

> It [the idea of America] is nothing but the inherent love of freedom in each one of us, and the great ideological struggle that we find ourselves engaged in today is not a new struggle. It's the same old battle. We met it under the name of Hitlerism; we met it under the name of Kaiserism; and we have met it back through the ages in the name of every conqueror that has ever set upon a course of establishing his rule over mankind. It is simply the idea, the basis of this country and of our religion, the idea of the dignity of man, the idea that deep within the heart of each one of us is something so God-like and precious that no individual or group has a right to impose his or its will upon the people so well as they can decide for themselves.

The great ideological struggle Reagan was referring to, of course, was the Cold War, the third major battle of the century. It's notable that he viewed the fight against communism as merely a continuation of the war against Nazism in WWII—the dangerous thread linking the enemies being their common totalitarianism.

What came next represents Reagan's first known public comment on the subject of America as a divinely selected nation:

> I, in my own mind, have thought of America as a place in the divine scheme of things that was set aside as a promised land. . . . I believe that God in shedding his grace on this country has always in this divine scheme of things kept an eye on our land and guided it as a promised land.[19]

From this early set of comments would emerge a theme—and a call—that Reagan would reiterate for forty years.[20] One can draw a straight line from his 1952 remarks at William Woods to his comment in an address to religious broadcasters during his presidency: "I've always believed that this blessed land was set apart in a special way, that some divine plan placed this great continent here between the two oceans to be found by people from every corner of the Earth—people who had a special love for freedom."[21]

Even after his presidency, Reagan never tired of expressing his faith in America's divine mission. Here he is in June 1990 in Carmel, California:

> You may think this a little mystical, and I've said it many times before, but I believe there was a Divine Plan to place this great continent here between the two oceans to be found by peoples from every corner of the Earth. I believe we were preordained to carry the torch of freedom for the world.[22]

Significantly, in the June 1952 speech, Reagan closed by issuing a call—a challenge, actually—to the young people assembled. He urged them to join the epic struggle against "totalitarian darkness" that confronted their nation, and did so by drawing an analogy to an incident that occurred during a nighttime football game he had recently attended at the Los Angeles Coliseum. A total of 103,000 people were in attendance. Simultaneously, each person lit a match and the lights were shut off—a grand glow, as Reagan put it, bathed the field below "in light that battled the darkness." He explained the parallel he was drawing:

> It was one of the most spectacular sights I have ever seen, just because each one of the people there did what he could to contribute a little light. . . . You have an opportunity to decide now whether you will strike a match and whether you will help push back the darkness over the stadium of humanity. . . . [W]ith your help I am sure we can come much closer to realizing that this land of ours is the last best hope of man on earth. God bless you.[23]

With that Reagan closed his commencement address, leaving his young listeners with a clear message: God had a divine plan that called upon His specially designated United States of America to confront the aggressive communist regime in Moscow. Moreover, it was up to them all—to himself, and to the audience assembled to hear him—to recognize the challenge, and heed the call.

The commencement address at William Woods College was also the commencement of Reagan's public anti-communist crusade. Among Reagan's first public speeches—even preceding his General Electric talks—it featured many of the themes he hammered home in the decades ahead, and it galvanized the William Woods graduates. "He was an excellent speaker," remembered a vindicated Swearingen. "I think it was one of the best commencement speeches we heard in our ten years at William Woods."[24] In the coming decades, much of America would respond to Reagan's favorite theme in much the same way.

CHOSEN AMERICA

Five years later Reagan was invited to deliver another commencement ceremony—this time at his alma mater. Speaking at Eureka College in June 1957, he offered a variation on his theme: "This is a land of destiny and our forefathers found their way here by some Divine system of selective service gathered here to fulfill a mission to advance man a further step in his climb from the swamps."[25] With their suggestion that Americans were specially chosen by Providence, such comments would attract charges of arrogance and ethnocentrism through the years.

Yet to indict Reagan on such charges is to overlook how thoroughly such sentiments have always been interwoven with the vocabulary of patriotism.[26] James H. Moorhead of Princeton Theological Seminary has written about this predilection among Americans in particular:

> It is a scholarly commonplace that Americans have believed themselves to be providentially chosen for a special mission. The Puritan settlers in the 1600s embarked on a divinely appointed errand in the wilderness. Subsequent generations pushed the boundaries of the nation relentlessly westward under the banner of Manifest Destiny and endowed their wars with apocalyptic meaning. Presidents have invoked the rhetoric of special mission.[27]

Similar thoughts regarding America's Providential role have been expressed through the whole course of American history, by the nation's founders and leaders, its most prominent theologians, and its finest men of letters.[28] Reagan's beloved John Winthrop, governor of the Massachusetts Bay Colony, may have been the first, preaching of the city on the hill as his ship approached the shoreline. Yet George Washington frequently used similar terms, invoking the Providential character of the American revolution and its role as a cause or event for all of mankind—a test of whether man was capable of democratic government. Like Alexander Hamilton in the *Federalist Papers*, Washington frequently spoke of the founding as a "great experiment" that was "entrusted into the hands of the American people," as he put it in his first inaugural and elsewhere.

Later presidents often sounded similar chords. William McKinley, who also inherited his piety from his devout mother, was one. Another, perhaps more surprising, was the liberal internationalist Woodrow Wilson. Wilson characterized his dream of a League of Nations, the crowning jewel of the Fourteen Points he offered the international community on America's behalf, as a matter of God's will:

> The stage is set, the destiny is closed. It has come about by no plan of our conceiving, but by the hand of God who led us this way. We cannot turn back. We can only go forward, with lifted eyes and freshened spirit, to follow the vision. It was of this that we dreamed at our birth. America shall in truth show the way. The light streams upon the path ahead, and nowhere else.[29]

Reagan's doctrine of American destiny has bothered liberal Democrats through the years, but many of their own presidential heroes expressed much the same belief. As president, Reagan relished the chance to remind Americans that FDR publicly yearned for divine intervention during the closing days of the Second World War.

"The Almighty God has blessed our land in many ways," Reagan declared, quoting FDR's Fourth Inaugural Address. "So we pray to Him
now for the vision to see our way clearly . . . to the achievement of
His will."[30]

Even John F. Kennedy, the Democratic icon of a later, more secular age, proclaimed: "We in this country . . . are by destiny, rather
than choice, the watchmen on the walls of world freedom."[31] In his
inaugural address, JFK asserted that in the long history of the world,
just a few generations had been granted "the role of defending freedom in its hour of maximum danger." He said he personally welcomed that responsibility. Moreover, he claimed that the energy,
faith, and devotion brought to that endeavor "will light our country"
and "the glow from that fire can truly light the world." And he closed
by exhorting his audience: "[L]et us go forth . . . asking His blessing
and His help, but knowing that here on earth God's work must truly
be our own."[32]

RONALD REAGAN, THEN, WAS NOT ALONE IN VIEWING
America as specially chosen, as a nation with a divine mandate. He
was alone in the single-minded passion with which he harnessed and
implemented that view in the Cold War.

Yet America's national destiny was hardly the only concept occu-
pying Reagan's mind in this period. The 1950s were a critical time in
the development of both an ideology and set of core issues that would
define the man and eventually carry him all the way to the White
House.

8.

The Freedom Crusader

"This irreconcilable conflict [the Cold War] is between those who believe in the sanctity of individual freedom and those who believe in the supremacy of the state."

—*Ronald Reagan, June 1957*[1]

"This evil enemy would deny us our God and . . . imbues his own youth and those of ours he can reach with a fervor of the false god of Marx and his false prophet Lenin."

—*Ronald Reagan, August 1965*[2]

As Ronald Reagan devoted more and more time to national and international issues through the 1950s and into the 1960s, his positions and public statements became more sophisticated. His core beliefs never changed: he continued to see America as a special place, and his notion of the nation's enemy remained sure. But as he traveled the country as a spokesman for General Electric, his thoughts turned from the *idea* of America to practical matters of political ideology and policy. For the first time, he took a long look at the principles of political conservatism. And all of this brought greater specificity to his speeches—of which there were many.

It may come as no surprise that a figure so committed to fighting totalitarianism abroad would eventually focus on the dangers of an overpowering federal government at home, as Reagan came to do during this period. In terms of domestic policy, he began to criticize government for becoming involved in far more than it should be—and especially for tax policies that he believed had become "confiscatory." The more money the federal government took from its citizens, Reagan believed, the more it also robbed individual freedom—especially for those (like him) whose income fell into the 91 percent federal tax rate. One of Reagan's most enduring messages, born in this period, was that Americans needed to be freed from such policies. Moreover, he grew convinced that American business must be liberated from "encroaching government controls."[3] Taken together, Reagan believed, high taxes and obtrusive government regulation represented a "creeping socialism" that might slowly but surely cripple the nation.

For Reagan, then, his GE years—1954 to 1962—in many ways represented his first concerted political campaign. Philosophically, the content of his many speeches in these years made the period a kind of Ronald Reagan freedom crusade.

Reagan thought in terms of defining principles and grand ideas, and among them he valued freedom more than any other.[4] Beginning in this period, freedom became the dominant theme in his speeches and public statements, appearing even more frequently than his numerous statements on God. Actually, the two concepts were inseparable to him—freedom, ultimately, was a God-given inalienable right.

Whether turning his spotlight on oppressive federal interference at home, or on the violations of human freedom perpetrated by communism abroad, Reagan called upon every audience he faced to join him in the cause of freedom.

WHEN REAGAN RETURNED TO EUREKA IN JUNE 1957 TO deliver a commencement address, he expressed a conception of a divinely ordained America. But he took his point much further: Eureka's graduating seniors got a richer Reagan than did those students at William Woods five years earlier.

Citing a possibly apocryphal story about the signing of the Declaration of Independence in Philadelphia, Reagan told the students about an unidentified man who was allegedly present in the state house on that day. "Were my soul trembling on the verge of eternity, my hand freezing in death," he quoted the stranger as saying, "I would still implore you to remember this truth: God has given America to be free."[5]

By itself, that line was no different from what Reagan would say repeatedly throughout his career. But where he went from there was remarkable. Here, said Reagan, in this "truth" that God had given America to be free, "was the first challenge to the people of this new land, the charging of this nation with a responsibility to all mankind. And down through the years with but few lapses the people of America have fulfilled their destiny."[6] God had not only chosen America to be free, Reagan was saying, but with that freedom, He had entrusted the nation with a larger responsibility *to all mankind.*

From these early days as a public speaker, we see evidence of how Reagan translated all of this into the Cold War struggle. "Today we find ourselves involved in another struggle, this time called a cold war," he told Eureka's upperclassmen. At William Woods he had held back those two key words—"cold war"—speaking only generally of a great ideological struggle. Now, five years later, he told his audience that the war wasn't "really a new struggle at all. It is the oldest struggle of human kind, as old as man himself." It was a "simple struggle between those of us who believe that man has the dignity and sacred right and the ability to choose and shape his own destiny and those who do not so believe." He drew a basic distinction that might have applied equally well to his burgeoning impatience with "creeping socialism" at home: "This irreconcilable conflict is between those who believe in the sanctity of individual freedom and those who believe in the supremacy of the state." And he continued with yet another characterization of communists—domestic and foreign—in stark moral terms: "In a phase of this struggle not widely known, some of us came toe to toe with this enemy this evil force in our own community in Hollywood, and make no mistake about it, this is an evil force."[7]

This was a new Reagan, bolder and more assured than just five years earlier. And his reference to Hollywood may have been less nostalgic than many would have thought at the time: even into the late 1950s Reagan felt the battle to protect the film industry from communist influence was far from over.[8] In 1959 he boycotted a 20th Century-Fox banquet for Nikita Khrushchev, and in May 1961 he charged that communists in Hollywood were "crawling out of the rocks," charging that the Communist Party had "ordered once again" a massive infiltration of television and motion pictures.[9]

As Reagan scholar Matthew Dallek has observed, "In his speeches and public statements" of the period "Reagan repeatedly depicted the Soviet Union as an evil and repugnant force"; he also painted the East-West conflict in "apocalyptic hues."[10] In a series of statements in 1961 and 1962, at the height of Cold War tensions, Reagan ratcheted up the intensity by using the rhetoric of literal war.

"The inescapable truth," he declared, is that the United States is "at war," and "we are losing that war simply because we don't, or won't realize that we are in it."[11] "This war," he said in Fargo, North Dakota in January 1962, "was declared a half century ago by Karl Marx and re-affirmed by Lenin when he said that Communism and Capitalism cannot exist side-by-side."[12] And the aggressor, as he charged in August 1965, was the USSR: an "evil enemy" that "would deny us our God."[13]

SOVIET COMMUNISM AND ETERNAL SALVATION

During this fundamental period in his ideological development, a fascinated Reagan watched and listened one day as fellow entertainer Pat Boone assailed the Red Menace before a crowd of 16,000 in the Los Angeles Sports Arena. As Reagan recalled, Boone had told the crowd: "I love my little girls more than anything. [Yet] I would rather see my little girls die now, still believing in God, than have them grow up under communism and one day die no longer believing in God." Reagan remembered:

> There were thousands of young people in that audience. They came to their feet with shouts of joy. They had instantly recognized the profound truth in what he had said with regard to the physical and the soul and what was truly important.[14]

To non-Christians and atheists, Boone's logic may seem absurd, even cruel. Yet the story had a profound resonance with Reagan. He retold it for years, speaking only of a "young father" or "well-known actor" he heard make the declaration. Boone's assertion (and Reagan's endorsement) was rooted in basic tenets of Christianity. Protestants believe that in order to attain salvation and "get into Heaven," one must accept Jesus Christ as personal Lord and Savior. A Christian must accept the deal offered in the New Testament: If followers accept Christ's sacrifice on the cross, they will receive the gift of salvation.[15]

Reagan expanded on his thinking in a later interview with the executive director of the Christian Booksellers Association. Asked his favorite Bible verse, Reagan cited John 3:16, which he quoted from memory.[16] When asked what the verse meant to him personally, Reagan explained by going to the same verse he quoted in his commencement speech at his high-school graduation: "It means that having accepted Jesus Christ as my Savior, I have God's promise of eternal life in Heaven, as well as the abundant life here on earth that He promises to each of us in John 10:10."[17]

This straightforward reliance on doctrine helps explain how Reagan and Boone could come to view the death of even their closest loved ones as preferable to life under communism. After all, denied the chance to learn about and thus accept Christ's gift, any unbelieving person who died might be denied eternal life. The unfortunate souls obliged to live under communism, in Reagan's eyes, were being prevented by the state from entering heaven—and this, in his eyes, was an abomination.[18]

Here it may be helpful to look to the writings of Christian philosopher C. S. Lewis, whom Reagan read and admired. "Christianity asserts that every individual human being is going to live for ever," wrote Lewis in his classic *Mere Christianity*.[19] "Now there are a good many things which would not be worth bothering about if I were going to live only seventy years, but which I had better bother about very seriously if I am going to live forever." Contrasting democracy and totalitarianism, he continued: "If individuals live only seventy years, then a state, or a nation, or a civilization, which may last for a thousand years, is more important than an individual." However, says Lewis, if Christianity is true, "then the individual is not only more important but incomparably more important, for he is everlasting and the life of a state or a civilization, compared with his, is only a moment."[20]

Reagan heartily subscribed to this worldview. He believed that individuals were incomparably more important than the state, and thus for a noneternal state to deny an eternal individual his or her right to heaven was intolerable and unacceptable. To Reagan, the outrage wasn't merely that Soviet officials shut down churches: the eternal salvation of millions was at stake. And as Reagan recognized, it was especially awful that the salvation of Russian people, whom he believed to be "deeply religious" at heart, had been sacrificed at the altar of communism.[21]

Maria Anne Hirschmann, a German émigré who was imprisoned in a communist work camp by the Soviets after WWII, has described this position with eloquence:

> Freedom is a gift from Heaven. The greatest gift that God gave the human race. And the first thing the communists take away from you is your permission, your freedom, to choose Jesus Christ. Hell hates freedom just as much as Hell hates salvation.[22]

It's hard to imagine a better summation of Reagan's views on Soviet communism.

FREEDOM, TAXATION, AND SCRIPTURE

The spiritual implications of communism may seem worlds apart from so prosaic a matter as American federal tax rates. Yet as Reagan's policy views evolved during this period, his thinking on foreign and domestic issues drew upon remarkably consistent sources and influences—from his wide reading to his overriding faith in God and freedom. It's easy to attribute Reagan's fixation on taxes to the punitive tax burden he experienced during his Hollywood years. Yet his reading of the Bible also influenced his thinking on taxation, as he made clear in a number of speeches he made throughout the 1950s and 1960s.

In one 1962 speech, Reagan spent four lengthy paragraphs eviscerating the American tax system, especially the 50 to 91 percent tax brackets. He promoted "proportionate taxation" over progressive taxation, in which the government levies a progressively higher tax rate on progressively higher incomes. And Reagan expressed his objections in explicitly biblical terms:

> For an illustration of the difference between proportionate and progressive taxation, we can look to the Bible. There, tithing is explained as the economic basis of our Judaic-Christian religions. The Lord says you shall contribute one-tenth and He says, "If I prosper you 10 times as much you will give 10 times as much." That is proportionate—but look what happens today when you start computing Caesar's share. A man of average income who suddenly prospered ten times as much would find his personal income tax increased 43 times.[23]

With its echoes of Nelle's teachings on tithing, this was a principle Reagan believed in deeply, and he had made the same point the previous year in speeches in New Jersey and Phoenix.[24] In the New Jersey speech, he basically argued for what today is called a flat tax, citing biblical teaching among his arguments for a flat-tax system.[25]

Declaring that there could be "no normal justification of the progressive tax," Reagan contended that modern American progressive taxation was received "direct" from the proud atheist Karl Marx, "who designed it as the prime essential of a socialist state." Indeed, it was encapsulated in one of Marx's best-known maxims, "From each according to his ability, to each according to his need."[26] Like so much of Reagan's political philosophy, it was a simple insight, but a trenchant one—and one that would propel him forward as he began his trajectory toward the White House.

A TIME FOR CHOOSING

In October 1964, the Soviet Union was in the midst of a leadership shift that would dislodge Nikita Khrushchev from office, to be replaced eventually by Leonid Brezhnev. As Reagan perceived it, however, the change in leadership had little impact on the Soviet war on religion.

Though it wouldn't become evident for another two decades, that same month was also a watershed for American leadership, and not just in terms of the two candidates squaring off in that year's presidential election. The American public may have been presented in 1964 with a choice between President Lyndon B. Johnson and Republican challenger Barry Goldwater, but that October is arguably the month that made Ronald Reagan president. Just as it was an October that birthed the Bolshevik revolution, it was also an October that spawned the man who would seek to unseat the revolution.

That month, Reagan was scheduled to make a televised statement on behalf of Goldwater; it would become known as the "Time for Choosing" speech. Key Republicans were so enthusiastic about the address that they pushed to air it nationwide. Perhaps the most instrumental among them was wealthy Republican contributor Walter Knott, whose role in arranging the broadcast has eluded history. It was Knott, the proprietor of California's Knott's Berry Farm, who first called the Republican National Committee to ask what it would cost to run Reagan's message for Goldwater on national television.[27] When the RNC gave him an estimate on the exorbitant price tag, he pointedly asked: If he raised the money, would the RNC ensure that the speech ran on national television? Yes, the RNC promised. A few days later a check arrived. Unsure of the wisdom of spending the money on a promotional spot for Goldwater, whose chances of prevailing against Johnson were slim, the committee telephoned Knott. "Could we invest the check elsewhere instead?" Knott was asked. "Absolutely not," he responded. He instructed the RNC to spend those resources "airing Reagan." If the speech failed to air, he promised that he would never raise another penny for the party.[28]

The RNC did as it was told. The speech was an enormous success, setting fund-raising records for the Republican Party nationwide. And for the first time it made Ronald Reagan a player in the national political debate.

The speech wove together all the themes Reagan had been nurturing for more than a decade, testing them around the country in his speeches for General Electric—from high taxation and excessive regulation, to the loss of freedom at home and abroad. Those messages were clear to anyone watching his delivery that day, and to those who have analyzed it in the years since. Neglected, however, have been the speech's religious underpinnings.

In the speech, Reagan assessed the state of freedom in the world, lamenting the "millions of people enslaved in Soviet colonies in the satellite nations." The speech's most memorable line may have referred to the American people's "rendezvous with destiny," yet Reagan used that phrase in a distinctly biblical context. Only a few sentences before he had mentioned Moses and Israel, and invoked the image of Christ on the cross. Reagan was setting very specific terms for his national audience: to him the cause of freedom was inextricably linked with God, and poised in direct opposition to the forces of aggressive, athestic communism.

"You and I have a rendezvous with destiny," he continued. It was a bold line, and an odd one, considering the circumstances: on October 27, 1964, Reagan had never been elected or even considered for any public office, let alone at the national or presidential level. Now, in his first foray into the national political spotlight, he had been recruited to make a statement on behalf of another person: Barry Goldwater, his party's nominee for president. Yet now Reagan wasn't speaking about Goldwater at all: he was talking about Ronald Reagan, the American people, and their common destiny.

The "Time for Choosing" speech, and that one line in particular, have since become such a familiar part of American political lore that it's difficult to appreciate how shocking they must have been in 1964. The phrase "a rendezvous with destiny" must have rung a distant bell for many viewers, for it had originated with none other than Franklin Roosevelt, Reagan's early hero. They were loaded words, packed with self-importance, though it has rarely been suggested they were arrogant. What was truly stunning was the confidence with which Reagan stepped into FDR's shoes: by "you and I," he *might* have intended merely to include himself among the millions of Americans summoned by FDR, but it's hard to escape the impression that he was already presenting himself as a leader for the American people.

Roosevelt had sounded the call at Franklin Field in Philadelphia in 1936, when the seeds of World War II were still being sown in Hitler's Germany. America was fast approaching a "rendezvous with destiny," he told his audience; as John McDonough and Robert Trout later observed, only a decade later was it apparent that it was the most prophetic line of the era. It would take somewhat longer for Reagan's rendezvous to play out, but before the end of his administration in 1989, the course of destiny had clearly shifted in America's favor.

The lines Reagan chose to follow the declaration were both challenging and apocalyptic:

> We can preserve for our children this, the last best hope of man on earth, or we can sentence them to take the first step into a thousand years of darkness. If we fail, at least let our children and our children's children say of us we justified our brief moment here. We did all that could be done.

Franklin Roosevelt wasn't the only politician who had used the phrase "rendezvous with destiny" in such a context: indeed, though few noticed it at the time, Reagan himself had used the phrase two years earlier in a televised speech supporting another nationally known Republican. In a November 4, 1962, speech for Richard Nixon's California gubernatorial campaign, he concluded: "You and I have a rendezvous with destiny; we'll meet the challenge in the days ahead or we'll trail in the dust the golden hope of mankind for years to come."[29]

To preserve the last best hope of man on earth, or take the first step into a thousand years of darkness; to meet the challenge, or trail in the dust the golden hope of mankind. It was a testament to Americans' longtime ease with Ronald Reagan that so many accepted such a stark challenge from a man whose only previous elected office was as leader of the Screen Actors Guild.

What might have possessed Reagan to thrust himself into the

spotlight in such a way in 1964? The speech made reference to the loss of freedom in all its forms, including through overly intrusive government in America itself. But with the Cuban missile crisis only two years past, the "darkness" Reagan envisioned was a far more direct reference to the threat of losing the Cold War to America's Marxist enemies and their "evil ways." His language may have been apocalyptic, but Reagan's inherent optimism shone through: by inviting the American people along with him on a shared mission to confront Soviet communism, he gave the first display of the confidence that would propel him to the White House a decade and a half later.

IN 1965, THE YEAR BETWEEN THE "TIME FOR CHOOSING" speech and his campaign for the governorship of California, Reagan gave an interview to the *New York Times*, laying out his policy positions to the public. For the *Times*, Reagan boiled his message down to a simple sentence: "I think basically that I stand for what the bulk of Americans stand for—dignity, freedom of the individual, the right to determine your own destiny."[30]

It was a message that would remain constant for the duration of his political career.

9.

God in Sacramento

"He who introduces into public office the principles of primitive Christianity will change the face
of the world."

> —*Ronald Reagan, first inaugural address as
> governor (1967), quoting Benjamin
> Franklin[1]*

"I'm not quite able to explain how my election
happened or why I'm here, apart from believing it
is part of God's plan for me."

> —*Ronald Reagan, interview with* Christian
> Life *(1968)[2]*

Before Reagan could take on communism from the national political stage, he needed real experience in public office. The California governorship, which he held from January 1967 to January
1975, provided that opportunity, but the job was more than a

stepping-stone to 1600 Pennsylvania Avenue. As a committed conservative, Reagan was drawn to the office by a series of domestic and statewide issues that attracted his attention and appealed to his evolving sense of the roles government should—and shouldn't—play in peoples' lives. And during this passage in his life, as in every other, his public statements and positions were marked by consistent religious orientation and commitment: once again he enlisted God in the charge.

This was clear as early as Reagan's first public act as governor. "It is inconceivable to me," he admitted only minutes into his January 1967 inaugural address, "that anyone could accept this delegated authority without asking God's help." And he appealed to a higher authority as he took on the challenges of his new position: "I pray that we who legislate and administer will be granted wisdom and strength beyond our own limited power; that with Divine guidance we can avoid easy expedients as we work to build a state where liberty under law and justice can triumph."[3]

In that first address Reagan also promised, explicitly and intrepidly, to conduct his public duties according to the teachings of Christ, borrowing a Benjamin Franklin quote about incorporating those teachings so as to "revolutionize the world."[4] This apparently unplanned remark has been reported in different versions—Reagan was speaking without notes, and there was no formal transcript—but in her 1980 autobiography, Nancy Reagan seemed to recall it best.[5] As she remembers, her husband paused, turned to the Senate chaplain who had opened the ceremony with an invocation, and said:

> Reverend, perhaps you weren't a part of my imagining of what this moment would be. But I am deeply grateful for your presence because you remind us and bring here the presence of someone else

without whose presence I certainly wouldn't have the nerve to do what I'm going to try to do. Someone back in our history, maybe it was Benjamin Franklin, said if ever someone could take public office and bring to that public office the precepts and teachings of the Prince of Peace,[6] he would revolutionize the world and men would be remembering him for 1,000 years. I don't think anyone could follow those precepts completely. I'm not so presumptuous as to think I can—but I will try very hard. I think it's needed in today's world.[7]

Revolutionizing the world, being remembered for a thousand years: Clearly this new governor was signaling that his interests were broader than those of the average state politician. One close listener, Reagan's colleague and fellow Christian Herbert E. Ellingwood, was pleased with the new governor's words, but found it difficult to believe he had no higher calling than Sacramento in mind when he uttered them.[8]

THE EARLY 1960S REMAIN A RELATIVELY UNDOCUmented time in Reagan's spiritual life. Beyond a few high points—the closing years of his General Electric period, the "Time for Choosing" speech—he steered relatively clear of the public eye. Yet it was the start of a decade of sweeping change in America, and in these quiet years, as he raised his second family with Nancy, Ronald Reagan encountered some of those changes in his own home.

Before moving to the governor's mansion, Reagan attended the Bel Air Presbyterian Church, which he joined after his marriage to Nancy. One Sunday morning, as his family was getting ready for church, Reagan found that his son, young Ron, was lingering in his room. Reagan walked in to check on him, only to find his son dressed in blue jeans and a T-shirt. He asked his boy why he wasn't wearing his suit. "I'm not going," said his son defiantly. "I don't believe it and I'm not going."

Some forty years later, Ron Reagan recounted the incident. "That bothered him for a long, long time," he said of his father. "I don't think it ever stopped bothering him. . . . [It was] one of the things that disturbed him more than anything else."[9] Reagan was very concerned over whether Ron, as well as his sister, Patti, were Christians. "I wish they would accept Christ," he more than once told his son Michael. One evening years later, during a family dinner in Washington in 1984, shortly before Patti married, Reagan grabbed Michael's hand and whispered, "I wish that Patti would accept Christ."[10]

For Reagan, the distinction between "believing in God" and "accepting Christ" was real and meaningful. He feared that Ron in particular had done neither. It troubled him so much that as president he mentioned his son's apparent atheism to Mikhail Gorbachev in their first one-on-one meeting at the Moscow Summit.[11]

Reagan had difficulty relating to his children's doubts over God; they were worlds apart from his own thinking as a child, and it must have perplexed him how he had failed to instill faith in his children the way that Nelle had in him.

And yet in 1995, Patti, probably the most controversial and difficult of the Reagan children, published a book called *Angels Don't Die: My Father's Gift of Faith*, a remarkable testimony to the gift her father bestowed upon his daughter. She writes:

> The world knows much about Ronald Reagan; it should also be
> known that he passed along to his daughter a deep, resilient faith
> that God's love never wavers, and that no matter how harsh life

seems, or how cruel the world is, that love is constant, unconditional, eternal. The world should know that Ronald Reagan was a father who patiently answered his child's questions about God, and angels, and miracles. That child grew into an adult who has never doubted the possibility of miracles and the presence of God, and who hears her father's answers even when the dark times seem overwhelming.[12]

Though it's not clear whether Patti became a Christian, her words make it plain that she did come to reject atheism. Her book appeared shortly after her father first announced the onset of Alzheimer's, at a point when his mind was still strong enough to converse regularly with Patti; he must have been moved by the gift she had given him in return.

During his time as a member of Bel Air Presbyterian in the 1960s, Reagan developed a close relationship with the church's senior pastor, Rev. Donn D. Moomaw; it would last through his governorship, his presidency, and his final lucid days. An all-American linebacker at UCLA and a founder of the Fellowship of Christian Athletes, Moomaw had passed up a pro-football career for the ministry. According to Moomaw, his relationship with Reagan eventually transcended that of a pastor and congregant; they became friends, and often sat and talked through issues of life and faith. Asked by former *New York Times* reporter Bob Slosser to describe these conversations, Moomaw demurred, citing pastoral privacy. But it was clear, said Slosser, that Moomaw was referring to "profound matters of salvation, eternal life, the divinity of Christ, the will of God, plus the day-to-day problems of living that touch upon these broader theological matters."[13]

Moomaw recalled that Reagan enjoyed discussing and even debating theological issues, sometimes in person, other times by phone. He sometimes called Moomaw after hearing a sermon, and though Reagan didn't always agree with the content, he always related the message to his own experience and understanding. Moomaw called Reagan's "a knowledgeable faith," saying Reagan was "very intelligent in his knowledge of the Scriptures." Reagan was "quite demonstrative in his love of the great hymns," and "always very attentive in worship. During a worship service, he became involved in the total experience—the sadness, the rejoicing, the singing. He was as alert to the full meaning of worship as anyone could be."[14]

During his governorship, Reagan continued to meet from time to time with close Christian friends from outside government, including Moomaw and Pat Boone. Indeed, immediately after the governor's election in November 1966, Reagan and Nancy came to the church for prayer.[15] Slosser reported that Reagan and Moomaw occasionally discussed and prayed over the major political, moral, and ethical issues facing the governor's administration.[16] Moomaw called Reagan "a man without guile—one of the most principled men I know. . . . In his decisions he tries to be morally right, use his common sense and seek the guidance of God." He prayed with Reagan often, and said that the two spent "many hours together on our knees."

Perhaps not surprisingly, from the moment he entered government in the 1960s, Reagan's religious beliefs seem to have informed his politics as well as his private conversations. Far from a passive parishioner, Reagan had so taken the pastor's sermons to heart that they regularly contributed to his political discourse: in a May 1968 interview, Moomaw remarked that he had heard many of his own illustrations from sermons come bouncing back at him in Reagan's campaign speeches.[17]

Remarks he made during these years reflect Reagan's belief that there was much the state could learn from the church. The governor told David Frost that Christ was the historical figure he most admired, and he believed that lawmakers could learn from Christ's teachings.[18] "Can you name one problem that would not be solved if we had simply followed the teachings of the man from Galilee?" he asked rhetorically in a September 1967 speech.[19] He said the answer to "each and every problem" could be found in the "simple words of Jesus of Nazareth."[20] In a later gubernatorial address, he asserted: "If we lived by the Golden Rule, there would be no need for other laws."[21]

Among the political issues during Reagan's gubernatorial tenure, there were certain challenges that prompted him to call upon his faith for answers. Among them was the death penalty.

Reagan believed that capital punishment conformed to biblical teaching, and it was a question to which he had devoted considerable thought. One of his bookshelves at the ranch still holds a 1925 book on the death penalty by a man named Lamar T. Berman; sections of the book that refer to God and Scripture have been underlined and bracketed in red ink.[22]

And yet, while Reagan seemed confident that the death penalty had biblical basis, during his governorship he was compelled to pray for guidance at least once over the issue. When thirty-seven-year-old Aaron Mitchell was sentenced to death for killing a Sacramento police officer (and a father of two, as Reagan usually noted) during an armed robbery, the question of clemency reached Reagan's desk. He would later recall the night before that decision, which he tried to postpone, as the worst of his governorship. He said no part of a governor's job is approached "more prayerfully" than a death penalty decision. As Reagan agonized over the matter, Donn Moomaw flew in to counsel him; the two knelt together by Reagan's coffee table to pray over the issue. Even after Moomaw said "amen," Reagan jumped in, asking for help to learn God's will and do what was right.[23]

In the end, Reagan refused to grant clemency to Mitchell, and the killer was put to death at 10:00 A.M. the following day in San Quentin's gas chamber. It was the only execution carried out during Reagan's eight years as governor.[24] That he ultimately chose not to prevent the execution suggested how firm his convictions were, but it was that moment of prayer with Donn Moomaw that offers a window into the real Reagan: a moment not just of conscience but of humility as he struggled to perceive God's way.

GOVERNOR REAGAN ON THE POWER OF PRAYER

Fairly early in his tenure as governor, Reagan saw that public life would dramatically affect his prayer life. In May 1968, just sixteen months into his first term, Reagan confessed that while prayer had always been a part of his life, he had spent more time praying in the previous few months than in any period he could recall: "The everyday demands of this job could leave me with many doubts and fears if it were not for the wisdom and strength that come from these times of prayer."[25]

Reagan's time as governor reveals his confidence that the country could solve its problems by "trusting in a power greater than ours." He placed great stock in the power of prayer, regularly urging it upon his audiences, both secular and nonsecular, from the earliest days of his public career. "I believe very much in His promise that, 'where two or more gather in My name, there will I be also,' " wrote Governor Reagan in a letter to Mr. and Mrs. L. W. Ripple of Bakersfield, California, thanking them for the prayers offered by the people at their church. "I think I have known and felt the power and help of those prayers."[26]

He also believed in the impact of prayer in his everyday private life. Nancy Reagan has said that he "prayed a great deal," "wherever" he was and "whatever" he was doing.[27] Prayer was "so important" to Reagan, according to Judge William P. Clark, that he prayed on a daily basis.[28] Next to Nancy, Bill Clark is probably the best authority on Reagan's spiritual life while in politics. A dedicated Catholic, Clark was Reagan's chief of staff as governor; later he followed Reagan into the White House, where he held a number of key positions, including national security adviser.[29] Edmund Morris dubs Clark the "most impressive" adviser within the White House inner circle, and the "most important and influential person" in Reagan's first presidential administration. He also names Clark as the only person in the two terms of the administration who had any kind of spiritual intimacy with the president.[30]

By his own account, Clark prayed frequently with Reagan.[31] Citing one of his earliest examples, he points to Reagan's first trip out of state as governor, on the way to Washington, D.C., aboard a TWA flight to Baltimore. Clark informed the governor that Martin Luther King, Jr., had been shot. He expected some comment from Reagan in return, but heard nothing. Clark stepped away; when he turned back around he found Reagan in prayer, looking down at his knees, lips moving in silence.[32]

Privately, Reagan attributed even physical healing to the power of prayer. In his second autobiography, he told the story of an ulcer he had once begun to suffer. Discussing the condition with no one but Nancy and his doctor, he prayed for it to go away. One morning he reached for his bottle of Maalox, until "something inside" told him "You don't need this anymore." An hour or two later he had a meeting with a man from southern California who wanted to discuss a problem. As the man was leaving Reagan's office, he turned and informed the governor that he was part of a group who prayed for him daily. Startled by the spontaneous offer, Reagan thanked him.[33]

Later that same day Reagan had another visitor, this one from northern California. As he was leaving, he, too, stopped, turned around, and told Reagan that he met daily with a group of people who prayed for him. Not long after, as Reagan told the story, he went to the doctor. Not only had the ulcer cleared up, he learned, but the affliction was so completely cured that no evidence of it remained. "The power of prayer?" Reagan contemplated. It was, he believed, more than a coincidence.[34]

Prayer was a rock of reliability to Governor Reagan. In one interview, the governor said that the two things he asked for most in prayer were wisdom and strength, a claim his pastor confirmed.[35] Countless times he borrowed a line from Lincoln, who reportedly said that he had been driven many times to his knees by the "overwhelming conviction" that he had nowhere else to go. "He lived that constantly," said Clark.[36]

The weight of the office, and the comfort he took in God, seems to have made Reagan think back to his Dixon childhood; it made him think of Nelle, who had passed away a few years earlier, and of Ben Cleaver. More than once as governor, he penned a letter to Ben thanking the pastor for helping instill the faith he relied on as governor. That faith, he said, prompted him to look upward when he faced adversity, rather than to someone else. "The Lord sometimes must tire of hearing me ask Him for strength, courage, and wisdom," he wrote to his childhood pastor. "I couldn't attempt this job for one day without His help."[37]

REAGAN EVANGELIZES: THE CALIFORNIA MINISTRY

It was during his governorship that Reagan's mind first began to turn seriously toward the idea that America needed a religious revival—a spiritual awakening. "I think our nation and the world need a spiritual revival as it has never been needed before," he argued as governor in a 1972 prayer breakfast.[38] In a later interview with *Christianity Today*, he said:

> There has been a wave of humanism and hedonism in the land. . . . However, I am optimistic because I sense in this land a great revolution against that. . . . I think there is a hunger in this land for a spiritual revival, a return to a belief in moral absolutes—the same morals upon which the nation was founded.[39]

Such comments weren't mere public attempts to appeal to religious conservative voters. In fact, they appear more often in Reagan's private letters to everyday citizens than in his public speeches. Here is a brief sample from letters he wrote in the 1970s:

To a narcotics control commissioner in Brooklyn: "What we need is a spiritual awakening and return to the morals of a Christian society."

To a common citizen: "I am deeply concerned with the wave of hedonism—the humanist philosophy so prevalent today—and believe this nation must have a spiritual rebirth . . . and we must have a spiritual rebirth very soon."

To another citizen: "I have felt for a long time that the people of our land are hungry for a return to things of the spirit."

To another: "This nation must have a spiritual rebirth, and we must have such a rebirth very soon."

To the graduating seniors of a public high school in Wayne, New Jersey: "No nation which has outgrown its God has ever lived to write additional pages of history. This nation is in need of a spiritual reawakening, and a reaffirmation of trust in God."[40]

In an article entitled "Ronald Reagan: 'God, Home, and Country,' " Herb Ellingwood shared a number of eyewitness accounts of Reagan spreading this message in the 1960s and 1970s:

> I overheard [Reagan's] personal conversation with Demos Shakarian after the Governor gave his testimony to a Full Gospel Business Men's Fellowship meeting in Sacramento. It was the same message I heard him tell his secret servicemen during the campaign in 1976. A group of ministers from Bob Mumford in Florida received the same answers to their questions. Publicly, before the California Association of Christian Schools; or privately, in letters to kids; it's the same story as the one he gave personally to Pope Paul VI— "The time has come to turn back to God and reassert our trust in Him for the healing of America."[41]

As governor, Reagan also endeavored to use his public office to bring the biblical message to Californians. Apparently unconcerned about any appearance of impropriety in bringing a church leader to the state house of the nation's largest state, Reagan invited members of the Supreme Court, executive branch, and others to hear the celebrated evangelist Billy Graham address a joint session of the California legislature. In introducing the preacher, Reagan stated, "There is no need in our land today greater than the need to rediscover our spiritual heritage." Graham challenged the official California leadership to lead spiritually. In the view of Herb Ellingwood, "that one event changed the lives of many in the state Capitol."[42] It was a broad and evidently successful appeal to a significant audience.

Many of Reagan's religious overtures at this time were explicitly Christian.[43] He often wrote of Jesus Christ in private correspondence with strangers, and he wasn't shy about Christian apologetics, frequently making the case for Christ.[44] In the 1970s, he asked an interviewer rhetorically: "How can you write off the prophecies in the Old Testament that hundreds of years before the birth of Christ predicted every single facet of his life, his death, and that he was the Messiah?"[45]

In a March 1978 letter to a liberal minister—who doubted Christ's divinity and accused Reagan of a "limited Sunday school level theology"—Reagan wrote:

Perhaps it is true that Jesus never used the word "Messiah" with regard to himself (although I'm not sure that he didn't) but in John 1, 10 and 14 he identifies himself pretty definitely and more than once.

Is there really any ambiguity in his words: "I am the way, the truth and the life: no man cometh unto the Father but by me?" . . . In John 10 he says, "I am in the Father and the Father in me." And he makes reference to being with God, "before the world was," and sitting on the "right hand of God." . . .

These and other statements he made about himself, foreclose in my opinion, any question as to his divinity. It doesn't seem to me that he gave us any choice; either he was what he said he was or he was the world's greatest liar. It is impossible for me to believe a liar or charlatan could have had the effect on mankind that he has had for 2000 years. We could ask, would even the greatest of liars carry his lie through the crucifixion, when a simple confession would have saved him? . . . Did he allow us the choice you say that you and others have made, to believe in his teachings but reject his statements about his own identity?[46]

Reagan frequently used this apologetic privately and publicly throughout the gubernatorial period—and beyond.[47] Some readers will here recognize an argument C. S. Lewis famously made in *Mere Christianity*.[48] Lewis advised people against taking what he called a particular, "really foolish" stance on Christ—the position that "I'm ready to accept Jesus as a great moral teacher, but I don't accept His claim to be God." Lewis protested:

> That is one thing we must not say. A man who was merely a man and said the sort of things Jesus said would not be a great moral teacher. He would either be a lunatic—on the level of the man who says he is a poached egg—or else he would be the Devil of Hell. You must make your choice. Either this man was, and is, the Son of God: or else a madman and something worse. You can shut him up for a fool, you can spit at Him and kill Him as a demon; or you can fall at His feet and call Him Lord or God. But let us not come with any patronizing nonsense about His being a great human teacher. He has not left that open to us. He did not intend to.[49]

Reagan's apparent familiarity with this position—known as Lewis's "liar, Lord, or lunatic argument"[50]—suggests just how willing he was to dig deeply into the philosophy of Christianity, on both his own behalf and that of correspondents like the Methodist minister to whom he made his argument. Reagan's faith was not shallow, as his evident appetite for apologetics and theological debate demonstrates.

He had clearly internalized Lewis's teachings; he cited the Oxford scholar frequently, and referred to his well-known *Screwtape Letters* as "brilliant."[51] No simple homily, Lewis's potent argument is the stuff of seminaries: that Reagan should muster it so casually suggests how sophisticated his understanding of the New Testament and Christ's teachings actually was.

"God's Plan"

By 1967, when he assumed the governorship, anyone who had watched Reagan's "Time for Choosing" speech was aware of the man's sense that America had been divinely chosen for a special purpose. Yet the wording of his call to action—"You and I have a rendezvous with destiny"—also suggested that Reagan felt personally compelled to fulfill a higher purpose. What are we to make of his sense of self, this evidence that Reagan felt that God's will might be expressed in his very own life?

Ronald Reagan's election as governor was a profound step for him. As his legacy of speeches and correspondence reveals, it appears to have crystallized and confirmed for him a modest yet long-held feeling that God had chosen to play a guiding role in his life.

Reagan was the antithesis of a deist. The deist believes that God created humanity, the earth, and the universe, and then essentially adopted a laissez-faire policy, stepping aside to allow human nature to take its course. Thomas Jefferson is generally accepted to have been a deist, but among American presidents he is a notable exception: most have perceived God's hand in daily events throughout the world, the nation, and their lives.

Ronald Reagan expressed a consistent belief that God was very much involved in the workings of the world, both in the grand sweep of history and in the daily course of human life. He believed that God chose people as His instruments, and that He had a plan for all, whatever their station in life.

In reflecting on his own life, Reagan credited God with the early "twists in the road" that had shaped his path. Many of his anecdotes seemed to turn on such turns of fate: "Then, one of those things happened that makes one wonder about God having a plan for all of us. . . ." To Reagan, it was surely "God's Plan"—in his writings he capitalized both the "G" and the "P"—that turned him away from that dream job at Montgomery Ward; then there was that new acting teacher who happened to arrive at Dixon High School just as Reagan got there. "Once again fate intervened," he interpreted, "as if God was carrying out His plan with my name on it." Above all, he saw divine intervention when he met his second wife: "If ever God gave me evidence that He had a plan for me, it was the night He brought Nancy into my life."[52]

The guarantee of "God's Plan" provided him with a kind of personal refuge during hard times. In the early 1950s, when Reagan's movie career was in the dumps—for good, it turned out—he settled for emceeing a third-rate vaudeville act at the aptly named Last Frontier hotel in Las Vegas.[53] But he didn't let the impasse get him down. "He again got back to the deep belief that everything happens for a reason," Nancy Reagan explained later. "Whatever happened to him, there was a reason for it."[54] Sure enough, shortly thereafter Reagan became host of the wildly successful GE Theatre, earning him a new national presence and making him a household name.[55]

It was during his time in Sacramento, though, that Reagan began to ruminate openly on the presence of God's hand in his political path. In a 1968 interview with Christian Life, he shared his feelings: "I've always believed there is a certain divine scheme of things. I'm not quite able to explain how my election happened or why I'm here, apart from believing it is part of God's plan for me."[56] William Rose, a reporter who wrote about the governor's religious views in a 1968 article, reported:

> Some of those who have attended conferences in Sacramento in which the Governor is faced with a decision, report that Reagan's reference to "God's will" or plan is very much a part of him. According to these sources, he frequently blurts out, after listening to the pros and cons of a proposal, "If it's God's will, let's do it."[57]

A *Newsweek* article at the time reported much the same thing, noting that Reagan saw himself as "His [God's] instrument."[58] Barely a year into his new life as an elected official, Reagan was asked whether his California governorship was a mere pause on his way to the presidency, and, if so, whether he would drop the post if called to the White House. He replied: "Let's not tempt fate." With a reverent look heavenward, George H. Smith reported, he explained: "The Lord willing, I'll complete my term."[59]

Writing in the *Washington Post* in January 1968, David Broder reported that some Reagan staff—those who wanted him to run for president—were encountering a certain difficulty: Governor Reagan had so resigned himself to things happening according to God's hand that he wasn't doing enough to make them happen on his own. "He is described by his associates as fatalistic almost to the point of naïveté in his belief that events will order themselves," reported Broder. He quoted a Republican colleague of Reagan: "Ron honestly believes that God will arrange things for the best. But some of the people who made him governor are willing to give God a hand in making him President, and they're not too happy with the slowdown."[60]

This abiding faith in the hand of God is yet another instance of Nelle Reagan's pervasive influence on her son's adult life.[61] In 1968, Reagan remembered his mother's example:

> She had an abiding faith in the necessity to believe and trust that everything that happens, happens for some good reason, and while you can't always see the reason at the moment, it happens for the best. She believed that if a person does have this kind of faith in God and faces up to the situation without rebellion or bitterness and is willing to wait for a time, he will learn the reason and discover its place in the Divine scheme of things.[62]

Even bad things may happen for a good reason, Nelle had always told him. Later on, she preached, "you'll find yourself thinking—'If I hadn't had that problem back then, then this better thing that *did* happen wouldn't have happened to me.' "[63]

Reagan's daughter Patti provides a telling example. Her father hated flying, and refused almost entirely to travel by air until the demands of public office left him no choice. After testifying before HUAC in Washington, D.C. in October 1947, he took a train all the way back to the West Coast.[64] During his GE days, he toured the country by train. Family excursions with Nancy and the children were always by car or train. But when he was finally obliged to fly as governor, Patti tells of how his comfort in God's will made the decision easier:

> He didn't make a big deal out of it; he seemed just to accept that it was a fear he had to get over. He seemed to glide past it; at least that's how it looked to me. Then he told me that every time the plane took off and landed, he closed his eyes and prayed.

"Do you pray that the plane won't crash?" I asked him assuming that would be a logical thing for which to pray.

"No," he answered. "I pray that whatever God's will is, I'll be able to accept it with grace, and have faith in His wisdom. We're always in God's hands. Sometimes it's hard to accept that, so I pray that He'll help me just to trust in His will." . . .

What my father had communicated to me, through his words and between them, was that he believed God was in charge of his fate and the fate of everyone on the plane. He had told me once before that when we die is God's business. So it wasn't his place to second-guess God or try to sell Him a particular agenda by praying, "Please don't let the plane crash."

And I thought of this, too: If I were falling through the sky, falling toward my death, would I want my last moments to be spent screaming at God for not obeying my wishes, or would I want to exit this earth in a moment of silent communion, a prayer for grace and acceptance? . . .

My father has chosen, on a daily basis, to try to accept the will of God.[65]

Reagan's confidence in "God's Plan" often entered into the personal advice and counsel he shared with others—those he hoped might be comforted by it just as he had. When WWII hero and actor Audie Murphy died in a plane crash during Reagan's turn as governor, he took the time to write a personal letter to Murphy's widow despite the fact that he hadn't known the actor well:

When tragedy strikes we inevitably ask why, and, of course, there is no answer. But of one thing I'm sure: our lives have a purpose known only to God, and God had a plan for Audie Murphy which was not completed with his magnificent wartime service.

Perhaps the fulfillment of that purpose is yet to come in the lives of Audie's sons. If that is so, then you are a very great part of God's plan.[66]

This was no rare letter: Reagan commonly wrote to strangers with such words of consolation, hopeful that his view of God's plan would comfort the reader. To one New York woman who had written of her handicapped son, he wrote:

I find myself believing very deeply that God has a plan for each one of us. Some with little faith and even less testing seem to miss in their mission, or else we perhaps fail to see their imprint on the lives of others. But bearing what we cannot change and going on with what God has given us, confident there is a destiny, somehow seems to bring a reward we wouldn't exchange for any other. It takes a lot of fire and heat to make a piece of steel.[67]

He also wrote to her son directly, adding that "things have a way of working out in life, and usually for the best, if we simply go forward doing our best and trusting that God does have a plan."[68] Even a difficult situation could be part of God's plan, he suggested: even if they look bleak in the short term, things often work out for the best.

In another letter of the time, he told the widow of a slain policeman that no one can be sure of "the why of God's plan for us. . . . Whatever God's plan is for each of us, we can only trust in His wisdom and mercy. . . . It isn't given to us to understand—we can only have faith. . . . [W]e must have faith in God's plan for all of us."[69]

In the years since Reagan's presidency, as his voluminous correspondence has gradually been made public, it became clear just how many such letters Reagan wrote: it was as if, during his time in the governor's office, he had elected to pursue a kind of personal grief ministry.[70] Even after he left Sacramento and failed in his first bid for the White House, he took his God's Plan theology to the airwaves in his syndicated radio show in the late 1970s;[71] he would continue it throughout his private and public life.[72]

A PROPHECY?

Among the many moments when Ronald Reagan felt personally moved by God, none is more dramatic than an incident that reportedly occurred at the home of Governor Reagan and his wife in Sacramento on a Sunday afternoon in October 1970.[73]

Reagan's run for a second term was almost complete; California voters would return to the polls the following month to decide whether to reelect him. Among Reagan's supporters, talk of a future presidential bid was already in the air.

Present in the Reagans' home that October 1970 Sunday was a group of evangelicals, some of them ministers—Harald Bredesen, Herb Ellingwood, George Otis—along with Pat Boone and his wife. As Otis later remembered, at one point the group joined hands in a prayer circle of seven, their eyes shut, Reagan's head bowed sharply. To the governor's left was George Otis, clasping Reagan's left hand in his right. Otis, a pastor with High Adventure Ministries in Van Nuys, California, remembered the few awkward seconds of silence that followed; they seemed more like minutes. He cleared his throat and began to pray.

"I was just sort of praying from the head," Otis told Bob Slosser. "I was saying those things you'd expect—you know, thanking the

Lord for the Reagans, their hospitality, and that sort of thing." This continued for ten or fifteen seconds—and then came a dramatic change. "Everything shifted from my head to the Spirit—the Spirit," Otis recalled. "The Holy Spirit came upon me and I knew it. In fact, I was embarrassed."

He was embarrassed because his arm had begun to tremble, shaking noticeably. "There was this pulsing in my arm. And my hand—the one holding Governor Reagan's hand—was shaking. I didn't know what to do. I just didn't want this thing to be happening. I can remember that even as I was speaking, I was working, you know, tensing my muscles and concentrating and doing everything I could to stop the shaking.

"It wasn't a wild swinging or anything like that. But it was a definite, pulsing shaking. And I made a great physical effort to stop it—but I couldn't."

As this was going on, the content of Otis's prayer changed completely. His voice remained constant, but the words came more steadily and intently. They spoke specifically to Reagan, referring to him as "my son." The words that came acknowledged the governor's role as leader of a state that was "indeed the size of many nations." The foyer where they stood in unison was still and silent. The only sound was Reverend Otis's voice. Everyone's eyes were closed. The voice concluded: "If you walk uprightly before Me, you will reside at 1600 Pennsylvania Avenue."

Otis learned from Ellingwood, who had been at Reagan's right, that the governor's other hand had been shaking in much the same way. Ellingwood said years later that he felt something like a "bolt of electricity" as he clasped Reagan's hand. Some of the participants apparently believed that Otis had somehow connected with God.

A decade later, just days after Reagan was elected president,

Boone called and asked him if he remembered "the time we joined hands and prayed, and we had a sense you were being called to something higher." "Of course I do," Reagan replied without hesitation.

Readers can make of this what they will. But the Reagans and the participants clearly felt that they had shared some kind of spiritual communion that day, one that spoke to a higher calling for Reagan—this time a very specific one.

REAGAN WAS REELECTED THE FOLLOWING MONTH, and during his second term as governor he maintained the same level of engagement with his spiritual life that had marked his first. He attended Bible study frequently in a small seminar room across from his Sacramento office, and though from time to time he was forced to forgo the meetings for some piece of urgent business, he looked forward to them and said he "always enjoyed" the study.[74]

One participant was Rev. Louis P. Sheldon, who founded the Traditional Values Coalition in Orange County, California, thirty years ago. (The organization, now based in Washington, D.C., currently represents more than 40,000 churches.) Sheldon remembers the Bible studies with Governor Reagan as "very effective and meaningful." Reagan "loved" to express concepts in simple parables, Sheldon noticed, and the group soon learned that when Reagan began telling a story, it was important to listen carefully, for even the simplest Reagan story would likely have some spiritual purpose.

Sheldon recalls certain Reagan phrases that seemed to capture the man. There were four in particular. "No acting on this one," he remembers Reagan saying frequently, signaling a moment of sincerity. Two other, related phrases—"this is the right way" and "this is not right"—were part of Reagan's common parlance, evidence of how much the idea of good and evil was "in the forefront of Reagan's mind" during these years. Even as governor, Sheldon says, Reagan spoke often of the Cold War in just such terms. Indeed, it was that kind of thinking that kindled the fourth Reagan phrase Sheldon recollects—"that's a communist trick."

The talk of good and evil during these get-togethers did often venture beyond the purely religious: the group talked regularly about the moral and spiritual bases of public policy. The subject of communism was never far from Reagan's mind. And, Sheldon recalls, there was a good deal of conversation about Reagan becoming president, which seemed a strong possibility. "No one ever stood up and explicitly said to him, 'You're going to be president,' but it was inferred. In a quiet way, there was definitely that feeling."[75]

10.

Two Campaigns

"The Russians have told us over and over again
their goal is to impose their incompetent and
ridiculous system on the world."

—*Ronald Reagan, 1975*[1]

The door to his Sacramento office had barely closed behind him
when Ronald Reagan began urging America and Americans to
assume their special responsibility to humanity. Within three weeks
after leaving the governorship, he was spreading this gospel in Washington, D.C. "We cannot escape our destiny," he said in a January
1974 speech in the nation's capital, "nor should we try to do so. The
leadership of the free world was thrust upon us two centuries ago in
that little hall in Philadelphia."[2] He lamented that the United States
"had begun to abdicate this historical role as the spiritual leader of
the Free World and its foremost defender of democracy."[3] With the
fog of Vietnam and the 1960s finally lifting, it was time for the Shining City to reemerge.

It was during this time that Reagan began frequently quoting a remark by Pope Pius XII in his public speeches and personal letters: "Into the hands of America, God has placed an afflicted mankind."[4] It was the penultimate line of Reagan's July 6, 1976, televised speech marking the bicentennial, followed only by his three-word sign off: "God bless America."[5] As Reagan noted, the Pope had made the remark after the global devastation of WWII, when America stood alone in strength. "The American people have a genius for splendid and unselfish action," said Pius XII, charging America with a divine mission to aid the struggling peoples of the world. Americans didn't seek this leadership role that Pius XII spoke of, Reagan stressed; it was thrust upon them by God.

With Sacramento behind him, Reagan launched the first of two successive campaigns for the presidency. His anti-communist language during these races picked up where it had left off in the early 1960s; his Cold War crusade against Soviet communism—particularly on the rhetorical front—was back with a vengeance. The late 1970s saw a new edge in Reagan's attacks on Marxism-Leninism; a national political figure at last, Reagan was on his way to becoming the face of the anti-communist movement.

As he campaigned for president, Reagan found that Moscow provided him with a righteous cause. As he said in March 1975, "Totalitarian communism is an absolute enemy of human freedom."[6] To Reagan, the USSR symbolized the larger atheistic-collectivist mindset threatening the globe. And he made that case to the world during this period.

On April 7, 1975, for instance, Reagan gave what is now essentially a lost speech to a group called the Pilgrim Society at the Savoy Hotel in London; only the first two handwritten pages from the speech exist today—and have not been published. On page two, Reagan told his audience, "The issue over which we struggle is very simple: Either we continue the concept that man is a unique being capable of determining his own destiny with dignity and God-given inalienable rights . . . or we admit we are faceless ciphers in a GOD-LESS [his caps] collectivist ant heap."[7] Moscow, of course, was Collectivist Central—the epicenter of that heap.

During this period, he was able to draw on the increasingly disturbing reports of Soviet brutality that were coming to light—both statistical and anecdotal evidence of the evils of the communist empire. Aleksandr Solzhenitsyn's *The Gulag Archipelago* had just been published, and his and other accounts of Soviet criminality by scholars and dissidents alike were being featured in favorite Reagan periodicals like *National Review* and *Human Events*—magazines he read cover to cover.

Appalled by the reports, Reagan focused national attention on them throughout the late 1970s through his campaign speeches and in the daily radio broadcasts he delivered over hundreds of radio stations from sea to sea. He did over a thousand such broadcasts from 1975 to 1979, writing the text himself for two-thirds of them—each roughly the length (and style) of a typical op-ed piece by a syndicated newspaper columnist.[8]

There were two aspects of Soviet communism that continued to raise Reagan's ire. One was the ongoing war on religious faith. The other was the Soviet regime's more general continuing oppression of its people, and its thirst to expand its empire. These further convinced Reagan of the USSR's wickedness—and inspired in him a fervent desire to defeat the nation and its empire.

To Reagan, the Soviet system was especially unacceptable when it took the leap of murdering—by the millions—in the name of what he saw as a blasphemous ideology. He was certain that the Soviet leadership intended to spread the system responsible for such human crimes worldwide, with Moscow as the headquarters for the pursuit of global communism. The Kremlin would usher in a Great Leap Backward.

And yet, as he set his sights on the White House, it was perhaps the religious repression of the Soviet system that continued to move him most deeply.

THE SOVIET WAR ON RELIGION CONTINUES

The Bolshevik assault on religion begun by Vladimir Lenin in the 1920s continued unabated through the Brezhnev era. One might open a chronology of the 1970s persecution by quoting the December 1970 message "To All Christians of the World" by the Second All-Union Congress of the E.C.B. Prisoners, a group dedicated to exposing the full brunt of Soviet religious repression. "The *aim* of the atheists is clear to us," said the message, with emphasis, "to destroy the church by any means, to destroy belief in God."[9]

As a July 1976 article in the *Washington Post* noted, while in theory the Soviet constitution granted freedom of religion, in reality evangelism was prohibited, all churches had to be registered with the government, no new churches were permitted, and informers were put in place to report on each congregation. The *Post* also noted the ongoing ban on sharing faith with children, and listed examples of Soviet torture as punishment for religious offenses.[10]

The Soviet constitution was one of Reagan's sore spots. He often pointedly listed the rights promised by the document—including religious freedom—and noted that Moscow had never honored those guarantees. For decades he blasted the constitution's insincerity, and charged the USSR with cruelly hiding behind its language as false proof of religious tolerance.[11]

The U.S. Congress was fairly vigilant in bringing accounts of communist persecution to the attention of the American public. In the summer of 1976, as Reagan was running hard to take the Republican presidential nomination from Gerald Ford, the U.S. House subcommittee on international political and military affairs heard testimony on Soviet torture of believers. Witnesses spoke of the routine mental abuse pursued in state experimental camps and psychiatric clinics, where, as one dissident put it, Christians were "treated for their faith," often by heavy drug sedation, as well as the newer tactic that dissidents termed "physical annihilation."[12] By the 1970s, Soviet religious repression had grown so atrocious that some referred to it as a "re-Stalinization." For the first time in U.S. history, the Congress went on record approving a resolution specifically condemning Soviet persecution of Christians. It passed 381 to 2 in the House in October 1976.[13]

The persecution intensified as the new decade dawned. In August 1980, shortly after Reagan gave his acceptance speech at the Republican convention in Detroit, one could open almost any newspaper and read about a lengthy report prepared by three major human-rights groups in Europe on religious liberty in the USSR. The well-publicized report pointed out, among other things, that under current Soviet legislation a group of believers—even three people—did not have the right to pray together, read the Bible, or discuss religious topics, without special written permission from Moscow.[14]

Throughout the late 1970s, Reagan excoriated this doggedly atheistic aspect of Soviet communism. "The Soviets are men who say we have no soul, there is no hereafter, there is no God," he thundered.[15] In an October 1975 radio broadcast, he called the USSR a "Godless tyranny."[16] In a February 1977 speech in Washington, he took aim at the Soviet "heart of darkness."[17] And just as in the previous two decades, the word "evil" resurfaced as a Reagan description for Soviet communism, including during a February 1978 radio address.[18]

In further broadcasts in September 1978 and June 1979, Reagan said that atheism "is as much a part of communism as is the gulag. Every kind of roadblock is thrown in the way of religion, up to and including imprisonment."[19] He pounced on the USSR for its "war" against "the very ideas of religion and freedom."[20] Twice in 1978 radio broadcasts, he said that Marx "swore that his paradise could only be realized by destroying the church. He had a special hatred for the Hebrews, possibly because the God of Moses is also the God of Christianity."[21]

Reagan decried the antireligious indoctrination of Soviet school children. On two different occasions in 1978 and 1979 he noted that Soviet children were "indoctrinated" in schools "from grade one" to believe the "falsehood" that there is no God.[22] He devoted a radio broadcast in July 1978 to examples of communist antireligious indoctrination of school children in Czechoslovakia.[23] Communist governments, he explained, wanted to ensure that only they teach children right and wrong.[24]

Reagan also focused attention on the hypocrisy of the Soviet attack on religious faith—hypocrisy in that the Soviet leadership treated Marxism-Leninism itself as a kind of religion. In two 1978 radio broadcasts, Reagan said pointedly that in the USSR "Karl Marx is hailed as the messiah."[25] But one of his most memorable and colorful critiques came in February 1978, when he spoke on what he called "the nativity according to Marx and Lenin." Political commissars in the Ukraine had taken a traditional Christmas carol and purged it of its Christian content. "Believers" in the lyrics became "workers"; the time of the season became October, the month of the glorious revolution; the image of Christ was replaced with "Lenin's glory hovering"; the Star of Bethlehem became the Red Star;[26] and so on. Reagan wryly welcomed the opportunity to share the new Soviet gospel with listeners.[27]

After decades of harrowing reports of Soviet horrors, by the time of Reagan's second run for the presidency in 1980 he had apparently had enough: in March 1980 Reagan flatly called the Soviet leaders "monsters."[28]

THE EVIL OF SOVIET CRIMES

"A single death is a tragedy," Joseph Stalin infamously decreed. "A million deaths is a statistic." The Soviet dictator practiced what he preached. No government in history—with the exception of Red China, which had many more victims at its disposal—killed so many of its innocent citizens. Millions perished in the gulag archipelago, the Soviet labor-camp system devised by Lenin.

Across the board, leading Bolsheviks from the start preached the necessity of "mass terror," from Lenin to his henchman, M.Y. Latsis, to KGB founder Felix Dzerzhinsky—all prior to the bloodthirsty Stalin. As one historian wrote, "terror was implicit in Bolshevism from the start."[29]

And, as Reagan was learning, this communist violence wasn't unique to Bolshevism.

Stephane Courtois, French editor of the journal *Communisme*, notes that government-orchestrated crime against citizens has been a defining characteristic of the communist system throughout its existence. Communism's most successful redistribution has been not of wealth, but of crime and murder. "Communism has committed a multitude of crimes not only against individual human beings but also against world civilization and national cultures," Courtois writes. "Communist regimes turned mass crime into a full-blown system of government."[30]

Martin Malia agrees. "Communist regimes did not just commit criminal acts," writes Malia, noting that noncommunist states have done likewise. "But they were criminal enterprises in their very essence: on principle, so to speak, they all ruled lawlessly, by violence, and without regard for human life." Here's a critical distinction, and lesson: under communism, totally different national cultures from all over the globe, completely unrelated to one another and sharing only communism as their common characteristic, all committed mass violence against the population. This violence was a deliberate policy of the new revolutionary order, done at a scope and inhumanity far exceeding anything in these nation's pasts.[31]

This common violence is evident in the record. *The Black Book of Communism*, a seminal study of communist repression and murder co-edited by Courtois and published by Harvard University Press, cited 20 million deaths by communist governments in the Soviet Union, 65 million in China, more than two million in North Korea and Cambodia, and a million or more in Afghanistan, Africa, Eastern Europe, and Vietnam, not to mention hundreds of thousands more elsewhere around the globe. The death toll worldwide approaches 100 million. Malia aptly writes that the communist record offers the "most colossal case of political carnage in history."[32]

Actually, the *Black Book*'s numbers may be conservative, especially in the Soviet case. The figure on the USSR is one of the lowest usually cited. Most accounts exceed 33 million, some twice that. Lee

Edwards, citing the epic work on "democide" by political scientist R. J. Rummel, as well as the research and accounts of the likes of Robert Conquest, Aleksandr Solzhenitsyn, and others, estimates that Soviet governments were responsible for the death of 61.9 million of their own from 1917 through 1987.[33]

Either way, 100 million total deaths dwarfs Hitler's genocide for sheer bloodshed by a factor of tenfold at least.[34] The figure approaches twice the total killed in WWI and WWII combined.[35] It is difficult to identify any ideology or belief system in history that has killed more people, let alone in such a concentrated period of time. The 100 million deaths primarily occurred during a roughly seventy-year period, and during those seventy years, the bulk of the slaughter transpired in half that time frame. One hundred million deaths over seventy years comes to an average of to 1.4 million deaths per year, or 119,000 per month, or almost 4,000 per day. It's almost impossible to imagine how one ideology could cause so much pain. As a point of comparison, during the sixty-four-year Spanish Inquisition (1481–1545), 31,912 citizens were killed—a smaller number than those felled per year under Lenin, and probably smaller than the weekly death toll in Stalin's Great Purge/Red Terror of 1934–38.[36]

Some of this data on communism has been published only recently, but hints at the scale of the killing were already plentiful by the time Reagan was campaigning in the 1970s. At that time, for instance, the nightmare orchestrated by Mao Tse-Tung in China was beginning to come to light; only half a decade earlier Mao hats and vests (and thoughts) had been fashionable on many U.S. college campuses. The communist slaughter in Cambodia, which took place from 1975 to 1979, also had an impact on American sentiment.

Reagan responded to the continuing carnage with one of his strongest statements on the problem, a May 1975 radio broadcast in which he labeled communism a "disease." "Mankind has survived all manner of evil diseases and plagues," conceded Reagan, "but can it survive Communism?" This disease had been "hanging on" for a half-century or more. It was imperative to remind us "just how vicious it really is." This was Reagan in classic attack mode—speaking forthrightly of this malice, calling out evil by name. "Communism is neither an economic or a political system," he added for good measure; "it is a form of insanity."[37]

Such rhetoric might strike some as hysterical Red-bashing, and indeed Reagan himself rarely used such extreme language. Yet in fact it's hard to find many contagions that have silenced so many in such a short time. In the twentieth century, probably the biggest killer among diseases was the influenza epidemic of 1918–19, which may have taken 10 to 20 million worldwide—nowhere near the toll of the "disease" of communism.[38]

For Reagan, the killing alone by Soviet communists was bad enough. Worse yet was the prospect that their system might spread further around the world, taking many more lives along the way. Simply put, Reagan perceived that the Soviet Union desired world domination in the form of a one-world communist state.

As soon as his presidential ambitions became clear, Reagan's statements to this effect began to alarm the USSR. In a 1975 radio broadcast he complained, "The Russians have told us over and over again their goal is to impose their incompetent and ridiculous system on the world."[39] In May 1977 he wrote that "every Soviet leader," including Brezhnev, "has sworn to carry out to the letter the words of Lenin," who, according to Reagan, had said, "It would not matter if ¾ of the human race perished; the important thing is that the remaining ¼ be communist."[40] In an April 1978 speech he warned:

"There is an evil influence throughout the world. In every one of the far-flung trouble spots, dig deep and you'll find the Soviet Union stirring a witches' brew, furthering its own imperialistic ambitions."[41]

During this time he found a friend in the recently declassified NSC-68, the Truman administration's seminal policy blueprint, which articulated the comprehensive national security policy and strategy that the United States would follow for decades. The core premise of the document was that the USSR was an aggressive and expansionist power that would try to expand at all costs. The USSR, it said, "seeks to impose its authority over the rest of the world." Reagan quoted this line in his radio broadcasts, telling listeners that NSC-68 "stated flatly that Russia is determined to impose its authority over the world; that we are the principal obstacle they would have to overcome; and if their expansionism wasn't checked or contained soon *no possible combination of the remaining free nations could assemble sufficient strength to stop them short of their goal*." (Italics are Reagan's.) "And that," he added, "was said 27 yrs ago."[42] Now, his implication was clear, the Soviets were well on that expansionary path.

THE USSR's EXPANSIONARY GOALS

To be sure, Reagan's suspicions weren't unfounded: expansionism was central to communist rhetoric from the very start. From its famous imprecation, "Workers of the world, unite!" Marx's 1848 *Communist Manifesto* urged revolution, declaring that the proletarians of the revolution "have a world to win." He declared himself joyous at the sight of "socialism spreading throughout the world."[43] "[I]t is our interest and our task to make the revolution permanent," said Marx in his 1850 Address of the General Council to the Communist League, "until the proletariat has conquered state power and until the association of the proletarians has progressed sufficiently far—not only in one country but in all the leading countries of the world."[44]

Lenin, who came to be synonymous with communism, said from the outset that the Soviet goal was "world revolution."[45] On the third anniversary of the 1917 Revolution, which coincided with the rout of the Menshaviks in the Russian Civil War, Lenin declared that true victory could come only "when our cause should conquer the whole world, for we began our work counting exclusively upon world revolution." Trotsky, who cited these words and endorsed them, also subscribed to a vision of "proletarian world revolution" and "overturning the world," noted that "more unassailable testimony could not be asked."[46] And from the start the enemy was clear: Lenin and Stalin spoke of capitalist encirclement and inevitable military conflict with the West. In his report to the eighth Party Congress in March 1919, Lenin declared:

> We live not only in a state but in a system of states, and the existence of the Soviet Republic side by side with the imperialist states for an extended period is unthinkable. In the end either one or the other will conquer. And before this result, a series of horrible conflicts between the Soviet Republic and the bourgeois states is unavoidable.[47]

"As long as capitalism and socialism exist," Lenin wrote, "we cannot live in peace: in the end, one or the other will triumph—a funeral dirge will be sung either over the Soviet Republic or over world capitalism."[48]

Lenin had his eyes on not only Europe but America.[49] In 1918, he wrote to a group of American workers: "We are in a besieged fortress until other armies of the international socialist revolution"—the American worker-troops—"come to our aid." In November of that year, he wrote:

> The facts of world history have shown that the conversion of our Russian revolution into a socialist revolution was not an adventure but a necessity, for there was no other choice. Anglo-French and American imperialism will inevitably strangle the independence and freedom of Russia unless world-wide socialist revolution, unless world-wide Bolshevism, conquers.[50]

To pursue his goal of a "full-fledged political project: world socialist revolution," Lenin established the Comintern—the Communist International,[51] a centralized authority under Moscow leadership, whose goal was "to replace the world capitalist economy by a world system of Communism." The "successful struggle" for the "dictatorship of the proletariat presupposes the existence in every country of a compact Communist Party, hardened in the struggle, disciplined, centralized and closely lined up with the masses."[52] In 1919 Grigorii Zinoviev, the head of the Comintern, was so impressed with the "dizzying speed" made by his movement that he confidently predicted that "in a year all Europe shall be Communist. And the struggle for Communism shall be transferred to America, and perhaps Asia and other parts of the world."[53]

Lenin's ambition, which followed Marx's, was carried on by Stalin and subsequent comrades. This Soviet fight to expand brought Reagan into the ring, and by the time his first presidential campaign was under way, it was clear to the world that he was throwing some serious punches.

THE TWO CAMPAIGNS

Ronald Reagan ran for president twice in the second half of the 1970s, first unsuccessfully challenging President Gerald Ford for the Republican nomination in 1975–6, then staging a second, successful campaign against Democratic president Jimmy Carter in 1979–80.

Reagan's candor about his religious background was striking, though it would hardly have startled anyone who knew him. On the 1980 campaign trail, Adrian Rogers, leader of the Southern Baptist Convention, asked Reagan whether he was "born again" and had "Jesus in his heart." He answered yes, replying that God was "real" to him, and that he had a personal experience when he "invited Christ" into his life. Rogers pressed: "Do you know the Lord Jesus or do you only know *about* Him?" Rogers said Reagan declared, "I *know* Him."[54]

In one 1976 exchange, he said he couldn't remember a time in his life when he didn't both call upon God and "hopefully thank Him" just as often. When asked if he "really believes somebody is listening up there," Reagan exclaimed: "Oh, my! If I didn't believe that, I'd be scared to death!"[55]

Did Reagan believe that God would make him president? Though he felt a sense of calling, his Christian humility kept him from being completely sure. As he wrote in a letter during his 1976 presidential run:

> I have to realize that whatever I do has meaning only if I ask that it serves His purpose. . . . I believe that in my present undertaking, whatever the outcome, it will be His doing. I will pray for understanding of what it is He would have me do.[56]

"If the task I seek should be given me," he said of his 1976 presidential bid, "I would pray only that I could perform it in a way that would serve God."[57]

What Reagan aimed to do in 1976 was remarkable: usually a loyal party man, he sought to unseat an incumbent president in a Republican primary. A stunning last-minute surge among a number of key states brought Reagan shockingly close to overtaking Ford. This led to a dramatic showdown at the Republican Convention at the Kemper Arena in Kansas City on August 19, 1976. In the end, Reagan missed by only 117 votes, grabbing 47.4 percent of delegates in an 1,187 to 1,070 contest. The winner needed 1,130. The exhausted Ford campaign breathed a huge sigh of relief, but Reagan had come breathtakingly close.

The 1976 loss seemed traumatic—for everyone but Reagan. His daughter Maureen said she was "just devastated" by the loss, so much that she cried for two days. "I just couldn't stop." Every time her father saw her during that period he'd ask, "Are you still crying?" He tried to cheer her up but couldn't. Finally, he pulled her aside and instructed: "There's a reason for this. I don't know what it is. But there's a reason." She said he told her, "Everything happens for a reason. . . . If you just keep doing what you're doing, the path is going to open up and you'll see what it is you're supposed to do."[58] He also told his aide and secretary Helene Von Damm not to worry about losing the race; it simply wasn't meant to be.[59] He wrote to his old Dixon role model, Garland Waggoner, now pastoring in Storrs, Connecticut, to say that he and Nancy were at peace with themselves and were awaiting whatever God had in mind for them.[60]

Yet Reagan didn't give up. He set his sights on the 1980 election, announcing his next candidacy at the New York Hilton on November 13, 1979. In a speech that had the Republican faithful teary-eyed, he closed as he had at the Kansas City convention in 1976, touching on now-familiar themes and expressing big ambitions for himself and his country: "A troubled and afflicted mankind looks to us, pleading for us to keep our rendezvous with destiny; . . . that we will become that shining city on a hill. I believe that you and I, together, can keep this rendezvous with destiny."[61]

After securing his party's nomination this time, he echoed those sentiments on July 17, 1980, at the Republican convention in De-troit.[62] The acceptance speech he gave there was his most prominent political moment to date—and he used it to offer one of his most powerful public displays of religious faith. For the close of the speech, he picked up a theme he had been publicly articulating since that commencement address in Fulton, Missouri, in June 1952: "Can we doubt that only a Divine Providence placed this land, this island of freedom, here as a refuge for all those people in the world who yearn to breathe freely?"

But it was an extemporaneous moment that gave the speech its dramatic close: "I'll confess that I've been a little afraid to suggest what I'm going to suggest—I'm more afraid not to: that we begin our crusade joined together in a moment of silent prayer." There it was: the most public confirmation yet that, for Reagan, this *crusade*—it was a pointed choice of words—had a profoundly spiritual dimension. A hush filled the convention center as the faithful bowed their heads, Gerald and Betty Ford (captured by TV cameras) among them. Then Reagan's emotion-ridden voice broke the silence with a crackly "God bless America."[63] This was not the Reagan of the broad grin or cocked head, but a man of grave demeanor and spiritual conviction, choosing to link his personal religious vision with his party's political destiny.

The event, of course, was also playing out on national television, and though Republicans present say there wasn't a dry eye in the house, upstairs among the press they were rolling. The crew of CBS Radio viewed the prayer as a display of "almost inexpressible corniness," according to one member who was present.[64] It was a sign of things to come: even before his election, the divide between Reagan's solemn piety and the clucking of cynical elites had begun.

Reagan's race against Democratic incumbent Jimmy Carter was tight right until the final week of the campaign, with polls showing the two men in a dead heat. Reagan continued to pound his message that Carter was weak on defense, weak on the Soviets, and responsible for a weak economy. He contrived a clever line to use against Carter in regard to the economic "malaise" gripping the country: "A recession is what happens when your neighbor loses his job. A depression is what happens when you lose your job. A recovery is what happens when Jimmy Carter loses his job."

In the final days of the campaign, the public apparently came around to Reagan's point of view. He trounced Carter, taking 44 of 50 states and winning the Electoral College in a landslide, 489 to 49. The American voters had accepted Ronald Reagan's call to crusade.

11.

The Oval Office

"What I have felt for a long time is that the people in this country were hungry for what you might call a spiritual revival. . . . And I always remembered that Teddy Roosevelt said this office was a bully pulpit, and I decided that if it was possible for me to help in that revival, I wanted to do that."

—*Ronald Reagan, October 14, 1984*[1]

Ever since his childhood, Ronald Reagan had had a recurring dream. Though he had lived in numerous homes in his lifetime—the actual number was thirty-seven[2]—he had always dreamed that he was living in a big white house. The dream "just kept coming back," he told Peggy Noonan. "And it was that I was going to live in a sort of mansion with big rooms like this one—high ceilings, white walls. And I'd have it over and over." That dream was about to stop—for good.[3]

On January 20, 1981, a drab day in the nation's capital, Ronald

Wilson Reagan took the oath of office and became the fortieth president of the United States. As Reagan was sworn in, Nancy stood aglow by his side, her eyes as wide and fixed as those of Amy Goodrich in *That Printer of Udell's* as Dick Walker prepared to head to Washington to save the world. For the swearing-in, Reagan had chosen to use Nelle Reagan's old, wrinkled Bible, opened to II Chronicles 7:14, her favorite verse and one her son treasured equally:

If my people, which are called by my name, shall humble themselves, and pray, and seek my face, and turn from their wicked ways; then will I hear from heaven, and will forgive their sin, and will heal their land.[4]

It was a verse in which Reagan had invested special meaning. He often quoted Scripture verses off the top of his head, especially those related to nations turning to prayer, and he recited II Chronicles 7:14 by heart in a number of proclamations and speeches over the years, major and minor.[5] It is engraved on the inside cover of his personal Bible, provided by the Cowboy Chapter Fellowship of Christian Athletes.[6] "When you go out across the country and meet the people," he had said in a failed presidential bid four years earlier, "you can't help but pray and remind them of II Chronicles 7:14." The Bible Reagan used at the inauguration bore an annotation next to the verse, in Nelle's hand: "A most wonderful verse for the healing of a nation."[7]

Nelle may not have lived to see her son ascend to the presidency, but she was very much on the mind of a number of Reagan's specially invited guests. Rev. Donn Moomaw was there, and Reagan's boyhood hero Garland Waggoner, the son of the pastor who drew Nelle to the First Christian Church in Dixon, made the trip with his wife, Neva, who had first met "warm, loving Nelle" in 1925. Reagan's words "So help me God," Neva recalled, brought Nelle to mind, and brought her to tears: "To the man who spoke [those words], it was an honest prayer from the heart," she felt. "They were not merely mouthed and meaningless."[8]

After completing the oath, Reagan approached the speaker's podium on the front side of the terrace of the grand Capitol building, in full sweep of the impressive view ahead. It was a departure from tradition, or rather an improvement upon it: His predecessors had been inaugurated behind the building, overlooking the appreciably less majestic parking lot.

In his first inaugural address, which he had written himself, Reagan began by hailing the nation's achievements, which he credited to a country that had long ago "unleashed the energy and individual genius of man to a greater extent than has ever been done before."[9] Freedom and the dignity of the individual, claimed Reagan, had been more available and assured in the United States than in "any other place on Earth."

He spoke of America's recent decline, insisting that such a path was never inevitable. "I do not believe in a fate that will fall on us no matter what we do," said Reagan. "I do believe in a fate that will fall on us if we do nothing." He urged an "era of national renewal." "Let us renew our determination, our courage, and our strength," pressed the new president. "And let us renew our faith and our hope."

He also urged his fellow Americans to "dream heroic dreams." "Your dreams, your hopes, your goals are going to be the dreams, the hopes, and the goals of this administration," promised Reagan, "so help me God." He challenged the country to face its problems and meet them head on. He quoted one of the less-known Founding Fathers, Massachusetts's Joseph Warren, who centuries earlier urged his fellow citizens to "Act worthy of yourselves." Reagan assured his countrymen: "We will again be the exemplar of freedom and a beacon of hope for those who do not now have freedom."

As he approached the end of his speech, he thanked people for their prayers:

> I'm told that tens of thousands of prayer meetings are being held on this day, and for that I'm deeply grateful. We are a nation under God, and I believe God intended for us to be free. It would be fitting and good, I think, if on each Inaugural Day in future years it should be declared a day of prayer.

He finished by claiming that if Americans believed in themselves, then they, together with God's help, could resolve the problems confronting them. "And after all," ended Reagan, "why shouldn't we believe that? We are Americans. God bless you, and thank you."

COMPARED WITH MANY OF HIS PREVIOUS STATEMENTS, including his convention speech, Reagan's first inaugural address wore its spirituality rather lightly. Yet those observing him at close range have described his ascension to the office in boldly religious terms— bolder, no doubt, than Reagan would have felt comfortable expressing in public. " 'I'm president of the United States by divine appointment,' " Donn Moomaw guesses that Reagan must have thought on assuming his new role. " 'This is God's plan.' . . . I think he really felt that."[10] Frank Van der Linden, a biographer attuned to Reagan's spiritual dimension, wrote in 1981 that Reagan "felt 'called' to lead the nation, as ministers are 'called' to their congregations and they pray that it is God's will." This, he felt, gave Reagan "a remarkable serenity." "Call it mysticism, fatalism, or predestination," wrote Van der Linden, "Reagan believes that he is ordained to fill his present role."[11]

CHURCH ATTENDANCE

In those first days of the presidency, most new presidents give careful consideration to the church they will attend in Washington, D.C. Reagan was no exception. In his case, however, the decision would soon be rendered moot: especially after surviving an assassination attempt in 1981, Reagan chose not to attend church regularly as president.

This religious truancy was difficult for even many of Reagan's most diehard Christian conservative supporters to countenance. To this day, many evangelicals will not excuse his failure to appear regularly at public worship services. To some that choice cast doubt on Reagan's faith. The Soviet press, lunging for any opportunity to portray Reagan as a hypocrite, especially on faith matters, took careful note. "[T]hough he shows . . . his religiousness," underscored an *Izvestia* journalist, "Reagan does not go to church."[12]

With the exception of his White House years, Reagan considered himself a "churchgoer all my life," even if he "didn't always attend every week."[13] The record bears this out: with the exception of his eight years in Washington, he attended services regularly throughout his life (and at times, as we've seen, was a dues-paying member of more than one congregation). Those who knew Reagan would confirm that his spirituality was always a personal matter; he apparently received guidance and fulfillment in his own daily relationship with God. Edmund Morris says most of Reagan's divine counsel came from "silent colloquies, usually at an open window."[14] Bill Clark agrees: "Formal religion to him was secondary to a one-on-one relationship with the Creator."[15] He did at times receive spiritual counseling in the White House. He had visits with many ministers and frequently exchanged meaningful letters with evangelists like Billy Graham.[16]

In 1984, during a presidential debate with former Vice President

Walter Mondale, reporter Fred Barnes asked Reagan about his lack of church attendance. The president explained by saying that he feared endangering not only his own life but those of others when he went to church. "I pose a threat to several hundred people if I got to church," Reagan explained. "I know all the threats that are made against me. We all know the possibility of terrorism."[17]

It was no bluff: even during his time in Sacramento, Reagan had been especially concerned about the threat of assassination. "He appears preoccupied with security," one contemporary biographer wrote of his first year as governor, listing many examples. By the time he reached the White House, both domestic threats and international terrorism were very much on the minds of the White House security detail, with unpredictable actors like Muammar Gadhafi and Yasir Arafat appearing regularly on the cover of *Time*. "We have seen the barricades that have had to be built around the White House," Reagan added during the Mondale debate. "I don't feel that I have a right to go to church, knowing that my being there could cause something of the kind that we have seen in other places, in Beirut, for example." His closing remark on the subject drew applause from the crowd: "And I miss going to church, but I think the Lord understands."[18]

In his memoir, he described the precautions required when he did choose to attend services: "Even if the Secret Service allowed us to go to church, we'd arrive there in a siren-screaming motorcade accompanied by legions of reporters and security people. No longer was going to church a pleasant Sunday morning experience, it was a news event." Helicopters swarmed overhead, and attendees were required to pass through a magnetometer before they could enter the sanctuary—not exactly the normal Sunday morning routine. He said that "things got worse" after he started getting reports about "terrorist hit squads."[19] According to one account, SWAT squad members even took posts on the church roof with rifles.[20] In a letter to one longtime friend, Reagan lamented the state of affairs: "I pray we can help bring back a more civilized world one day."[21]

"He hated to inconvenience people," explained Bill Clark as he sat in the front pew of the beautiful chapel Clark built himself high upon a majestic hill in Paso Robles, California. "He didn't want to do that," Clark said. "We discussed this. He didn't want to bother people"—and certainly not while they were attending church.[22]

One eyewitness to this unease was a parishioner at the Santa Ynez Presbyterian Church, located near Reagan's beloved Rancho del Cielo—his ranch near Santa Barbara. As president, Reagan attended the church just once, during an Easter Service. Asked if she remembered anything about Reagan on that day, the parishioner, without prompting, recalled just one thing: he seemed preoccupied with the notion that he was "burdening" (her word) the congregants.[23]

A critic might retort that security concerns in the age of terrorism didn't prevent George H. W. Bush or Bill Clinton from attending church as president. That is true, though of course neither of those men had had a bullet fired into his chest.

Security concerns, and the fear of disturbing others, weren't the only things that kept President Reagan from attending church.[24] He also didn't relish the prospect of worshipping in a church and turning around to see hundreds of eyes fixed on him to see if he was singing, praying, staying awake, or bungling the Apostle's Creed. "[A]nd once we were seated in church," Reagan lamented, "Nancy and I often felt uncomfortable because so many people in the other pews were looking at us instead of listening to the sermon." "Very unhappily," wrote Reagan, "we just had to stop going to church altogether, and we really missed it."[25]

An illuminating account is provided by New York radio personality Joey Reynolds. Reynolds, who attended Reagan's church in Bel Air, recalls a moment in the late 1970s when Rev. Moomaw told him that he asked Reagan to quit attending church because "people were now coming to worship Ronald Reagan instead of God." Reagan had become a distraction in church, a painful reality that only magnified once he moved to Washington.[26]

Etched in his son Michael's memory, was an Air Force One flight in Easter 1988, nearing the end of his presidency. At one point, Michael came upon his father counting on his fingers. When he stopped at nine, Michael asked what he was doing. In nine months, the president replied, he could go to church again.[27] And indeed he resumed regular attendance once he returned to California. Until recently the most powerful man in the world, Reagan even attended "new member" classes upon rejoining his old church.[28]

Reagan's decision to forgo church attendance may have engendered some public disapproval during his presidency, but he didn't concern himself with the political fallout. The irony is that if he had had a phony faith, and exploited religion merely for political purposes, he could have visibly appeared in church. In any event, he was secure enough not to be fazed by the arrows.

SPIRITUAL REVIVAL: THE BULLY PULPIT AS PULPIT

Rather than bringing himself to church, President Reagan brought the church to his presidency. Once he was ensconced in the Oval Office, his testimonies and demonstrations of faith were ubiquitous. A Soviet news analyst for TASS once sneered that "whenever Mr. Reagan delivers a speech, he always mentions his religious feelings."[29] "Always" was an exaggeration—but it wasn't far off.

The Presidential Handwriting File at the Reagan Library today is filled with examples of religious phrases and verses handwritten into speechwriters' texts by Reagan.[30] Speechwriter Peter Robinson, who penned the Berlin Wall address for Reagan, recalls a meeting in the Oval Office in which Reagan stood up, walked to a bookshelf, grabbed a Bible, and turned to a passage he wanted inserted into a speech.[31] It was inserted.

The public had little sense of how thoroughly such material characterized Reagan's personal as well as public thinking. Most Americans were aware of his habit of closing nearly every presidential speech with the words "God bless America," which quickly became a trademark sign off for him. What the country didn't know was that he also ended many of his private letters with a customary "God bless." Throughout his presidency his private correspondence was filled with religious symbolism and invocation.[32]

But Reagan's public faith was overt—and not merely for show. As president, Reagan showed an extraordinary inclination to use the bully pulpit *as* a pulpit. As governor, he had lamented that "Not enough of us use our talents and our positions in testimony to God's goodness."[33] As president, he would use his position to do just that. In private letters to citizens in his first term, he characterized his presidency as an "opportunity to serve God"; this, he said, was his "daily prayer."[34] He would carry that hope through his second term as well. "My own prayer is that I can . . . perform the duties of this position so as to serve God," he wrote to Bernard Cardinal Law, Archbishop of Boston, in March 1987.[35]

To Reagan, the presidency was also his best opportunity to serve a grand purpose: to help spark the "spiritual revival" he had always envisioned, in America and around the world.[36] It's important to note, in this context, that Reagan appears to have distinguished carefully between national and spiritual matters, in both his private reflections and his public statements. When Reagan spoke of "restoring" or "renewing" the American spirit, he was referring to American morale—an entirely patriotic meaning of "spirit." But he consistently used the term "revival," rather than "renewal," to describe this spiritual or religious rebirth. It is stunning to see his consistency in this specific choice of terms—and equally telling to reflect on how prevalent both these distinct, though similar, ideas were in his thinking.

In this, he may have been driven by public sensitivities about mixing church and state. Reagan was always at risk of angering reporters for daring to introduce religious statements into his public discourse, especially distinctly Christian statements. If it became clear that he was trying to encourage a religious revival in America he knew well that a backlash among the nation's secular elite (not to mention the editorial pages of the *New York Times* and *Washington Post*) would follow, especially from those who feared the religious right. Thus, in his public statements, he was far more circumspect about matters of religious revival than he was about the nation's need for patriotic renewal.

Yet Reagan sometimes let his guard down, as in this Oval Office interview with reporter Bob Slosser:

> What I have felt for a long time is that the people in this country were hungry for what you might call a spiritual revival, a return to values, to things they really believed in and held dear. And I always remembered that Teddy Roosevelt said this office was a bully pulpit, and I decided that if it was possible for me to help in that revival, I wanted to do that.[37]

And that wasn't the only time he went out on a limb as president, openly declaring his desire to use the bully pulpit for a "spiritual revival."[38] Speaking in an unsympathetic setting, Reagan told an audience at Kansas State University in 1982: "I think the American people are hungry for a spiritual revival."[39] A year later, he said candidly: "It's something that I have been speaking of for quite some time—that the American people are hungry for a spiritual revival in this land."[40]

On at least one occasion, a challenge from a skeptical reporter compelled him to go further. On February 13, 1984, a Knight Ridder reporter took Reagan to task about his outspoken Christianity, expressing concern over Reagan's "divisive" preaching of "the Gospel of Christ" from the Oval Office. Reagan defended his actions, advising the reporter that "there is a great hunger for a kind of spiritual revival in this country, for people to believe again in things that they once believed in—basic truths and all." He told the reporter that he didn't want America to be another great civilization that began declining because it had forsaken God. He then openly said: "And I also feel that there is a responsibility in this position also—as Teddy Roosevelt called it, 'a bully pulpit'—to do those things."[41]

It was an extraordinary admission for Reagan, especially to a hostile reporter. Around the White House, though, Reagan's sense of mission was understood. Speechwriter Ben Elliott, a committed Christian, specialized in writing Reagan's religious speeches; in an interview he confirmed Reagan's inclination to use his office as a "bully pulpit" to "support what he felt was a national groundswell for a religious revival in the United States." "He absolutely intended that," said Elliott categorically.[42]

It was a daunting task, of course, and given the nature of his office, making the occasional strategic speech on the subject was about as much as Reagan could do for the cause himself. Ever the optimist, though, from time to time he allowed himself a moment of hopefulness about his progress. In 1982 and 1983 letters, the optimist said he believed he was seeing evidence that his long-awaited "Christian revival in our land" was beginning.[43]

CHRIST'S NAME

Christian politicians generally tread carefully when invoking Christ by name, out of fear of being labeled narrow-minded or divisive. In a survey of presidential inaugural addresses, Paul H. Boase of Ohio University has found that every single American president has mentioned God—usually in the peroration, and often utilizing colorfully broad terms such as "Benign Parent," "Great Maker," "Giver of Good," "Fountain of Justice," "Patron of Order." Only William Henry Harrison, however, mentioned Jesus Christ by name in his first official address as president.[44]

Reagan refrained from invoking Christ's name in his inaugural, and used caution on other occasions when Christian imagery might have been deemed insensitive—even among ecumenical religious audiences. Ben Elliott is at pains to point out that Reagan was a "very sensitive man" who tried to reserve such words for Christian listeners. Reagan was sensitive to Jews in the audience, for example, and tried to avoid Christ-specific remarks on those occasions.[45]

But when he faced a Christian audience, said Elliott, "Reagan was not fearful or embarrassed to speak of Jesus Christ."[46] In reviewing speech drafts as president, for instance, he was known to alter specific passages to conform to his beliefs about the divinity of Christ. One such draft by Elliott and Peggy Noonan, for instance, included a line calling Christmas "the day that marks the birth on Earth of the Son of God"; Reagan changed it to read "the birthday of the *promised Messiah*, the Son of God" (italics added).[47] Such changes were common. "He didn't make a big deal about it," said Elliott. "He would want a change like that and would just write it in."[48]

More than a few times, he invoked Christ in completely secular situations—including speeches at nonreligious universities like Kansas State. In his 1982 speech there, he made another text insertion himself, reminding his audience of the "admonition of the Man from Galilee to do unto others as you would have them do unto you."[49] But Christ's name appeared most frequently in Reagan's talks to the annual National Prayer Breakfast and the organization of National Religious Broadcasters.[50] To the latter in January 1984, he spoke openly:

> If the Lord is our light, our strength and our salvation, whom shall we fear, of whom shall we be afraid? No matter where we live, we have a promise that can make all the difference—a promise from Jesus to soothe our sorrows, heal our hearts and drive away our fears. He promised there will never be a dark night that does not end. Our weeping may endure for a night, but joy cometh in the morning. He promised if our hearts are true, His love will be sure as sunlight. And by dying for us, Jesus showed how far our love should be ready to go: all the way.[51]

This was too much for the editorial board of the *New York Times*, which unleashed the wrath of its judgment. Reagan, the *Times* complained, had presented the speech "not while worshiping in his church but in a Washington hotel." The only appropriate venue for such remarks, the *Times* implied, was in church. "You don't have to be a secular humanist to take offense at that display of what, in America, should be private piety. . . . It's an offense to Americans of every denomination, or no denomination, when a President speaks that way." After all, the *Times* scolded, Reagan was "the President of a nation whose Bill of Rights enjoins Government from establishing religion, aiding one religion, even aiding all religions."[52] Reagan's interview with a hostile Knight Ridder reporter took place ten days later.[53]

There's abundant evidence that Reagan thought carefully about when *not* to mention Christ by name: he took care never to use it in vain. Like George Washington, whom Reagan loved to quote on religious matters, he believed it was folly to ask for God's blessings if he impugned His name at the same time.[54] Yet Reagan returned to speak to groups like the National Religious Broadcasters year after year— and to mention Christ. According to Ben Elliott, condemnation from the likes of the *New York Times* hardly broke his stride. "He wore it like a badge of honor."[55]

12.

Religion and the Reagan Presidency

"[Americans] must seek Divine guidance in the
policies of their government and the promulgation of their laws."

—*Ronald Reagan*[1]

For Reagan, then, spiritual faith was not something to hang in the
closet upon taking political office. As governor he had often relied on prayer for guidance, and after entering the White House he felt
he needed prayer as much as ever. And politics, he held, needed faith.
He frequently invoked George Washington's aphorism that religion
and morality were "indispensable supports" to political prosperity.[2]

He also felt that America and Americans needed the Bible. The
Bible, argued Reagan, held all the answers. "I'm accused of being simplistic at times," he said, more than once. "But within that single
book are all the answers to all the problems that face us."[3] When the

president shared the thought before the National Broadcasters convention, as Ben Elliot remembered, it "brought the house down." The audience responded with a standing ovation, and Reagan was delighted. Years later, Elliot recalled that the White House Staff originally objected to the line. As they expressed reservations, Reagan pleaded: "But that is what I believe!"[4]

He saw God as the preeminent source of wisdom and moral guidance, the fount "from whom all knowledge springs."[5] "When we open ourselves to Him," the president told a group of students in December 1983, "we gain not only moral courage but also intellectual strength."[6] It was a line he had used for years.[7]

And his faith in spiritual guidance had a geopolitical dimension: Reagan was earnestly afraid of what might happen to free, democratic societies if they scrapped religious faith. "At its full flowering, freedom is the first principle of society; this society, Western society," he told a crowd at Georgetown University on its bicentennial. "And yet freedom cannot exist alone. And that's why the theme for your bicentennial is so very apt: learning, faith, and freedom. Each reinforces the others, each makes the others possible. For what are they without each other?"

Reagan instructed his audience that day to pray that America be guided by learning, faith, and freedom. He cited the author of *Democracy in America*: "Tocqueville said it in 1835, and it's as true today as it was then: 'Despotism may govern without faith, but liberty cannot. Religion is more needed in democratic societies than in any other.' "[8] With a sly nod to his academic audience, he warned, "Learning is a good thing, but unless it's tempered by faith and a love of freedom, it can be very dangerous indeed. The names of many intellectuals are recorded on the rolls of infamy, from Robespierre to Lenin to Ho Chi Minh to Pol Pot."[9]

In particular, Reagan believed that biblical wisdom was indispensable in devising intelligent law. One thing that "must never change" in America, he contended, is that men and women must "seek Divine guidance in the policies of their government and the promulgation of their laws." They must, he urged, "make our laws and government not only a model to mankind, but a testament to the wisdom and mercy of God."[10]

A belief in the power of prayer, and an inclination to extend the lessons of religion to the challenges of policy: in these and other ways Ronald Reagan's spirituality shaped his presidency.

PRAYER AND THE PRESIDENCY

Throughout the 1980s, Reagan often seized the opportunity to preach the power of prayer.[11] Twice during the presidential debates with Walter Mondale, he said he couldn't imagine how someone could carry out the "awesome responsibilities" of the presidency without prayer. To think otherwise struck him as "absurd." He didn't think he could carry on without trust in a higher authority.[12] He expressed this sentiment repeatedly in private letters throughout his presidency, frequently invoking the image of Lincoln on his knees.[13]

One of the best chances of getting a letter or phone call from the president was to let him know that he was in the correspondent's prayers. A letter from Father Robert J. Baffa, informing Reagan that the Catholic Student Association at the University of Vermont and Norwich University was planning a twenty-four-hour interfaith prayer vigil to coincide with the Washington summit, prompted a personal telephone call from Reagan.[14]

On one occasion, Secretary Margaret Heckler of Health and Human Services suggested that Reagan's cabinet meetings should open with a prayer. It was an unorthodox proposal; only Dwight Eisenhower is on record as opening such meetings with prayer on a regular basis. To Heckler's suggestion, Reagan simply replied "I do." That is, he was already in the habit of praying, alone and to himself, before each meeting. Don Hodel, then secretary of energy and now president of Focus on the Family ministries, witnessed the exchange. "He both responded to the suggestion and closed the subject," said Hodel. "There was no debate. No controversy. That was it. He prayed himself."[15]

Reagan personally penciled into a February 1983 speech the following lines: "I know at times we feel that perhaps in our prayers we ask too much. Or possibly we feel something isn't important enough to be bothering God with it." He advised placing that decision in God's hands: "Maybe we should let Him decide these things."[16]

One of Reagan's favorite images was that of George Washington praying at Valley Forge, which he called the "most sublime image in American history."[17] Washington kneeling in the snow, he said in a radio address in December 1983, "personified a people who knew it was not enough to depend on their own courage and goodness; they must also seek help from God, their Father and their Preserver."[18]

If there was one passage in time that shed light on Reagan's penchant for prayer while in office, it was the period before 241 marines were killed by a suicide bomber in Beirut, Lebanon, in October 1983.[19] Those days saw a series of sporadic deaths in the ruined city. Troops were steadily picked off, slowly bleeding the strength and morale of the forces. Reagan insisted on being immediately notified of these deaths, regardless of the time of day. "He wanted to be awakened as soon as possible," recalled Bill Clark, then Reagan's national security adviser. Often, the Pentagon informed Clark in the middle of the night, and it was his job to bring Reagan the news. The president would express regret; then, sometimes, a pause would follow as Reagan stopped to pray in silence.

Reagan always took the names of the marines and the phone numbers of their next of kin, and when he called to offer his condolences he would often pray with the families. "By custom," said Clark, "he would say: should we say a little prayer?" The answer was usually *yes*, and the president prayed with the grieving loved ones over the telephone.

Speaking at the National Prayer Breakfast in February 1983, Reagan had reminded his listeners that America had relied on God in the past, and must be willing to do so again. In these calls and many other expressions of faith during his time in office, he made plain his belief in the power of prayer.[20]

RELIGION AND POLICY

Reagan's foundation of faith also closely affected his presidential leadership. His belief in God was a key source of his optimism and boldness, his daring and self-security, and his confidence; these essential intangibles carried him throughout his presidency—and career as a whole—and enabled him to achieve what he did.

His confidence, for example, was so formidable that it almost seemed as though he were reaching outside of himself to summon it. This evident self-security suffused his approach toward the Cold War, encouraging him to pursue an extraordinarily daring strategy to attempt to defeat Soviet communism, particularly through very risky covert economic warfare.[21] The very notion that he thought he could undermine the USSR suggested immense confidence, especially at a time when no one else thought such a goal possible. To *pursue* the goal took yet more confidence—one rooted in his faith.

It also took what Reagan often called his "God-given optimism"[22]—a sense of hope, he said after his presidency, that came directly "from my strong faith in God."[23]

Another key to his success, of course, was the legendary storytelling skill that earned him the title "the Great Communicator." As noted, his early experience in reading and teaching from the Bible had taught him the power of stories;[24] as he once told a reporter, "I believe an illustration, like a picture, is worth a thousand words. Jesus used parables to make His points and help people understand."[25]

Taken together, these attributes constituted a powerful arsenal in Reagan's efforts to direct American policy at home and abroad. But his faith influenced more than simply his leadership abilities; it also informed his positions themselves. The arenas in which Reagan drew on his religious beliefs to shape his policy preferences as president are legion.

One of these was education policy. The issue of prayer in public schools was very much in the air during his presidency, and Reagan's ardent position on the matter was no surprise.[26] "God isn't dead," quipped Reagan in a line he'd been using since the 1960s. "We just can't talk to Him in the classroom anymore."[27] He lobbied incessantly for the right of children to pray in public schools, rarely missing an opportunity to raise the issue. "Can it really be true that the First Amendment can permit Nazis and Ku Klux Klansmen to march on public property, advocate the extermination of people of the Jewish faith and the subjugation of blacks, while the same amendment forbids our children from saying a prayer in school?" he wondered aloud in a February 1984 radio address.[28]

Reagan argued for prayer in public schools every chance he could,[29] sometimes taking his message straight into the lion's den—public schools themselves.[30] He chose venues as consequential as the annual meeting of the National Association of Secondary School Principals, as well as a State of the Union speech, to air his views.[31] Beginning in 1982, he pushed hard for a constitutional amendment to allow prayer in public schools.[32]

His faith clearly affected a number of his other positions on education. In a March 1987 letter to a friend, he complained of the secularized manner in which sex education was taught in public schools. "Well-intentioned though it may have been," he began, "it is taught in a framework of only being a physical act—like eating a ham sandwich. The educators are fearful that any references to sin or morality will be viewed as violating the church and state separation."[33]

Abortion was another issue he found inseparable from biblical precepts.[34] In a January 1984 speech to religious broadcasters, he said: "God's most blessed gift to his family is the gift of life. He sent us the Prince of Peace as a babe in the manger."[35] Like the nineteenth-century clergymen who led the movement to abolish slavery, as a Christian Reagan considered himself duty-bound to fight abortion, which he equated with slavery in terms of moral outrage. He made that analogy in January 1984 when speaking to the National Religious Broadcasters, quoting Christ in the process:

> This nation fought a terrible war so that black Americans would be guaranteed their God-given rights. Abraham Lincoln recognized that we could not survive as a free land when some could decide whether others should be free or slaves. Well, today another question begs to be asked: How can we survive as a free nation when some decide that others are not fit to live and should be done away with?
>
> I believe no challenge is more important to the character of America than restoring the right to life to all human beings. With-

out that right, no other rights have meaning. "Suffer the little children to come unto me, and forbid them not, for such is the kingdom of God."[36]

Together, Reagan assured the religious broadcasters, he and they could convince their fellow countrymen that America "should, can, and will preserve God's greatest gift"—the right to life. This was a very strong statement that did not escape criticism by pro-choice liberals in the media.[37]

He was frequently vocal about God and abortion. To cite just one other high-profile example, in his 1986 State of the Union address he lamented: "Today there is a wound in our national conscience. America will never be whole as long as the right to life granted by our Creator is denied to the unborn."[38] And he was as good as his word: on many issues Reagan was more flexible than conventional wisdom suggests, but abortion was a moral issue on which he refused to compromise as president.

The same was true when it came to racial and religious prejudice. Reagan's hatred of bigotry toward blacks, Jews, Catholics, and other groups was derived from the example of his parents, and from their understanding of fairness and right and wrong.[39] In a letter to a friend as president, he said that being the son of a Catholic meant he didn't have "even a tinge of religious prejudice."[40] Bill Clark, a devout Catholic, agrees. "He was very tolerant of other faiths," said Clark, "especially the Jewish faith."[41]

Though Reagan learned his opposition to bigotry through his parents' example, it was also deeply grounded in his faith.[42] In Reagan's mind, the biblical opposition to prejudice and injustice was straightforward: "The commandment given us is clear and simple: 'Thou shalt love thy neighbor as thyself.' " That commandment itself, Reagan insisted, rejected racism. From his personal letters to the Evil Empire speech, Reagan missed few chances to scorn bigotry and racism as a "sin" and a "moral evil," and to acknowledge his Christian responsibility to "denounce" and oppose it "with all my might."[43]

As liberals would note, Reagan's prescription for alleviating poverty marked one of his administration's most radical shifts in policy from previous administrations. Yet here, too, Reagan was drawing on his own faith and belief system.[44] As we've seen, his thinking on poverty and welfare can plausibly be traced directly back to *That Printer of Udell's*; there may also be links between Reagan's ideas and the social gospel practiced by the Disciples of Christ from the turn of the century through the Great Depression of the 1930s.[45] The Disciples came to believe the purpose of the church was to work for the "redemption of society as well as the saving of the individual." By the first decade of the twentieth century, this theology had permeated the Disciples' thinking—and certainly inspired Nelle Reagan's own life of good works.[46]

By the 1980s, it was clear that the New Deal, big-government solutions of the Roosevelt and Johnson administrations had grown bloated and counterproductive. As an alternative to more spending, Reagan proposed private-sector remedies, with an emphasis on the contributions of faith-based organizations. Thomas McDill, an evangelical member of a group of church officials who met with Reagan in the White House one afternoon during the first term, was struck by the president's dedication to the work of faith-based groups. Reagan spoke up, stressing to the group that the religious community must "step up to the plate" to help the hungry and homeless. Citing food pantries, soup kitchens, and other such programs, he insisted that churches had a "duty" to assist the needy.[47]

Another such occasion was a March 1982 luncheon with African

American clergy. Insisting that America's churches have a vital role in the life of the nation, Reagan quoted " 'Our Savior': inasmuch as ye have done unto the least of these, my brethren, you have done unto me." "Well," he followed, "too many churches are Sunday morning churches and not seven-day-a-week churches."[48]

Reagan's Christian approach to foreign policy was no different. Even aside from his position on communism and the Cold War, as president there is ample evidence that Reagan brought a Christian frame of mind to issues ranging from foreign aid to nuclear arms.

One of Reagan's longest-standing convictions about American foreign policy was that the United States had a Christian duty to extend aid to less fortunate countries. As early as 1962, he had said: "I think that Christian charity—charity of the God of Moses, requires that we should share of our superfluous goods with our needy neighbors."[49] As president, he told Mother Teresa in a December 1984 letter that the United States "can offer assistance" to the needy abroad "only because God has granted us abundance."[50]

That Reagan took God's lead in extending foreign aid may not be all that surprising, but some readers may be surprised to realize that Reagan was inclined to view even a cold policy matter such as arms control in Christian terms. As he reported on the historic INF treaty with the Soviet Union, which abolished a full class of nuclear weapons, the president spoke boldly of Christ before a nationwide television audience on December 10, 1987. Reagan noted that all "God's children" should take hope in the fact that "we're moving away from the so-called policy" of Mutual Assured Destruction (MAD), by which "nations hold each other hostage to nuclear terror and destruction." With Christmas a little more than two weeks away, Reagan called on the image of Jesus in this very secular context:

How that cry echoes down through the centuries, a cry for all children of the world, a cry for peace, for a world of love and understanding. And it is the hope of heeding such words—the call for freedom and peace spoken by a chosen people in a promised land, the call spoken by the Nazarene carpenter . . . standing at the Sea of Galilee, the carpenter whose birth into the poverty of a stable we celebrate—it is these words that we remember as the holiday season approaches and we reflect on the events of this week here in Washington.

Let us then thank God for all His blessings to this nation, and ask Him for His help and guidance so that we might continue the work of peace and foster the hope of a world where human freedom is enshrined.[51]

Agree or disagree, it was quite a statement: in a moment of important political transition, Reagan was calling on all Americans from the Oval Office, *on prime-time television,* to remember the words of Christ as they reflected on what happened at the Washington Summit the previous week. It was one of the most dramatic spiritual overtures of his presidency.

13.

In the Stars

"Astrology was simply one of the ways I coped
with the fear I felt after my husband almost died."

—Nancy Reagan[1]

Only two months after his first inauguration, Ronald Reagan's
routine was violently disrupted. March 30, 1981, began as a
regular presidential day. Yet it was cut short by an event that the new
president soon became convinced was not just out of the ordinary but
a Providential experience.

At 2:25 P.M. that afternoon, Reagan was leaving the Washington
Hilton through a side door after speaking to a crowd of union officials. Outside was a gaggle of staff, secret service, reporters, and
bystanders—including one who was determined to end Ronald Reagan's life at that moment. That face in the crowd belonged to an un-
stable man named John Hinckley, there to gain the attention of, and
prove his love for, the young actress Jodie Foster.

As the president headed toward the open car door, a reporter barked out a question. With a smile, Reagan raised his left arm to deflect the query. But he could not deflect what was about to fly in his direction. A few feet from the safety of the backseat of the limo, Reagan heard what sounded like firecrackers. It was gunfire.

Secret Service agent Jerry Parr thrust Reagan into the car, landing on top of him. "Jerry, get off," cried Reagan, "I think you've broken one of my ribs." The pain Reagan felt was actually the result of a bullet that had torn into his chest. Noticing the frothy blood bubbles percolate through Reagan's lips, Parr commanded the driver to get to a hospital fast. They managed to reach George Washington University Hospital in only a few minutes.

Parr's call was the first good news of the day. His snap diagnosis and order to the driver may have saved Reagan's life. The second bit of good news came when the president was stretched out on the table in the operating room. It just so happened that the hospital was holding its monthly meeting of department heads. For this profoundly fortunate man, it was another of those divine twists of fate: the university's chief brain surgeon *and* chief thoracic surgeon were both on hand, and they rushed to the president's side.[2] Reagan later recalled his thoughts prior to their arrival:

> I focused on that tiled ceiling and prayed. But I realized I couldn't ask for God's help while at the same time I felt hatred for the mixed up young man who had shot me. Isn't that the meaning of the lost sheep? We are all God's children and therefore equally beloved by him. I began to pray for his soul and that he would find his way back into the fold.[3]

Reagan had learned the power of forgiveness from his mother, Nelle; he saw it not only as his Christian obligation but as a practical means for "conquering anger and bitterness," as he had written years earlier to the pastor of Westminster Presbyterian Church in Los Angeles.[4]

Only once the president was on the operating table did the doctor determine the full extent of his injury. Hinckley had used .22 Devastator bullets, designed to explode on impact. One of the bullets had ricocheted off the armored car, flattened, and sliced into his body through his left armpit, leaving a small, barely perceptible slit like a knife wound—so tiny that the doctors discovered it only after finding a hole in the president's jacket. The projectile traveled downward, bounced off a rib, punctured a lung, and finally halted in Reagan's chest—less than an inch from his seventy-year-old heart.

Reagan had survived a perilously close call. Asked later by Donn Moomaw whether he would have been ready to meet God if Hinckley had succeeded, Reagan grew pensive and replied simply, "Yes." Moomaw prodded further: How was he certain he was ready? Reagan returned: "I'm ready to meet God because I have a Savior."[5]

REAGAN'S DAUGHTER PATTI WRITES OF HER VISIT TO the hospital immediately after the shooting:

> He actually didn't look frail; he looked almost ethereal. There was a light in his eyes that made me think, then and still, that he saw something—visited with God, listened to the counsel of an angel—something. My mother has since told me that he woke up at one point after the doctors had operated on him, unable to talk because there was a tube down his throat. He saw figures in white standing around him and scrawled on a piece of paper, "I'm alive, aren't I?" My mother still has the note.
>
> This story has become one that gathers more truth as it is shared with more listeners. When my mother first told it to me, we

discussed how logical it is to assume that the figures in white, standing around my father, were the doctors and nurses who were tending to him. But maybe not, we said; maybe he did see angels. We
left it with a question mark. Then I repeated it to a friend—a
nurse—who pointed out to me that no one in a recovery room or in
intensive care is in white; they're all in green scrubs. I phoned my
mother and told her, and her reaction was "I didn't even think of
that, there was so much that day—but you're right." I give endless
prayers of thanks to whatever angels circled my father, because a
Devastator bullet, which miraculously had not exploded, was finally found a quarter inch from his heart. Without divine intervention, I don't know if he would have survived.[6]

That was Patti's view, one her parents wouldn't have questioned. After the attempted assassination, though, Nancy Reagan looked anywhere she could for comfort—and found it in an unlikely place, one
that would give members of Reagan's Christian following some pause
when it came to light.

NANCY REAGAN AND ASTROLOGY

After her husband's shooting, Nancy Reagan's concerns about security grew exponentially. She agonized over his health and his schedule, and suffered an unshakable fear that the president would once
again be put in harm's way.[7]

Just after the shooting, she was told by her Hollywood friend
Merv Griffin that a Hollywood astrologer named Joan Quigley had
warned that March 30 was a "dangerous day" for the president. Nancy
recalled:

"Oh my God," I remember telling Merv, "*I could have stopped it!*" I hung up the phone, picked it up again, and called Joan. "Merv tells me you knew about March 30," I said. "Yes," she replied. "I could see it was a very bad day for the president." "I'm so scared," I told her. "I'm scared every time he leaves the house, and I don't think I breathe until he gets home. I cringe every time we step out of a car or leave a building. I'm afraid that one of these days somebody is going to shoot him again."[8]

"Astrology was simply one of the ways I coped with the fear I felt after my husband almost died," she said later. She was attracted to astrology as a "crutch," a way to channel the trauma and grief she had suffered, and in Quigley she felt she had found a comforting friend. At the time, astrology also felt like another means to do everything she possibly could to ensure her husband's safety. As she said, she "wasn't about to take any chances." Of course, Reagan survived the rest of his two-term presidency without further attacks. "Was astrology one of the reasons?" asked Nancy in her memoir. "I don't *really* believe it was, but I don't *really* believe it wasn't. . . . Why take chances? [Astrology] may be nonsense, but does anybody *really* know? . . . But I do know this: It didn't hurt, and I'm not sorry I did it."[9]

"She was frightened," explained Mrs. Reagan's press secretary, Elaine Crispen. "I don't think any of us appreciated how much. So if she could get a little comfort and consolation from astrology, why not?"[10]

Those who knew Nancy Reagan might not have been surprised at this mystical side. Long concerned for her husband's safety, she had also shown a willingness to consider supernatural danger signs in looking out for him. One extraordinary account, never before reported, illustrates Nancy's trust in the mystical when it came to protecting her husband.

Joan Sieffert, president of the Pittsburgh chapter of Reagan's fan club in his Hollywood days, exchanged letters with Reagan well into the 1970s. Reagan is characteristically candid and personal in his letters, many of which run longer than a full page. So close was the pen-pal relationship that Sieffert also received letters from Nelle and even some from Reagan's sister-in-law (Moon's wife).[11]

One night in 1974, Sieffert said she awoke from a dream—"a nightmare"—in which she pictured Reagan running for president, winning the presidency, and then being shot. "He was shot before entering a car," she envisioned, "and it really terrified me." The next morning she sent off a letter to the Reagans informing them of her dream.[12]

Even more interesting than the dream itself was Nancy's reaction. A few days after sending the letter, Sieffert said she received a phone call from a traumatized Nancy Reagan in California. Nancy said that she feared something like this could happen someday, and so did her husband. But, she said, in Sieffert's words, "Ronnie really believes that it's God choice that he run the country. And I feel that way, too."

It was the only call Sieffert ever received from Nancy, prompted by a supernatural sign of impending danger. Already plagued by an acute fear that her husband could be assassinated, Reagan's wife was fully capable of being rattled by something as nebulous as a fan club president's dream—and just as willing to place faith in a mystic's astrological charts.

Though she has said that she was "far from a true believer,"[13] only Nancy Reagan herself knows the true nature, and level, of her devotion to astrology during her husband's political career. Some reports have claimed that she was consulting seers as early as the gubernatorial days.[14] In any case, the Reagans were certainly both exposed to astrology via the Hollywood culture, especially during its heyday in the 1960s.

It is difficult today to convey Hollywood's (and the general public's) fascination with astrology at the time. For instance, in a 1966 appearance on the popular *Mike Douglas Show*, astrologer Jeane Dixon was credited with predicting the deaths of John F. Kennedy, Mahatma Gandhi, Dag Hammarskjold, and more. Douglas, who presented her claim at face value, sat spellbound as Dixon predicted that the Chinese would invade Russia, and that the United States and USSR would ally together to repel them. She also predicted that the Soviets would beat America in landing a man on the moon.[15] That on the same program she spoke cryptically of Ronald Reagan one day becoming president may not have escaped Nancy's notice.

On the other hand, a number of accounts, including her own, agree that Nancy Reagan also believes in God, and perceived no conflict between her Christianity and astrology. She is extremely private in what she simply terms her "faith." "It's the essence of my faith that's sheltered, never spoken but fiercely guarded." She says that she has drawn upon this faith countless times, in periods of "great personal crisis and darkness." When she felt tested, she said, it revealed itself time and again, giving her strength. It is "one of the few things I have left," she says, "which is strictly my own."[16]

ASTROLOGY'S ROLE IN THE PRESIDENCY

Toward the end of Reagan's presidency, the public learned that Nancy Reagan had regularly consulted astrologer Joan Quigley, even making some scheduling decisions for her husband based on Quigley's ruminations on "the stars."

Nancy maintained—and the facts appear to confirm—that "While astrology was a factor in determining Ronnie's schedule, it was never the only one, and no political decision was ever based on it."[17] The critical latter half of that statement seems correct. The First Lady herself took time to emphasize the point more than once in her own memoir, once writing in italics for emphasis: "I want to state one thing again, and unequivocally: *Joan's recommendations had nothing to do with policy or politics—ever. Her advice was confined to timing—and to Ronnie's schedule, and to what days were good or bad, especially with regard to his out-of-town trips.*"[18]

The public's interest in astrology's place in the Reagan White House was inflamed by former chief of staff Donald Regan, who gave a very different account of Quigley's role. In his own book, Regan charged that "virtually every major move and decision the Reagans made during my time as White House Chief of Staff was cleared in advance with a woman in San Francisco who drew up horoscopes to make certain that the planets were in a favorable alignment for the enterprise."

Regan's claim, alas, appears to have been uncareful at best. Certainly his reference to "virtually every major move and decision" is an exaggeration, denied by other members of the Reagan White House and belied by decisions the president and his advisers, including Don Regan himself, made at places like Reykjavik.

Regan's assertion might have some basis in fact. His account does offer a convincing case that astrology played a role in certain key scheduling decisions during Reagan's presidency.[19] Close aide Michael Deaver says that Quigley's role was reserved strictly to "large public events," not the entire presidential schedule. If Quigley identified "two or three" so-called "bad days," Deaver said he would schedule around them, simply for Nancy's peace of mind.[20]

If Ronald Reagan was "influenced" by astrology, then, it was only to the extent that particular moments in his schedule were influenced by Joan's interpretations, relayed to Nancy. It's hard to believe that this practice extended to major events, such as international summits: Reykjavik, for example, was scheduled according to suggestions by the Soviets.

Nancy contends that her husband was initially unaware of her consultations with Quigley. "At first," she says, "Ronnie knew nothing." She wanted to tell him about what she was doing, she says, but "wasn't exactly *dying* to tell him, and I kept putting it off." Then one day Reagan walked in when she was on the phone with Joan and asked: "Honey, what was that about?" When she told him, she says, he responded: "If it makes you feel better, go ahead and do it. But be careful. It might look a little odd if it ever came out." She said he foresaw that the issue "could have serious consequences for us."[21]

Indeed, during his Sacramento days Reagan had already had a taste of such "consequences." After his inauguration as governor was scheduled for one minute after midnight, his executive secretary was forced to dismiss accusations that the time was chosen for astrological reasons: "He does not believe in astrology. He is not guided by the stars!"[22]

Astrology and Ronald Reagan

It is critical to understand that most of the voices who describe Nancy Reagan's dalliance with astrology do *not* allege that the president himself was a follower. From Regan and others to Nancy herself, the primary sources pin the blame on Nancy. Only a few secondary sources have attempted to extend the claim to the president.

The two prominent voices who have publicly claimed that Reagan himself was a follower of—or interested in—astrology are Joan Quigley herself, and the celebrity biographer Kitty Kelley. Quigley, not surprisingly, puffs up her role.[23] Even so, she concedes that she never gave the president advice directly. At best, she notes that Nancy was her "line" to the president. On two or three occasions, she claims, Reagan sought her opinion through Nancy, once supposedly asking, "What does Joan say?" That one line managed to become the title of Quigley's book. Quigley is correct in speculating that Reagan "had to have known about me and the advice I was giving Nancy"; as we've seen, eventually he was.[24] Inasmuch as Quigley had any influence on Reagan, though, it was through Nancy's maneuvering.

The other source is Kitty Kelley, who penned the scandalous unauthorized biography of Nancy Reagan that sent the First Lady and her husband into a rage. The sensational book dared to report material no one else would touch, including sexual innuendo about the Reagans. Kelley also questioned the Reagans' religious faith, and went further than anyone in contending that Reagan himself was devoted to astrology deep into his Hollywood years. She even featured pictures of three astrologers she claims served the Reagans over the years—Jeane Dixon, Carroll Righter, and Quigley.[25]

Reagan was eventually forced to deny publicly the allegations that he was influenced by astrology.[26] When one reporter yelled to him as he left a Rose Garden ceremony, "Mr. President, will you continue to allow astrology to play a part in the makeup of your daily schedule?" Reagan responded: "I can't, because I never did." He said that "no decision was ever made by me on the basis of astrology."[27]

On another occasion, he said unequivocally: "No policy or decision in my mind has ever been influenced by astrology."

And, indeed, there's little evidence that Ronald Reagan had any kind of commitment to astrology. His devotion to his Christian faith was solid and serious, enough so to support his repeated rejection that he believed in or "practiced" astrology.

Others who knew him concur. Speechwriter Ben Elliott saw astrology as "completely foreign" to Reagan. "To me, that just wasn't him," he said. "I never heard anything like that from Reagan."[28] That was also true for Ed Meese, whose relationship with Reagan dated back to the 1960s: "I don't ever remember him having said anything about [astrology]," he said.[29] Richard V. Allen, who traveled the world with Reagan in the 1970s as his foreign-policy adviser and later served in his White House, uses almost the very same words, saying that he "never heard him [Reagan] ever say anything about astrology. Absolutely not."[30]

He did, however, read his horoscope. In *Where's the Rest of Me?*, he talked about reading the popular astrological columnist Carroll Righter, whom Reagan was also friendly with.[31] His son Michael remembers sitting at the breakfast table in the 1960s as his father read Righter. "But it was no big deal!" he protests. "It was like reading the comics. He would laugh and say to us, 'Hey, listen to this today. . . . ' " Michael adds with emphasis: "You need to understand that *everyone* in Hollywood read him [Righter] in those days. *Everyone*."[32] Ed Meese also remembers Reagan reading his horoscope for "entertainment" and "amusement." "At no time," said Meese, "did he ever to my knowledge use astrology for anything [to do] with his presidency. I never saw it. That's been way overblown."[33]

Of course there's a difference between reading a newspaper's horoscope column and actively consulting an astrologer, and there's little to suggest that Reagan ever did the latter. Indeed, it's hard to imagine Reagan feeling much need for the kind of comfort astrology purports to offer: the Christian God guided and moved him more than any alignment of the stars. Among the thousands of private Reagan letters reviewed in research for this book—letters dating from his adolescence through his presidency—there were endless references to God. Not one addressed anything remotely related to the zodiac.

ANOTHER REASON TO BELIEVE REAGAN'S DISAVOWALS of astrology? He rarely showed an inclination to hide his views on anything—even when his advisers might have wished he had kept his own counsel. Reagan was a man of supreme confidence in his beliefs, who often flummoxed people with his candor: he was known to speak freely of flying saucers, aliens, ghosts, and spiritual visitations. He was criticized, on the 1980 campaign trail and thereafter, for expressing doubts about evolution.[34] He also freely talked about Armageddon, the Antichrist, and prophecy.[35]

His talk of the Apocalypse made his advisers very nervous. Once, when Reagan was speaking openly of the Second Coming with biographer Edmund Morris, chief of staff Howard Baker walked in, saw Morris's tape recorder, and fretted: "I tell you, Mr. President, I wish you'd quit talking about that. You upset me!" Reagan didn't care. He went on, speaking of Gog, Meshech, Ten Kings.[36] He talked of Armageddon so often that some biographers suggested it was an obsession of Reagan's.[37] The man was an open book on mystical matters.

Nonetheless, for a while the astrology rap stuck, and Reagan paid quite a price in the public eye. Garry Wills's criticism was typical: "Why would evangelicals and others reject a sincere believer in the gospel, like [President Jimmy] Carter, for Reagan's profession of a hodgepodge of make-believe beliefs?"[38] Wills exclaimed: "President Reagan's religiosity barely rises above the level of superstition."[39] Wills is no conservative, but many evangelical Christians echoed his concern. One evangelical, referring specifically to astrology, told me: "Reagan was a real disappointment to us." To this day, many hold it against him. At the time, columnist Cal Thomas, a conservative Christian, was blunt: "This is the last straw for a lot of religious people who treated Reagan as their political savior. He used to say, 'The answer to all life's problems can be found in the Bible.' I guess he put God on hold and consulted Jeane Dixon."[40]

Even to this day, for some evangelicals sizing up Reagan's faith, astrology remains the eight-hundred-pound gorilla in the room. It's the first concern they express when considering President Reagan's faith. Many Christians insist that one cannot be a "serious Christian" while engaging in the "cultish" practice of seeking careful counsel from stargazers. As David Neff asserted with "indignation" in *Christianity Today*, "Biblical Christianity clearly condemns astrology."[41]

To the contrary, the astrologers linked with the Reagans felt otherwise. On *The Mike Douglas Show*—in that same appearance where she rubbed her crystal ball to view Reagan's road to the White House—Jeane Dixon wore a shiny crucifix dangling from her necklace, and rooted her "gift" of "prophecy" in the Bible, calling it a "blessing" and "the Lord's gift."[42] And Joan Quigley claimed that astrology is not inconsistent with Scripture, maintaining that the prophet Isaiah and the Wise Men were astrologers; according to her, in fact, "the Bible praises astrology."[43]

OF ALL JOAN QUIGLEY'S REVELATIONS ABOUT THE Reagans, perhaps the most telling moment in her book comes when she finally meets the president in person after a White House party.

Following that brief meeting, she told Nancy: "It amused me so much when I talked to Ronnie after dinner, and he told me that he felt God had entrusted him with a mission and that his strength came directly from God."[44] When presented with the chance to solicit an astrologer's opinions, what did Ronald Reagan do? He shared his own brand of spiritual wisdom.

14.

God's Will and the Demise of the Soviet Empire

"I have decided that whatever time I have left is for Him. . . . Whatever happens now I owe my life to God and will try to serve him every way I can."

—Ronald Reagan to Terence Cardinal Cooke, Good Friday 1981[1]

"There is a purpose to this. . . . This has happened to you at this time because your country and the world need you."

—Mother Teresa, to Reagan on his surviving near-assassination, June 4, 1981[2]

Ronald Reagan's reaction to his brush with death was quite different from his wife's. Where she looked west, to Hollywood seers, he looked upward.

Reagan later said he was sure God had spared him. What happened to him on that day was not just physical but spiritual. Indeed, while the physical effects of the shooting slowed him down for a few weeks, spiritually Reagan was transformed by the attack; it fueled his feeling of divine purpose for the next eight years.

If Reagan's sense of mission began to come into focus with his inauguration in January of 1981, it became clearer in the aftermath of the March attack. One might have expected what happened that day to dampen his enthusiasm. Instead, it seemed to give Reagan new momentum—an ever more confident belief in a calling.

Only a week and a half before the shooting, Reagan told an audience: "Our Nation's motto—'In God We Trust'—was not chosen lightly. It reflects a basic recognition that there is a divine authority in the universe."[3] His survival only enhanced his trust in a divine authority. Similarly, before Reagan left the office the morning of the shooting, he held a 10:00 A.M. meeting with 140 sub-Cabinet appointees. At the conference he quoted one of his favorite lines, from the American revolutionary Thomas Paine: "We have it in our power to begin the world over again."[4] How ironic that Reagan would soon feel a heightened call from God to shake up the world—renewed through the intervention of Hinckley's assassination attempt later that day.

In his public and especially private statements, Ronald Reagan left ample evidence that he felt God had chosen him for a special purpose in the Cold War struggle. And it seems clear that he wasn't the only one who felt that way: many of the religious figures who met with him, including three of the world's prominent Catholics, offered a form of external confirmation to his internal thinking. One was Pope John Paul II, with whom Reagan forged an extraordinary relationship and a mutual mission.

"Whatever Time I Have Left Is for Him"

While recovering in the hospital, Reagan told his daughter Maureen that he felt God had spared him for a reason, and that he would devote the rest of his time on earth to whatever it was God intended him to do.[5]

It was a thought he wouldn't leave behind in the hospital bed. On his first evening back in the White House he confided to his diary: "I know it's going to be a long recovery. Whatever happens now I owe my life to God and will try to serve him every way I can."[6] As he sat in the White House solarium in robe and pajamas one morning, awaiting his doctors' go-ahead to resume a full work schedule, he pondered how to start the negotiating process with the Soviet Union. Reagan figured: "Perhaps having come so close to death made me feel I should do whatever I could in the years God had given me to reduce the threat of nuclear war; perhaps there was a reason I had been spared."[7]

It was a conviction that had a slow but certain ripple effect on Reagan's Cold War strategy. The following month he wrote a four-and-a-half-page letter directly to Leonid Brezhnev. It went to the NSC and the Kremlinologists at the State Department, who rewrote it entirely. Reagan got it back and shrugged in deference: "Well, maybe they know more about this than I do." Michael Deaver heard the comment and spoke up, reminding the president that *he* had been elected with a mandate, not the State Department. Reagan agreed and thanked him. "You know, since I've been shot," he told Deaver. "I think I'm going to rely more on my own instincts than other people's. There's a reason I've been saved."[8] The letter was mailed, beginning a process of consistently reaching out to the Soviets.[9]

That same month, Reagan's feeling of being saved for a certain reason was affirmed—on Good Friday—when he sought and received face-to-face counsel from New York's Terence Cardinal Cooke. "The hand of God was upon you," Cooke told Reagan. Reagan grew very serious. "I know," he replied, before confiding to the Cardinal: "I have decided that whatever time I have left is for Him."[10] As Edmund Morris explains, Reagan meant, "among other things, a coming to terms with Evil. Not the . . . evil . . . of John Hinckley's assault, but that institutional murder of all liberties known as Soviet communism."[11]

Reagan didn't keep such feelings private for long; he would take his conviction public in his speech to the 1982 National Prayer Breakfast the following February. "I've always believed that we were, each of us, put here for a reason, that there is a plan, somehow a divine plan for all of us," Reagan told the room. It was an observation he had made countless times before, but this time he shared what he told Cardinal Cooke privately: "I know now that whatever days are left to me belong to Him."[12]

APRIL-MAY 1981 — AMERICA'S "CHALLENGE"

Reagan's recovery was startlingly quick, especially for a seventy-year-old. In those initial weeks after the attack he stepped up his public comments about the Cold War challenge facing America, and about its God-given duty to respond. Once again he revived the remark of Pope Pius XII: "Into the hands of America, God has placed an afflicted mankind." In the April and May immediately following the attack he incorporated the line into major addresses, including a commencement speech at the U.S. Military Academy;[13] he would return to it again and again throughout his presidency, often before college audiences.[14]

The Soviets understood that Reagan was reviving Pius's forty-year-old observation with one thing in mind: his belief that God had chosen the United States—*not* the Soviet Union—as a beacon of hope for all mankind. In a discussion on the Moscow TV program *International Observers Roundtable*, commentator Viktor Nikolayevich Levin observed that the pontiff's words were "very close to Reagan's heart, and moreover it is precisely this postulate that he is attempting to pursue in the realm of practical politics. This is the origin of the problems that we are encountering."[15]

That same May, Reagan laid out the challenge in a commencement speech at the University of Notre Dame.[16] The address has since been recognized as one of his first presidential predictions on the demise of communism:

> The years ahead are great ones for this country, for the cause of freedom and the spread of civilization. The West won't contain communism, it will transcend communism. . . . It will dismiss it as some bizarre chapter in human history whose last pages are even now being written.[17]

In retrospect, the visionary quality of the speech is almost startling. Though no one else was making such audacious predictions at the time, those "last pages" Reagan referred to were being written even as he spoke. Unbeknownst to the world, communism's grip on Eastern Europe was fading; it would not survive the decade. Even within the Soviet Union, communism had only a handful of years

left: the USSR would disintegrate peacefully in 1991, expiring sym-
bolically on December 18, 1991, when the Soviet hammer and sickle
that had flown over the Kremlin for decades was replaced by the flag
of the new Russian Federation. A week later, on Christmas Day, a
helpless Gorbachev resigned as leader of the USSR, formally bringing
to a close the Soviet empire.

In 1981, however, Reagan's prediction was scoffed at, dismissed as
naïve or arrogant. Even some conservatives may have shrugged it off
as idealistic rhetoric. Yet Reagan's Notre Dame speech is noteworthy
for several reasons besides its bold predictions. A highly personal talk,
it began with lengthy extemporaneous remarks by Reagan prior to
the formal address. Weaving together quotes and anecdotes, both impromptu and prewritten, the speech sounded Reagan's theme of a
larger cause and challenge—a challenge he placed before America by
addressing his audience on a personal and spiritual level, invoking a
higher authority.

It was a complex, enigmatic speech—idiosyncratic and open to
interpretation. He announced its unorthodox nature in his opening
lines:

> The temptation is great to use this forum as an address on a great
> international or national issue. . . . Indeed, this is somewhat tradi-
> tional. So, I wasn't surprised when I read in several reputable jour-
> nals that I was going to deliver an address on foreign policy and the
> economy. I'm not going to talk about either.[18]

This, as we'll see, wasn't quite true. The principal focus of the address seemed to be to drive home Reagan's notion that Americans
were part of a larger cause. In doing so, he drew on a set of remarks
made by Winston Churchill during the most ominous days of the

Battle of Britain. "When great causes are on the move in the world," Churchill had said, "we learn we are spirits, not animals, and that something is going on in space and time, and beyond space and time, which, whether we like it or not, spells duty."[19] The words were eerily Reaganesque, with their emphasis on a great cause and their spiritual dimension. To Reagan, the obligation Americans must meet was their duty to fight expansionist, atheistic Soviet Marxism. Was America worthy of that challenge? He responded in the affirmative, citing a protracted history of Americans meeting tests.

He followed the Churchill passage with a personal story from his movie *Knute Rockne, All-American:*

> Now, today I hear very often, "Win one for the Gipper." . . . But let's look at the significance of that story. [Coach Knute] Rockne could have used Gipp's dying words to win a game any time. But eight years went by following the death of George Gipp before Rock revealed those dying words, his deathbed wish.
>
> And then he told the story at halftime to a team that was losing, and one of the only teams he had ever coached that was torn by dissension and jealousy and factionalism. The seniors on that team were about to close out their football careers without learning or experiencing any of the real values that a game has to impart. None of them had known George Gipp. They were children when he played for Notre Dame. It was to this team that Rockne told the story and so inspired them that they rose above their personal animosities. For someone they had never known, they joined together in a common cause and attained the unattainable.
>
> We were told when we were making the picture of one line that was spoken by a player during that game. We were actually afraid to put it in the picture. The man who carried the ball over for

the winning touchdown was actually injured on the play. We were told that as he was lifted on the stretcher and carried off the field he was heard to say, "That's the last one I can get for you, Gipper."

Now, it's only a game. And maybe to hear it now, afterward—and this is what we feared—it might sound maudlin and not the way it was intended. But is there anything wrong with young people having an experience, feeling something so deeply, thinking of someone else to the point that they can give so completely of themselves? There will come times in the lives of all of us when we'll be faced with causes bigger than ourselves, and they won't be on a playing field.[20]

Why this story in this speech? Reagan, of course, had played George Gipp in the film; it was his character who uttered the unforgettable deathbed line "Go out there and win one for the Gipper." Throughout his political life he used that line as a kind of signature, often referring to himself as "the Gipper." Yet here, as he used the story as a metaphor for a larger cause, he appeared to be linking himself to Rockne, not Gipp.

Just as Rockne had rallied a team torn apart by "dissension and jealousy and factionalism," Coach Reagan seemed to be rallying his own team. He seemed anxious to convince the group to join "someone they had never known"—apparently himself—to "attain the unattainable," just as that Notre Dame football team had for a Gipp they'd never met.

It wasn't the first time he had rallied a group of students to the cause. Indeed, this challenge was quite similar to the appeal a younger Reagan had made to the students at William Woods College in June 1952, when he asked them to join him in the grand ideological struggle to "push back the darkness over the stadium of humanity."[21]

In May 1981, Reagan used his Notre Dame appearance to reach out to a "team" of college kids who "never experienced any of the real values that a game has to impart." His audience on that day had no real experience with the world, or with the Cold War that had defined it for a generation—an infinitely more sober game than football.

Reagan was bent on motivating his young countrymen to rise above their personal animosities. A country divided, factionalized could not meet the Cold War challenge with confidence. After the Gipp story, Reagan cast his gaze in a loftier direction:

> When it's written, the history of our time won't dwell long on the hardships of the recent past. But history will ask . . . Did a people forged by courage find courage wanting? Did a generation steeled by hard war and a harsh peace forsake honor at the moment of great climactic struggle for the human spirit? . . . [T]he answers are to be found in the heritage left by generations of Americans before us. They stand in silent witness to what the world will soon know and history someday record: that in its third century, the American Nation came of age, affirmed its leadership of free men and women serving selflessly a vision of man with God, government for people, and humanity at peace.[22]

Someday, Reagan believed, history would judge that America reached maturity by affirming "its leadership of free men and women serving selflessly a vision of man with God"—an implicit recognition of the atheistic Soviet vision.

There is no question that the struggle between God and communism was very much on his mind as he uttered these words. Only four paragraphs earlier in the speech, he predicted that communism was nearing its final days; the next three paragraphs continued that theme. More broadly, though, it's key to remember that just a few weeks had passed since Reagan's brush with death, and his pledge to Cardinal Cooke that "whatever time I have left is left for Him." This awareness of a greater calling, to serve God's purposes whatever they may be, is reflected throughout the speech.[23]

Reagan continued:

> For the West, for America, the time has come to dare to show to the world that our civilized ideas, our traditions, our values, are not—like the ideology and war machine of totalitarian societies— just a facade of strength. It is time for the world to know our intellectual and spiritual values are rooted in the source of all strength, a belief in a Supreme Being, and a law higher than our own.[24]

"The time has come": it was another a grand moment, another invitation to destiny. Those values, which America should dare to show the world, said Reagan, derive from the greatest of strengths—from God, from belief in God, and from the wisdom of God's law.

How odd that Reagan should preface such a speech by saying he was not going to talk about foreign policy. It was as if he felt that what he had to say transcended foreign policy—as if, to Reagan, the very notion of "foreign policy" seemed belittling in light of the big picture.

Reagan himself recognized, and remembered, the impact of these remarks. Seven years later, when he returned to Notre Dame for a final rally, he mentioned that in 1981 he had come to give "one of the first major addresses of my Presidency," and that his remarks included his prediction that the West would transcend communism. He said that America was able to achieve that objective because its spiritual values and inner strength were so great. He then revisited the legend of Knute Rockne: "And that inner strength is what Notre Dame and the legend of Rockne are all about."[25]

This time, however, he turned to the subject of Rockne's religious faith. While Rockne was known for his influence on his players, Reagan said, not enough attention had been paid to the spiritual influence *they* had on *him*. Rockne had remembered watching his team slumber up to the Communion rail at Sunday Mass despite a severe lack of sleep following a rough game the previous afternoon. It was then, the coach said, that he understood "what a powerful ally their religion was to them in their work on the football field."[26] It wouldn't be too great a stretch to conclude that Reagan's own battle with communism was on his mind when he made this remark.

Reagan concluded his address by reflecting on how Rockne found his religious faith at Notre Dame, and how eager he was to share it with others. Rockne, he noted, had once told a friend: "I believe I've found my way, and I shall travel it to the end." He concluded by pointing out that after Rockne's plane crashed, his limp body was found next to a prayer book, a rosary in his hand. "Someone put it so well at the time," he eulogized. "Knute Rockne did more spiritual good than a thousand preachers."[27] Reagan must surely have hoped he would one day be praised in similar terms.

A few months after the Notre Dame speech Reagan again tackled the notion of challenge, this time during a talk observing the 200th anniversary of the Battle of Yorktown. He addressed the question of whether Americans would prove worthy of the divine burden he believed God had placed before them. "Will we meet the challenge?" he asked on the old battlefield. "Will we act worthy of ourselves? Each generation before us has struggled and sacrificed for freedom. Can we do any less?"[28]

And where to get the strength and will to summon that challenge?

For Reagan, of course, the answer was a spiritual one. Americans, he said, needed "to reassert our commitment as a nation to a law higher than our own . . . to renew our spiritual strength." "Only by building such a wall of spiritual resolve" could Americans meet this challenge.[29]

Here again, he invoked Thomas Paine's challenge: "We have it within our power to begin the world all over again." To Reagan, Paine's was no quixotic goal; it was a real charge, one he would strive to achieve on a geopolitical plane. He followed the Paine line with this close: "We only have to act worthy of ourselves."[30] This was Reagan working to convert the legions toward what he believed: That God had chosen this course for Americans, they were worthy of the task, and merely needed to accept the challenge.

Within that "we," of course, he included himself.

MOTHER TERESA AND POPE JOHN PAUL II

In April, Reagan had met with Cardinal Cooke. In May, he spoke to a large group of Catholic students and faculty at Notre Dame. Now he would soon have encounters with two particularly prominent Catholics—each quite meaningful. Jack Reagan, his Irish Catholic father, would have been proud.

In June, during a private meal with the Reagans and a few selected guests, Mother Teresa made an immediate impact upon the host. Gesturing toward a younger sister who was joining them, she said, "Mr. President Reagan, do you know that we stayed up for two straight nights praying for you after you were shot? We prayed very hard for you to live."

Reagan thanked her, but Mother Teresa wasn't finished pursuing her point. She looked at Reagan directly, and addressed him dramatically: "You have suffered the passion of the cross and have received grace. There is a purpose to this. Because of your suffering and pain you will now understand the suffering and pain of the world." Her words were uncannily resonant with his own private beliefs: "This has happened to you at this time because your country and the world need you." Nancy Reagan dissolved into tears; the president was almost speechless.[31]

A year later, in June 1982, came an even more powerful visit with Pope John Paul II at the Vatican.

The Pope liked Reagan for a number of reasons. He rightly recognized him as a Protestant who was friendly to Catholicism, and who counted many Catholics among his intimates. Reagan was surrounded by Catholics on his staff, especially the chief foreign-policy players—his first national security adviser, Richard V. Allen; CIA director William J. Casey; ambassador Vernon Walters; speechwriter Tony Dolan; and his second national security adviser, Bill Clark, to name a few. Clark, a committed Catholic, was Reagan's closest prayer partner. Of course, John Paul II was overjoyed when Reagan later became the first president to extend diplomatic recognition to the Vatican—a move long resisted by Protestants as far back as the administration of Harry Truman.[32]

Reagan and John Paul II were in many ways a perfect match, their respective religious faiths giving them an extraordinary amount of common ground. The Pope himself had suffered an assassination attempt in 1981, only six weeks after Reagan's, and each man was able to rise above his personal suffering when it came to his assassin: just as John Paul II forgave his would-be assassin, even visiting him in prison, Reagan prayed for forgiveness for Hinckley. John Paul's passionate association with his Polish homeland, moreover, rendered him a fierce and faithful ally to Reagan in their shared anticommunism. The two appeared to believe equally in God's will, and shared a faith-based optimism that made them hopeful about the future.[33] The Pope, in his own words, held a self-professed "conviction that the destiny of all nations lies in the hands of a merciful Providence."[34]

On June 7, 1982, the two men sat face-to-face for the first time. They discussed the assassination attempts, as well as their shared sense of special purpose. In a later cover story for *Time* magazine, Carl Bernstein reported that both the Pope and Reagan believed that God had saved them for a chosen mission—that mission, the article implied, was the defeat of communism in the Soviet bloc.[35]

At that first meeting together, the two men met and talked alone for fifty minutes in the Vatican Library. As Pio Cardinal Laghi, the apostle delegate to Washington, was told afterward, Reagan said to the Pope: "Look how the evil forces were put in our way and how Providence intervened." Bernstein reported that Reagan's national security adviser, Bill Clark, said that both men referred to their survivals as "miraculous." He said they also shared "a unity of a spiritual view and a unity of vision on the Soviet empire: that right or correctness would ultimately prevail in the divine plan."[36]

Clark expanded on this in a November 1999 interview:

The Pope and the president shared the view that each had been given a spiritual mission—a special role in the divine plan of life. Both are deeply prayerful—in Reagan's case, without public display. . . .

These common characteristics became apparent on the occasion when the two men came together at the Vatican in June 1982, to pray together and talk about life. . . . The two men discussed the unity of their spiritual views, and their concern [for] the terrible oppression of atheistic communism. . . .

The two men shared the belief that atheistic communism lived a lie that, when fully understood, must ultimately fail. . . . [E]ach was successful in translating a personal vision into an underlying policy, and implementing the strategy to defeat Soviet aggression and oppression.[37]

This mutual special thinking led to real action. Following this meeting, the two men and their teams agreed to aid the Solidarity movement in Poland, aiming to sustain and keep it alive as a wedge that could potentially split the USSR's empire in Eastern Europe. Each man believed that Solidarity could be the splinter to crack the Iron Curtain and hasten the downfall of the communist bloc and the USSR. Reagan had believed as much for years, long before his presidency.[38] Reagan and the Pope translated their divine mission into a practical mission to maintain Solidarity.[39] And their estimate of the historic importance of the movement was indisputably on target: Mikhail Gorbachev later agreed that once Poland held free elections in June 1989, the Soviet bloc was doomed.[40]

Bernstein quotes a cardinal who was one of the Pope's closest aides:

> Nobody believed the collapse of communism would happen this fast or on this timetable. But in their first meeting, the Holy Father and the President committed themselves and the institutions of the church and America to such a goal. And from that day, the focus was to bring it about in Poland.[41]

The extraordinary fact—not to mention the details—of Reagan's collaboration with the Pope on the defeat of communism remains largely unknown to the public. Most of the correspondence between the Reagan administration and the Vatican remains classified, with the few documents that have reached the public mostly or fully redacted.[42] We know only generally, for example, that the influence of their informal alliance spread into the Western Hemisphere: John Paul II supported the administration not only in Poland but throughout Latin America, resisting communism and supporting the spread of democracy there. The "American formula" for dealing with left- and right-wing regimes in the Western Hemisphere, write Carl Bernstein and Marco Politi in their biography of the Pope, "was now the Vatican's policy as well."[43]

As Bernstein and Politi dramatically concluded, "For the Pope, Reagan had been . . . an instrument in the hands of God." John Paul II disliked the excesses of capitalism and materialism in America, and didn't hesitate to condemn them in global terms. Yet, according to Bernstein and Politi, because the Pope believed Reagan was an instrument of God, "at no point in the eight years of Reagan's presidency did the Vatican or the Pope openly criticize the White House." The pontiff even prevailed upon U.S. bishops to water down their criticism of Reaganomics. Over the strong objections of bishops, he generally accepted Reagan's rationale for the military buildup of the 1980s, which Reagan justified to him in a January 1982 letter declassified in July 2000.[44] When the Vatican Academy of Sciences prepared a report sharply critical of Reagan's Strategic Defense Initiative (SDI), the Pope—following lobbying from Vice President Bush, Ambassador Walters, and Reagan himself—ordered it buried. Bernstein and Politi write: "Not until the Persian Gulf War in 1991—after the fall of communism in Eastern and Central Europe—did the Pope or his Church publicly oppose a single major feature of American policy."[45]

What Was the "Special Purpose?"

There's little question that Reagan perceived a divine plan for America in combating the USSR. And he publicly pledged his own life to serve God's wishes. But did he specifically see himself as chosen by God to attack and defeat the Soviet empire?

Any close Reagan associate will insist that this is no easy question. Reagan's faith is certain, yet his feelings about his particular mission, as we've seen, appear to have been marked by modesty and caution. Reagan himself was not always sure of God's plan for him when it came to his general conduct of the presidency, let alone the prospect of a presidential assault on Soviet communism. When it came to interpreting God's will, Reagan felt compelled to wait and pray for guidance.[46]

What is difficult to determine with certainty is whether Reagan believed that God had chosen him specifically to pursue the course of action he did. This crucial issue requires careful and precise attention, for it speaks directly to Reagan's motivation and conviction in confronting the USSR.

We do know that Reagan had set his sights on conquering communism well before the power to do so was within his grasp. Richard Allen, a longtime Reagan foreign policy adviser, will never forget Reagan telling him categorically in California in January 1977 that his intent was to take on and defeat the Soviet empire. "Dick, my idea of American policy toward the Soviet Union is simple," said Reagan. "It is this: 'we win and they lose.' "[47] Throughout the 1980s, of course, Reagan did predict the demise of Soviet communism repeatedly. And he did feel that God had a special plan for America generally in facing down the Soviet empire. Since he believed that God's hand guided events, he must have suspected that the Almighty was behind that plan. It might have been natural for Reagan to have surmised, then, that God was guiding his own hand, and that perhaps he was doing God's work in confronting the USSR.

Richard Allen has separately noted that Reagan generally saw himself as a "handmaiden" or "instrument" of God. Many others have noted this as well, from the Pope and Bill Clark to Reagan himself.[48] And yet both Allen and Clark, interviewed separately, insist that Reagan was too humble to talk or even *think* that way about his role in the end of the Cold War. Allen chooses his words carefully:

> I don't believe Reagan believed that God chose him to defeat the Soviet empire. But he did believe America was a chosen place. He would look back [after his presidency and the Cold War ended] and say something like: "Our team has fulfilled God's purpose." I think he would look back and say that. "We were part of the Divine Plan." He did, in fact, have a vibrant, vigorous faith that we could and would prevail against the USSR.[49]

For Reagan, it was one thing to assert that America fulfilled that special role for God; Allen and Clark claim that their longtime friend would never say or even think such a thing about himself.

Clark says that he never heard Reagan say explicitly that he knew God had chosen him for the specific purpose of taking on the USSR and its empire, nor that God had selected him in particular to *defeat* Soviet communism. "No," said Clark. "He did not say that because that would be out of character for him. He would speak more in the passive voice. 'The wall or Iron Curtain will come down.' 'It will come apart.' 'The Divine Plan,' or 'DP' as I called it, 'will prevail.' . . . He said things like that."

And yet, Clark clarifies, Reagan "did feel a calling, as I did, to this effort and the idea that truth would ultimately prevail. Not that *he* would prevail, but the truth will prevail."[50] In a March 2000 speech in San Francisco, Clark said that Reagan confidently told him and his staff, "several times both as governor and many times later as president," that "the wall around atheistic communism is destined to come down within the Divine Plan because it lives a lie."[51] Most dramatically, Clark says that Reagan fully expected communism to fall "in his lifetime"—a belief that would have been dismissed in the 1970s or even much of the 1980s.[52]

In an August 2001 interview, Clark continued:

> I remember one day I was with him when someone congratulated him for taking down the wall. He said, "No, I didn't bring the wall down. That was part of the Divine Plan, teamwork, and God's Will." His number one maxim is that we can accomplish anything if we don't concern ourselves with who gets the credit. . . . He just had total confidence in the Divine Will. He was there as an instrument of God, and one of many. He would refer to teamwork. . . .
>
> He would not consider making a statement like, "I have been chosen by God to lead a crusade against the Evil Empire." He would consider that to be false pride. . . . This is an amazingly humble person. True humility. There was no pride there at all.[53]

According to Clark, Reagan was too humble to credit anyone but his overall "team" as acting by God's hand. When one admirer congratulated him for "your success in ending the Cold War," Clark saw Reagan smile and reply, "No, not my success but a team effort by Divine Providence."[54]

Edwin Meese, another longtime Reagan ally, confirms the impression left by Allen and Clark: Meese never heard Reagan say he felt chosen by God to defeat the USSR.[55]

The same is true for Caspar Weinberger, Reagan's secretary of defense throughout the 1980s. Like Meese, Allen, and Clark, Weinberger knew and worked with Reagan well before the presidency, serving as Reagan's director of finance in California.

Weinberger does, however, recognize the power of Reagan's personal sense of calling. "I heard him say to me and others two to three times that he had a very strong feeling after he was spared in the assassination attempt," he remembered, "that he felt he had been spared for a particular purpose, which made him all the more determined to carry out the things he wanted to do. . . . It was for a purpose, not just a random occurrence." When asked if this purpose was specifically to undo the Soviet empire, Weinberger demurs: "I don't think it was quite that specific. He had a lot of ideas that were difficult to enact. I think it was more of a general purpose regarding his ideas, persevering amid criticism and ridicule, and following his course." "That included," Weinberger added, "him continuing his war against communism."[56]

IN THE END, THEN, WHAT DO WE KNOW ABUT REAgan's sense of divine mission? We know that he believed that he— and America—had a special purpose. And, as Meese acknowledges, the special purpose Reagan had in mind was "probably something important relating to the USSR. I believe his 'special purpose' was related to setting in motion the forces that would ultimately lead to ending the Cold War."[57]

Of course, the record shows that as president Reagan poured extraordinary effort into directing his nation and himself toward the goal of rolling back an atheistic ideology and empire.[58] And though he avoided using the first person in this regard, Reagan's explicit assertion that God had chosen his "team" to defeat the USSR speaks volumes: there was no doubt about who was head of that team.[59]

15.

Washington's Anti-Communist Crusader

"Freedom is the universal right of all God's children. . . . [T]he cause of freedom is the cause of God. . . . I believe God intended for us to be free."

—*President Ronald Reagan*[1]

His sense of Cold War purpose reinvigorated, Reagan went on the verbal offensive after surviving his assassination attempt in 1981. The Ronald Reagan who had been attacking the Soviets from the 1950s onward returned, his passionate defiance only enhanced by the gravitas of his office. The themes he articulated, and the language he used, were strikingly consistent with his rhetoric and positions throughout his public career. Yet now there was a difference: Reagan's spiritually inflected brand of anti-communism, aired until then in private correspondence or before small audiences, was suddenly on display before the world at large. And from living rooms in Eastern Europe to the halls of the Kremlin, the Soviet bloc was listening.

THE ATHEISM OF SOVIET COMMUNISM

If all the statements Reagan ever made blasting the USSR for its anti-religious stance could be laid end to end, they would stretch from Washington to Leningrad. They also extended through nearly every week of his presidency. Though he inherited a nation with its own domestic problems, Reagan's obsessive focus on the Soviet threat never wavered.

This became abundantly clear in his very first presidential press conference, on January 29, 1981. Prompted by a question from ABC's acerbic Sam Donaldson, Reagan's answer left no doubt that Jimmy Carter was gone for good. The new president maintained that the Soviet leadership had "openly and publicly declared that the only morality they recognize is what will further their cause, meaning they reserve unto themselves the right to commit any crime, to lie, to cheat." The Soviets considered such behavior "moral, not immoral," said Reagan. This was something that the United States needed to "keep . . . in mind" when doing "business" with Moscow.[2]

His rejoinder was a shot across the bow of Soviet moral relativism, and in the weeks that followed its effects rippled through the American media. The press corps pressed Reagan repeatedly for clarification: had he misspoken?

He elaborated on his position in an interview the following month, saying of the Soviet leadership: "They don't subscribe to our sense of morality. They don't believe in an afterlife; they don't believe in a God or a religion. And the only morality they recognize, therefore, is what will advance the cause of socialism."[3] Pressed to de-

fend his view, he told an incredulous Walter Cronkite on March 3:
"Remember their ideology is without God, without our idea of moral-
ity in a religious sense."[4] Two weeks later, on March 20, he called the
Soviet Marxists leaders men "who would deny man has a place before
God."[5] Such statements laid any confusion to rest.

It's important to understand how revolutionary Reagan's plain
talk about communism was within the realm of American political
discourse in the early 1980s. In the first two decades of the Cold War,
most Americans—from the press to the general public—had accepted the moral dichotomy between the U.S. and the USSR as a
given. However, the decade that followed saw the bloody stalemate of
Vietnam, the moral disappointment of Watergate, and a détente with
the Soviet Union orchestrated by Richard Nixon and Henry
Kissinger; by 1980, Jimmy Carter's malaise-ridden America had lost
its sense of moral strength, and grown uneasy with the prospect of
baiting the increasingly militaristic Soviets. The last American
politician to confront the Kremlin so passionately from the national
stage had been Reagan's old ally Barry Goldwater. It's hardly surprising that the domestic media appeared so completely unprepared for
Reagan's charges.

To Reagan, however, any such complacency was a recipe for dis-
aster. To his Christian worldview, any thought of reconciliation or
détente with the Soviet Union smacked of moral acquiescence. And
few in the press corps seem to have recognized that Reagan's remarks
on Soviet amorality were simply a paraphrase of Lenin's famous 1920
remark before the All-Russia Congress of the Russian Young Communist League:

> We repudiate all morality that proceeds from supernatural ideas
> that are outside class conceptions. Morality is entirely subordinate

to the interests of class war. Everything is moral that is necessary
for the annihilation of the old exploiting social order and for uniting the proletariat.[6]

Reagan took some heat for citing this quote—some claimed he had
misinterpreted Lenin's remarks—but it was a fair summation, and
merely the tip of the iceberg when one considers the whole of Lenin's
incendiary public statements.[7] As *Washington Post* reporter and Reagan biographer Lou Cannon would point out, regardless of any dis-
pute over Reagan's paraphrase, the words he chose had the virtue of
accuracy.[8]

Reagan lambasted Soviet atheism nearly every chance he got.
The new president could be colorful in assessing the relationship between God and Soviet communism: he liked to joke that "communism works only in Heaven, where they don't need it, and in Hell,
where they already have it."[9] The Soviet leadership was "contemptu-
ous of the worship of God," said Reagan in August 1983; it believed
that "governments should dominate human action and that individuals must live like sheep."[10]

Shortly into his second term, Reagan addressed the subject at
length at a conference on religious liberty held in the Old Executive
Office Building in Washington, D.C. He told his audience that one
truth must be understood: for the USSR, he said, "Atheism is not an
incidental element of communism, not just part of the package; it *is*
the package." In countries that had fallen under communist rule, "it
is often the church which forms the most powerful barrier against a
completely totalitarian system. And so, totalitarian regimes always
seek either to destroy the church or, when that is impossible, to subvert it." He frequently illustrated his arguments with stories of actual
persecuted Christians behind the Iron Curtain. And in a thought

that could have come from Nelle Reagan herself, he observed that "History has taught us that you can bulldoze a church, but you can't extinguish all that is good in every human heart."[11]

Reagan assured listeners that this communist resentment was rooted in the fundamental teachings of both Marx and Lenin: "Marx's central insight when he was creating his political system was that religious belief would subvert his intentions. . . . Marx declared religion an enemy of the people, a drug, an opiate of the masses." And he never stopped quoting Lenin: "Religion and communism are incompatible in theory as well as in practice. . . . We must fight religion."[12] The communists' own record was Reagan's best weapon.

No doubt harkening back to his own days teaching Sunday school at the First Christian Church in Dixon, Reagan even took time to express chagrin at the lack of Sunday schools in the USSR. TASS quickly responded, claiming "it is well known that in the United States, too, the insistent calls of the present [Reagan] administration for the introduction of compulsory prayers in schools are, to put it mildly, not being greeted with understanding."[13] The agency's attempt to liken the Soviet ban on religious education with the debate over prayer in American public schools might have amused Reagan if it were not so sad.

COMMUNISM AND THE THREAT TO RELIGION WORLDWIDE

Reagan perceived that communist ideology posed a danger to religious practice not only in the Soviet Union but around the world. He blasted antireligious actions by communists from China to Africa to Central America. And he spoke in defense of all religions, stressing that communist efforts were under way to undercut Buddhism in

Cambodia, Confucianism in China, even Islam in Afghanistan.[14] Jews in particular had suffered cruel persecution under communism, he noted; the Sandinistas in Nicaragua had used threats and harassment to force "virtually every Nicaraguan Jew to flee [the] country."[15] The story of the persecution endured by a Nicaraguan named Prudencio Baltodano became one of his most frequent, and affecting, anecdotes.[16]

As president, Reagan clipped and kept on hand a chilling article by Nina Hope Shea, the Washington director of the Puebla Institute, a lay Catholic human-rights group. After touring Nicaraguan refugee camps in Honduras and Costa Rica, Shea described her experiences in a *Wall Street Journal* article entitled "The Systematic Destruction of Faith in Nicaragua." The piece laid bare the Sandinista persecution of believers, replete with the mocking of God so common among interrogators in prisons behind the Iron Curtain. Reagan copied the article and mailed it to his pastor and old friend, Rev. Donn Moomaw.[17] In one fiery speech, he took his crusade against communism from Moscow to Managua:

> Why do those who claim to represent the most enlightened thought on Central America refuse to listen to the testimony of one of the greatest moral leaders of our time, His Holiness Pope John Paul II? Last year, John Paul went to Nicaragua on a mission of peace, armed only with love and a message of goodness. This is what happened to the Pope when he went into the land of the Sandinista regime.
>
> He was forced to stand in the brutal sun, this man who'd languished so long in a hospital bed after being shot. He was forced to stand in the brutal sun as Daniel Ortega, the leader of the Sandinista government, delivered a long and hate-filled diatribe against

the West. Then he was booed and jeered by the Sandinistas when he tried to speak. The Sandinistas tried to humiliate His Holiness. They didn't know that it's not possible to humiliate that kind of greatness. When they booed him and jeered him, he said, *"Silencio"*—silence—and they were silenced by the sheer force of his majesty.

Two weeks ago Pope John Paul II stood on the balcony overlooking St. Peter's Square, and he said that the Sandinista government is oppressing the Catholic Church of Nicaragua. He deplored the arrest and deportation of priests. . . .

Why can't those who claim to represent the most enlightened opinion on Central America come to grips with what is happening there? Why can't they admit that the Sandinistas are only totalitarian thugs who are squelching freedom in their country, including freedom of religion? . . .

[I]n Central America, we're more inclined to listen to the testimony of His Holiness the Pope than the claims of the Communist Sandinistas.[18]

There were other Marxists he indicted for religious repression in the 1980s. He cast stones at "the Godless tyranny of communism" as represented by the North Vietnamese forces that American soldiers had faced in the 1960s and 1970s;[19] the communist guerrillas in El Salvador, likewise, were to him a cadre of revolutionaries who wanted to plunge the Salvadoran people into the "darkness of godless communist rule."[20] In November 1983, a year in which he leveled innumerable such attacks, he described the Stalinist state of North Korea as founded on "hatred and oppression," charging that it "brutally attacks every form of human liberty," and "declares those who worship God to be the enemies of the people."[21]

And yet somehow Reagan managed to maintain his basic optimism, his belief that such repression would inevitably backfire. At the aforementioned conference on religious liberty held at the start of his second term, he sparked a glimmer of hope:

> Throughout the world the machinery of the state is being used as never before against religious freedom. But at the same time, throughout the world new groups of believers keep springing up. Points of light flash out in the darkness, and God is honored once again.
>
> Perhaps this is the greatest irony of the Communist experiment. The very pressure they apply seems to create the force, friction, and heat that allow deep belief to once again burst into flame.[22]

He cherished anecdotes that relayed how communist attempts to stifle religion produced the opposite result. One of his favorites came from Polish Solidarity leader Lech Walesa, who said of his country's heirs to Lenin: "Our souls contain exactly the contrary of what they wanted. They wanted us not to believe in God, and our churches are full."[23] Reagan found these words as comforting as a Christmas hymn.

GOD, FREEDOM, AND COMMUNISM

During these years, Reagan's freedom offensive was so fierce, and so nonstop, that Yuri Kornilov, a commentator for TASS, complained of one speech, "It would evidently require a modern computer to estimate how many times Ronald Reagan used the word 'freedom' in his remarks."[24]

The Soviets weren't the only ones who registered Reagan's passion for the twin subjects of liberty and religion. French president François Mitterand described Reagan as a man who "communicates through jokes, by telling . . . stories, by speaking mainly about California and the Bible. He has two religions: free enterprise and God—the Christian God."[25]

It was a message he preached constantly as president. "The freedom to choose a Godly path is the essence of liberty," Reagan claimed in a proclamation just six weeks into his presidency.[26] On the contrary, he asserted in January 1982, the Soviets "believe that freedom is precious, too, so they ration it like all the other goods their people don't have."[27] He consistently maintained that "Nothing is less free than pure communism."[28]

Speaking in Vatican City after a meeting with Pope John Paul II, Reagan claimed that "all men and women yearn for the freedom that God gave us all when he gave us a free will."[29] The Pope himself provided another favorite Reagan quote: "Freedom is given to man by God as a measure of his dignity. . . . As children of God, we cannot be slaves."[30]

Reagan often spoke of freedom as God's specific dictate. Twice as president, once before a joint session of Congress and another time in front of the U.N. General Assembly, he declared freedom the "universal right of all God's children."[31] In observance of Captive Nations Week, he spoke in words aimed directly at the Iron Curtain: "[T]he cause of freedom is the cause of God."[32] Pointing to Scripture, he declared that "Where the Spirit of the Lord is, there is liberty."[33]

He went so far as to maintain that God had "placed" the "dream of freedom" within the human heart. That was the last line in his second Inaugural Address; it is a profoundly important proclamation to understanding Reagan. Just as profound were the words with which he opened his first inaugural: "We are a nation under God, and I believe God intended for us to be free." Both lines were Reagan's own.[34]

The president took this homily around the world. "Each of us, each of you," he urged in West Germany, "is made in the most enduring, powerful image of Western civilization. We're made in the image of God, the image of God, the Creator."[35] Earlier, he appealed to an audience of communist dissidents to make their voices of religious liberty heard by the leadership in their home countries. "Tell them," Reagan implored with religious conviction: "You may forbid the name of Jesus to pass their [your people's] lips. But you will never destroy the love of God and freedom that burns in their hearts."[36]

Reverend Cleaver would have been proud of Dutch's fervor.

GOD, FREEDOM, AND THE AMERICAN EXPERIMENT

Reagan thought it critical to use the presidential platform to contrast the Soviet experiment with the American experiment. He had long believed that "God intended this land [America] to be free."[37] "We Americans understand the truth of these words," he preached. "We were born a nation under God, sought out by people who trusted in Him to work His will in their daily lives."[38]

Reagan even went so far as to contend that all Americans belong equally to the Kingdom of God. "And most of all," he claimed in remarks upon returning from his only trip to Moscow, "let us remember that being an American means remembering another loyalty, a loyalty as, the hymn puts it, 'to another country I have heard of, a place whose King is never seen and whose armies cannot be counted.' "[39] It was a bold assertion, one that no doubt thrilled some and outraged others. Reagan's words appear to suggest that being an American means having a dual loyalty, both to the nation and to God. That is a tight definition of an American, one many citizens would neither meet nor accept.

In Reagan's view, the Bible was fundamental to the American experiment, because it taught the inherent worth and dignity of each individual. He gladly proclaimed 1983 the Year of the Bible, and in his formal proclamation reminded listeners that biblical precepts had helped shape the Founding Fathers' abiding belief in the inalienable rights of the individual.[40] There was no group of historical individuals that Reagan held in higher esteem than the Founders, and as president he celebrated their wisdom often. He admired the Declaration of Independence, whose language he had borrowed throughout his public life, and put great stock in the ideals of government the Founders had instilled in the Constitution. Beyond their written legacy, though, Reagan respected the Founders' religious awareness, and believed they had shared his conviction that God intended people to be free. As he said in March 1983, he shared their belief that faith in God was the key to Americans being a "good people" and America becoming a great nation:

> The basis of [America's] ideals and principles is a commitment to freedom and personal liberty that, itself, is grounded in the much deeper realization that freedom prospers only where the blessings of God are avidly sought and humbly accepted.
>
> The American experiment in democracy rests on this insight. Its discovery was the great triumph of our Founding Fathers, voiced by William Penn when he said: "If we will not be governed by God, we must be governed by tyrants." Explaining the inalienable rights of men, Jefferson said, "The God who gave us life, gave us liberty at the same time."
>
> The evidence of this permeates our history and our govern-

ment. The Declaration of Independence mentions the Supreme Being no less than four times.[41]

Reagan was enamored of the three inalienable rights cited by Thomas Jefferson in the Declaration—life, liberty, and the pursuit of happiness—and took to heart Jefferson's famous observation that these rights were endowed in humans by their Creator.[42] He referred to the passage as an "explicit promise" in the Declaration, and called it "a principle for eternity, America's deepest treasure." In a 1983 address in Atlanta, he quoted a theologian who said that these rights are "corollaries of the great proposition, at the heart of Western civilization, that every . . . person is a *ressacra*, a sacred reality, and as such is entitled to the opportunity of fulfilling those great human potentials with which God has endowed man."[43]

To Reagan, then, it was an obvious corollary that an ideology such as communism, with its history of murdering its own citizens, violated God's will by trampling on this inalienable right to life. Likewise, the communists' systematic seizure of property, and other infringements on individual liberty, were further violations of the inherent rights God granted to all individuals. To Reagan, a loss of inalienable rights through seizure by a repressive government meant a consequent loss of freedom and dignity. At its core, he asserted that government's essential function was to protect life, liberty, and property.[44]

Reagan saw no greater intrusion on freedom than a government effort to suppress or control or try to eliminate one's freedom to worship God, as the communists did. This violation of freedom of conscience was an attempt to contain the soul itself. Freedom of the press, freedom of speech, freedom over one's wallet—all of these were material, tangible concerns. Religious liberty was of a different order altogether. In fact, Reagan singled out "the right to worship" as "the most important human right being violated" in the USSR.[45]

In July 1983 Reagan revisited one of his messages of the late 1950s, laying out his view of the two basic "visions of the world." He used his observance of Captive Nations Week to spell out these two visions while condemning the Soviet system:

> Two visions of the world remain locked in dispute. The first be-
> lieves all men are created equal by a loving God who has blessed us
> with freedom. Abraham Lincoln spoke for us. . . . The second vi-
> sion believes that religion is opium for the masses. It believes that
> eternal principles like truth, liberty, and democracy have no mean-
> ing beyond the whim of the state. And Lenin spoke for them.[46]

In Reagan's view, the American Revolution was anchored in Judeo-Christian values; the Bolshevik Revolution was deliberately estab-lished upon an antithetical premise. The founders of Soviet communism divorced their "faith" from Christianity. Alone among other revolutionary movements in history, claimed Reagan in the same statement, "only one so-called revolution puts itself above God."[47]

REAGAN AND COMMUNIST EXPANSIONISM

Even if it had been nothing more than an isolated bastion of commu-nism, the USSR would probably have come in for regular condemna-tion during the Reagan presidency. But Ronald Reagan believed deeply that the evils of Soviet communism constituted a dangerous virus that threatened to multiply the world over. As he had in the late 1970s, from the start of his presidency Reagan warned of Soviet expansion and of Moscow's goal of a one-world Marxist state. Every Soviet leader since Lenin, he proclaimed, had aimed to "Communize the world." The Soviets had been "consistently and religiously devoted" to that single purpose.[48]

In May 1982, he told Western European journalists that the USSR's "worldwide aggression" stemmed from "the Marxist-Leninist theory of world domination";[49] in July he declared that the USSR's "self-proclaimed goal is the domination of every nation on Earth."[50] His formal speeches, campaign appearances, interviews—all were filled with similar pronouncements.[51] He saw Soviet actions in Nicaragua as an attempt to reach into new territory, and understood the Soviet war in Afghanistan in the same terms: "[T]his invasion by the Soviet Union is just further proof that they are following an expansionist policy that is based on the Marxian doctrine, and the Marx-Lenin doctrine, that communism must become a one-world Communist state, that is their goal."[52] And until the advent of Mikhail Gorbachev,[53] he made a point of naming each Soviet leader—and top officials like Andrei Gromyko[54]—as personally hell-bent on expansion and world domination.[55]

At one point during the presidency, Reagan was taken to task on the question of expansionism by two Soviet journalists, who grilled him on the sources of his "allegation" that Lenin and Soviet communists had "expansionistic aims."[56] One of the interviewers pressed: "Soviet specialists, insofar as I know, in the U.S. press and people who work in the Library of Congress have studied all of the compositions of Lenin's, and they haven't found one similar quotation or anything that's even close to some of those quotations." The pair tried to corner Reagan: "So, I would like to ask you what works of Lenin did you read, and where were those quotations that you used taken from?" Reagan held his ground:

Karl Marx said your system, communism, could only succeed when the whole world had become Communist. And so, the goal had to be the one-world Communist state.

Now, as I say, I can't recall all of the sources from which I gleaned this, and maybe some things have been interpreted differently as in modern versions, but I know that Lenin expounded on that and said that must be the goal. But I also know—and this didn't require reading Lenin—that every leader, every General Secretary but the present one had, in appearances before the Soviet Congress, reiterated their allegiance to that Marxian theory that the goal was a one-world Communist state. So, I wasn't making anything up; these were the things we were told. For example, here in our government, we knew that Lenin had expressed a part of the plan that involved Latin America and so forth. And the one line that sounded very ominous to us was when he said that the last bastion of capitalism, the United States, would not have to be taken; it would fall into their outstretched hand like overripe fruit.[57]

Godless, repressive, opposed to the fundamentals of liberty, eager to expand its reach to every corner of the world: the charges brought against the Soviet Union by Ronald Reagan were exhaustive. Yet none would have quite the impact of two words he uttered in one speech on March 8, 1983.

16.

The Evil Empire

"He called us the 'Evil Empire.' So why did you in
the West laugh at him? It's true!"

—*Arkady Murashev, Moscow police chief, a
leader of Democratic Russia*[1]

Throughout his presidency, Ronald Reagan heard regularly from
men and women who had escaped the Iron Curtain. They informed and confirmed his understanding of Soviet oppression, and
offered crucial moral support to his convictions. Some wrote to tell
him they were praying for him, and he responded to many of these individuals.

One such person was Reverend John Kmech of Chicago, for
three and a half years a prisoner in a Siberian concentration camp.
Reagan took encouragement from a particularly timely letter that
Kmech wrote to him on December 10, 1982. "I know how deceitful
the Soviet government is," he wrote to the president. "They propose
peace to the world while they build-up their war machinery to con-

quer the world." He wrote in capital letters for emphasis: "DO NOT BELIEVE THEM! DO NOT TRUST THEM!!" Kmech, a Catholic priest, was furious at the protests by some bishops over Reagan's weapons policies: "I back you 100%," he wrote, "and I apologize for the silly ramblings of the American bishops." Borrowing the words of Christ, he advised Reagan: "Forgive them for they know not what they do. Be strong even though you are opposed by many, for you are doing the right thing."[2]

Moved by the letter, Reagan responded personally to Kmech on February 1, 1983. "I can't tell you how much your letter . . . meant to me and how grateful I am." Clearly he wished that Kmech's message could be broadcast for general consumption: "If only more people and, yes, if the Bishops could hear and heed the words of someone like yourself who knows firsthand the Godless tyranny of Soviet totalitarianism."[3]

What John Kmech couldn't do, Ronald Reagan soon would.

On March 8, 1983, at a moment when the impasse between the United States and USSR seemed almost unbridgeable, Ronald Reagan gave a speech in Orlando, Florida, before the National Association of Evangelicals that became a defining moment of his presidency. Deeply influenced by his religious orientation, the address became known as the "Evil Empire" speech. In its language and impact it recalled the March day four decades earlier when Winston Churchill, speaking in Fulton, Missouri, declared that an "Iron Curtain" had descended across the European landscape. No one familiar with Reagan's longtime antipathy for the Soviet Union should have been surprised at his rhetoric. Nonetheless, Reagan's stinging claim shocked sensibilities worldwide, and elicited abrupt howls that could be heard from the Washington press corps all the way to Moscow—again, much like Churchill's proclamation.

Thomas McDill, president of the Evangelical Free Church, was there in Orlando that afternoon. It was a sunny, perfect day—the kind best found in Florida in the early spring. The ballroom was crowded with several hundred people; McDill was seated at the platform on the stage, just a few feet from Reagan.

When Reagan came to those memorable words—the Soviet Union was the "focus of evil in the modern world"; it was an "evil empire"—McDill glanced instinctively down at the White House press corps seated below. He stared at reporter Sam Donaldson, Reagan's nemesis, to gauge his response, and saw "the most unbelievable smirk" come over Donaldson's face. "It was a surprise to all of us," said McDill of Reagan's choice phrases, "but especially to the reporters down in front."[4]

In the short term, it was one of the most polarizing speeches Reagan ever gave. In the ensuing years, however, many who followed the Soviet disintegration would mark it as one of the critical gestures of challenge that helped end the Cold War.

REAGAN SPOKE AT 3:04 P.M. IN THE CITRUS CROWN Ballroom at the Orlando Sheraton Twin Towers Hotel. He began by thanking all those present for their prayers, saying that their intercession had "made all the difference" in his life. He cited his favorite quote from Lincoln, about being driven to his knees by the conviction he had nowhere else to go. He then commended the role of religious faith in American democracy. "[F]reedom prospers only where the blessings of God are avidly sought and humbly accepted," he maintained. "The American experiment in democracy rests on this insight," he said; its discovery was the "great triumph" of the Founders.

Characteristically, he cited Jefferson on God and liberty and

Washington on the indispensability of religion and morality to politics. Much of the speech concerned domestic matters: Reagan bemoaned "modern-day secularism," which he believed had discarded the "tried and time-tested values" upon which American civilization was based. He expressed deep concern over the rising number of illegitimate births and abortions in the United States. He pushed to restore prayer in public schools. That was fitting, since earlier that day he formally transmitted to Congress a proposed constitutional amendment on prayer in public schools; March 8, 1983 was a day of religious promise for the president.[5]

Reagan then took a more philosophical, indeed theological, turn. He spoke of sin and man's fallen nature: "We know that living in this world means dealing with what philosophers would call the phenomenology of evil or, as theologians would put it, the doctrine of sin." Here, he inserted a distinctly Christian claim: "There is sin and evil in the world, and we're enjoined by Scripture and the Lord Jesus to oppose it with all our might." This assertion set up the crucial sections of the speech, including items both well remembered and well forgotten. He continued:

> Our nation, too, has a legacy of evil with which it must deal. . . .
> [T]he long struggle of minority citizens for equal rights, once a source of disunity and civil war, is now a point of pride for all Americans. We must never go back. There is no room for racism, anti-Semitism, or other forms of ethnic and racial hatred in this country.
>
> I know that you've been horrified, as have I, by the resurgence of some hate groups preaching bigotry and prejudice. Use the mighty voice of your pulpits and the powerful standing of your churches to denounce and isolate these hate groups in our midst.

The commandment given us is clear and simple: "Thou shalt love thy neighbor as thyself."

This part of the speech ought to have been well-received by liberals and conservatives alike: before applying the word "evil" to the USSR in this speech, Reagan first applied the charge to America. That application of evil was never questioned by his detractors.

Only then did Reagan turn his attention offshore—toward the Soviet Union. He revisited the Bolshevik godfather's conception of morality, drawn from the same quote he had cited two years earlier:

[A]s good Marxist-Leninists, the Soviet leaders have openly and publicly declared that the only morality they recognize is that which will further their cause, which is world revolution. Lenin . . . said in 1920 that they repudiate all morality that proceeds from supernatural ideas—that's their name for religion—or ideas that are outside class conceptions. Morality is entirely subordinate to the interests of class war. And everything is moral that is necessary for the annihilation of the old, exploiting social order and for uniting the proletariat.

The refusal of "many influential people" to accept this "elementary fact of Soviet doctrine," Reagan claimed, was indicative of a historical reluctance to see totalitarian powers for what they truly were. That reluctance, he said, was a phenomenon the world had witnessed in the 1930s, tacitly referring to the Nazis, and which protected the Soviets through the current day. Importantly, he told his audience that recognizing the Soviets' conception of morality should not preclude the United States from trying to find peace with the USSR. "At the same time," though, the Soviets "must be made to understand we will never compromise our principles and standards. We will never give away our freedom. We will never abandon our belief in God."

As Reagan moved on, he shared one of his favorite, and most highly charged, anecdotes—the story of Pat Boone (whom he didn't identify by name), and Boone's contention that he'd rather see his girls die, still believing in God, than watch them grow up faithless under communism. Reagan told the Florida crowd that when this "young actor" had made the remark years earlier, it sent thousands in the audience to their feet with shouts of joy. These celebrants, said Reagan, instinctively understood the "profound truth" in what had been said; they recognized the crucial difference between the physical and the soul, the temporal and the eternal.

Reagan's first mention of Soviet evil in the speech, it should be noted, followed a prayerful plea by Reagan on behalf of the Soviet people:

> [L]et us pray for the salvation of all of those who live in that totalitarian darkness—pray they will discover the joy of knowing God. But until they do, let us be aware that while they preach the supremacy of the state, declare its omnipotence over individual man, and predict its eventual domination of all peoples on the Earth, they are the focus of evil in the modern world.

There was an unfortunate ambiguity in this passage: Reagan begins by entreating prayer for the Soviet people, praying that "they" will embrace religion. By the end of the passage he has shifted his focus, however; his charge that "they are the focus of evil in the modern world" clearly refers only to the country's Marxist-Leninists leaders. Though those who knew Reagan knew he never considered the Soviet people themselves evil, Reagan's remarks may have been thought less intemperate if the wording of this paragraph had been more precise.[6]

Then came the memorable two words that earned the oration its name. He rallied his fellow Christian soldiers:

> I urge you to speak out against those who would place the United States in a position of military and moral inferiority. . . . I urge you to beware the temptation of pride—the temptation of blithely declaring yourselves above it all and label both sides equally at fault, to ignore the facts of history and the aggressive impulses of an evil empire, to simply call the arms race a giant misunderstanding and thereby remove yourself from the struggle between right and wrong and good and evil.

He was nearing the end of his talk. The Reagan of years past might have reached for a quote from Whittaker Chambers. So did the Reagan of 1983:

> The real crisis we face today is a spiritual one; at root, it is a test of moral will and faith. Whittaker Chambers, the man whose own religious conversion made him a witness to one of the terrible traumas of our time, the Hiss-Chambers case, wrote that the crisis of the Western World exists to the degree in which the West is indifferent to God, the degree to which it collaborates in communism's attempt to make man stand alone without God. And then he said, for Marxism-Leninism is actually the second oldest faith, first proclaimed in the Garden of Eden with the words of temptation, "Ye shall be as gods."
>
> The Western World can answer this challenge, he wrote, "but

only provided that its faith in God and the freedom He enjoins is as great as communism's faith in Man."

Here again, as he had many times before the presidency, and had done at Notre Dame and Yorktown in 1981, Reagan spoke of a challenge—a Cold War challenge he connected to God. He finished his talk by predicting the demise of communism, followed by one of his beloved biblical verses from the book of Isaiah:

> I believe we shall rise to the challenge. I believe that communism is another sad, bizarre chapter in human history whose last pages even now are being written. I believe this because the source of our strength in the quest for human freedom is not material, but spiritual. And because it knows no limitation, it must terrify and ultimately triumph over those who would enslave their fellow man. For in the words of Isaiah: "He giveth power to the faint; and to them that have no might He increased strength. . . . But they that wait upon the Lord shall renew their strength; they shall mount up with wings as eagles; they shall run, and not be weary. . . ."
>
> Yes, change your world. One of our Founding Fathers, Thomas Paine, said, "We have it within our power to begin the world over again." We can do it, doing together what no one church could do by itself.
>
> God bless you, and thank you very much.

The speech seemed to capture a lifetime of Reagan's thinking on the subject. The sentiments in the address made news around the world, though to Reagan they were old and familiar themes. Bill Clark put it this way: "The 'Evil Empire' speech . . . was not so much about the Soviet Union as it was about Ronald Reagan. It was condemned by so many people, but to many of us it was probably his greatest speech because it was so much the real Ronald Reagan."[7]

First and foremost, the speech was a brutal lesson in the art of effective communication. Reagan knew the case he wanted to make, and he insisted upon using a vocabulary that he knew would make an impact. And he had the confidence to speak in such blistering language, even when he knew it might well generate a hailstorm of criticism, around the world and even among his own countrymen.

For years, Reagan had been derided in some quarters as simplistic. Now, in condemning the USSR in such morally absolute terms, he was accused by many of reducing a complex situation to inappropriately black-and-white terms. As C. S. Lewis once observed, many believe that the wiser one becomes, the less one desires to call anything good or bad.[8] After the Evil Empire speech, many such "wise" people agreed that they knew better than this rube of a president.

But Reagan had looked close enough, and thought hard enough, to feel confident proclaiming what he felt was obvious—that the Soviet empire was rotten. It *was* evil. The matter was that simple. "For many years now, you and I have been shushed like children and told there are no simple answers," he had told a crowd three years earlier. "Well, the truth is that there are simple answers."[9] And this, he felt, was one of them.

REAGAN'S FORGOTTEN FOREBEARS

Reagan was hardly alone among American presidents who had directed fierce words at the Soviet leadership. Indeed, Reagan's more partisan detractors might have been surprised to know that three of the century's most celebrated Democratic leaders—Woodrow Wilson, Franklin Roosevelt, and Harry Truman—had condemned the

Soviet Union in terms equally harsh, if not harsher, during their pres-
idencies.

Wilson, the genteel former Princeton professor who sent U.S.
troops to Russia to fight the Bolsheviks, had called them "barbarians,"
"terrorists," and "tyrants," engaged in a "brutal" campaign of "mass
terrorism" and "indiscriminate slaughter" through "cunning" and
"savage oppression." He used such language openly and often, including to a joint session of Congress. He constantly denounced the Bolsheviks for "poisoning" the Russian people with an "expansionist"
ideology they wanted to export throughout the world and against the
United States.[10]

During World War II, of course, America had entered an alliance
with the Soviets to defeat Hitler. Yet when he was asked about the
moral implications of siding with Stalin in WWII, FDR analogized
Stalin's USSR to the Devil: "My children," FDR famously remarked,
"you are permitted in time of great danger to walk with the Devil until you have crossed the bridge."[11] (FDR also characterized the war
with Japan in WWII as a battle between the forces of "religion" and
"irreligion"; and the Nazis, he maintained, were seeking to enforce
"their new German, pagan religion all over the world.")[12]

Few presidents were as blunt and "simplistic" as Truman, whose
administration counted among its ranks George Kennan, Dean
Acheson, and the other architects of American Cold War strategy.
One of Reagan's favorite presidents, Truman referred to Bolshevism
as "godless communism."[13] In one of his many colorful ruminations,
Truman wrote a memo to himself:

> I've no faith in any totalitarian state, be it Russian, German, Span-
> ish, Argentinian, Dago [Italian], or Japanese. They all start with a
> wrong premise—that lies are justified and that the old, disproven

Jesuit formula, the ends justify the means, is right and necessary to maintain the power of government. I don't agree, nor do I believe that either formula can help humanity to the long hoped for millennium [a Christian term for Christ's return]. Honest Communism, as set out in the "Acts of the Apostles," would work. But Russian Godless Pervert Systems won't work.[14]

In another example of the one-time haberdasher's candor, on the day the Nazis invaded the USSR on June 22, 1941, Senator Truman shared this bit of advice on the situation: "If we see that Germany is winning we ought to help Russia, and if Russia is winning we ought to help Germany, and that way let them kill as many as possible."[15] (Scholars have always given Truman a pass for such extreme language, while pouncing on Reagan for less radical remarks.)

There were other big-name Democrats who issued similarly tough language.

In New York City on August 27, 1952, Democratic standard-bearer Adlai Stevenson, the party's presidential nominee, commented on what he called America's "healthy apprehension about the Communist menace within our country." His blistering assessment was laced with religious overtones:

Communism is abhorrent. It is strangulation of the individual; it is death for the soul. Americans who have surrendered to this misbegotten idol have surrendered their right to our trust. And there can be no secure place for them in our public life.[16]

Though Reagan was vocal in the fight against domestic communism in the 1950s, he never said anything so vicious about fellow Americans, usually referring to them as mere "dupes" led down the wrong path. Stevenson, known as a liberal's liberal and an intellectual, then told his American Legion audience that it and other "patriotic organizations" needed to protect the nation from its "evil enemies."

John F. Kennedy, who presided over the Cuban Missile Crisis, referred specifically to the USSR as America's "atheistic foe." The "fanaticism and fury" of communism and the "communist conspiracy," he said with foreboding, "represents a final enslavement." In language indistinguishable from Reagan's, he claimed: "The enemy is the communist system itself—implacable, insatiable, unceasing in its drive for world domination. . . . This [is] a struggle for supremacy between two conflicting ideologies: freedom under God versus ruthless, godless tyranny."[17]

In these early Cold War years, the view of communism as evil was common currency; the rhetoric of Democrats like Truman and Kennedy, and even Stevenson, was par for the course. One of the major factors in the broad American revulsion for Soviet communism was its blasphemous nature. This was an influential factor in the decisive period when America first moved to confront the Soviets.

By the 1980s, of course, the rhetoric of Democrats had tempered considerably, and Reagan opponents such as House Speaker Tip O'Neill (D-Mass.) erupted in protest whenever Reagan rained fire and brimstone upon the Soviets—in terms their own party had once embraced. The reception he received makes it easier to understand Reagan's assertion that he didn't leave the Democratic Party, the party left him.

REAGAN'S CONTRIBUTION

Those who had been with Reagan throughout his political career were perhaps least surprised by the rhetoric of his March 8 address.

Bill Clark, his cabinet secretary in Sacramento, said that he personally heard Reagan describe the USSR as an "evil empire" "years before" the speech.[18] Ed Meese also recognized the phrase as long part of Reagan's repertoire.[19] As recently as June 7, 1982, after meeting with Pope John Paul II, he condemned the "forces of evil" and the spread of "godless tyranny" in the communist bloc. Two days later, before the Bundestag in Bonn, West Germany, he borrowed a quote from Friedrich Schiller about how the "pious man" grapples with his "evil neighbor."[20]

As for the phrase "evil empire" itself, some debate persists over its coinage. Reagan's address was drafted by speechwriter Tony Dolan, then a thirtysomething Yale graduate and Pulitzer Prize winner.[21] While reluctant to suggest anyone other than Dolan coined the main phrases—and it was Dolan who appears to have first written them into the draft[22]—Edmund Morris cites two foreign writers who used similar language in ways that grabbed Reagan's attention. One was Aleksandr Solzhenitsyn, who told the AFL-CIO in 1975 that the USSR was "the concentration of world evil."[23] Reagan read Solzhenitsyn frequently, citing him at length in his radio addresses of the 1970s—some of which were focused solely on Solzhenitsyn[24]—and in his stump speeches in 1980.[25]

The other was Alexandre de Maranches, the chief of French intelligence, who Morris says "flew all the way to Los Angeles in December 1980 to warn Reagan against '*l'empire du mal*.' " With Arnaud de Borchgrave, *Newsweek*'s foreign correspondent, translating, Maranches dramatically predicted: "You are the American president who will lead the free world to final victory over communism." Morris remains convinced that the phrase *l'empire du mal* sank in with Reagan. De Maranches would use it repeatedly, predicting that "Once their fighter bombers and fighter tanks can no longer fly" after what he hoped would be a U.S.-aided campaign to defeat the USSR in Afghanistan—"the evil empire will begin to disintegrate."[26]

Such voices probably registered with Reagan. As we've seen, though, the lifetime cold warrior had been using similar language long before he had heard from these knowledgeable men. Certainly a longer-term influence was Whittaker Chambers. In the end, however, the label is essentially Reagan's, a turn of phrase that captured perfectly his turn of mind. Dolan himself has said that when he chose the words "evil empire" he was essentially using Reagan's own words. "They're the president's phrases," Dolan confirmed seventeen years later.[27]

Aside from those most memorable words, other crucial passages in the speech were demonstrably Reagan's own. As with many of the critical Reagan presidential speeches,[28] it was Reagan's own editing hand that made the difference in the speech's most indelible, effective spots. While Dolan obviously deserves immense credit for the speech, he himself has pointed out that Reagan "toughened" its characterization of the Soviets. And a review of the March 5 draft, which shows Reagan's editing, reveals that the president himself contributed critical parts of the text. Those who seek confirmation needn't venture all the way to the Reagan Library; Reagan's collection of speeches, Speaking My Mind, contains an actual photograph of the draft, complete with a full handwritten page by Reagan himself.

Reagan edited the text so thoroughly that it's fair to consider him the co-author of the final speech. He cut fifteen entire paragraphs from Dolan's original draft, and nixed dozens of additional sentences and hundreds of words; he also penciled in fourteen new paragraphs, including the Pat Boone story, and roughly thirty complete lines of text changes.

Reagan's changes to the speech's critical passage illustrate how his contributions helped make the address memorable. Dolan's initial draft read: "Surely, those historians will find in the councils of the Marxist-Leninists—who preached the supremacy of the state, who declared its omnipotence over individual man, who predicted its eventual domination of all peoples on the Earth—surely historians will see there the focus of evil in the modern world." Reagan changed the passage to point out that though the Soviets "preach the supremacy of the state, declare its omnipotence over individual man, predict its eventual domination of all peoples on the Earth, they are the focus of evil in the modern world."[29]

A few subtle alterations, but they made all the difference. Reagan changed the lines from past to present tense, transforming the passage from a gentle rumination on the opinions of future historians to a direct assessment of the here and now. And by changing the words "historians will see there" to "they are," he clarified and *personalized* his message. Reagan's message was unmistakable: the "focus of evil in the modern world," he charged, was not just the monolithic Soviet system itself but the leaders who kept it going. It was a rhetorical cruise missile aimed directly at the Kremlin.

Another little-recognized change of Reagan's speaks directly to the spiritual context in which he viewed the struggle against communism. Just before the passage cited above, Reagan himself added the line expressing hope that the Soviets "who live in that totalitarian darkness" would "discover the joy of knowing God." Moreover, he asked his audience to pray for the "salvation" of these Soviets. These sentiments were added after Dolan's original draft; at least two variations of the new language were considered and scratched by Reagan and either Dolan or another staffer.[30] And the idea would live on in Reagan's repertoire: when he returned the following March to address the same convention in Columbus, Ohio, he said he hoped the Soviet people might come to know the "liberating nature of faith in God."[31]

As with the SDI speech, delivered only two weeks later—coming so close together, the two served as a double blow to the USSR—there was tremendous internal opposition to the speech among Reagan's staff. David Gergen remembered that he was disturbed by some of the "outrageous statements" of the speech and worked with Bud McFarlane to try to tone it down.[32]

The year before, when initial drafts of Reagan's Westminster speech had included references to evil, the "pragmatists" in the White House had purged all but one innocuous use of the word.[33] Now the battle over "evil" was rejoined. In his initial Evil Empire draft Dolan included the word as many as seven times. He submitted his draft on March 3, while Reagan was in California. At the White House, speechwriting director Aram Bakshian reviewed the draft. He saw the references, and particularly liked the term "evil empire." Both Bakshian and Dolan hoped to route it past the White House's gatekeepers as a "low priority speech" for a prayer breakfast, not a major speech and not even a foreign-policy speech. "I made a point of not flagging it," said Bakshian later. "It was the stealth speech."[34]

On March 5, Reagan returned. By then, just three days before the speech, the West Wing pragmatists—Gergen and others—had discovered Dolan's draft and begun hacking. Dolan remembers his text coming back with "a lot of green ink" and the whole "evil empire" section crossed out. Whoever axed the section expected it to be deleted before the president saw it, but Dolan refused. "I just won't go along with those [changes]," he protested. "Let's just let the president decide on this." He explained that he "rarely took a stand like this, but I was disgusted because this stuff was crossed out."[35]

So the decision was left to Reagan. And, as he would with Peter Robinson's "Tear Down This Wall" speech four years later, Reagan rejected the advice of State Department and White House staff to tone Dolan's language down. "He really insisted on it and kept it in," said Ed Meese.[36]

REACTIONS TO REAGAN'S SPEECH

Reagan's address drew a wide array of reactions. His use of the phrase "evil empire" sent some in the United States into a rage. To the contrary, it struck a resonant chord in less expected quarters. The multifaceted reactions are as much a story as the remarks themselves.

The strongest denunciations of Reagan came from leftists in the American media and academe, the Western European political left, and the Soviet press.

Two days later, Anthony Lewis of the New York Times described the speech as "sectarian," "dangerous," "outrageous," "simplistic," before ultimately concluding it was "primitive—the only word for it." "To the most difficult human problem," he charged, Reagan had applied "a simplistic theology." Lewis ended his column: "For a President to attack those who disagree with his politics as ungodly is terribly dangerous."[37]

Historian Henry Steele Commager asserted, "It was the worst presidential speech in American history, and I've read them all." He was particularly angered by what he saw as Reagan's "gross appeal to religious prejudice."[38] George Ball, a high-level official in the Kennedy and Johnson administrations, published an open letter to Reagan months later in which he referred with contempt to "your obsessive detestation of what you call 'the evil empire.' "[39]

A particularly damning indictment came from the New Republic, the bible of the American left. In a sarcastic, biting April 4, 1983 editorial titled "Reverend Reagan,"[40] the journal charged:

> According to Ronald Reagan, history is reaching a climax. He portrayed his country as embattled, set upon by enemies from without and within. . . . The enemy without is Communism . . . the speech left friends and foes around the world with the impression that the President of the United States was contemplating holy war. The enemy within is "modern-day secularism." With his implication that the two are working toward a single end, which is the weakening of America, Mr. Reagan insulted multitudes.

The editors of the *New Republic* noted that Reagan had "thrilled his audience" with the "tale of a man" who said he would rather see his little girls die now, still believing in God, than have them grow up under communism; they seemed to take special offense at this story (as did TASS). In the area of foreign policy, the *New Republic* editorial board complained, this was hardly the "question at issue."[41] The magazine also complained that Reagan was guilty of "staggering oversimplification." The editorial accused Reagan of slandering secularism—and, worse, doing so on the dubious authority of Whittaker Chambers. Citing Reagan's use of the Chambers line about "Communism's attempt to make man stand alone without God," the magazine called the speech "an orgy of cheap shots."

It was the religious aspect of the address that ultimately seems to have disturbed the *New Repubic*. Reagan's rhetoric was "deeply divisive," its editors claimed. The editorial insisted that Reagan used "very poor history," that he "profoundly misunderstands" the "nature of secularism" and the "profoundly secular character of democracy." Reagan had given not a speech but a sermon, a homily, the magazine roared: "We elected a President, not a priest." "The President should cease these celestial navigations," the editors advised. "There is business on earth. He is not in the White House to save our souls, but to protect our bodies; not to do God's will, but the people's."

Two months after the speech, some were still seething. Apparently motivated by these and other spiritually inflected comments Reagan had made recently, columnist Richard Cohen launched a flurry of salvos from the editorial page of the *Washington Post*.[42] He began his column with this charitable Q & A: "Question: What does Ronald Reagan have in common with my grandmother? Answer: They are both religious bigots." With the righteous certainty of a convicted Baptist preacher, Cohen then fired away:

> It was my grandmother's conviction until the day she died . . . that anyone not of her religion was less than human. She ascribed to that person all sorts of animalistic qualities, specifically a total lack of respect for either life or property, particularly hers.
>
> It is not, I think, going too far to say that our president holds the same views. . . . Time and time again, the president has gone into this business that the difference between "us" and "them" is that we have religion and they don't. We, of course, is the United States of America and "they" is any communist country and any communist or communist sympathizer—regardless, I might add, of religious affiliation.
>
> It must be comforting to think this way, undeterred by either common sense or the facts, but it cannot be easy. . . .
>
> [Reagan] likes to see things in black and white and so he has enlisted God on our side in the Cold War. He understands that we all have different ways of worshiping God, so the president makes no endorsements of the manner or the methods of worship—just

the Deity himself (herself, Ron?). In his mind, he would love to es-
tablish an amorphous state religion—a kind of parade ground God
who, among other things, is on our side in El Salvador. . . .

In previous speeches, he has talked of this God as one of the
prime differences between us and the communist states, although it
was when one of those states (Russia) was deeply religious that my
grandmother became understandably intolerant of other people's
beliefs. In the name of God they were forever trying to hit her over
the head.

[R]eligion or the lack of it does not necessarily have anything
to do with morality. The president is proof of that. He's got religion.

What he lacks is tolerance.

More than a year later, House Speaker Tip O'Neill was still furious,
fuming from the podium at the Democratic National Convention:
"The evil is in the White House at the present time. And that evil is
a man who has no care and no concern for the working class of
America and the future generations of America. . . . He's cold. He's
mean. He's got ice water for blood."[43] Naturally, no one on the political left complained about O'Neill's use of the word "evil."

In Western Europe, as Edmund Morris has noted, Reagan was
variously perceived as either the archetypal American naïf or a "bi-
nary-minded simpleton" who thought all issues could be reduced to
check boxes marked YES or NO.[44] (When it came to an assessment
of communist morality, of course, Reagan wouldn't have agonized for
a moment before checking the right box.)

Yet not all the reactions from overseas were negative. Andrew
Sullivan—who would spend much of the post–Cold War 1990s as editor of none other than the New Republic—was a British teenager at

the time. "I will never forget the moment I heard his 'evil empire' speech," Sullivan later recalled in an op-ed piece for the London *Sunday Times*. "It was broadcast on Radio 4, with skeptical British commentary about this inflammatory new president who knew nothing about the complexities of late communism." "But for all the criticism," Sullivan remembered, "what came through to my teenage brain was an actual truth. Yes, the Soviet Union was evil." Merely hearing those words spoken out loud, simply and directly, made a profound impression on the young man. "Who now doubts that?" he asks today.[45]

Reagan also found support in a letter he received that month from another Brit—Malcolm Muggeridge. Muggeridge, who had made the journey from left-wing agnosticism to anti-communist Christianity, reported to Reagan that when he was a young journalist in Moscow in 1932, he encountered "anti-God museums, the total suppression of the scriptures and related literature, the ridiculing of the person of Christ and his followers, the whole force of the most powerful and comprehensive propaganda machine ever to exist, including the schools and universities, geared to promote Marxist materialism and abolish Christianity forever." In his crusty British candor, Muggeridge proclaimed to Reagan the fundamental difference between Christianity and Marxism—"Christianity happens to be true, and Marxism . . . 'unresisting imbecility.' "[46]

From the American right, one intriguing appraisal came from William F. Buckley, Jr., founder of the *National Review*. Buckley made two points in particular:[47] he was among the few who noted that Reagan had reminded America that its own history was not blameless, that the nation had its own "legacy of evil" to deal with. But Buckley's most interesting insight was to draw "a notable analogue [between] what Mr. Reagan was attempting" and the words of Abraham Lincoln in his second inaugural. Just after delivering the address, Lincoln had told one enthusiast that he didn't expect the speech to prove immediately popular. "Men are not flattered by being shown that there has been a difference of purpose between the Almighty and them," Buckley quoted Lincoln as saying. "It is a truth which I thought needed to be told."

Just as Lincoln cast an eye on Confederate defenders of slavery, Buckley pointed out that the Soviet leadership believed in its own form of slavery. Of course, he noted, there was one difference: even Jefferson Davis's men prayed to God for help, whereas those around Andropov caught in such an act "would cease to be those around Andropov." But Buckley's point stands: Lincoln and Reagan were each confronted with an unquestionable evil, and each judged it imperative to acknowledge and condemn the iniquity—even if doing so disturbed the sensibilities of others.

Buckley understood what some seemed too irate to recognize: Reagan's words were chosen deliberately, and for a purpose. He had indeed *attempted* something, as Buckley put it. And he succeeded in making his impact.

REACTIONS FROM THE EVIL EMPIRE

Soviet reaction to Reagan's words came from General Secretary Yuri Andropov, from the Soviet official news agency, and from Soviet media. Of course the Soviet media outlets were fully controlled by the state, so their reaction was identical with government reaction.

The day after the speech, in an official response circulated by the government press agency TASS, Andropov called Reagan's remarks deliberately "provocative," a sign that he and his administration "can think only in terms of confrontation and bellicose, lunatic anticommunism."[48]

A March 10 piece in *Pravda* began by noting that Reagan "had made his latest provocative speech, once more confirming" that he could "only think in terms of confrontation and militant, unbridled communism." The "occupant of the White House" exhibited the "extreme militarism" of the administration. Reagan had accused the USSR of "aggressive impulses," "without bothering to cite any evidence."[49]

As it often did, the Soviet press cited negative American media reactions to bolster its own case. *Pravda* reported that the "UPI called attention to Reagan's pathological hatred of socialism and communism, noting that his statements resurrected the worst rhetoric of the cold war era." (The Soviet army organ, *Krasnaya Zvezda*, also cited the UPI statement.)[50] It also reported that ABC television, in a commentary on the speech, "made special note of the fact that it had an 'openly militaristic bias.'"

A day after the *Pravda* piece, TASS also assailed Reagan's "extreme militarism" and his "fits of anti-Soviet bellicose hysteria."[51] Denouncing Reagan's "crusade against communism," TASS blasted the president's "McCarthyism" and added: "The White House boss is quite prepared to sacrifice them [American children] in the name of his rabid anti-communism and militarism."[52]

On March 13, Reagan was excoriated on Soviet TV by reporter Gennady Gerasimov. "[I]n the eyes of the president," the USSR looked like a "demon or a devil," stated Gerasimov. Reagan had spoken "almost as though he were God's vicar on earth." He continued:

This is not the first time the President has used similar moral categorizations: on the one side good, which naturally means him and America, which is the embodiment of this good, and on the other side evil. And here the president says exactly what he is talking

about, pointing the finger [at the USSR] as he says: Behold the empire of evil. In other words: Look out, holy ministers and others[,]
lest you should become the Devil's accomplices.

    An easy scheme of things for those too lazy to think.[53]

The Soviet television reporter's critique echoed those from the
American left: Reagan was a lazy man and lazy thinker who boiled
down the Cold War to a simplistic moral struggle between good and
evil, and who had the audacity to claim that God was on his side.
This kind of thinking was "very dangerous," charged Gerasimov.
Then, without pausing a moment to consider the contradiction, he
returned the fire: "And if one is to talk about evil in our world then
the most important source of this is American imperialism."[54]

    Gerasimov wasn't the only Soviet commentator to turn the ta-
bles on Reagan: On Moscow television that November, reporter Eduard Grigoryev spoke openly of "the evil will of the current Reagan
administration."[55] A few days later, on March 17, 1983, Soviet propagandist Georgi Arbatov published a typically lengthy diatribe in
Pravda. "Frenzied calls are being made for crusades," he wrote. "[This
is] outright medievalism. And all this is covered up by hypocritical
talk about faith and God, about morality, eternal good and eternal
evil."[56] One Soviet press clip, calling Reagan a "criminal against
mankind," was mailed to the president with a letter of reassurance.
"There exists no better compliment for you than to be attacked by
the Communists," wrote seventy-five-year-old survivor of communist
torture Richard Wurmbrand.[57]

    Reagan never tired of pointing out that the Soviets had said the
same and worse about him and the United States, before and after the
Evil Empire speech. (Andropov himself had once declared Reagan
"mad" and likened him to Hitler, a comparison common at the time

among Soviet commentators.) In January 1984, when pressed by *Washington Post* journalists to defend his rhetoric, Reagan observed that for years the Soviets had been calling American leaders "imperialists," "aggressors," and worse.[58] Six months later, again on the defensive, he told reporters: "I don't think that I've said anything that was as fiery as them referring to the funeral service for the unknown soldier as 'a militaristic orgy.' If we're going to talk about comparisons of rhetoric, they've topped me in spades."[59] He later noted that the Soviets had "called us 'cannibals.' "[60] Ambassador Jack Matlock agreed: "It didn't seem to me [that] the Soviets should be angry. After all, they had been calling us imperialists and warmongers for decades."[61] Edward Luttwak of the Center for Strategic and International Studies said that thanks to Reagan, the "U.S. is now speaking to the Russians the same way the Russians have been speaking to the U.S."[62]

Beyond the immediate protests, however, it is clear from reading Soviet media archives that Reagan's "evil empire" remark was carved indelibly into the Soviet consciousness. For years thereafter, at least until Reagan left office in 1989, Soviet media and official news releases harped on the phrase hundreds of times.[63] To some extent that was Reagan's goal, and he succeeded wildly.

REACTION FROM THE FORMER SOVIET EMPIRE

A decade later, once former Soviet and Eastern European citizens were free to speak their mind, dramatically different reactions began to emerge. In a post–Cold War piece in *Foreign Affairs*, John Lewis Gaddis, probably the top contemporary Cold War historian, wrote: "Now that they are free to speak—and act—the people of the former Soviet Union appear to have associated themselves more closely with

President Reagan's famous indictment of that state as an 'evil empire' than with more balanced academic assessments."[64]

There were many such Soviet reactions, even at the highest levels. Andrei Kozyrev, Boris Yeltsin's foreign minister, explicitly endorsed the phrase in August 1991. It was a mistake to call it "the Union of Soviet Socialist Republics," said Kozyrev. "It was, rather, [an] evil empire, as it was put."[65]

Genrikh Trofimenko, the academic and onetime director of the prestigious Institute for U.S. and Canada Studies of the Russian Academy of Sciences, said in 1993 that Reagan's description of the USSR as an evil empire "was probably too mild on the background of the facts that are now being presented to the world from Russia itself."[66]

Another concurring reaction came from Sergei Tarasenko of the Soviet foreign ministry, who went on to become the principal policy assistant to Foreign Minister Eduard Shevardnadze from 1985 to 1991. Speaking in Princeton, New Jersey in 1993, he prefaced his remarks by explaining that when the Soviet general secretary or American president said something that would "heat up the atmosphere," the Soviet foreign ministry immediately jumped into "damage control mode" to deal with the matter. One would have thought, Tarasenko agreed, that Reagan's "evil empire" remarks would have sent the foreign ministry scrambling. Such was not the case, however. "I would say that at the foreign ministry we didn't take Reagan's speech seriously," said Tarasenko. "Maybe we knew that we were evil. So, what else is new? So the president said, 'It is an evil empire!' Okay. Well, we are an evil empire." "You know," Tarasenko finished, "it was not a problem with us."[67]

Theologian and scholar Michael Novak tells of a joyful dinner between U. S. and Soviet arms negotiators years after the Soviet collapse. When the group began speculating on which straw had finally broken the bear's back, a former senior general in the Red Army, a little flush with vodka, heatedly interrupted. "You know what caused the downfall of the Soviet Union? You know what did it?" he thundered, slamming his fist on the table. "That damned speech about the evil empire! That's what did it." The general was standing now. To the questioning eyes of one American, he added: "It *was* an evil empire. It was."[68]

"A lot of Russians will tell you that when he used that language, that biblical language—'Evil Empire'—that was when they, for the first time, began to accept the fact that they were an evil system," said Edmund Morris.[69] It helped "the motherland realize . . . it was indeed evil."[70] Later, Morris wrote, evidence would gather that the word "evil" had "penetrated the Russian soul as surely as the cadmium poisoning Russian beets." Well-connected Western travelers in Moscow at the time relayed a feeling of instant shock in the USSR. "Within twenty-four hours," one of them told Morris, "I was hearing of the reaction spreading through society—of self-disgust and self-acknowledgment." While other presidents had bad-mouthed communism before, the observer conceded, none had done so quite as "directly" and in "such plain language."[71]

Today, it is hardly difficult to find sympathy for Reagan's description among former Soviet citizens.

One is Arkady Murashev, Moscow police chief, a leader of Democratic Russia and close associate of Boris Yeltsin. Murashev told the *Washington Post*'s David Remnick that Reagan "called us the 'Evil Empire.' So why did you in the West laugh at him? It's true!"[72]

Another such citizen is Alexander Donskiy, born in 1954, a Ukrainian who served in the Red Army and then worked at the prestigious Strategic Rockets division of a military-weapons plant. Donskiy, a Jew who observed Soviet religious oppression firsthand, said he wasn't offended by Reagan's use of the words "evil empire." "I agreed with them," he explained. "It was true. At that time we had no freedom politically, socially, economically, religiously. That was true. He was correct."[73]

Speaking in October 2000, Donskiy was eager to share some of his reasons. His town had only one Orthodox church, he said—a fact that bothered him greatly, considering his country's "fifteen-hundred-year" religious tradition—and that church "cooperated very closely with the KGB." According to Donskiy, it was illegal for a father who was a member of the Communist Party to get his child baptized. "The constitution of the Soviet Union permitted freedom of religion, but that was false," he said. He concluded with this assessment: "The USSR was a 99 percent atheistic country."[74]

Asked if Reagan's phrase "helped or hurt" in any way, Donskiy offered: "It hurt the US-Soviet relationship a bit maybe, but helped to destroy the USSR and create a better country. It influenced Gorbachev. It may [have] speeded up reforms in the USSR." Donskiy has always held a favorable opinion of Gorbachev, and believes both the general secretary and Reagan deserve credit for ending the Cold War. Yet he says of Reagan's "evil empire" remarks: "These things, and Reagan's policies, helped end the Cold War."[75]

As Donskiy spoke, his wife, Ukrainian Olena Doviskaya, nodded vigorously. Asked whether she agreed with the Evil Empire description, she added emphatically: "That was absolutely true. Totally true."[76]

Another person who welcomed Reagan's candor was Vladimir Bukovsky, who suffered twelve years in the Soviet gulag, shifting between work camps, prisons, and lunatic asylums—dismissed as a madman for not enjoying the utopian paradise. Speaking on March 5,

2003—the fiftieth anniversary of Stalin's death—Bukovsky, who now lives in Cambridge, England, confirmed that Reagan's speech was a "major event" to political prisoners and dissidents. He said the expression "evil empire" became "incredibly popular" behind the Iron Curtain, and remains so today.[77] What an irony: denounced by American detractors as inapt and unfair, the term Reagan chose to describe the evil empire was eagerly adopted by its own citizens.

Many a career diplomat has also testified to the effect Reagan's words had on high-level Soviet-American relations. Though conceding that "this is a tricky area," Jack Matlock, who served as U.S. ambassador to the USSR in the 1980s, wrote in his memoir *Autopsy of an Empire* that "there is no question that American statements can bolster favorable trends and undermine unfavorable ones. An obvious example is Ronald Reagan's use of the term 'evil empire.' While this offended the Soviet rulers at the time, it did much to undermine the claim to legitimacy of the Soviet empire."[78] James Billington, another authority on Soviet reactions, calls Reagan "by far the most important" among American presidents who contributed to winning the Cold War.[79] During the May-June 1988 Moscow summit, two "Soviet reformist politicians" told Billington that they had used the "unprecedentedly undiplomatic" Evil Empire speech to help convince Soviet leaders to accommodate the West rather than confront it.[80]

In Eastern Europe, where citizens bore the daily brunt of Soviet persecution, Reagan's description of the USSR as an evil empire was regarded as "nothing more than a statement of the obvious," according to George Weigel, author of the bestselling biography of Pope John Paul II, *Witness to Hope*.[81] Those were the same words used by Jan Winiecki, an economic adviser to Poland's Solidarity underground in the 1980s and now a professor at the University of Frankfurt, to describe reaction in his circles. "To us, it was, of course, true," he said of Reagan's description. "The leftist intellectuals in the West thumbed their noses at it, but we said 'What's the big deal?' What he said was a statement of the obvious. This was not [a] mystery."[82]

Sadly, many such expressions of gratitude from Eastern Europe and the former Soviet Union came too late for Reagan to comprehend. One exception was the case of Anatoly Sharansky, a former prisoner of conscience. In March 1977, twenty-nine-year-old Sharansky had been abducted by the KGB outside his apartment on Gorky Street in downtown Moscow. Charged with espionage and treason against the USSR—crimes punishable by death—he was sent to Lefortovo Prison. He spent nine years there, where he symbolized Reagan's description of the "religious dissident trapped in that cold, cruel existence."

After his release, Sharansky met with Reagan and his staff near the end of his presidency. "I told him that his speech about the Evil Empire was a great encourager for us," Sharansky said. Reagan "was one who understood the Soviet Union is [an] evil empire and we could change it. . . . [He] was calling a spade a spade—he understood the nature of the Soviet Union. I told [that to] Reagan, and he turned and said to his colleagues, 'Hear what he is saying, listen to him.' Shultz was there, McFarlane too, Poindexter, maybe Baker."[83]

POST–COLD WAR AMERICAN REACTIONS

Within two decades, of course, the shape of the world had changed altogether—so much so that in a 1999 speech the day before the tenth anniversary of the fall of the Berlin Wall, no less than Bill Clinton, the first Democratic president to follow Reagan, commended "President Reagan, who said so plainly . . . that the Soviet empire was evil."[84]

The academy, too, eventually reconsidered Reagan's words. Historian Alonzo Hamby called Reagan's address "actually a very interesting speech" that had been "miscaricatured."[85] "For those who read it carefully and fully, the speech belied those who argued that Reagan avoided serious ideas." He notes that the speech was "a statement about human nature in terms of what once had been called 'neo-orthodox theology,' " a movement in vogue among liberals in the 1940s and 1950s.[86]

The reaction of historian Garry Wills, a Catholic liberal, is interesting. "It seemed to many (and to me) that Reagan's talk of an Evil Empire was irresponsible," Wills wrote. "Moral absolutism looses fanaticism, a dangerous thing when nuclear weapons lie ready to a trembling hand." But at length Wills reevaluated the speech, and came to see Reagan's "dangerous" words as a "gamble" that "might not have worked. It might have blown us up. But it didn't."[87]

"Reagan's comments on the Soviet Union," Wills went on, "were not a ploy but, for him, a statement of the obvious." Wills makes a powerful point:

> His evident sincerity, even simplicity, gave weight to his view—not only abroad but at home. David Hume said that political efforts are sustained more efficiently by moral arguments than by appeals to mere advantage or self-interest. People will sacrifice for what they are persuaded is deeply right.
>
> And, besides, the Soviet Union was evil. Weak, but evil. Few could see the obvious weakness. But he made us see the obvious evil.[88]

"He called it an Evil Empire," Wills wrote in a bout of surprising hyperbole, "and it evaporated overnight."[89]

MOTIVATIONS AND RESULTS

In retrospect, Reagan's reasons for unleashing his strongest rhetoric on the Soviets in 1983 may seem self-evident. By "calling a spade a spade," as Sharansky put it, he forced the issue on every front, causing everyone from dissidents in Eastern Europe to diplomats in the Kremlin to reassess the moral standing of the oppressive regime.

But there were many reasons he took the precise course of action he did. Among them was a Christian motivation: both Scripture and Jesus Christ command Christians to oppose evil with all their might,[90] and Reagan would doubtless have felt remiss in his Christian duty if he had failed to denounce and oppose the Soviet Union. Like Dick Walker, the hero of *That Printer of Udell's*, Reagan the practical Christian had a duty to speak out against evil.[91]

There's also ample evidence that Reagan spoke so frankly about the USSR because he saw himself as a voice for the voiceless. Just as he was compelled to speak out for the voiceless victims of abortion—another issue he addressed at length in the Evil Empire speech—Reagan felt obliged to speak for the voiceless in the USSR. As Ben Elliott notes, the president "had enormous sympathy for these Soviets who lived under captivity." As Reagan said on another occasion: "To prisoners of conscience throughout the world, take heart; you have not been forgotten. We, your brothers and sisters in God, have made your cause our cause, and we vow never to relent until you have regained the freedom that is your birthright as a child of God."[92]

Reagan himself said that simple honesty compelled his frank words toward the USSR. After his presidency, he described his motivations:

For too long our leaders were unable to describe the Soviet Union as it actually was. The keepers of our foreign-policy knowledge—in other words, most liberal foreign-affairs scholars, the State Department, and various columnists—found it illiberal and provocative to be so honest. I've always believed, however, that it's important to define differences, because there are choices and decisions to be made in life and history.

The Soviet system over the years has purposely starved, murdered, and brutalized its own people. Millions were killed; it's all right there in the history books. It put other citizens it disagreed with into psychiatric hospitals, sometimes drugging them into oblivion. Is the system that allowed this not evil? Then why shouldn't we say so? Even the Soviets themselves are now admitting to annihilating their own people during Stalin's era.[93]

To Reagan, this honesty was necessary, because it helped eliminate illusions. As national security adviser Bud McFarlane explained, "Realism had to be one of the pillars of the new relationship. We had to say we had no illusions about Marxists."[94]

Reagan said such talk was needed to "philosophically and intellectually take on the principles of Marxism-Leninism." "We were always too worried we would offend the Soviets if we struck at anything so basic," he said after he left the presidency. "Well, so what? Marxist-Leninist thought is an empty cupboard. Everyone knew it by the 1980s, but no one was saying it."[95] Of course, not everyone knew it. But *he* was willing to say it.

Reagan craved such Cold War clarity. In an interview with a disapproving British reporter ten days after the Evil Empire speech, Reagan explained that his purpose was to express his "willingness to face up to what the differences are in our views and between us, to be realistic about it. . . . We've seen, under the guise of diplomacy and détente and so forth in the past, efforts to kind of sweep the differences under the rug and pretend they don't exist. I have stated, very frankly, what I believe the differences are."[96]

He wanted the Soviets to know precisely where he was coming from. In his memoirs, he wrote:

> I wanted to remind the Soviets we knew what they were up to. . . .
> I wanted to let Andropov know we recognized the Soviets for what
> they were. Frankly, I think it worked, even though some people—
> including Nancy—tried persuading me to lower the temperature of
> my rhetoric. I told Nancy I had a reason for saying those things: I
> wanted the Russians to know I understood their system and what it
> stood for.[97]

But Reagan also had tactical reasons for making that speech at the moment he did—reasons that stemmed from the delicate diplomatic relationship that was emerging between the U.S. and the USSR at the time. Reagan saw that a moment of American bombast could be a useful peace-through-strength weapon in the effort to *improve* relations with the USSR—a rhetorical volley that would help prompt negotiations.

One great misunderstanding about Reagan holds that he fired away at the enemy indiscriminately, with no real purpose. In fact, he delivered the Evil Empire speeech with careful, deliberate intent. As he later explained: "Although a lot of liberal pundits jumped on my speech at Orlando and said it showed I was a rhetorical hip-shooter who was recklessly and unconsciously provoking the Soviets into war[,] I made the 'Evil Empire' speech and others like it with malice aforethought."[98]

Reagan's choice of language, in other words, was aimed at bringing the Soviets to the negotiating table, where the real progress could be made. As members of his administration have since confirmed, the president was undertaking a kind of two-track diplomacy, blasting the USSR in public while also offering to negotiate.[99] Donald Regan, Reagan's chief of staff, was among those who saw the dual approach as it related to the big picture. "Reagan's every action in foreign policy," wrote Regan—listing the military buildup, rejection of Soviet adventurism, pursuit of SDI, and "public rhetoric of confrontation and the private signals of conciliation toward the Soviets"—had been carried out with "the idea of one day sitting down at the negotiating table with the leader of the USSR and banning weapons of mass destruction."[100]

One who grasped the dual approach at the time, probably better than anyone, was speechwriter Tony Dolan. In his 1993 piece "Premeditated Prose: Reagan's Evil Empire," Dolan relayed how in key Reagan speeches, particularly his most abrasive, the president pushed "a new, intensely controversial approach to the Soviet-American dialogue and mutual relations: candor as part of a strategy to exploit the psychological vulnerabilities of totalitarianism and weaken its intransigence."[101]

Bill Clark confirms that the president was following a deliberate strategy.[102] Reagan was "incredibly careful about use of bellicose language," he says, and "did not at all" shoot from the hip. When he ratcheted up the rhetoric, Clark maintains, it was for a conscious purpose. Indeed, Reagan fully understood the dangers of such incendiary language, on occasion even removing particularly "seething" (Dolan's word) lines from his speeches.[103]

Finally, in the Evil Empire speech Reagan saw an opportunity to attack the atmosphere of moral equivalency that had characterized the American foreign-policy debate for decades. Much of the political left had long held the United States and the Soviet Union equally responsible for the Cold War; neither side, by this view, could claim the moral high ground.

To Reagan, this was rubbish. It was the USSR that had severely repressed God's inalienable rights since its inception, killing millions of its own along the way. America, on the other hand, was a democratic country "where all people enjoy the right to speak, to worship God as they choose, and live without fear." As he told a crowd in Miami, "don't let anyone tell you we're morally equivalent with the Soviet Union. . . . We are morally superior, not equivalent, to any totalitarian regime, and we should be darn proud of it."[104]

Reagan ripped into this notion of moral equivalency in the Evil Empire speech. He reminded his audience that during the 1940s, when the United States had enjoyed a nuclear monopoly, it had refused to use it to conquer or dominate the world. It was a point he had been making since the 1950s, even hand-writing it into letters he sent to Soviet general secretaries.[105] His implication was clear, and hard to deny: Stalin and the Soviets would never have behaved so peacefully had they held the world's nuclear monopoly.

Reagan urged his audience of evangelicals to "speak out against" those who would place the United States in a position of moral inferiority, and urged them not to "blithely" proclaim themselves above the debate and declare both sides equally at fault. They could not in good conscience "ignore the facts of history," nor "the aggressive impulses of an evil empire." The arms race, he said, was no mere misunderstanding, but a real battle between right and wrong.[106]

Revisiting the speech a decade and a half later, George Will observed that a key purpose of Reagan's Evil Empire remarks was to "remoralize" American foreign policy, after the era of détente had attempted to "de-moralize" it.[107] Around the same time, Ed Meese explained that Reagan's aim with the words was "to engage the Soviet Union on a moral plane."[108] In Augustinian fashion, Reagan was laying the groundwork for a "just war"—cold though it may have been—with the Soviets.

Historian Alonzo Hamby has ascribed the early criticism of Reagan's remarks to a pervasive postmodern tendency to abandon all clearcut distinctions, especially those pertaining to morality and truth, in favor of pervasive moral ambiguity.[109] As Allan Bloom wrote in *The Closing of the American Mind*, "What was offensive to contemporary ears in President Reagan's use of the word 'evil' was its cultural arrogance, the presumption that he, and America, know what is good."[110]

REAGAN'S EVIL EMPIRE ADDRESS HELPED CHANGE SUCH attitudes around the world. When, after the Soviet Union's dissolution, the *Los Angeles Times* ran an op-ed piece about the newly opened Soviet archives under the headline "The Soviet Union's Endless Paper Trail of Evil Comes to Light," no one blinked an eye.[111] Ten years before, such a line would have been unthinkable.

In his August 1992 speech at the Republican National Convention, Reagan expressed a measure of pride in his tough talk: "We stood tall and proclaimed that communism was destined for the ashheap of history. We never heard so much ridicule from our liberal friends. The only thing that got them more upset was two simple words: 'Evil Empire.'" He drew a connection between his caustic vocabulary and positive Cold War developments: "But we knew then what the liberal Democrat leaders just couldn't figure out: The sky would not fall if America restored her strength and resolve. The sky would not fall if an American president spoke the truth. The only thing that would fall was the Berlin Wall."[112]

17.

A Message for Communist Peoples Worldwide

"[I]n many countries people aren't even allowed to read the Bible. It is up to us to make sure the message of hope and salvation gets through."

—*Ronald Reagan, December 9, 1983*[1]

"Our mission extends far beyond our borders; God's family knows no borders."

—*Ronald Reagan, January 30, 1984*[2]

A t 3:00 A.M. on November 10, 1982, America's top national-security official got an urgent call in Washington.[3] On the line was Soviet Ambassador Anatoly Dobrynin. *This must be important,* national security adviser Bill Clark thought. Dobrynin told Clark that Soviet General Secretary Leonid Brezhnev had died at seventy-six. And the Soviet Union, he said, fully expected President Reagan to come to Moscow for the funeral.

When Clark woke the president to report the news, Reagan told him he wouldn't be attending the funeral. "No, no, Bill. I don't want to do that. The vice president can handle that. When I go to Moscow for the first time I want it to be a matter of substance." The following day his top advisers unanimously suggested he reconsider, but Reagan refused. "His thinking," Clark said, "was [that] it would be hypocritical to show up at his funeral having never met the man." Instead, Reagan decided that he, along with Clark and Nancy, should go to the Soviet embassy to offer his condolences. Clark recalled the scene:

> When we arrived there it was morgue like. Of course, maybe it al-
> ways was morgue like. We signed the condolence book in total si-
> lence. [Reagan] then leaned over to the two of us and said, with a
> little twinkle in his eye: "Think they would mind if we just said a
> little prayer for the man?" So we said a short Christian prayer for
> the repose of the soul of Chairman Brezhnev.

To Brezhnev and his comrades, Reagan's prayer would have surely appeared a futile, silly act of piety. To Reagan, it was the right thing to do—and a rare opportunity to bring the word of Christ into a god-less house. Whether it did Brezhnev any good, none of us can know.

Garry Wills once surmised that "Reagan's God prefers Americans to his other creatures."[4] Quite the contrary: Ronald Reagan's expressed Christian beliefs and actions show he believed otherwise. "I recognize we must be cautious in claiming that God is on our side," he said on a number of occasions as president, "but I think it's all right to keep asking if we're on his side."[5] To Reagan, prayer was the best way to ask.

As the "focus of evil" passage in the Evil Empire speech suggested, Reagan was moved by a Christian duty to pray even for communists themselves. He felt an obligation to part the Iron Curtain so that God's word could pass freely inside. If conversion wasn't his explicit goal for the Soviet empire, he certainly sought at least to promote Christian ethics, religious freedom, and a general belief in God. Reagan's moment of prayer for Brezhnev at the embassy captures his thinking: He wanted to crush Brezhnev's system, yet also pray for his soul.

The Soviet journal *Literaturnaya Gazeta* fumed that there were "no doubts at all" as to Reagan's intentions for the USSR. "To crush the Soviets would be a mission of purification pleasing to the Almighty," the magazine imagined Reagan thinking. "Let us save the Russians by dispatching them to the Christian paradise in heaven!"[6]

Reagan himself might have laughed at the writer's tone—but recognized the kernel of truth in his words.

A MISSIONARY'S DUTY

Ninteen eighty-four saw Ronald Reagan launch his final election campaign. On January 30 that year he gave two interviews regarding the coming political season—one with reporters at 9:00 A.M. in the Rose Garden, the other at 3:30 P.M. with David Hartman of ABC's *Good Morning America*. Coincidentally, at that very moment the Soviets were also facing the prospect of leadership change—one brought about not through election cycles but by life cycles. By the end of January Yuri Andropov's health had plummeted; he died on February 9, a week and a half later. He was succeeded by an ailing

Konstantin Chernenko, whose lungs were so filled with emphysema that he couldn't even raise his arm to salute the procession at his inauguration. Chernenko lasted only thirteen months; Reagan later quipped that he wanted to negotiate with the Soviet leaders "but they keep dying on me."

The Soviets' wariness of the U.S. president had not abated. In a *Pravda* article that January, political observer Vitaliy Korionov reminded readers that "the present White House incumbent, invoking God, [has] declared the 'crusade' against socialism."[7] Korionov hoped this would be an unsuccessful year for the incumbent.

In between press interviews on January 30, President Reagan traveled to the Grand Ballroom of the Sheraton Washington Hotel to address the annual convention of the National Religious Broadcasters. There he made a curious pronouncement:

> Our mission extends far beyond our borders; God's family knows no borders. In your life you face daily trials, but millions of believers in other lands face far worse. They are mocked and persecuted for the crime of loving God. To every religious dissident trapped in that cold, cruel existence, we send our love and support. Our message? You are not alone; you are not forgotten; do not lose your faith and hope because someday you, too, will be free.[8]

Our mission: an intriguing phrase for a president to use in addressing an evangelical group. He made the remarks after commending groups like Mt. Zion Baptist Church, the Moody Bible Institute, and the Christian Broadcasting Network for their global outreach and missionary programs. As comments like these reflected, Reagan saw the presidency in part as a chance to launch his own global outreach. On an earlier occasion he had thanked a group of Catholic clergy—and specifically the Catholic Information Service—for providing "inspiration to a world seeking desperately to find men who can make the message of the Gospel a reality in their lives and times"; he might as well have been talking about himself.[9]

A few weeks before his January 30 speech, Reagan had said unequivocally: "[I]n many countries people aren't even allowed to read the Bible. It is up to us to make sure the message of hope and salvation gets through."[10] At the end of the year, in a December letter to Mother Teresa, Reagan cited Scripture in expressing a desire to help those suffering abroad, noting it was Christ who spoke of the need "to bind up the broken-hearted, to proclaim liberty to the captives."[11]

While all of this had special application for the Soviet Union, Reagan also carried a spiritual message to the communist, and officially atheist, nation of China. In April 1984 he traveled to Beijing; standing beside Chinese leaders on April 27, he fearlessly preached not just self-government and the words "trust the people," but the fact that "America was founded by people who sought freedom to worship God and to trust in Him to guide them in their daily lives."[12]

He went to greater lengths in an April 30 speech to Chinese students at Fudan University in Shanghai. He was always vocal about faith issues when he had a student audience, where diplomatic tact wasn't such a necessity. Halfway through the speech he recited his treasured lines from the Declaration of Independence: "that all men are created equal, that they are endowed by their Creator with certain unalienable rights." As he closed, he added that there was "one other part of our national character I wish to speak of. Religion and faith are very important to us." He noted that America was a nation of many religions. "But most Americans derive their religious beliefs from the Bible of Moses, who delivered a people from slavery; the Bible of Jesus Christ, who told us to love thy neighbor as thyself, to do unto your neighbor as you would have him do unto you." And this, too, he said, "has formed us."[13]

In mentioning that Moses had "delivered a people from slavery," Reagan was surely thinking of the Chinese people's need to be delivered from communism. As he delivered these words, Chinese Christians were languishing in prison, some for uttering words less provocative than what Reagan had just publicly proclaimed. Yet Reagan had faith that God could help to deliver them all from communism, just as it had Whittaker Chambers. It was as if Dutch Reagan had picked up Nelle's post as president of the Missionary Society, but with a much larger audience at his disposal.

Reagan chose to bring this message to China's youth—an auditorium full of students, all of them bright, inquisitive, and utterly proscribed from religious practice. Here was the hope for China's future, not those Communist Party octogenarians sleeping in their seats at the People's Congress, and Reagan saved his best shot for them, just as he would for youngsters at Moscow State University four years later.

As he flew home, White House reporters jostled with him aboard Air Force One. "How did they [the Chinese leadership] like preaching—your preaching at them about democracy, God, capitalism, freedom?" one reporter asked. "Do you think that they thought you were trying to propagandize their people?" Reagan was sad to learn from them that his message had been censored from broader circulation. But he did know that his remarks were carried on live television, as they would be in Moscow four years later.[14]

A week later, Pope John Paul II complimented the president on his effort in China, saying he was "deeply honored" by Reagan's presence during a mutual stop in Fairbanks, Alaska. The pontiff noted that Reagan had just returned from an "important trip" to China.[15]

He was surely impressed by his friend's success in bringing God to Beijing—a China mission John Paul II had always wanted, but found frustratingly elusive.

PRAYING FOR THE CLERK AND THE COMMUNIST

Reagan's most strident anti-Soviet rhetoric occurred during his first term. Though he did not shelve the tough talk after his reelection, the latter half of his presidency featured considerably more dialogue between him and the Kremlin. During his first administration the United States and Soviet Union held no summit meetings; the second Reagan term, in contrast, would see summits in Geneva in November 1985, Reykjavik in October 1986, Washington in December 1987, and in the belly of the beast itself—Moscow in May-June 1988. Four summits in just four years: ample evidence for the belief of diplomats like James Billington that the president's bellicose language may have helped push the Soviets to the bargaining table.

In early November 1985, with the Geneva summit fast approaching, Reagan prepared a draft of an address to the nation. He penciled in a statement that it was "most important" that, in regard to the USSR, "our young people . . . would learn that we are all God's children."[16] Though it only became clear in retrospect, this was the start of a decidedly spiritual crusade to Moscow that would carry Reagan through the rest of his time in office.

Two months later, Reagan expressed his spiritual openness in a message observing the Orthodox Christmas, when he said the birth of Christ "brought forth good tidings of great joy to *all* people" (his italics). Citing the "gift" of Christ, he told listeners that "We are told there are up to 100 million believers in the Soviet Union alone. Whether you are from Russia, Ukraine, Byelorussia, Armenia, Georgia, the Baltic states, or elsewhere inside the Soviet Union—please know that we in America join you as one family under the Fatherhood of God . . . for today and tomorrow and for all time." "May we pray together," he asked, "that God's message of peace may touch the hearts of all His children." Reagan cited Christian teaching in explaining his concern for the religious well-being of all people— "God's commandment that we love our neighbor as we love ourselves."[17] (Shades, once again, of missionary Nelle, who had written in November 1947 that the church must support missionary work because God decrees, "Love thy neighbor as thyself.")[18]

Reagan made such statements all the time as president.[19] Before the Geneva summit, he insisted: "[W]e are all God's children. The clerk and the king and the Communist were made in His image. We all have souls." Thus, he said, "I'm convinced, more than ever, that man finds liberation only when he binds himself to God and commits himself to his fellow man."[20] In February 1988 he commented that "God's gift . . . is for all mankind."[21] And in October of that year he urged a group of American and Soviet students to understand that "we're all God's children."[22]

Reagan feared sincerely for the souls of the Soviet people. This was palpable in his prayers not just for persecuted Russian believers but also for committed atheists like Brezhnev, whose regime regularly dispatched people of faith to the snows of Siberia. He was always careful to say that his problems were with the Soviet system, not the people. He called the Soviet people "the warmest, friendliest, nicest people you could ever meet," and said "I pray that the hand of the Lord will be on the Soviet people."

And he recognized that government was the one thing that stood between God and many of his children: "It isn't people, but governments that make war. And it isn't people but governments that erect barriers that keep us apart."[23]

REAGAN WAS FOND OF A PARTICULAR PRAYER, AND shared it often with Bill Clark. It typifies how he perceived his role toward communist peoples and nations in his second term as president:

> *Lord, make me an instrument of your peace . . .*
> *Where there is doubt, let me sow faith.*
> *Where there is despair, let me sow hope.*
> *Where there is darkness, let me sow light.*[24]

In a letter to the president written on stationery bearing the legend "Jesus to the communist world," Pastor Richard Wurmbrand suggested to Reagan, "Perhaps the American government should now also consider the use of the ideological bomb. A bomb in which religion would be an important component."[25]

That was exactly what Reagan had in mind.

18.

Missionary to Moscow

"The heretofore impregnable edifice of Communist atheism was being assaulted before their very
eyes by [Reagan]."

*—Soviet translator Igor Korchilov on Rea-
gan's actions in Moscow in May 1988*[1]

"He wants to see Christianity in Moscow, it's as
simple as that."

—Edmund Morris[2]

On May 3, 1988, the East Room at 1600 Pennsylvania Avenue was marked by hope and promise. At 2:44 that afternoon, President Reagan held a press conference with four Russian
religious dissidents—Father Vladimir Shibayev, Reverend Stefan
Matveiuk, Mykola Rudenko, and Iosif Begun. He elevated the event
by asserting that while the White House had seen many important
people—presidents, diplomats, world statesmen—none were "more

important, none of greater faith and moral courage, than these four men."[3]

Reagan perceived few things as more courageous than standing for God under persecution—particularly communist persecution. To Reagan, these men were spiritual heroes. He made a public vow to the four men:

> I promise that the witness of faith that you have brought here today will not be confined within these four walls, or forgotten when this meeting is ended. I will carry it in my heart when I travel to the Soviet Union at the end of this month. And I will say that the most fitting way to mark the millennium of Christianity in Kiev Rus would be granting the right of all the peoples and all the creeds of the Soviet Union to worship their God, in their own way.

Reagan would carry that witness not merely in his heart but also in his words and deeds: four weeks later, he would keep his vow.

The president told his audience that "The presence of these four men here today is testimony to the fact that our witness here in the West can have an impact." Indeed, Reagan felt keenly that his own witness was having an impact, and in this final year of his presidency he was preparing to extend that witness all the way to Moscow. In lieu of enlisting the Pentagon's army in the closing days of the Cold War, he would marshal his own salvation army.

The actions he took to bring the word of God directly to everyday citizens in the Soviet Union were remarkable. "He didn't have the slightest compunction about sharing his religious views with the Russian people," said Richard Allen.[4] George Shultz, the secretary of state who sat at his side in many meetings with Soviet officials, emphasized that such "religious freedom was very important to him."[5]

This Reagan mission was manifest in his trip to Moscow for a fourth summit with Mikhail Gorbachev, which took place from May 29 to June 2, 1988. All of Moscow became his rooftop that spring; Soviet-supplied microphones became his bullhorns. Ben Elliott concedes that his boss was trying to evangelize the Soviet people: "On such a historic trip, Reagan wanted every word to have meaning. He wanted every word to be heard."[6] Edmund Morris agrees: "He want[ed] to see Christianity in Moscow, it's as simple as that."[7] It was indeed: Reagan seemed to be following the exhortation to Christians in Matthew 28:19–20: "Therefore go and make disciples of all nations. . . . And surely I will be with you always, to the very end of the age."

Just as Reagan had yearned to reach the lush greens of the Disciples' Eureka College as a seventeen-year-old, he now craved the gray confines of atheistic Moscow as a seventy-seven-year-old. Paradoxically, he harbored a Christian impulse for each. In preaching the gospel of God and religious freedom in the USSR in 1988, Reagan hoped to spread religious belief.

Most intriguing, he may have had an added motivation. In a July 1981 letter, Reagan had written to a private citizen, "I have had a feeling . . . that religion might well turn out to be the Soviets' Achilles' heel." He pointed to Pope John Paul II's earlier visit to Poland, and how it had undercut communism there.[8] Eager to find every means possible to undermine Soviet communism, Reagan must have believed from the start that in making God—and particularly biblical Christianity—a constant refrain during his 1988 trip to the USSR, he stood a real chance to weaken Soviet communism and even help change the country. Indeed, in another letter during his presidency, he hoped that "the hunger for religion" in the USSR—which he long sensed—"may yet be a major factor in bringing about a change in the present situation."[9]

A conventional history of the Reagan administration might focus on the diplomatic and geopolitical matters at issue during this final Reagan-Gorbachev summit. Yet if one is to judge from the statements Reagan himself made during the trip, it's impossible to overlook the fact that religious belief and freedom seem to have been the primary issues on his mind. And those statements may astound readers today, just as it did Soviets then.

For Reagan, the Moscow summit was evidently also a mission—perhaps first and foremost. He dedicated much of his public schedule there to promoting spiritual freedom and belief, in a series of events that came as close to evangelization as any president ever had. And his intentions were not lost on the Soviets, who watched the American president speak right over the heads of their leadership directly to the people.[10]

LAYING THE ROAD TO MOSCOW

Reagan's eagerness to help spread religion behind the Iron Curtain was evident well before he landed in Moscow in May 1988. He had arguably been preparing the groundwork for his mission since at least 1983.

During his first term, with a particular eye toward the Soviet empire, Reagan announced a concerted effort to expand and improve the religious broadcasts carried on Voice of America (VOA). It was one of the Great Communicator's pet projects. In January 1983, he happily announced that for the first time VOA would broadcast a religious service worldwide—Christmas Eve from the National Presbyterian Church in Washington, D.C. "Now, these broadcasts are not popular with governments of totalitarian powers," said Reagan with a wink. "But make no mistake, we have a duty to broadcast."[11] Again, his use of language was deliberate and suggestive: to whom did "we"—he and his nation, presumably—owe this duty to reach beyond U.S. borders and carry the word of God?

Reagan followed the VOA announcement by shaking a frank finger at Soviet authorities:

> To those who would crush religious freedom, our message is plain: You may jail your believers. You may close their churches, confiscate their Bibles, and harass their rabbis and priests, but you will never destroy the love of God and freedom that burns in their hearts. They will triumph over you.[12]

"Think of it," he said, piling it on in the same announcement. "The most awesome military machine in history [the USSR], but it is no match for that one, single man, [that] hero, [that] strong yet tender, Prince of Peace." That Prince of Peace—"His name alone"—was Jesus Christ.[13]

But at the same time Reagan was also taking private action to improve religious freedom in the USSR. Among his first steps was a February 1983 meeting with Soviet ambassador Anatoly Dobrynin. The first of Reagan's long-cherished one-on-one meetings with high-level Soviet officials, the meeting should be recognized as an early turning point in diffusing the Cold War confrontation.

It came about almost accidentally. Secretary of State Shultz had just returned from a trip to China. On that Friday and Saturday, there was a blizzard in Washington, leaving the city at a standstill. Unable to make the flight to Camp David, the Reagans called the Shultzes and invited them to dinner.[14]

During dinner, George Shultz commented on the usefulness of his private meetings with Ambassador Dobrynin, which had been opposed by some in the administration. On Tuesday, he told the president, Dobrynin would be dropping by his office again. Shultz asked Reagan if he would like to surprise the ambassador by joining in. "The president said, 'great,' " remembered Shultz. "He was itching to engage these people [the Soviets]." Shultz figured the meeting would take ten minutes. It went on for over an hour.[15]

Reagan carried the conversation, raising a number of topics. He zeroed in on Soviet persecution of a group of Russian Pentecostal Christians who had taken refuge in the U.S. embassy in Moscow five years earlier and had been living there ever since. The Pentecostals wanted to practice their beliefs, and to emigrate from the Soviet Union. They had been denied both requests. "If they attempted to set foot off the embassy grounds, they would be arrested," Reagan complained. "Their crime: belief in their religion and belief in God."[16]

In the meeting with Dobrynin, Shultz recalled, Reagan "came down very hard on human rights," particularly the Pentecostals' rights. He told the ambassador that some positive act by the Soviet leadership might make it easier to resume overall U.S.-USSR negotiations, and suggested that the Pentecostals might serve as that token.[17] If the Soviet leadership were to take action to resolve the impasse he would be delighted, and would not embarrass the USSR "by undue publicity, by claims of credit for ourselves, or by 'crowing.' " They cut a deal, the Pentecostals were set free, and Reagan kept his word.[18]

From the meeting, Shultz came away with two lessons. One, the Soviets learned the depth of Reagan's concern about human rights. Second, they learned that he was a man who kept his word. Both were crucial to future negotiations and summits.[19]

Later that summer, a second group of Pentecostals was permitted to leave the USSR. Reagan recalled this gesture in his memoirs: "In the overall scheme of U.S.-Soviet relations, allowing a handful of Christian believers to leave the Soviet Union was a small event. But in the context of the time I thought it was a hope-giving development."[20]

The "practical Christian" in Reagan could take comfort that he had helped further the wishes of a group of committed Russian believers. He had served his Lord. He had also kept his word, never publicizing the incident despite the potential propaganda value it might have had for the American cause—this at a time when the nuclear-freeze movement, much of the political left, and even some theologians were demonizing him as a nuclear-weapons-craving warmonger.

The episode is enlightening: Reagan had raised a number of points during this first major encounter with the Soviet leadership, but the key one—the issue that led to the quickest and most decisive action—concerned the fate of Christians. This quiet overture, which extended religious liberty to a group of persecuted Russian believers, actually stands as Reagan's first agreement with the USSR.

But then, persecuted Soviets were frequently on his mind. Secretary of Defense Frank Carlucci recalled that the president "would walk around with lists in his pocket of people who were in prison in the Soviet Union." Each time the secretary of state prepared to travel to the USSR, Reagan pulled out the names—"some of whom we'd heard of but most of whom we hadn't," said Carlucci—and say, "I want you to raise these names with the Soviets." And sure enough, said Carlucci, "George [Shultz] would raise them and one by one they would be released or allowed to leave."[21]

RUSSIAN SOULS AND PRESIDENTIAL PRESSURE

The years 1985, 1986, and 1987 brought three summits to the two Cold War adversaries—each a prelude to the fourth summit in Moscow. Throughout this period of intense diplomatic initiative, Reagan's many statements on the Soviet Union were sprinkled with remarks about God.

Hard-line Soviet communists were perturbed by Reagan's constant "God talk." "I'm afraid," lamented Aleksandr Bovin in *Izvestia* in October 1985, "that the President feels strongly tempted to play the role of emissary of the forces of good and of light embarking on a theological argument with the forces of evil and of darkness."[22] He was right. Commenting on another typical Reagan speech, *Pravda* commentator Georgi Arbatov sighed in November 1986: "[I]n this speech, too, the President could not get by without references to the faith and religious values."[23] Right again: as far as Reagan was concerned, annoying the likes of Arbatov and Bovin was a greater badge of honor than irritating the editorial board of the *New York Times*.

And he looked for ways to deliver his message directly to the Soviet people—as in the New Year's radio address he broadcast to the Soviet people on December 31, 1986.

Reagan and Gorbachev had each agreed to wish a happy new year to the other's people, without any state censorship of their comments. Gorbachev's message was conventional, but Reagan's differed sharply from expectations. He did discuss the summits at Geneva and Reykjavik, the latter of which had occurred just two months earlier. But first he beelined to the issue that was foremost on his mind. This was a season, he said, of love and hope, reflection, expectation—"a time when people in America, just like people all over the world, gather with family and friends to remember the blessings of God and to look to the future with hope. That's what I would like to do with you, the Soviet people, tonight."[24]

By the time Reagan had finished with that opening passage, the Kremlin must have cursed its miscalculation—and, in fact, thereafter, Soviet officials were more mindful of the "dangers" of an uncensored Reagan on their airwaves.[25] For a moment, the president toned things down, turning his attention to earthly things like summits and nuclear missiles. Halfway through, however, his focus returned to the linked issues of spirituality and human rights: "The American people are deeply concerned with the fate of individual people wherever they might be throughout the world. We believe that God gave sacred rights to every man, woman, and child on Earth." After four more paragraphs about peace and individual rights, he finished with a final paragraph that invoked saints and martyrs, mentioned prayer twice, and included the word "soul" five times—including a dangerously provocative mention of the "Russian soul."[26]

What was that? Soviet citizens must have been wondering. For possibly the first time ever on radio, the Russian people had just heard a politician discussing their *souls*—a concept Lenin himself had worked all his life to deny and abolish. Even Reagan's signature signoff, "God bless you," must have bewildered many Soviet ears.[27]

Approaching the December 1987 Washington summit, in a November 30 speech Reagan blasted the Soviets for continued human-rights abuses, especially religious persecution. His strong words concerned some in his administration, since the Soviets were coming to town to sign the INF Treaty and, with luck, make some progress on human rights. The State Department didn't want Reagan's tough words to jeopardize its backroom diplomatic efforts.

But he did so on that day, and in face-to-face talks he lectured a testy Gorbachev on religious freedom.[28] "Few moves on the part of the Soviet government could do more to convince the world of its sincerity for reform than the legalization of the Ukrainian Catholic Church," he said in the November 30 speech. "One of the truest measures of *glasnost* [political openness] will be the degree of religious freedom the Soviet rulers allow their people—freedom of worship for all." Until such changes were made, said Reagan, glasnost was "a promise as yet unfulfilled."[29] Gorbachev—the first Soviet leader to make any real attempt at reform, the man who had introduced the very concept of glasnost —must have been incensed: wasn't he doing enough?

Reagan's concern was not unjustified, as demonstrated by a front-page *Pravda* editorial entitled "Fostering Committed Atheists" that had run the previous year—well into the era of glasnost. The editorial cited an "urgent need" to "foster committed atheists," and thanked the 27th CPSU Congress for taking that lead in "communist building." "Atheist education," it said, "is an inalienable constituent part" of the "transforming force" of Marxist-Leninist ideology. The editorial declared:

> Lenin's instruction about a class and party approach to religion as a thoroughly false system of views of the world remains in force to this day. Ideological cadres must take care to improve the forms and methods of atheist work. What is needed is a clear, systematic approach, a well-thought-out program of activity, and close interaction with other spheres of ideological educational work. . . .
>
> [I]t is important to find the optimum combination of mass, group, and individual forms of influencing people. . . . [L]abor collectives have every opportunity to surround their comrade with concern and to prevent him from being drawn into a religious association or sect. . . .

V. I. Lenin repeatedly reminded people that the more scientifi-
cally the struggle against religious ideology is waged, the greater is
the success achieved in it. . . . An acute need is arising to investi-
gate, for example, the essence and nature, the specific causes, the
degree of religiosity in various regions of the USSR, [and] the individual reasons why people turn to religion. . . .

The struggle against religious ideology requires all conscious
working people and communists, above all, to be drawn into the
ranks of champions of atheist education.[30]

With messages like that coming from the editorial board of the nation's state-controlled newspaper—on the front page no less—
Reagan could be forgiven for thinking that even Gorbachev's reforms
might not be enough. Reagan pressured the Soviet leader publicly
and privately, and the lobbying got under Gorbachev's skin.

That said, Reagan was hopeful about the USSR's receptivity to
Christianity. He read widely about the problem, and heard the testimony of dissidents, often firsthand; in their words he saw that a
yearning for religious liberty persevered in the hearts of many Soviet
citizens.

One of those who agreed was his fellow crusader Billy Graham.
On December 1, 1987, immediately before the Washington summit,
Reagan promised publicly that he and Gorbachev would "have a few
words" about religious persecution in the USSR. He said that Graham had told him that underlying "everything" among the Soviet
people was a "hunger for religion." Though the Soviet people didn't
"dare admit it," he said, he believed Graham's testimony.[31]

In a letter Reagan had received from Graham a week earlier, Graham had reported that "under those babushkas of those little shuffling
figures" going to church in the USSR were hidden some youthful

faces—an indication that Soviet youth were "hungry for God." He urged Reagan to keep that fact "in the back of your mind at all times in your dealings" with the Soviets.[32]

Reagan shared this hopeful report on December 1—not in a chapel but in a public school in Jacksonville, Florida, before an audience of youthful faces in his own country. He described with excitement the makeshift "Bibles" sent to him from the USSR. When Soviet citizens "get their hands on a Bible—it is so difficult there, and they're not supposed to have them—they cut them up and make them into these little books so that everybody has just a few verses of their own of the Bible," he reported. "And one of those was sent to me to show me what they do."[33]

Sporadic though they were, such occasional sunny reports buoyed Reagan's spirits about the prospect of spiritual revival in the Soviet Union. He even heard good news from the usually pessimistic Malcolm Muggeridge. The "most important happening" in the world, Muggeridge had said, was the "resurgence" of Christianity in the Soviet Union, which, he claimed, had demonstrated that "the whole effort sustained over sixty years to brainwash the Russian people . . . has been a fiasco."[34] The thought stuck with Reagan, and he and Muggeridge corresponded on the subject at length; in one letter, Muggeridge insisted that the Western media was blowing it by failing to report on this major historical development in the USSR.[35] As Edmund Morris details, Reagan became obsessed with the notion that an underground religious movement was rising—like a water table, as Morris put it—beneath the surface of Soviet society.[36]

All of Reagan's hopeful talk about burgeoning religious faith in the land of Lenin, however, was a mere warm-up to the message he would bring to the Soviets themselves come late May 1988.

Moscow: The May-June 1988 Mission

In his press conference with the four Russian religious dissidents on May 3, Reagan had signaled that his Moscow trip would be a human-rights crusade, with special emphasis on his call for religious freedom. After promising to carry witness of their faith with him to the Soviet Union at the end of the month, Reagan momentarily took a positive tack in those remarks, listing a number of "encouraging signs" of religious freedom in the USSR. These signs, he said, were signs of change in a nation that had devoted itself "to reshaping man" and denied "one of the most basic teachings of the Judeo-Christian belief: that after God shaped Adam from dust, he breathed into him the divine principle of life." In typical fashion, however, he then cranked up the pressure on the Soviets and Gorbachev, listing examples of continued persecution. "While every positive step taken by the Soviets is welcomed," he granted, "we realize that this is just the beginning."[37] An impromptu story closed his remarks, including a prod to Gorbachev:

> I have to add a little something here. Recently, a woman wrote a letter and enclosed in the letter was a copy of what can only be called a prayer. But the story of that—it's in that single page—of a young Russian soldier in a shellhole in World War II, knowing that his unit was going to announce—or going to advance the attack, looking up at the stars and revealing for the first time that he had been taught all his life that there was no God. But now he believed there was. And he looked up at the heavens and spoke so sincerely and said. "Maybe before the night is over I'll be coming to You. And I hope You will forgive what I believed for so long, the foolish-

ness, because I know now there is a God." And that letter was found on the body of the young soldier who was killed in the coming engagement. I thought sometimes of taking it to Moscow with me—maybe the General Secretary might like to read it.

Well, thank you all very much. God bless you.[38]

He did in fact take that letter to Moscow, reading it to Gorbachev personally in their first one-on-one meeting together on May 29.[39] Yet even before he was able to walk the message into Red Square, TASS political observer Anatoly Krasikov throttled Reagan for his remarks of May 3. The president's "hopelessly unrealistic appeals," said Krasikov, "provoke only an ironic smile in the USSR. It will be better if they [the U.S. president and Congress] take up problems of freedom of conscience at home." Insinuating hypocrisy on Reagan's part, Krasikov said there were "quite a few people" in the "upper echelons" of American government who, "while advertising their own piety, demonstrate by their whole way of life that faith for them is no more than a covering for extremely unevangelical doings."[40]

On May 4, Reagan gave what might be considered his own "Four Freedoms" speech. In it, he listed the four freedoms he would push in his human-rights campaign in the USSR at the end of the month—freedom of religion the first among them.[41]

Reagan's statements pushing religious freedom continued throughout the month. He promised in his May 25 departure statement that he would press the Soviet leadership to increase religious liberty within their borders.[42] Stopping in Western Europe on his way to Moscow, he continued to hammer that cause. In one of his first formal pre-summit addresses, on May 27 in Finland, he conjured up images of Russia's zealous past, noting that Moscow's 1,600 church belfries had once earned it the moniker "City of the Forty Forties." "The world welcomes the return of some churches to worship after many years," said Reagan, "but there are still relatively few functioning churches and almost no bells." He then quoted a Gorbachev statement in which the general secretary said that "Believers are Soviet people . . . and they have the full right to express their conviction with dignity." While he applauded Gorbachev's statement, Reagan pushed for more: "What a magnificent demonstration of good will it would be for the Soviet leadership for church bells to ring out again not only in Moscow but throughout the Soviet Union."[43]

The Soviet press noted each of Reagan's repeated religious statements as his arrival approached, heartily disapproving each step of the way. Article after article complained bitterly of the pressure he was bringing to bear, with those appearing in *Izvestia* perhaps the most resentful.[44] *Izvestia* mocked his Finland speech, noting sarcastically that "a bitter tear moistened the President's eye" when he recalled the Forty Forties.[45]

Reagan preferred the arrival message of Patriarch Pimen of Moscow, who proclaimed on May 29, that "God's heavenly will" was about to bring them all together—Reagan, Gorbachev, and their peoples.[46]

THE ARRIVAL

As Reagan's plane cut a path across the blue sky that May 29, Soviet handlers took pride in the day ahead. It was the first such meeting at the Soviet capital since Richard Nixon's 1974 trip, and the host country's advance team had attended to every detail. The streets near Spaso House, where the Reagans would stay, had been mercifully repaved; two dilapidated structures nearby had been miraculously fixed and whitewashed. The ugly buildings across the street from the Kremlin were repainted in bright pastels, the lawn at the public school Nancy Reagan would visit replanted.[47] Even the prostitutes who frequented hotels where the American press and Reagan's entourage would be staying were cleared out. Igor Korchilov, the Soviet government translator of thirty years, called it a latter-day Potemkin village. Before Reagan's arrival, city authorities had boasted that the lilacs would be in bloom to greet him, and the sun itself would shine upon him—two predictions that actually came true.[48] As if under orders from the Politburo, even the pollution seemed to depart to accommodate the distinguished stranger.

The president's plane touched down shortly before 2:00 P.M. at Vnukovo-2 airport. He and Nancy touched Soviet soil at 2:05 P.M., where they were greeted with banners and perfect skies. They were also welcomed by the uninviting countenance of foreign minister Andrei Gromyko, once described by Reagan as "that frosty old Stalinist."

The motorcade transporting the Reagans entered Kremlin grounds through the Borovitsky Gate before proceeding to the Grand Kremlin Palace building. As they stepped from their car, the Reagans were welcomed by a flurry of American and Soviet flags. From there, they climbed to the top of the endless Grand State Staircase—where Reagan was met by a fifteen-foot canvas of Lenin holding forth before the Komsomol (the Communist Youth League) in 1920. After the long climb, he might have hoped for a better reward. Reagan grinned and muttered, "I sort of expected him to be there."

They shuffled to the Kremlin's majestic St. George's Hall—a dazzling room, the largest ceremonial chamber in the Grand Kremlin Palace. As the Reagans strode in from one end, the Gorbachevs entered from the other. The two couples met in the middle of the room on a red carpet.

They exchanged pleasantries and handshakes. Each man quoted a Russian proverb or two. After that, both followed by offering official statements.

By design or happenstance, that May 29 was a Sunday. And Reagan's self-appointed role of religious emissary started in that initial ceremony. He finished his remarks by pausing, looking up, and delivering this direct, closing salutation to the general secretary and his comrades: "Thank you and God bless you." As the words left his lips and were translated into Russian, the hardened Kremlin atheists present visibly blanched. Gorbachev's translator said that Reagan's words rang like blasphemy to the Soviet officials present, and they reacted with wry expressions. "The heretofore impregnable edifice of Communist atheism was being assaulted before their very eyes by [Reagan]," the translator recorded in his notes.[49] For unregenerate Red atheists, it was a discomfiting moment.

The two leaders held their first one-on-one meeting at 3:26 P.M. that day. It lasted an hour and eleven minutes. The conversation opened with remarks from Gorbachev, but when Reagan's turn came he immediately raised the issue of religion in Russia. He spoke of Muslims, Jews, Protestants, and Ukrainian Catholics, and insisted that all have a right to go to the church of their choice. If Gorbachev improved religious liberty, Reagan told him, he would greatly enhance his image worldwide and be viewed as a "hero."[50]

Gorbachev responded by claiming there was no serious problem with religion in Russia, though he acknowledged the earlier "excesses" after the Revolution. Reagan was not convinced. He invited Gorbachev to examine how religious rights were granted by the U.S. Constitution. The debate continued, lasting long enough that it comprised two and a half of the nine pages of official notes by the American note-taker—over a quarter of the conversation.[51]

By now, Mikhail Gorbachev could not have been blindsided by Reagan. At the summit in Washington six months earlier, his host had chosen unexpected moments to talk about religion. At one dinner for the Soviet general secretary he raised his glass to make a toast, invoking the Spirit of the approaching season without a hint of reluctance:

> General Secretary Gorbachev, you've declared that in your own country there is a need for greater *glasnost*, or openness, and the world watches expectantly and with great hopes to see this promise fulfilled. . . . Thomas Jefferson, one of our nation's great founders and philosophers, once said, "The God who gave us life, gave us liberty as well." He meant that we're born to freedom and that the need for liberty is as basic as the need for food. And he, as the great revolutionary he was, also knew that lasting peace would only come when individual souls have the freedom they crave. What better time than in this Christmas and Hanukkah season, a season of spirit you recently spoke to, Mr. General Secretary, when you noted the millennium of Christianity in your land and spoke of the hopes of your people for a better life in a world of peace. These are hopes shared by the people of every nation, hopes for an end to war; hopes, especially in this season, for the right to worship to the dictates of the conscience.[52]

Now, on Gorbachev's home turf, Reagan was even more intense. This Midwesterner turned Californian, who had lived through the Russian Civil War as a church boy in Dixon, unleashed a nonstop assault against religious repression throughout his Moscow visit.

DANILOV MONASTERY, SPASO HOUSE, AND THE FACETED CHAMBER

In one of his most personally enriching and exciting moments in Moscow, on the second day of the summit, Ronald Reagan emptied his soul in a meeting with religious leaders at the restored Danilov Monastery. Founded in 1282 and named for a canonized prince, the monastery was an oasis of Orthodox Christianity amid a spiritual desert.

From the outset, Reagan's remarks suggested his larger intent. "It's a very good pleasure to visit this beautiful monastery and to have a chance to meet some of the people who have helped make its return to the Russian Orthodox Church a reality," he began. "I am also addressing in spirit the 35 million believers whose personal contributions made this magnificent restoration possible."[53] He continued:

It's been said that an icon is a window between heaven and Earth through which the believing eye can peer into the beyond. One cannot look at the magnificent icons created, and re-created here under the direction of Father Zinon, without experiencing the deep faith that lives in the hearts of the people of this land. Like the saints and martyrs depicted in these icons, the faith of your people has been tested and tempered in the crucible of hardship. But in that suffering, it has grown strong, ready now to embrace with new hope the beginnings of a second Christian millennium.

We in our country share this hope for a new age of religious freedom in the Soviet Union. We share the hope that this monastery is not an end in itself but the symbol of a new policy of religious tolerance that will extend to peoples of all faiths. We pray that the return of this monastery signals a willingness to return to believers the thousands of other houses of worship which are now closed, boarded up, or used for secular purposes.[54]

In expressing his hopes for the USSR, Reagan was appealing to those travails that have rallied persecuted Christians for 2,000 years—the testing of faith, the hardship, suffering, and martyrdom that had marked the lives of the saints.

As was his custom, Reagan told his audience that Americans "feel it keenly when religious freedom is denied to anyone anywhere." He predicted that "soon all the Soviet religious communities that are now prevented from registering, or are banned altogether, including the Ukrainian Catholic and Orthodox Churches, will soon be able to practice their religion freely and openly and instruct their children in and outside the home in the fundamentals of their faith." He called the restoration of the monastery a "first" that he hoped would be followed by a "resurgent spring of religious liberty." He directly coaxed Gorbachev, this time on his home turf: "We may hope that *perestroika* will be accompanied by a deeper restructuring, a deeper conversion, a *mentanoya*, a change in the heart, and that *glasnost*, which means giving voice, will also let loose a new chorus of belief, singing praise to the God that gave us life."[55]

Citing a Solzhenitsyn quote that echoed the thoughts of De Tocqueville in *Democracy in America*, Reagan finished prayerfully:

There is a beautiful passage that I'd just like to read, if I may. It's from one of this country's great writers and believers, Aleksandr Solzhenitsyn, about the faith that is as elemental to this land as the dark and fertile soil. He wrote: "When you travel the byroads of central Russia, you begin to understand the secret of the pacifying Russian countryside. It is in the churches. They lift their belltowers—graceful, shapely, all different—high over mundane timber and thatch. From villages that are cut off and invisible to each other, they soar to the same heaven. People who are always selfish and often unkind—but the evening chimes used to ring out, floating over the villages, fields, and woods, reminding men that they must abandon trivial concerns of this world and give time and thought to eternity."

In our prayers we may keep that image in mind: the thought that the bells may ring again, sounding through Moscow and across the countryside, clamoring for joy in their newfound freedom.[56]

Predictably, the Soviet press took quick offense at Reagan's salvo from the monastery. "It is not quite appropriate to visit someone and to talk about problems in the host's home," complained one editorial. "To put it mildly, we were amazed by what we heard from the president. The same old lament about 'freedom of worship in the Soviet Union.' "[57] Most of the press appeared distinctly offended by Reagan's rhetoric, and tried to squash the message.

Two hours later, however, the rude guest from the Oval Office spoke again, this time from the U.S. ambassador's residence at Spaso House in Moscow. His audience included dignitaries and dissidents; the latter were summarily trashed the next day in *Izvestia* and especially *Pravda*, which printed a hate-filled hatchet job on the event on its front page—intended to discredit the invitees Reagan sought to honor.[58]

Unlike the monastery group, the Spaso House attendees were not a religious audience; they surely expected a secular message,[59] and for 90 percent of this quite formal address, that was what they got, as Reagan listed his human-rights priorities—his "four freedoms"—for the USSR.

But not entirely. "And here I would like to speak to you not as a head of government but as a man, a fellow human being," he told his audience. "I came here hoping to do what I could to give you strength." It was a line that may be unparalleled in the history of presidential rhetoric: Reagan seemed to be offering himself less as a political leader than as a prophet or even priest. Then, anchoring that redemptive vision within a broader spiritual structure, he ended extemporaneously with a religious apologetic:

> If I may, I want to give you one thought from my heart. Coming here, being with you, looking into your faces, I have to believe that the history of this troubled century will indeed be redeemed in the eyes of God and man, and that freedom will come to all. For what injustice can withstand your strength, and what can conquer your prayers? . . .
>
> Could I play a little trick on you and say something that isn't written here? Sometimes when I'm faced with an unbeliever, an atheist, I am tempted to invite him to the greatest gourmet dinner one could ever serve and, when we finished eating that magnificent dinner, to ask him if he believes there's a cook.
>
> Thank you all and God bless you.[60]

It was an odd way to close—a little abrupt, more oblique than Reagan usually was. Nonetheless the image was somehow vintage Reagan, his eye twinkling as he cast his gaze heavenward. It must have surprised the secular audience, this ad lib that amounted to a pitch for creationism.

But theologians would have recognized in Reagan's parable a variation on a story told in Christian circles, ascribed to the sixteenth–seventeenth century astronomer Johannes Kepler. As a Christian,

Kepler frequently argued with an atheist colleague, and one day he chose a creative apologetic to convince his friend that there was a Creator. Kepler constructed an elaborate, wondrous working model of the solar system, equipped with a sun encircled by rotating planets as well as moons moving around planets. When his unbelieving friend saw the model, he was amazed and asked who made it. *Nobody,* Kepler said. *It just happened. A strong wind must have come in one afternoon,* Kepler speculated fantastically, *and blown around a bunch of laboratory debris, dust, and other particles from outside. Somehow this elaborate model is the result.* When his friend asked if Kepler really expected him to believe such nonsense, the astronomer said *Of course not. And yet,* Kepler reprimanded his friend, *you're willing to believe that the actual solar system, with its unspeakable complexities, simply created itself. Now that is ridiculous.*

The Proletariat may have been taken aback by the American president's story, but not Gorbachev: Reagan had ended their first one-on-one meeting with the very same story.[61] (And the parable would stay with him even after he returned from his trip: a few weeks later he would tell it again, this time to a group of American evangelical students.)

Reagan's extemporaneous close to the Spaso House speech may have seemed a little awkward, even ill-fitting with the venue and the rest of the president's address. For Reagan, though, every word he spoke to the Soviet people was an opportunity to bring even a hint of religion to a spiritually starved nation. This particular event, he knew, was being broadcast on live television in the Soviet Union; with such an open opportunity to reach millions with a spiritual message, it's hard to imagine Ronald Reagan making any other choice.

Perhaps the huge Soviet television audience explained the swift denunciation of the speech that followed in the communist press. As a live message, Reagan's address couldn't be successfully censored by an evening blackout on *Vremya*, the TV news broadcast—so instead it was pilloried. Unlike the monastery talk, which was dismissed as a mere annoyance, the Spaso House speech was viewed, by one Soviet official's account, as "positively anti-Soviet."[62] And in a way that's precisely what it was.

DAY TWO OF THE MOSCOW SUMMIT ENDED WITH A dinner hosted by Mikhail Gorbachev at Granovitaya Palata, the Faceted Chamber of the ancient Palace of Facets. After the general secretary spoke, Reagan startled him with a few remarks of his own, and a gift: he handed Gorbachev a videotape of the 1956 Gary Cooper movie *Friendly Persuasion*.

The film concerns an Indiana Quaker family caught in the Civil War. The Quakers' faith teaches that war is not an option; they simply want to worship, farm, and live in peace. In a climactic scene, a Union major confronts the prayerful in their meeting house, pleading with them to fight for their lives and property. He asks the devout Cooper character what he would do if enemy troops threatened his wife and family. "If the test comes," Cooper answers stoically, "all I can say is I hope and pray I can be an instrument of the Lord. Let us pray that . . . we be given the strength and grace to follow His will."

Another key scene comes when Confederate raiders burn down the barn of a fellow Quaker. The vengeful Quaker debates Cooper over how to respond. Cooper's conscience is racked by thoughts of peace, war, and what God wants. Reagan, according to Gorbachev's translator, "plunged into a complicated discussion" of this scene.[63]

The president then raised his glass with a toast. And he did it again, shell-shocking his Soviet hosts by concluding, "God bless you."[64]

From Moscow State University to Gethsemane

On May 31, the third day of the summit, the president arrived at the Kremlin at 10:00 A.M. for a negotiating session with the general sec-retary. From there, the two leaders shifted to Red Square. Gorbachev tried to guide his counterpart toward Lenin's Tomb—but the presi-dent caught on and awkwardly offered a polite, if unconvincing, de-murral, putting his arm around Gorbachev and steering him away. As it had throughout his journey to the historically brutal communist state, Reagan's principles overruled any fatuous courtesies. Gor-bachev should not have expected the lifelong anti-communist to pay his respects to the cold, stiff Lenin; Reagan had none to give.

From there on, though, the tone of the day grew steadily more uplifting. The two men shared their famous afternoon stroll through Red Square, an emboldened St. Basil's Cathedral arching proudly heavenward in the background; the image of the two leaders seemed to symbolize the new era in U.S.-Soviet relations. That same day, Reagan gave an address on freedom to students at Moscow State Uni-versity, the alma mater of both Mikhail and Raisa Gorbachev. For Reagan, the speech would be the summit of the summit.

For months, Reagan and Secretary of State Shultz had pushed the Soviets to air the speech on state TV. Television was the Great Communicator's medium of choice; Reagan wanted the opportunity to address millions of Soviet citizens directly in their homes, just the way he reached the people of America. Gorbachev was inclined to accommodate the president, but Soviet officials bristled at the re-quest, knowing full well that Reagan would use the occasion to preach American values to the wide viewing audience. Especially wary of the president's tendency to sermonize, as he had in his 1986 and 1988 New Year's messages, the Soviet advisers preferred to limit any Reagan address to "safe" excerpts to be edited and broadcast at a later time.[65]

This pull-and-tug was recollected by Gorbachev's translator, Igor Korchilov, as he enthusiastically watched Reagan deliver the speech. "I wasn't disappointed," he observed. "It was a real tour de force by the president-turned-professor. . . . I think it may have been his finest oratorical hour. . . . It was one of the finest examples of oratory I had ever heard." "Like a real professor," said Korchilov, Reagan offered what amounted to an American civics lesson.[66]

Among America's finest freedoms, Reagan told his massive audience, was freedom of religion. He told the viewing audience that Americans "are one of the most religious peoples on Earth" and that if they should travel to "any American town" they would encounter "dozens of churches" and "families of every conceivable nationality worshiping together." Why were Americans so religious? Because, he told the Soviet students—whom he saw as the next generation of leaders—"they know that liberty, just as life itself, is not earned but a gift from God." And those Americans "seek to share that gift with the world."[67] As did, evidently, their president.

Reagan's sentiments were decidedly uncommon for the venue: atheism had been a mandatory course at Moscow State University, and its graduates were obliged to recite a profession of faith to the state upon receiving their diplomas.[68] Reagan spoke before a giant marble bust of Lenin, which towered atop a high yellow pedestal—so imposing that he later remembered it as fifty feet tall.[69] Before he began, the president turned back, looked once more at the angry Bolshevik's grim visage, and sighed; when the students gave him a standing ovation, Reagan later joked that he turned and saw the statue weep.[70]

Later that day Reagan returned to Spaso House, where he hosted a state dinner. In his toast to Gorbachev—the general secretary might have seen it coming—he made a stunning statement of religious symbolism. In a quivering, dramatic tone, he spoke mystically of "the voice":

> Mr. General Secretary . . . I believe . . . we both hear the same voice, the same overwhelming imperative. What that voice says can be expressed in many ways. But I have found it in vivid form in Pasternak's poem "The Garden of Gethsemane." Listen, if you will, to Pasternak's account of that famous arrest:
>
> "There appeared—no one knew from where—a crowd of slaves and a rabble of knaves, with lights and swords and, leading them, Judas with a traitor's kiss on his lips.
>
> "Peter repulsed the ruffians with his sword and cut off the ear of one of them. But he heard: 'You cannot decide a dispute with weapons; put your sword in its place, O man.' "
>
> That's the voice. "Put your sword in its place, O man." That is the imperative, the command. And so we will work together that we might forever keep our swords at our sides.[71]

It's hard to know whether Gorbachev could have appreciated what Reagan was talking about, beyond recognizing that it had something to do with Christianity and the putting down of swords—that is, weapons—in the interest of peace. Of course Reagan *was* talking about putting swords away, but he didn't need a story about Gethsemane to make that point. The subtext of Reagan's latest parable was that it *was* a parable—that it was an account from the gospel of Jesus Christ. Regardless of what Gorbachev comprehended in the moment, what really mattered to Reagan was that, once again, he was bringing a spiritual message to a much larger audience beyond the Soviet general secretary.

A FEAST OF THE TRINITY

Ronald Reagan dropped religious messages wherever he could during the trip, even after his major appearances were over. On the heels of his appearances at Spaso House and Moscow State University, one of these meaningful religious gestures was actually delivered by Nancy Reagan. Raisa Gorbachev took the First Lady on a tour through the Cathedral of the Assumption in the Kremlin. There, Nancy politely but openly inquired why the cathedral was no longer the center of worship it had once been—a very uncomfortable question for Raisa, who was a proud atheist. The next morning, Nancy awoke early and asked to see Russia's greatest icons—a collection of beautiful sacred works in the reserve collection of the Tretyakov Gallery that had been removed from public view by the communists. Her request was immediately granted, and her visit, too, was broadcast on Russian television—thereby giving the Russian people a glimpse of these hidden treasures for the first time in years.[72]

The fifth and final day of the summit, Thursday, June 2, ended with a brief farewell ceremony, held in the morning at St. George's Hall. The president had one last quick statement. In the spirit of St. George, he said, he hoped that with God's help peace and freedom would prevail, launching a new era in human history. He pointed out to the Gorbachevs that he had arrived five days earlier on a Sunday. In saying goodbye, he borrowed a Russian proverb—*Troitsa: ves' les raskroitsya*. This meant: At the feast of the Trinity on Sunday, the whole forest blossoms. Gorbachev's translator later said that while the proverb might have been known by Russian believers, it once again baffled the general secretary and atheist officials attending the ceremony. They were not, however, confused by the president's closing. For a final time, Reagan closed with the words "Thank you and God bless you."[73]

With that benediction Reagan's visit was over, his mission completed. He left behind a Kremlin bereft once more of divine discourse—though not for long.

GORBACHEV'S SOUL

Reagan was intensely interested in whether Mikhail Gorbachev was a Christian. According to Reagan press secretary Larry Speakes, the White House had received word prior to the summits that Gorbachev was known to invoke God's name in conversation—an unprecedented breach for a Soviet leader.[74] And both before and during the Moscow summit, Reagan found reason to suspect that the Soviet leader did hold some basic Christian beliefs, acquired in childhood.[75] That suspicion of a tiny fissure of faith within the monolith of Soviet atheism became a subject of fascination to Reagan the crusader.

Gorbachev himself invoked God's name on a number of occasions in Reagan's presence, typically in expressions like "only God knows" or "God help us."[76] It was a habit the president had noticed at the first summit in Geneva. In their first plenary meeting there, the head of the Evil Empire chimed in: "We have never been at war with each other. Let us pray God that this never happens."[77] Gorbachev dropped God's name again in a casual reference during his and Reagan's fireside chat at Geneva, and that evening struggled to borrow a Biblical quotation in an impromptu toast.[78] (In his reply toast, Reagan acknowledged Gorbachev's quotation and himself quoted a passage from Acts 16.)[79] Reagan actually counted these divine utterances, and a few months later admitted that they "stuck" in his mind and formed "a nagging question that won't go away."[80]

In a very telling incident, Mike Deaver describes how Reagan called him excitedly a week after his return from the Geneva summit for a debriefing. Deaver perceived a "festive tone" from Reagan that was "infectious." When Deaver arrived, he asked the president what he had learned about the Soviet leader in their time together. Reagan might have been expected to go on about Gorbachev's demeanor— his openness, his charm, even his concern over SDI. But Reagan responded by whispering two simple words: "He believes." Deaver knew what Reagan meant, but he also knew that religious believers didn't run the USSR. "Are you saying the general secretary of the Soviet Union believes in God?" Deaver asked. Reagan responded: "I don't know, Mike, but I honestly think he believes in a higher power."[81] To Reagan, at that moment, Gorbachev's religious beliefs were the paramount issue on his mind.

Two years later, at the Washington summit, Gorbachev would tell Reagan, "I am convinced it's God's will that we should cooperate."[82] The remark was noted at the time, but some have raised the possibility that the general secretary was exploiting Reagan's religious sympathies to benefit the USSR's negotiating position.[83] Reagan himself was not naïve to such tactics: In 1978, he had noted in a radio address that Leonid Brezhnev had been quoted as telling President Carter at their summit that God would never forgive them if they failed in their mission. "I'm sorry that I can't believe in his sincerity," said Reagan of Brezhnev at the time. "Indeed I think he was hypocritical and deliberately using the Lord's name to curry favor or soften up the President, who does believe in God as Brezhnev does not."[84]

So Reagan was likely to be on guard for tricks by a Soviet general secretary. The question remains: was such talk about the Almighty a deliberate tactic by Gorbachev, or was it genuine?

Reagan and Gorbachev did speak briefly about religion at the Geneva and Washington summits, a conversation that apparently went beyond small talk. As Reagan reported later, Gorbachev told him that his wife, Raisa, was an atheist—but that he himself had had the Bible read to him as a child by his Christian grandmother.[85]

Raisa Gorbachev was a Marxist-Leninist to the bone—a Lenin scholar who admired the Bolshevik leader's defiance of religion, and had actually taught a course on atheism herself. Transcripts declassified in May 2000 show that the Gorbachevs proudly described Raisa's atheistic credentials to the Reagans in a dinner conversation at Geneva.[86] The Reagans were unimpressed.

But the general secretary himself was another matter. "The president was convinced," Speakes remembered, that "the childhood exposure . . . had an influence" on Gorbachev.[87] Reagan noted that Gorbachev singled out Raisa as an atheist, but was noncommittal when it came to his own spiritual life—and for some reason felt compelled to admit that he'd been familiar with the Bible from childhood. As Gorbachev would report in another context, his mother, both of his grandmothers, and one grandfather were all Christians, and one grandmother was "deeply religious." She prayed for him, for Russia, and for the world. Perhaps even more telling, his one nonbelieving grandfather was a communist who nevertheless "considered it a personal obligation to respect believers." In his grandparents' house, a table with his grandmother's religious icons also featured portraits of Lenin and Stalin, forming a sort of icon corner/Lenin corner. Gorbachev's grandfather, in other words, offered an early model of peaceful coexistence—an example of religious tolerance that obviously had a lasting effect on the leader.

Former president Richard Nixon, long a student of communist ways himself, caught wind of Gorbachev's surprising comfort level with religion—and found it curious enough that he sent Reagan a letter on the subject. Nixon speculated that Reagan "sensed from the way" Gorbachev responded that "he was implying that he probably was not" an atheist. Nixon recalled an incident that occurred when he was at a Kremlin dinner Khrushchev hosted for him in 1959:

> Khrushchev was trying to impress me with the fact that he really had an open mind and was not just a doctrinaire Marxist. He looked down the table to where Vice Premier Koslov was sitting. Koslov had welcomed me at the airport with a typically bombastic tirade about the glories of communism. Khrushchev in an obviously contemptible manner said, "Comrade Koslov is a hopeless communist."
>
> I assumed that what he was trying to tell me was that he, Khrushchev who was then the top leader of the whole communist bloc, was *not* a hopeless communist! What all of this seems to indicate is that the Russians like to make points subtly, without directly admitting that they are not hewing to the straight party line. Whether in Gorbachev's case it is an act or a fact, of course, is something you will be able to judge far better than I.[88]

An act or a fact: alas, Reagan replied to Nixon's letter with a phone call, so we don't know what he concluded.[89] Either way, the president was an avid collector of intelligence about Gorbachev's beliefs. From Tip O'Neill, who met with Gorbachev as head of a congressional delegation to Moscow, he had learned that the general secretary was very upset with the "evil empire" remark. "[I]t seemed to upset him more than anything else," O'Neill reported.[90] All of this suggested to Reagan that the general secretary might be a "closet Christian."

Admittedly, Gorbachev has never been particularly clear about his spiritual faith. In a book published in 2000, long after he had any reason to drop misleading hints on the matter, he referred to *Homo sapiens* as "God's highest creation."[91] On the other hand, his book is entirely secular in its orientation. He quotes leading humanists and identifies them directly as such, and immediately after the *Homo sapiens* remark writes that "A return to age-old, spiritual, moral, life-affirming values, to a humanist and genuinely optimistic worldview is one of the decisive tasks of our era." If the book contains some passing evidence that Gorbachev believes in God, it offers a far more compelling case that New Age thinking has influenced him in later years.[92]

And yet the hints of Christian thinking in Gorbachev excited Reagan. Perhaps he figured that God might have chosen the Soviet leader, as he'd chosen Reagan and John Paul II, to help lead the nation out of spiritual bondage.

Reagan's and Gorbachev's Religious Openings

This we do know: Under Mikhail Gorbachev, religious faith in the USSR began to flourish. Of all the Soviet leaders, he was the only one who wasn't hostile to religion; in fact, Gorbachev halted seventy years of Soviet religious repression, sparking a genuine religious revival in Russia by the 1990s.

Whatever Gorbachev's true dispensation toward religion, there's a clear case to be made that Reagan's pressure influenced the religious changes Gorbachev made. The general secretary's first major reforms were set in motion in the spring of 1988, from April through June—precisely the period surrounding Reagan's full-court press.

In April, a month before Reagan's arrival for the summit, Gorbachev held an important symbolic meeting with the Patriarch Pimen and other church leaders. This step was widely publicized as the first encounter between a Communist Party leader and church leadership since WWII. Gorbachev gave his personal political blessing to the reopening of hundreds of Orthodox churches, as well as to the return of other sanctuaries, such as Moscow's Danilov Monastery and Kiev's Pechersky Monastery, which had been seized and held by the state since Stalin. In ceremonies broadcast to 150 million viewers on *Vremya*, the main evening newscast, the Kremlin museum returned religious relics to the Church, long after the Bolsheviks worked so hard to confiscate them. Only days after Reagan left Moscow, Gorbachev permitted a week of celebrations of the millennium of the Orthodox Church. While he didn't take part, his nonbelieving wife was a conspicuous participant at the main opening ceremonies held on June 10 at Moscow's Bolshoi Theater.[93]

In 1988 to 1989, the Orthodox Church opened 2,000 parishes all over the USSR, including two hundred new ones. The expansion of religious freedom was so intense that the church found itself at a loss for priests, and new seminaries and religious academies began opening to fill the need. The church's sphere in public activity expanded; church leaders were permitted to appear on TV, work in hospitals, run charitable organizations, meet with scholars, expand church activities, and even be elected to the Congress of People's Deputies.[94]

By 1992, American missionary Fred Mueller noted, religious freedom had been so fully restored in Russia that he was able to walk into a Russian public school or college, knock on a classroom door, ask the teacher if he could come in and share the Christian gospel message with students, and was frequently able to do so. "We had freedoms then in Russia that didn't even exist in America," recalls Mueller, "particularly in public schools."[95]

By the end of 1988, even Reagan was regularly commenting on these early improvements in Russia—although he made clear that there was still a long way to go. How directly did his pressure on Gorbachev lead to these changes? Gorbachev has never said outright whether Reagan was a motivation in his actions. His religious liberalization was at least partly a component of the general improvement ushered in by glasnost. But Reagan himself seemed to conclude that his actions may have made a difference.

In recalling his May-June 1988 trip in his memoirs, for instance, the former president put particular emphasis on the human-rights objectives he'd held for Russia, particularly in the realm of religious freedom. He noted that he tried to link that goal to any help he offered to the USSR in economics and trade. "At our first session alone [at the Moscow Summit], Gorbachev again expressed his desire for increased U.S.-Soviet trade," he remembered. "I was ready for him. I'd thought about what I was going to say when he brought up the issue: One reason we have trouble increasing trade with your country, I said, was that many members of Congress as well as many other Americans oppose it because of what they consider Soviet human rights abuses." He went on by singling out religious freedom:

> "Our people have diverse backgrounds," I told Gorbachev, "but they are united when they see any people discriminated against simply because of their ethnic origin or religious belief." Then I raised an issue that had been on my mind for a long time: religious freedom in the Soviet Union. "This isn't something I'm suggesting we negotiate," I told him, "just an idea. I'm not trying to tell you

how to run your country, but I realize you are probably concerned that if you allow too many of the Jews who want to emigrate from the Soviet Union to leave, there'll be a 'brain drain,' a loss of skilled people from your economy. [According to estimates I'd seen, something like 400,000 to 500,000 Jews wanted to leave the Soviet Union.] I can see where this could present problems. These people are part of your society and many of them must have important jobs. But did it ever occur to you, on this whole question of human rights, that maybe if the Jews were permitted to worship as they want to and teach their children the Hebrew language, that maybe they wouldn't want to leave the Soviet Union?

"That's how our country was started, by people who were not allowed to worship as they wished in their homeland, so they came to our shores, a wilderness across the Atlantic, and founded our nation. I'm sure a lot of your people who are asking to leave wouldn't want to leave if they had freedom of religion. They say they want to leave, but they're Russians. I know they must love their country as much as other Russians do, so perhaps if they were allowed to reopen their synagogues and worship as they want to, they might decide that they wouldn't have to leave and there wouldn't be that problem of a brain drain."[96]

Reagan stopped short of claiming credit for the religious revival in the USSR, but he made his own suspicions clear: "Whether my words had any impact or not I don't know, but after that the Soviet government began allowing more churches and synagogues to reopen."[97]

There's little doubt that Reagan had a positive impact on religion in the USSR, though without Gorbachev's relative openness toward religion it's hard to believe any American president would have made much headway in the matter. In 2000, Gorbachev wrote that under glasnost and perestroika "a firm course was taken toward freedom of conscience. I based this on my belief that religious people are worthy of respect." He added: "Religious faith is an intensely private matter"—in the USSR, of course, that was the only option for believers—"and each citizen should have the unqualified right to his or her own choice."[98]

Ultimately, neither Reagan nor Gorbachev alone reopened church doors in the waning days of the Soviet Union. Nonetheless, without Reagan's years of political pressure—and his extraordinary overtures to the Soviet people in Moscow in 1988—Gorbachev may never have felt compelled to effect change as swiftly and completely as he did. Of course, what made the difference was the convergence of these two leaders at the right moment in history—a convergence Reagan, at least, might have ascribed to the hand of Providence.

TESTIMONY

The true measure of Reagan's impact on religious freedom in the USSR might be found in the testimony of the Russian people themselves, especially in the wake of the Moscow summit.

Most Soviet citizens had never known anything but atheism. And yet it's surprising how warmly even nonbelievers seemed to greet Reagan's religious overtures. "I'm not religious," one Muscovite woman assured an interviewer, "but I was delighted to hear [Reagan] end his speeches by saying 'God bless you.' We never heard it said before on television."[99] That much was certainly true: prior to Gorbachev's changes in 1988 and 1989, church leaders had not appeared on Soviet TV.[100] Daniil Granin, a Russian novelist whose *Bison* was one of the major books in Russia in 1987, said of Reagan, "One thing pleased me especially—his religiousness. Hearing religious vocabulary from a politician is something we're not used to."[101]

Word of Reagan's mission had reached some in the Soviet Union long before he arrived in Moscow. Among them were Anatoly Sharansky, the Russian Jew and former Soviet prisoner who met with Reagan near the end of his term in office.[102] Sharansky's time in prison was marked not merely by periods of isolation and hunger strikes but also special interrogation and indoctrination. "They wanted to use me to destroy the two groups I worked for," he said, "Jews who hoped to leave for Israel and dissidents who spoke out on behalf of human rights."[103]

During his prison stay, Sharansky fell in with his old camp friend Volodia Poresh—a Christian. Sharansky's portrait of Poresh recalls Solzhenitsyn's Alyoshka, the imprisoned Baptist in *One Day in the Life of Ivan Denisovich*. Both Alyoshka and Poresh drew support and peace of mind through their religious faith, standing out among the other poor souls in the gulag.[104]

Poresh endured hunger and work strikes in an attempt to get his Bible back from prison authorities. He and others were surprised when he actually got it back by the end of 1983. It was impossible to know why the KGB allowed the Bible. In any case, Sharansky followed suit and decided not to let the occasion pass without trying to obtain a Bible of his own. Though he failed, he was able to read the Bible with his Christian friend. He and Poresh began their Bible study every morning after returning from the exercise yard, reading both the Old and New Testament and discussing what they read.

The two men called their Bible sessions "Reaganite readings." Sharansky explained why they chose the name:

First, because President Reagan had declared either this year or the preceding one (it wasn't exactly clear from the Soviet press) the Year of the Bible, and second, because we realized that even the slightest improvement in our situation could be related only to a firm position on human rights by the West, especially by America, and we mentally urged Reagan to demonstrate such resolve.[105]

Even in the gulag, Sharansky and his fellow inmates had heard Reagan's call to religious freedom. Reagan had attracted scorn among both American leftists and Soviet leaders for his Year of the Bible initiative in 1983; on one Moscow radio program, a commentator from *Literaturnaya Gazeta* countered that it ought to be declared "the Year of Karl Marx." And yet to religious dissidents in the USSR, Reagan's Year of the Bible was an inspiration. Dutch Reagan, who had led his own Bible study groups in Dixon in the 1920s, must have been thrilled.

Reagan eventually learned what such actions meant to people like Sharansky and his Christian friend. On July 13, 1988, six weeks after the Moscow summit, he received a letter from a group of Soviet dissidents. "Mr. President," they wrote, "We can hardly envisage the struggle for human rights without a struggle for the national rights of nations. And as today, so in the future, the freedom of nations is one of the main guarantees for human rights. We are convinced that the true history is not written on paper but in the hearts of people, and the good Lord reads these." Reagan was personally assured by Sharansky, Armando Valladares (a longtime prisoner of Castro's gulag), and others that the messages of religious tolerance he had broadcast from America and Moscow could be heard, in Reagan's words, in the "remote dungeons of the Communist world."[106]

A week and a half before he left the Oval Office for the last time, Reagan presented Sharanksy with a Congressional Gold Medal. During the ceremony, Sharansky told Reagan that if he should ever encounter any "sad moments" after leaving the presidency, he should think of Sharansky's "happy family," and of the "thousands and thousands of people who are praying—in Soviet camps." And he thanked Reagan on behalf of the Soviet citizens who were "free today not because of some good will of Soviet leaders but because of their struggle and your struggle."[107]

19.

Rendezvous

"The Lord is faithful. . . . And there is Victory
ahead for all who make their resolves and do not
grow weary."

—*Rev. Ben Cleaver, closing line of 1924*
statement to the Dixon church[1]

"We must all thank God that we have been
allowed, each of us according to our stations, to
play a part in making these days memorable in
the history of our race."

—*Ronald Reagan in Oxford, borrowing from*
Churchill, December 4, 1992[2]

A s Air Force One left Moscow, Ronald Reagan took a measure of
comfort and fulfillment in what he had accomplished at the
summit. It had been a long sojourn from Dixon to Moscow, and the
prospects for faith in the evil empire suddenly seemed brighter. Rea-

gan had not remained silent; he had found a way to speak for the voiceless. In the spirit of Dick Walker and his own mother, he had acted as a practical Christian.

Reagan had begun 1988 by asking "Is there any truth that gives more strength than knowing that God has a special plan for each of us?"[3] And even after his success in Moscow, he continued his efforts to fulfill that plan. With the final year of his presidency only half over, he stopped in Britain on his way home from Moscow.

Spiritually speaking, Britain and the United States had an obvious common heritage. Britain had a proud record of religious freedom, extending back from Wycliffe and the Protestant Reformation, through Wesley and Tyndale, to modern-day practical Christians like William Wilberforce, J. R. R. Tolkien, and C. S. Lewis. Yet by the 1980s, as Reagan well knew, that record was obscured by the nation's dwindling number of professing believers: by June of 1988, the United Kingdom was arguably in greater need of a spiritual revival than America.

Like many of Western Europe's social democracies, Britain had seen religion wane among its people in recent decades. Fewer than 20 percent of Britons said they believed in God, and fewer than 10 percent attended church regularly—a rate much lower than in America. Labour Party leader Neil Kinnock, who stood to succeed Margaret Thatcher as prime minister if the Tories should lose, was an avowed atheist, and his electorate didn't hold it against him.

In short, Britain in 1988 was symptomatic of what Reagan meant when he had long lamented that "the world is crying out for a spiritual revival."[4] Indeed, he saw a need throughout Europe and lent a hand when he could. In one case involving the especially secular nation of France, Reagan asked a favor of President François Mitterand:

that he meet with Billy Graham, Reagan's emissary to the California legislature two decades earlier.[5]

In Britain on that June 3, 1988, Reagan was scheduled to speak to members of the august Royal Institute of International Affairs in London—and God and communism were still on his mind. His audience knew, of course, that Reagan had just exited the Moscow summit. But it's hard to imagine that many of them recognized his remarks for what they were—a kind of valedictory sermon, teeming with religious fervor and capturing everything Reagan's spiritual crusade had been about.

He began the speech by quoting favored words from the prophet Isaiah, as he had five years earlier in the Evil Empire speech: "He giveth power to the faint, and to them that have no might, he increased their strength, but they that wait upon the Lord shall renew their strength. They shall mount up with wings as eagles. They shall run and not be weary."[6] He might have been speaking of those in the gulag. But he was also invoking the faith of the American people, of his British hosts, and of crusaders for liberty everywhere—himself among them.

Six decades earlier, Ben Cleaver had spoken similar words to the Reagan family's Dixon congregation: "God is not wearied; why should we be?" Following God's way, he told them, would ensure victory: "The Lord is faithful. . . . And there is Victory ahead for all who make their resolves and do not grow weary." "His leading is ever onward," said Ben, "and the victory of faith is assured us if we follow bravely on."[7] Now it was as if Ben Cleaver's ghost had entered the fifteenth-century Guildhall where Reagan spoke.

The message Reagan drew from Isaiah's words that day was revealing. "Here, then, is our formula for completing our crusade for freedom," he continued, once again drawing a direct link between God and his global crusade. "Here is the strength of our civilization and our belief in the rights of humanity. Our faith is in a higher law." Yes, he added, "we believe in prayer and its power." And, "like the Founding Fathers" in both the United States and Great Britain—and unlike the founders of the empire he just left—"we hold that humanity was meant not to be dishonored by the all-powerful state, but to live in the image and likeness of Him who made us."[8]

In his remarks that day, Reagan came full circle from the promise he had made in his "Time for Choosing" speech in October 1964: "More than five decades ago, an American President [FDR] told his generation that they had a rendezvous with destiny; at almost the same moment, a Prime Minister [Churchill] asked the British people for their finest hour." United, the American and British people had taken that charge from their leaders to the totalitarian enemy. "This rendezvous," Reagan now said, "this finest hour, is still upon us."[9] *He* was now the leader exhorting Brits and Americans to continue the battle against the enemy of totalitarianism—an enemy whose Nazi brown had simply been replaced by Bolshevik red.[10]

Reagan concluded his remarks that day with a simple call to higher mission: "Let us seek to do His will in all things, to stand for freedom, to speak for humanity."[11] Among all his recorded speeches, it is difficult to find one that had better encapsulated his thinking. In his closing words he had cited Scripture, drew upon the guidance of God in what he called his "crusade for freedom," invoked a higher law, and commended both American and British Founding Fathers for their wisdom in appealing to that higher law.

Most tellingly, he had reminded listeners of their shared rendezvous with destiny. It was a point he had made not only in "A Time for Choosing," but in his nomination acceptance speech in July 1980.

Speaking with a palpable awareness that he would indeed soon be president, Reagan had quoted Thomas Paine—"We have it in our power to begin the world all over again"—and followed his words with the reminder that "I believe, too, we have a rendezvous with destiny."[12] The Republican faithful were no doubt reminded of Reagan's October 1964 speech; now, in 1988, they were reminded again.

Ronald Reagan led America during a pivotal moment in history—the closing of a struggle between the two competing systems that dominated the modern world for nearly a century.[13] He took it upon himself to confront the Soviet empire, and the Marxist-Leninist ideal that motivated it, more forthrightly than any American leader before him. And he did so in fulfillment of a role he believed God had assigned to America. By the end of 1991, there was no longer any question about the outcome: Soviet communism lay smoldering on the ash-heap of history Reagan had foreseen.

THE FINAL RENDEZVOUS

Aleksandr Solzhenitsyn, the author of *The Gulag Archipelago*, recognized Reagan's contribution to the defeat of communism. "I rejoice that the United States at last has a president such as you," he said to Reagan, "and I unceasingly thank God that you were not killed by that villainous bullet."[14]

Reagan must have delighted in that remark from a man he admired so much. No doubt he also thanked God for standing by him along the road from Dixon to Moscow, from the solitude of those endless Illinois apartments in the 1910s and 1920s to the remote atheistic Soviet Union in 1988.

From his earliest days in the public eye, Reagan sensed that he was called to bigger things. In his first inaugural address as governor, he had invoked the words of Benjamin Franklin: "He who introduces into public office the principles of primitive Christianity will change the face of the world."[15] In June 1968, he told an audience at the Indiana state fairgrounds:

> In the days just ahead, whether we like it or not, you and I are going to write a page in history. It can describe the rise and fall of the United States of America or it can be a recital of our finest hour. Men will live a thousand years in the shadow of our decision.[16]

In the last line of his second inaugural address as president, he declared that God was calling upon Americans "to pass" that "dream of human freedom" to "a waiting and hopeful world."[17]

In Reagan's vision, God's plan for America long predated him. It was in place from the days of the Mayflower Compact; it was there with Winthrop on the Arabella, with Bradford and the settlers, with the founders at Philadelphia. The divine plan would continue into the Cold War years, as America faced the challenge posed by Soviet Bolshevism. America plainly was "the last best hope of man on earth"—as Reagan had told the young women graduating from William Woods College in 1952.[18] And within that grand scheme, he, of course, had his own role—one that included a Christianity to be used, not put on a shelf.

In a speech at Oxford University in 1992, after communism and the USSR were consigned to history's dustbin, Reagan borrowed from Churchill:

> We must all thank God that we have been allowed, each of us according to our stations, to play a part in making these days memorable in the history of our race.[19]

The part Reagan played in ending the Cold War—thereby securing liberty for millions of oppressed members of the human race—will remain his enduring legacy.

For now, however, Ronald Reagan continues a lonely drift to that ultimate rendezvous with his maker. He began life as a lonely boy in Illinois, surrounded by strangers, a caring woman, and a source of stability in a God ever at his side. Today he ends it the same way, with Nancy as his caretaker, and a faith that sustained him for more than nine decades. Still now, he is never alone.

Epilogue

Ronald Reagan's path to the presidency, as we've seen, was marked by a series of extraordinary public speeches. In each, he made impassioned and meaningful references to his faith. From "A Time for Choosing" in 1964, through his Republican convention speeches, his four inaugural addresses, and his Farewell Address from the Oval Office, he carried on a tradition begun at his very first "presidential" speaking engagement, as president of his high-school senior class: he made sure that God was invited. His final two public statements were no exception.

In his August 1992 address to the Republican convention—as many guessed at the time, it would be his farewell speech to the nation—Reagan made five references to God or Christ. He connected his "God-given optimism" to the Shining City. And he closed: "And finally, my fellow Americans, may every dawn be a great new beginning for America, and every evening bring us closer to that Shining City Upon a Hill." He signed off for himself and Nancy: "My fellow Americans, on behalf of both of us, goodbye, and God bless each and every one of you, and God bless this country we love."[1]

Reagan's last public act was his November 5, 1994, letter informing the world that Alzheimer's disease—a foe every bit as malevolent as Soviet communism—was inexorably carrying him into "the sunset of my life." In that brief letter to the American people, he mentioned God and faith four times. "When the Lord calls me home," he wrote, "I will leave with the greatest love for this country of ours and eternal optimism for its future." For the final public time, he concluded, "May God always bless you." It was a fitting goodbye.

While he was president, Ronald Reagan's religious faith was, at best, dismissed or ridiculed. For me personally, it has been a moving experience to discover, and help bring to light, this overlooked side of the historical Reagan—a side he would have wanted to be recognized.

In the course of putting this book together, I had countless conversations with Reagan associates in California and around the country. At first I always asked simply, "Well, how's he doing?" The responses were rarely encouraging. Like the man's disease, the answers kept getting worse.

Long before it consumed him, Reagan understood and denounced the scourge of Alzheimer's disease. He made eight separate statements on Alzheimer's as president—an average of one for each year in the White House.[2] It is chilling to read those words today. In his final presidential statement on the disease, made November 5, 1988—six years to the day, eerily, before his farewell letter to the nation—he spoke words that could have described his own condition in those final years:

Alzheimer's disease ranks among the most severe of afflictions, because it strips people of their memory and judgment and robs them of the essence of their personalities. As the brain progressively deteriorates, tasks familiar for a lifetime, such as tying a shoelace or making a bed, become bewildering. Spouses and children become strangers. Slowly, victims of the disease enter profound dementia.[3]

Reagan knew well that that his own mother, Nelle, had ebbed away from what doctors at the time still called "senility"; today it would likely be diagnosed as Alzheimer's. As Moon's wife, Bessie Reagan, wrote in a letter two years before Nelle's death, "She [Nelle] has become so senile that it is necessary to have someone stay with her all the time. It is so too bad for she was so good and did so much for others."[4]

Nelle and her boy would share not only the same faith but the same fate. And, just as Dutch had felt that Nelle's passing was for the best, Reagan's own son carries on his father's faith and optimism. "I know where my dad is going," says Michael Reagan. "When he dies, I'll have no reason to be sad. I'll be saddened that he'll be leaving this place. But I'm overjoyed over where he's going. I guarantee he would be overjoyed—thrilled."[5]

AT ONE POINT IN LATE 2002, AS REAGAN'S CLOSEST friends and family struggled to cope with the fact that he no longer recognized them, I received an e-mail from Floyd Brown, director of the West Coast headquarters of the Young America's Foundation, which owns and operates the ranch that Reagan once cherished. For some time, it was known that Reagan's physical health had outlasted his mental awareness; now, however, Brown informed me that Reagan's body was slowly going as well. Later that day I spoke face-to-face with a longtime California conservative and Reaganite Cold Warrior, who described how even in his frailty Reagan had one day mustered the cognizance to take his secret service agent's strong hand, pull it to his lips, and kiss it in appreciation. "Can you believe it?" the man asked me. Looking heavenward, he lifted his hands and wondered: "Where's God?"

It was not the first time I'd heard the question. The previous year, driving through Pittsburgh, I had heard a radio talk-show host convey the latest news on the former president's unhappy condition, and then demand aloud: "God, please take Ronald Reagan!" Michael Reagan, too, wished for an end to his father's suffering. "I sit with him, grab his hand, and silently pray," he said. "I pray that God takes him and relieves him of his situation."

I understood the thought. In those waning days, images of the vigorous Reagan felt almost too painful to recall: the robust young lifeguard who pulled seventy-seven swimmers from the swirling Rock River in Lowell Park; the actor who became one of Hollywood's most winning faces in the 1940s; the stirring campaigner for Republican causes, who lent his emotional resonance to Barry Goldwater's cause. I thought particularly of a clip I'd watched of Reagan sparring with Robert F. Kennedy in a nationally televised debate on Vietnam, a moment now all but forgotten by the annals of history. Even in the 1980s, when he was in his seventies, Reagan's physical presence always enhanced his air of resolve: from his denunciation of the USSR in that first press conference, to his performance before a joint session of Congress following the assassination attempt, to the Evil Empire and Berlin Wall addresses—not to mention the foreign summits at Geneva, Reykjavik, and that moment when he stood in Red Square with his arm around Gorbachev—Reagan's unmistakable energy had never failed to move his audiences.

In Reagan's twilight years, then, the question of God's continued presence in his life weighed heavily on my own mind. But I remembered what Reagan had told the party faithful at the Republican convention in New Orleans in August 1988: "I'm grateful to God for blessing me with a good life and a long one." And though this was now clearly Reagan's time to suffer, I saw no reason to conclude that God wasn't there with him. "[W]hen we die is God's business," he had told his daughter Patti years before. In the words of his son Michael: "God does what He believes is best. My dad always believed that."[6] As Reagan himself wrote in 1982 to a friend whose wife had just died: "It isn't given to us to understand the why of such things. We can only trust in God's infinite mercy and in His purpose that we go on to a better life where there is no pain or sorrow. Believe in that and have faith in His wisdom."[7]

Like his mother, as a boy Ronald Reagan sometimes expressed his thoughts in poetry. At the age of seventeen, he captured his feeling of eternal hope in a poem he called "Life." A few lines from that poem seem especially fitting as Reagan's passing approaches:

> [W]hy does sorrow drench us
> When our fellow passes on?
> He's just exchanged life's dreary dirge
> For an eternal life of song.
>
> What . . . makes us weep at the journey's end?
> Weep when we reach the door
> That opens to let us in
> And brings to us eternal peace
> As it closes again on sin.
>
> Millions have gone before us,
> And millions will come behind,
> So why do we curse and fight
> At a fate both wise and kind?[8]

God's final fate for all of us, Reagan believed, is one both wise and kind. The eternal optimist in him would likely have found a spiritual answer—a comforting one—even for the kind of death that conquered him. He told friends and loved ones that death was merely a window to something better. Some six decades after he wrote this poem, he and Nancy were returning to the White House from the funeral of the First Lady's mother in Phoenix. As they flew aboard Air Force One, a speechwriter asked him how Mrs. Reagan was holding up. The president noted that she was quite upset. To console her, he said: "I just told Nancy that the Lord closed the door to this life and opened the door to a new life, and had her mother join Him."[9]

Reagan had come to terms with his own mother's death in much the same way. In a November 1962 letter to a friend, he said of Nelle's recent passing: "in a way it was for the best." There was, he assured, "no pain or distress."[10] Death, to him, was simply that final "twist" or "fork" in the road Reagan incessantly spoke of: as Nelle had taught him, when things seemed bad it was likely just a precursor to brighter skies. He might have viewed even his own death the same way—as a transition to something better, a step through that eternal window, the denouement of God's plan. No matter how completely Ronald Reagan was compromised by the evil of Alzheimer's, the disease could never take that away from him.

AFTERWORD

On Saturday afternoon, June 5, 2004, Ronald Reagan lay unconscious. He had been suffering from pneumonia for two weeks, and from Alzheimer's for ten years. Most Alzheimer's victims succumb within four to five years of being diagnosed, but Dutch's strong body, so long a blessing, was now a curse. Earlier that morning Nancy Reagan told longtime friend Mike Wallace of CBS News: "This is it."

At Reagan's bedside were Nancy, son Ron, and daughter Patti; a doctor and nurse were nearby to measure the patient's struggling breathing. His breath soon grew heavy and labored. Then something shocking happened: At the last moment, Ronald Reagan's eyes somehow opened one final time, and he stared directly at the love of his life, at Nancy, with eyes that had not opened for days. "They weren't chalky or vague," said Patti. "They were clear and blue and full of love, and then they closed with his last breath."[1] Ron confirmed: "[L]iterally, with his last breath, he turned his head, opened his eyes wide, and . . . looked right at my mother, and then he was gone." Ron recalled that his father had once written to Nancy that he wanted her to be the first thing he saw every morning and the last thing he ever saw—that is precisely what happened.[2]

Stunned, sobbing, Nancy summoned a handful of parting words, telling her husband that his goodbye glance was the greatest gift he could have given her; then she told him, "I love you." Just a month earlier, Nancy had stoically admitted that "Ronnie's long journey has finally taken him to a distant place where I can no longer reach him."[3] Now, Nancy's husband of fifty-two years had somehow reached *her*, one final time.

Dr. Gary Small, an Alzheimer's specialist from nearby UCLA, was asked if it was possible that a man who years earlier stopped recognizing his family could recognize Nancy when death called. Small said it was "certainly possible," explaining that at the end-stage of the disease there have been instances where there seems to be a sense of recognition.[4] The explanation seemed more providential than scientific, as if God in His never-ending grace had granted Ronald Reagan one last look of appreciation to the woman who cared for him all those years, who held his hand until the very end.

The clock at the Reagan home in the Bel Air section of Los Angeles announced the time of death as 1:00 P.M. Pacific time. Michael Reagan hurried to get there before the end, but he arrived too late. Still, he was the first Reagan child to issue a press release, which read:

> I remember with great clarity my father's emotion when Nelle Reagan, my grandmother, passed away. Until today I didn't understand the feeling of loss and pain which comes when a parent leaves you. . . .
>
> He played an important role in pointing me to God. . . . The greatest gift my father ever gave me was the simple knowledge that I would see him in heaven one day.[5]

A press release also immediately followed from Reagan's spiritual partner William P. Clark. As he did so often, Clark extolled Reagan's commitment to life, from defending the voiceless in the womb to the voiceless in communist dungeons of Eastern Europe and the USSR. Clark called Reagan "a defender of the innocent, young and old alike."[6]

Thoughts were also shared that day by Orland, Illinois, Park Police Chief Timothy McCarthy, the secret serviceman who in March 1981 had taken a bullet for the president, turning himself into a human shield as John Hinckley's bullets zipped toward Reagan. "It's a sad day for the country," said McCarthy, whose brave actions had ensured eight years in the White House for Ronald Reagan, not to mention another two decades of life.[7]

Flags everywhere were lowered to half-mast. At ballparks and the Belmont Stakes, spectators bowed their heads in moments of silence. Tributes flowed in from all around the world.

From Paris, a traveling President George W. Bush announced, "A great American life has come to an end." Reagan had left behind "a nation he restored and a world he helped save." Because of Reagan's leadership, said Bush, the world laid to rest an era of fear and tyranny; now Americans would lay their leader to rest. He concluded: "He always told us that for America, the best was yet to come. We comfort ourselves in the knowledge that this is true for him, too. His work is done, and now a shining city awaits him. May God bless Ronald Reagan."[8]

Bush's predecessor, President Bill Clinton, remarked: "It is fitting that a piece of the Berlin Wall adorns the Ronald Reagan Building in Washington." He was joined by fellow Democrats, Senator Bob Graham of Florida, who called Reagan "a man who changed history," and

Senator Ted Kennedy of Massachusetts, who said that the 40th president "will be honored as the president who won the Cold War."[9]

This new consensus on Reagan's legacy seemed to be shared even in quarters that once treated him with skepticism. In the *Washington Post*, a newspaper hardly sympathetic to the president in the 1980s, David E. Hoffman's page-one story on Reagan's death was titled simply "Hastening an End to the Cold War."[10] NBC's Tim Russert agreed that Reagan's legacy was "winning the Cold War." Russert said that by challenging the Soviets to an arms buildup they couldn't match, Reagan had forced Mikhail Gorbachev to "reform" and the Kremlin to "cry uncle."[11]

For his part, Mikhail Gorbachev sent a letter to Nancy Reagan, telling her: "Your husband has earned a place in history and in people's hearts."[12] He told reporters: "I take very hard the death of Ronald Reagan."[13]

Religious leaders came forward with reflections and new information. Billy Graham confirmed that Reagan had been one of his "closest personal friends for many years" and that he and his wife had "hundreds of hours of conversation" with the Reagans. He described visiting with Reagan on "numerous occasions in recent years." Unknown to reporters, Graham had often visited Reagan as he lay suffering; though Reagan was unable to respond, Nancy told Graham softly, "When you prayed, I think he knew you were here."[14]

D. James Kennedy, a prominent evangelical, told of a private exchange he had with Reagan in 1980. He asked the governor, "If you were to die and stand before God and He were to say to you, 'Why should I let you into My Heaven?' what would you say?" Kennedy said Reagan acted as if he had been punched in the gut. He doubled over, put his head down, and stayed in that position for forty-five seconds. Slowly, Reagan sat up and replied somberly, "I don't deserve to go to

Heaven. The only thing I could say would be, 'For God so loved the world, that He gave his only begotten Son, that whosoever believeth in Him should not perish, but have everlasting life.' "[15]

From the Holy See, Vatican spokesman Joaquin Navarro-Valls said that Pope John Paul II, the man Reagan partnered with to undermine the Soviet grip on Poland, recalled Reagan's contribution to "the historical events that changed the lives of millions of people, especially in Europe." Philadelphia Archbishop Emeritus Cardinal Anthony Bevilacqua, who hosted Reagan at the Cardinal's residence in 1988, called Reagan "a stalwart advocate for protecting the most vulnerable—the unborn human person."[16]

From Israel, Anatoly "Natan" Sharansky, now free to express his opinions and faith, remembered a day in March 1983 when he was confined to his eight-by-ten-foot prison cell in Siberia. Sharansky's jailers allowed him the privilege of reading the latest *Pravda*. There, splashed across the front page, was a condemnation of Reagan's description of the USSR as evil. Using Morse code, Sharansky tapped out the president's missive to the next cell, from where it was sent around the camp via walls and toilets. "We dissidents were ecstatic," said Sharansky. "Finally, the leader of the free world had spoken the truth—a truth that burned inside the heart of each and every one of us."[17]

An intriguing story was told by Dr. Roger Peele, chief psychiatrist for Montgomery County, Maryland, who divulged a secret he carried for decades: That Reagan had forgiven John Hinckley—and even, similar to Pope John Paul II, had wanted to forgive his would-be assassin in person. As a result, in 1983, he tried to arrange a private meeting. Hinckley was at St. Elizabeth's Hospital, a Washington psychiatric facility, where Roger Peele was the head of psychiatry. Peele discussed the option with Reagan. "[H]e really wanted to do it," Peele recalled more than twenty years later. But Reagan "said he only wanted to do what was in Mr. Hinckley's best interests," and when Peele advised against the meeting, the president accepted his decision. When Hinckley's lawyer, Barry Levine, learned of the revelation, he remarked that it demonstrated "the magnanimity of the president, a man of grace, great grace."[18]

Over the next few days after Reagan's death, Americans witnessed an outpouring of emotion for a president that had not been seen since the deaths of John F. Kennedy and Franklin Delano Roosevelt. Little-noticed by American eyes was the affection that poured from the former Soviet bloc and former USSR. These former "captive peoples" now had uncensored voices, and they stepped up to pay tribute to the man that many of them credit for their freedom.

In Romania, unshackled from the chains of the Iron Curtain and dictator Nicolae Ceauşescu, one newspaper editorialized Reagan as "The political leader who contributed the most to the fall of the totalitarian communist system."[19] Romanian President Iliescu stated: "Romanians highly praise President Reagan for his decisive contribution to the end of the Cold War and to paving Romania's way towards a United Europe."[20]

From liberated Estonia, a former Soviet Baltic nation, a writer named Juri Estam wrote a piece titled "Ronald Reagan: the late 'President of Eastern Europe.' " Ronald Reagan, said Estam, "will be gratefully remembered by all of Eastern Europe as 'our American President.' May he rest in peace."[21]

In unified Berlin, Germany, a proposal was immediately offered to name a square or a street after Reagan.[22]

In free Prague, former Czech president Václav Havel said he was deeply moved by the news of Reagan's death, calling him a man who "undoubtedly contributed to the fall of Communism." The nation's current president, Václav Klaus, added: "He was certainly one of the greatest statesmen of the recent era. I think that without him, the end of the communist regime would not have been so fast and even would not have been so calm as it really was."[23]

Also from the former communist bloc, encomiums came from Hungary. In the *Budapest Business Journal*—its mere existence a symbol of the triumph of Reagan's ideals—one Hungarian wrote: "Everyone doing business in the free markets of Central and Eastern Europe, or voting in their democratic elections, owes it all to Ronald Reagan. Or, if that's too eulogistic, let's just say 90% of it."[24] The business journal printed another testimony claiming that if Ronald Reagan had been president in 1956, during the Hungarian uprising, Hungarians might have achieved freedom decades sooner:

> I always hoped that finally the forces of freedom would defeat the empire of lies, which tried to wash the brain of every citizen. I genuinely thought my country was in the deadly grip of the Devil. That is why Reagan's fervent anti-communism, his hard line in dealing with the "Evil Empire" . . . made me his unconditional supporter and admirer.
>
> Reagan was one of the greatest statesmen who ever served the United States. At present, every country of the former Eastern bloc is a functioning democracy. I feel a sympathy with Thatcher's words: "He will be missed . . . by millions of men and women who live in freedom today because of the policies he pursued." It is symbolic that Reagan passed away just one day before the 60th anniversary of D-Day, when Allied troops began to liberate Europe from another totalitarian rule. Mr. President! Through your life's work, "there will always be a bright dawn ahead," not only for America, but for the whole world. God bless your soul![25]

These voices rose from precisely the freedom Reagan sought for that once repressed part of the world. Collectively, they comprised his finest eulogy.

In fact, praise was heard in the heart of the former Evil Empire itself. "America has lost one of the greatest public figures in its history," said Professor Eduard Ivanyan, the author of the first Russian book on Reagan.[26] Gennady Gerasimov, a top spokesman for the Soviet Foreign Ministry in the 1980s, said that "Reagan bolstered the U.S. military might to ruin the Soviet economy, and he achieved his goal." Yelena Bonner, the widow of Soviet dissident Nobel Peace Prize winner Andrei Sakharov, said that she considered Reagan "one of the greatest U.S. presidents since the World War II because of his staunch resistance to communism and his efforts to defend human rights."[27]

Of course, not everyone was teary-eyed. Some old adversaries, at home and abroad, could not hold back their continued distaste for Reagan. *Pravda* remains alive, and little changed. *Pravda* writer David R. Hoffman remembered Reagan thus: "A popular adage goes: 'Never say anything but good about the dead.' Ronald Reagan is dead. Good!"[28] At home, commentator Christopher Hitchens called Reagan "an obvious phony and loon," and "dumb as a stump."[29] Political cartoonist Ted Rall, a Pulitzer Prize finalist and two-time winner of the Robert F. Kennedy Journalism Award, whose work is distributed by Universal Press Syndicate to 140 publications including the *New York Times* and *Los Angeles Times*, celebrated the notion that Reagan was "turning crispy brown right about now." He called Reagan an "idiot" and a "Christianist"—which Rall describes as "the radical-right equivalent of Islamist"—who unjustifiably depicted foes as evil.[30]

Nonetheless, most of the commentary was quite kind. The sentiment expressed by Secretary of State Colin Powell, Reagan's onetime national security adviser, was typical: "America flowed through him to the rest of the world," Powell said of Reagan.[31]

Back home, Reagan was remembered throughout his home state of Illinois. In Peoria Heights, a spot along the Reagan Trail that winds through northwestern Illinois, the Village Board, which hangs two presidential portraits in its meeting room—Teddy Roosevelt's and Reagan's—sent a care package to Nancy Reagan. A local barber-shop quartet stood next to a four-foot-tall portrait of Reagan and sang "God Bless the USA."[32] At Eureka College, five hundred mourners gathered in folded chairs aside a garden built to Reagan.

In Dixon, a memorial service was held at the First Christian Church on 123 South Hennepin. Among the dignitaries were Illinois Governor Rod Blagojevich, the Rev. Dr. Chris Hobgood, president of the Disciples of Christ denomination, and the speaker of the House, U.S. Representative J. Dennis Hastert (R-IL), whose congressional district includes both Dixon and Tampico. Hobgood said that Reagan showed how far a person of modest beginnings can go: "A boy grew up in a small town, nurtured by the thousands of Christians in that town to become the most powerful person in the world, but never losing that touch of his hometown." He hailed a person he said had been touched by God's love: "God grew Ronald Reagan into the leader he was, and God is drawing Ronald Reagan into eternal life."

Congressman Hastert added that it was "a proper thing that we gather here in this church where Ronald as a boy of eleven years of age was baptized. It was here in this church he learned his values, he learned right from wrong, he learned his Christian faith."[33]

Governor Blagojevich agreed that Reagan was a product of that sanctuary in the heartland: "The idyllic view he had of the United States, what he envisioned for America, really is rooted in his experience growing up here." The Democratic governor said that because he was in a church, he had a confession to make: He himself was a Reagan Democrat. Being from Chicago, he joked, he'd voted for Reagan twice—in the same election.

The town mayor, James G. Burke, said that Reagan had no pretenses or excessive pride: "You could take Ronald Reagan out of Dixon, but you couldn't take Dixon out of Ronald Reagan."[34] Church member Wanita Trader said, "He was our hero, our hometown boy made good. At the church we feel that we nurtured a president."[35]

The congregants left the chapel for the humidity outside, where a warm, gentle rain met them for the eight-block walk to Reagan's boyhood home. A sea of umbrellas hovered outside the one-time residence of Jack, Nelle, Moon, and Dutch. As the band began playing "The Star-Spangled Banner," State Senator Todd Sieben faced the flag, put his hand on his heart, and began to sing softly, prompting the rest of the crowd to follow suit. According to the *Dixon Telegraph*, when the band played "The Battle Hymn of the Republic," one of Reagan's favorite songs, the sky opened in earnest, "drenching rich and poor, humble and proud, old and young, treating everyone equally, just as Ronald Reagan always had done."[36]

Back in California, a black hearse with a flag-draped coffin began its rounds, with its first destination in Simi Valley, the location of Reagan's presidential library and museum. One of the four men who carried Reagan's casket from location to location was Army Specialist David Milder of State Center, Iowa, near Des Moines, where the Great Communicator began honing his craft nearly seventy years earlier. Escorting the Reagan family from spot to spot was Army Major Jason Garkey, of Eureka, Illinois, whose parents both graduated from Eureka College and whose grandmother knew Ronald Reagan as a lifeguard in Dixon.[37]

As the Reagan hearse readied to leave the Santa Monica mortuary for Simi Valley, a contingent of Russian and East European immigrants came out to pay their respects. They placed placards and flags in the grass outside the mortuary. SIR—YOU TOLD GORBACHEV TO "TAKE DOWN THIS WALL." WE HELPED. THANKS FOR YOUR COURAGE AND LEADERSHIP, read one sign, affixed there along with two quarter-sized bits from the Berlin Wall. Another, accompanied by a Lithuanian flag, read PRESIDENT REAGAN, THANK YOU FOR LITHUANIAN FREEDOM. Still another read: SOLIDARNOSC! WITH LOVE FROM POLAND.[38]

Rabbi Velvel Tsikman, who leads a vibrant Russian Jewish retirement center in West Hollywood, spoke of how in the USSR he was forbidden to wear a yarmulke. Pointing to the elderly people at the center, Tsikman explained, "They are living in a paradise here. It's like God is paying them for a terrible life in Russia." In Russia, he said, "these people were sitting home waiting to die. When they came here, they came alive again." Tsikman pointed to Reagan: "[W]hat he did was very helpful to destroy the monster that was there in Europe."[39]

Also present was Aleksandr Shakhnovich, a former shipbuilder for the Soviet navy, who said of Reagan: "This is a guy who changed the world. It wasn't only his speeches—it was his actions. . . . He did something that not only changed my life, but changed the lives of everyone in the Soviet Union."[40] Another bystander, an Armenian named Paul Khostikyan, called Reagan "the best president in U.S. history."[41]

By Tuesday, June 8, more than one hundred thousand people had visited Reagan's casket in Simi Valley.[42] When his body arrived in Washington it was treated to a solemn but poetic state funeral that captured the nation's attention.

The late president was carried unhurriedly to Capitol Hill on a horse-drawn caisson. Along the way, his corpse passed the E. Barrett Prettyman Federal Courthouse, where John Hinckley had been tried.[43] A riderless black horse carried a pair of Reagan's favorite boots turned backward in the stirrups. The caisson came to a stop and a twenty-one-gun salute followed: a sign for the coffin to be lowered by an honor guard of eight military officers, from where it was slowly walked up the steps into the Capitol Rotunda as Nancy looked on.

Inside the Rotunda, Reagan's coffin lay in state on a black velvet-covered catafalque that had once bore the casket of President Lincoln, guarded by a soldier, sailor, airman, and Marine, all upright, completely silent, moving only in robotlike motions during the changing of the guard. A stream of thousands waited hours in intense heat to pass by. Once inside, onlookers slowed slightly, took an appreciative glance, and moved on. Some held small flags, others held babies or pushed strollers, one blind man held a walking stick and the leash of a seeing-eye dog. Some bowed, some kneeled, some made the sign of the cross. Ex-military men snapped a salute. Two young sailors, in uniform, hats off, halted, mumbled something inaudible to one another, refit their hats as perfectly as possible, then faced Reagan, stood ramrod straight, and gave a sharp salute. It was a gesture that would be repeated by people along the California highway when Reagan returned to Simi Valley.[44]

On Thursday, a ceremony was held at the Rotunda. The nation watched and wept as a frail Nancy Reagan lumbered to the casket, caressed it, gave it several gentle pats, kissed it, and quietly talked to her husband. The featured eulogy that evening was delivered by Vice President Dick Cheney, who, more than any speaker all week, talked about Nelle and Jack. "When you mourn a man of ninety-three," said Cheney, "no one is left who remembers him as a child in his mother's arms." He noted that while Nelle and Jack lived long enough to see the kind of man they raised, "they could never know all that destiny had in store for the boy they called Dutch. And if they could witness this scene in 2004, their son taken to rest with the full honors of the United States, they would be so proud of all he had done with the life they gave him." Speaking of Nelle's spiritual influence, Cheney acknowledged, "This was the Ronald Reagan who had faith. It was the optimism of a faithful soul, who trusted in God's purposes, and knew those purposes to be right and true." The vice president concluded by calling the 40th president "more than an historic figure"; he was "a providential man, who came along just when our nation and the world most needed him. . . . [W]e commend to [the] Almighty the soul of His faithful servant, Ronald Wilson Reagan."[45]

The service at the National Cathedral the next day was gripping, as church bells far and wide rang forty times at noon in Reagan's honor. Remarks were delivered by President George W. Bush and his father, Reagan's vice president, whose voice crackled with emotion as he informed those gathered that he had learned more from Ronald Reagan than from anyone he encountered in all his years in public life. Margaret Thatcher, former British prime minister and Reagan's friend and political soulmate, gave a memorable talk via videotape, her seventy-eight-year-old frame wracked by a series of small strokes. She heralded Reagan as "The Great Liberator." She signed the condolence book, "To Ronnie, 'Well done, thou good and faithful servant.' "[46] Another tribute came from Reagan's friend Canadian prime minister Brian Mulroney.

America's four living ex-presidents were there, as were dozens of world leaders, including Mikhail Gorbachev, Polish Solidarity leader Lech Walesa, the first president of a democratic Poland, and Anatoly Sharansky. The music was beautiful but very mournful and sad, from Mozart's crushing "Requiem" to Ronan Tynan's breathtaking rendition of Schubert's "Ave Maria." "Hail to the Chief" was played at dirge tempo.[47]

The service was officiated by former Senator John Danforth (R-MO), an Episcopal priest who had supported Reagan's two historic tax cuts and assault on Soviet communism. The speakers were ecumenical, befitting Reagan's respect of other faiths and the nondenominational quality of his own Protestant faith.

First was Rabbi Harold Kushner, who read from Isaiah: "But they that wait upon the Lord shall renew their strength; they shall mount up with wings as eagles." The rabbi knew this as one of Reagan's favorite passages; the president's "formula," as he had said in Britain in June 1988, for completing his "crusade for freedom." Rabbi Kushner could not have known that the verse was also a favorite of Ben Cleaver, the most spiritually formative male figure in Dutch's life, and who, like Nelle, had something to do with all of this happening. Borrowing from that Isaiah verse eighty years earlier, in 1924, Ben had promised his congregation that there was "Victory ahead" for those who "make their resolves and do not grow weary." Indeed, that June 11, 2004, was a celebration—a victory. As Reverend Danforth would say in his closing: "There is no better time to celebrate the triumph of life than in a service for Ronald Reagan."

Justice Sandra Day O'Connor, appointed by Reagan as the first woman on the Supreme Court, read John Winthrop's 1630 sermon that inspired Reagan's vision of a shining city on a hill. Next, Theodore Cardinal McCarrick read Matthew 5:14–16, the New Testament section in which Jesus talks of a "city on a hill" and letting one's "light shine before men, that they may praise your good deeds and praise your Father in heaven." As one watched the ceremonies, one could not help but think that Nelle would have loved the tribute that Nancy had meticulously arranged.

Given the throng that came to see Reagan in Washington—more than one hundred thousand visited during extended hours—it was impressive that the final service in California on Friday evening started as planned. Governor Arnold Schwarzenegger, the Gretzkys, and Reagan's Hollywood friends—Merv Griffin, Tom Selleck, Bo Derek, Mickey Rooney—all stood dressed in black outside the Reagan Library.

By and large, Ronald Reagan would have been thrilled with the eulogies given by his three surviving children. The heirs of the Great Communicator presented excellent orations, perfectly timed, with wit, a drop of humor, and with minimal to no use of notes. All three of the talks were different and managed meaningful spiritual references—though Ron's statement contained a political slap at the current president that many found out of place.

Michael Reagan went first. He called himself the "lucky one" of the Reagan children because he was "chosen" by Ronald Reagan in 1945. And yet, said Michael, his dad never mentioned that he was adopted. He spoke of how at the early onset of Alzheimer's he and his dad began a habit of hugging each other and saying they loved one another. As the disease set in and Reagan couldn't verbalize his son's name, he recognized him as the man who hugged him. Once, when Michael forgot to hug him, Reagan strolled outside with arms open; Michael saw him from the car and ran to embrace the elderly man. "It was a blessing truly brought on by God," said Michael.

Michael relayed a 1988 conversation that took place on a flight to California, where his father told him "about his love of God, his love of Christ as his Savior." Said Michael: "I didn't know then what it all meant. But I certainly, certainly know now." Now, Michael closed, he knew where his father was: "[A]nd I can only promise my father this: Dad, when I go, I will go to Heaven, too. And you and I and my sister Maureen that went before us, we will dance with the heavenly host of angels before the presence of God. We will do it melanoma [the cause of Maureen's death in 2001] and Alzheimer's free."

Patti's testimony featured her sardonic sense of humor, evident in a wonderful parable. "My father never feared death," she began. "He never saw it as an ending." She shared a childhood story about the death of her goldfish. In the garden, her father dug a hole with a spoon and made a cross with two sticks and twine. In his eulogy, he explained that the fish was now swimming in the clear blue waters of heaven, as far and wide as it wanted, free forever, never growing tired or hungry, never fearing pain or danger or death. When they returned to the house, Patti looked at her remaining goldfish and suggested they kill them, so they, too, could enjoy the magical fruits of fish heaven. Her smiling father tenderly explained that in "God's time" the other fish would join their deceased friend, and although that timing seems a mystery, we should trust that God is right and wise. "In God's time," said Patti's dad, "we'd all be taken home."

Even Reagan's son Ron, a self-described atheist, mustered a string of inspirational words concerning the hereafter, suggesting (perhaps unintentionally) that his father was resting with his heavenly Father. Ron did not sound like an atheist when he averred: "My father is in a better place."[48]

The 40th president's body was lifted to a platform a few feet from its final resting place. The Reverend Michael Wenning, the Reagans' pastor and an immigrant who had come to this country decades earlier, took over. In very personal words, he explained what Reagan had meant to him and his own father, and he commended Nancy for her dignity and dedication. He described the Ronald Reagan he saw in church, singing hymns by memory. He called Reagan "a gift of God to us all" who didn't shirk in the face of communism, and claimed that "the fruit of the holy spirit was deeply embedded" in Reagan's

DNA. Reagan was now "touching the face of God," said Wenning, just as the president had once said of those victims of the space shuttle Challenger. Wenning concluded by reading II Chronicles 7:14, which he knew was a favorite Reagan verse; he may not have known it was also a favorite of Nelle.

The flag covering the coffin was folded and presented to Mrs. Reagan by the commander of the USS *Ronald Reagan*, who whispered some words on bended knee. He stood slowly and saluted her. Nancy was then left alone with the casket. She rose, laid the left side of her head on top of the coffin, stroked it with her right hand, and spoke some words through her sobs. The Reagan children rushed to console her. They all kissed her, felt the casket one last time, and walked away.

The procession began, each friend walking to the casket to say goodbye. The choir sang a mellow version of "God Bless America," and the band played "Holy, Holy, Holy." After the first dozen or so paid respects, the sun descended halfway below the horizon. After a few more guests, Lady Thatcher, who more than any Western leader supported Reagan's anti-communist crusade, and who had flown to California from Washington despite her weak condition, stepped to the casket alone and gradually bowed. The gesture would have put a lump in the throat of even the most hardened London nuclear-freezer. And it was literally at that moment that the sun dropped completely below the horizon.

President George W. Bush had closed his tribute earlier that day: "When the sun sets tonight off the coast of California, and we lay to rest our 40th president, a great American story will close." The sunset of Ronald Reagan's life, which he had spoken of ten years earlier, had at last drifted below its horizon.

According to Nielsen, 21 million viewers watched the Friday ceremony in Washington; another 35 million tuned in for the evening burial in Simi Valley.

On Saturday, June 12, Ronald Reagan's body was sealed away inside a crypt on the hilltop of his presidential library. The solid mahogany casket was placed inside a bronze-lined vault seven feet underground. Workers closed the tomb just before 3:00 A.M. Secret service agents stood at attention; their services as Reagan's bodyguards were no longer needed—their work, too, was finished. Also observing Reagan's final connection to the world were a few library personnel and people from the mortuary. Ronald Wilson Reagan was gone—removed from public view forever.

Yet perhaps Reagan's end should have brought to mind not the cold grimness of a sealed vault, but the sunny optimism of a rainbow, an image born of his eternal optimism, a characteristic that now had a meaning it never had before. Nelle, after all, had taught him about a rainbow always waiting around the bend. When she died in 1962, her son had carried on her tradition of optimism. His mother's death, he told friends—later he would say the same of Nancy's mother's death—was a step through an eternal window, to a rainbow waiting around the bend.

Now, in June 2004, Ronald Wilson Reagan could finally rest in peace, step through that eternal window, and enjoy that permanent rainbow.

ACKNOWLEDGMENTS

L ike its subject, a book has a life of its own. It has characters, surprises, turning points, frustrations, and joys. In compiling these acknowledgments, I have tried to remember to list anyone who provided even the smallest assistance, with sincere thanks to all. My deepest apologies to any individual I neglect to mention.

A handful of people were especially crucial. First was Peter Schweizer, whom I first met in 1998. We spoke about his first book on the Reagan administration and the Cold War, *Victory*. I noted that while I enjoyed the book, it said little about the very specific role of Reagan himself in the Cold War effort. "Ah, yes," said Peter. "Reagan is an enigma." Then he spoke the words that changed everything for me: "Maybe *you're* the one to write that one."

Also crucial was the help of Charles W. Dunn, dean at Grove City College, who has mentored and encouraged many faculty members. Arriving at Grove City College four years ago, not long after I did, Chuck asked why I was spending so much time struggling to get journal articles past academic gatekeepers. "Those four journal articles you're talking about," he said of some ideas I ran past him, "could comprise at least half a book."

Third and just as vital is my wife, Susan. Like Chuck, she constantly encouraged me to persevere while publisher after publisher warned me that only a minute audience would be interested in a book on Reagan's religious faith. Moreover, despite the demands of our three children—including "six-and-three-quarters"-years-old Paul, five-year-old Mitch, and eleven-month-old Amanda—Susan ensures that I have time to write. I have an ideal situation: During each writing day, I can focus on my book while still watching my children grow.

For financial support in my travels to Dixon, Illinois; to the Reagan Library in Simi Valley, California; and to the Reagan Ranch north of Santa Barbara, the assistance of the Earhart Foundation, the Historical Research Foundation, and B. Kenneth Simon was indispensable. Ken Simon in particular has been wonderful: a longtime Pittsburgher who achieved great business success, he now supports a number of causes. In addition to financial support, Ken has become a good friend.

I received research and editorial support from a number of sources, including some phenomenal students. One such student was John McCay. For week after week, John sat in GCC's Buhl Library with thick volumes of the *Public Papers of the Presidents of the United States: Reagan*, more than ten thousand pages in total. Armed with a list of key words—God, religion, communism, evil, Pope John Paul II—John read through all of the papers and flagged items of interest. He volunteered his time, refusing pay, out of sheer love for what he was doing. This book is the first testimony to his assistance; my second Reagan book will be as well.

Among the researchers or readers of early drafts of the manuscript were: Bethany Nichols, Cory Shreckengost, Melinda Haring, Mike Price, Gary Smith, Michael Coulter, Paul Kemeny, Gil Harp, Andrew Busch, M. William (Bill) Lower, Melissa Harvey, Jen Velencia, Wade Ewing, Matt Scheff, Hans Yehnert, Elaine Rodemoyer, Mike Liptak, Caroline Koopman, Brian Hutchinson, Travis Barham, Dawn Blauvelt, Nate Adams, Brian Donovan, Nick Emery, Karen Deitrick, Scott Sweeney, Matt Divelbiss, J. D. Dunston, Peter Williams, Adrian Monza, and Tasha Halevi. Among the most enlightening group of readers were the twenty-five students who comprised my Humanities 302 intersession course at GCC—one of the most enjoyable classes I've ever taught, in part because they taught me as well. I'd like to pay special tribute to Hugh Heclo of George Mason University and Jeff Chidester for their insightful comments. Hugh is well established as one of the best and fairest minds among academic presidential observers. Jeff will one day occupy such a spot as well.

A word on the earliest of those readers: This book began as two lengthy "religion chapters" in a larger work on Reagan that is still in progress. Naïvely, I circulated those two shoddy, unorganized chapters among some close colleagues here at GCC in June 2001. In a shining example of Christian charity, a handful of GCC religion professors looked the chapters over and offered suggestions for improvement, without ever telling me the painful, embarrassing truth. Shortly thereafter, in a conversation in my muggy office with my colleague Michael Coulter, I realized that I should splinter off those two religion chapters into a separate work on Reagan's faith. This book was truly born at that moment.

Structurally and stylistically, a turning point for the book came in the summer of 2002. Most significant was the guidance of Tim Bent, an editor at a major publishing house in New York, who convinced me to overhaul the book, making it less of a thematic, academic work, and more of a narrative. Near the end of 2002, my agent, Leona Schecter, and a brilliant GCC student, Matt Sitman, pointed me toward further improvements. Weeks later, Cal Morgan at ReganBooks called to say he wanted the book. Cal's editing made the book more readable, without sacrificing content and sections I felt were critical. Cal Morgan is an exceptional editor; it is because of him and Judith Regan that that manuscript has become this book.

There are others who deserve many thanks. At GCC these include President John Moore, Sam Casolari, Diane Grundy and her tireless library staff, and Carole and Lorraine at the copy center. Outside of GCC, Andrea Millen-Rich offered endless patient advice. Lee Edwards recommended Leona Schecter. Matt and Elizabeth Spalding provided encouragement. Among editors at other houses, Peter Ginna and Mary Carpenter saw the book's potential and provided very helpful input, as did their reviewers (most notably, Reviewer #4 at Peter's house). Jim Miller of the Wisconsin Policy Research Institute offered many suggestions and, in an indirect way he may not recognize, even provided financial support.

My biggest cheerleaders were my parents, Paul and Gloria Kengor; Pastor Bob McCreight; and Lee Wishing, GCC's magnificent PR guy.

Certain former Reagan staffers were especially accessible, insightful, and supportive—Richard V. Allen, Ben Elliott, William P. Clark, and Ed Meese. Meese gave me his home phone number and told me I could call him anytime. Judge Clark is simply a wonderful man and a model of faith and virtue.

On the West Coast, my appreciation goes to the staff at the Reagan Library and Foundation—Mark Burson, Kirby Hansen, Holly Bauer, Greg Cumming, and others. The staff of the Reagan Ranch and West Coast branch of the Young America's Foundation was great, particularly Andrew Coffin and Floyd Brown. From Ventura, California, my entire family thanks Peggy and Uri Halevi for their hospitality during our stay there.

Finally, in Dixon, Illinois, I'm grateful to Marion Emmert Foster, the daughter of Reagan's Sunday school teacher, who escorted me and my family around Dixon in late June 2001, from the beach at Lowell Park to Reagan's boyhood home to the First Christian Church. I urge any Reagan researcher to make that trip to Dixon: no book on Reagan can be complete without that understanding.

I'd like to especially thank Dixon's excellent local historian Ron Marlow. A diligent researcher and a kind, gentle soul, Ron was indispensable in sharing clips from the *Dixon Telegraph* in the 1920s, which he vetted through his exhaustive research efforts. Ron's continuous hard work on those early Reagan years has been one of the great, continued blessings emanating from the Dixon church at 123 S. Hennepin.

Ultimately, it is to the people of Dixon, Illinois, that this book owes the most, particularly a small group of individuals who lived there in the 1920s and 1930s: especially the Cleavers, the Waggoners, and Jack and Nelle Reagan.

Paul Kengor
Grove City, Pennsylvania
May 5, 2003

NOTES

ABBREVIATIONS

ES   Executive Secretariat files at the Reagan Library
FBIS   Foreign Broadcast Information Service
HSF   Head of State Files at the Reagan Library
Memcons   the Memoranda of Conversation formal notes transcribed by the official notetaker at the various US-USSR summits during the two Reagan terms
NSC   National Security Council files at the Reagan Library
PHF   Presidential Handwriting Files at the Reagan Library
PR   Presidential Records files at the Reagan Library
PS   Presidential Speeches files at the Reagan Library
Public Presidential Papers   *Public Papers of the Presidents of the United States, Ronald Reagan* (Washington, D.C.: U.S. Government Printing Office, 1981–89).
RRL   Ronald Reagan Library
YAF   Young America's Foundation collection of Reagan letters

PREFACE

1. Anatoly Krasikov, commentary for Soviet news agency *TASS*, November 22, 1986, printed as "TASS Examines Reagan's Remarks on Religion," in *FBIS*, November 24, 1986, p. A11. Note: FBIS is a U.S. government service that transcribed and translated all media from the USSR and around the world.
2. Letter is located in PHF, PR, RRL, Box 18, Folder 282.
3. I'm referring to the multivolume collection of presidential speeches, statements, and more—formally known as the *Public Papers of the Presidents of the United States, Ronald Reagan* (Washington, D.C.: U.S. Government Printing Office, 1981–89). These documents are available in most large libraries and most college libraries. The majority of these papers are now also available on-line through the Reagan Library website; the on-line version does not include page numbers. In this book, Reagan presidential

statements from these papers will be referenced by title, location (if outside of Washington, D.C.), and date.

4. Reagan was private about his faith with certain people at certain times, particularly if the issue wasn't raised. Also, he did not seem to prefer to openly or at length speak of his faith in a personally introspective way. To the contrary, he was willing to speak of God in an apologetic way. In a letter or to an audience, he was much more likely to say things like "here is why prayer is important" or "America needs a spiritual renewal" or even "here is why Christ is the Messiah." He would do that rather than detail matters like "this is how my heart changed when I accepted Christ" or "here is what being 'born again' did for me personally in my relationship with my wife."

5. According to the Julian calendar, the Bolshevik revolution took place on October 25, 1917. According to the Gregorian calendar, it occurred November 7, 1917. America operates by the Gregorian calendar, meaning that the revolution took place on November 7 by the timing of Reagan's Dixon, Illinois. The Universalist church burned on the night of Sunday, November 25, 1917, when the flames from a burning automotive garage spread to the church. In this book, I refer to the revolution as the "October" revolution.

6. My goal is not to determine whether he was devoted to, say, Reformed Protestant theology. Later, I'll note that Reagan seemed to subscribe to more of a general Christianity; more specifically, a general Protestantism. Having said that, he was very open to religious consultation with Catholics. While clearly not a Catholic, he was in no way hostile to Catholicism. Also, some religion scholars may tend to see Reagan's expressed Christian beliefs as reflecting more of a sort of "civil religion." While that term does partly explain some of his remarks and thinking, it does not at all suffice as a full explanation. The two classic works on civil religion are: Jean Jacques Rousseau, *The Social Contract*, translated by G. D. H. Cole (Buffalo, NY: Prometheus Books, 1988); and Robert N. Bellah, *Beyond Belief: Essays on Religion in a Post-Traditional World* (New York: Harper & Row, 1970).

7. This is the focus of my next work on Reagan. I detail at length the fact that he intended this Soviet end.

8. Reagan, "Address Before a Joint Session of the Irish National Parliament," Ireland, June 4, 1984. Note: A reader might interpret Reagan's use of such words in a general way, not necessarily a religious way. As readers will see, however, that would generally be a mistake. It indeed applies from time to time, but Reagan usually employed such words with religious connotation.

9. TASS statement, September 11, 1984, published as "Reagan Uses Religion to Support Anti-Soviet Policy," in *FBIS*, FBIS-13-SEP-84, September 13, 1984, pp. A4–5.

CHAPTER 1

1. Cited in Gordon P. Gardiner, "Nelle Reagan: Mother of Ronald Reagan, President of the United States," *Bread of Life*, Vol. 30, No. 5, May 1981, p. 6.

2. Jack arrived in the world 11 days earlier on July 13, 1883. Source: "Geneological Information on Ronald Wilson Reagan," Office of the Press Secretary, The White House, provided by the Ronald Reagan Library. Another source lists the couple as married at St. Emanuel's Catholic Church in Fulton, Illinois. One source lists the marriage date as November 18, 1904, whereas another says November 8, 1904.

3. Anne Edwards says that Reagan's father was so lacking in outward faith that his brother, Neil, claims he didn't know that his father was Catholic until he was almost 18 years old. See: Anne Edwards, *Early Reagan: The Rise to Power* (New York: Morrow, 1987), pp. 33–39 and 58.

4. Reagan said this in an undated 1980s letter to Kenneth J. Bialkin, published in Kiron Skinner, Annelise Anderson, and Martin Anderson, editors, *Reagan: A Life in Letters* (New York: Free Press, 2003), p. 2.

5. As will be shown shortly, the testimonies to this are numerous.

6. Fran Swarbrick, ed., *Remembering Ronald Reagan* (Dixon, IL: Creative Printing, 2001), pp. 5 and 12.

7. This was by Reagan's own account. See his letters in Skinner, Anderson, and Anderson, *Reagan: A Life in Letters*, pp. 3–5.

8. I'm fairly confident in estimating that he was probably five years old at the time; if not five, then six.

9. Ronald Reagan, *An American Life* (New York: Simon & Schuster, 1990), p. 24; and Ronald Reagan with Richard Hubler, *Where's the Rest of Me?* (New York: Duell, Sloan & Pearce, 1965), p. 11.

10. Ibid.

11. This is my speculation. To my knowledge, Reagan never said this, but he likely wouldn't disagree.

12. Reagan and Hubler, *Where's the Rest of Me?* p. 13.

13. Reagan used this description in a May 22, 1984, letter to John Morley of Laguna Hills, California. The letter is published in Skinner, Anderson, and Anderson, *Reagan: A Life in Letters*, p. 5.

14. Source: "Residences of Ronald Reagan," document assembled by the Reagan Library.

15. Aside from Reagan himself, a number of biographers have shared this account.

16. The source for this is literature provided by the Reagan Boyhood Home, 816 South Hennepin Avenue, Dixon, Illinois.

17. Patti Davis interview on television documentary "Ronald Reagan: A Legacy Remembered," History Channel production, 2002.

18. Laxalt interviewed by Lou Cannon. Lou Cannon, *President Reagan: The Role of a Lifetime* (New York: Public Affairs, 2000), p. 194.

19. Reagan and Hubler, *Where's the Rest of Me?* pp. 7–8. Among more recent accounts, see: Edmund Morris, *Dutch: A Memoir of Ronald Reagan* (New York: Random House, 1999), p. 39; and "Reagan," *The American Experience*, television documentary produced by PBS, WGBH-TV Boston, 1998.

20. The Christian Church designation, because of its vagueness, is confusing. Other Christian denominations are much more distinctive in name, such as Quaker, Lutheran, Presbyterian. A local Disciples congregation seldom uses "Disciples of Christ" in its name, even though some have begun placing it in parentheses on church stationary to clear up confusion. Typically, a Disciples church will have a name like "First Christian Church" or "Community Christian Church" or "Walnut Grove Christian Church."

In writings on Reagan, Edmund Morris refers only to the Disciples of Christ, whereas earlier biographer Anne Edwards refers only to the Christian Church. Some use the two designations side by side. For instance, both Kenneth Teegarden, a president of the denomination, and Lester McAllister and William Tucker, who wrote one of the most authoritative histories of the denomination, spell out the church title as the "Christian Church (Disciples of Christ)"—each use that exact designation each time they discuss the church in their respective books.

Two other presidents were Disciples, James A. Garfield and Lyndon Johnson. Garfield also served as president of Hiram College, a Disciples-related school, and as a former minister. See: Kenneth L. Teegarden, *We Call Ourselves Disciples* (St. Louis, MO: The Bethany Press, 1975), pp. 9–10 and 112; Lester G. McAllister and William E. Tucker, *Journey in Faith: A History of the Christian Church (Disciples of Christ)* (St. Louis, MO: The Bethany Press, 1975); and Winfred Ernest Garrison and Alfred T. De-Groot, *The Disciples of Christ: A History* (St. Louis, MO: The Bethany Press, 1948), pp. 251, 268, 307, 333, 336, 340, 356, and 534.

21. Teegarden, *We Call Ourselves Disciples*, pp. 1–17. Also see: Wilfred Ernest Garrison, *An American Religious Movement: A Brief History of the Disciples of Christ* (St. Louis, MO: Bethany Press, 1951), pp. 28–41. For more on the spread of the Disciples into Illinois, see: Garrison and DeGroot, *The Disciples of Christ*, pp. 220–22 and 303–6.
22. Quoted in Garrison and DeGroot, *The Disciples of Christ*, p. 303.
23. On the preaching, Reagan biographer Norman Wymbs wrote: "There is every reason to believe that Nelle also did much of the preaching at the time." This may well be true, but I could not find a second source to confirm it. No one that I interviewed found the claim unreasonable. The problem is a lack of information on the Tampico church. Norman E. Wymbs, *Ronald Reagan's Crusade* (Lauderdale-by-the-Sea, FL: Skyline Publications, 1997), pp. 40–43.
24. Source: "Enrollment Directory for the Year 1922," First Christian Church, Dixon, Illinois.
25. On this, see: Reagan and Hubler, *Where's the Rest of Me?* p. 10; Peggy Noonan, *When Character Was King: A Story of Ronald Reagan* (New York: Viking Penguin, 2001), p. 153; Anne Edwards, *Early Reagan*, pp. 59–60; and Swarbrick, ed., *Remembering Ronald Reagan*, p. 17.
26. Sources: " 'The Pill Bottle,' " *Dixon Telegraph*, May 12, 1924; "Regular Meeting of W.C.T.U. Held Friday," *Dixon Telegraph*, June 19, 1926; and "Mrs. J. E. Reagan in Program in Tampico," *Dixon Telegraph*, July 29, 1925.
27. Sources: "Armistice Day Poem," *Dixon Telegraph*, November 11, 1926; and "American Legion Auxiliary Meeting," *Dixon Telegraph*, February 17, 1927.
28. Sources: "Christian Church Notes," *Dixon Telegraph*, August 3, 1925; "Most interesting discussion on prayer," *Dixon Telegraph*, January 8, 1926; and "Christian Church Notes," *Dixon Telegraph*, October 26, 1925.
29. Source: "Christian Church Notes," *Dixon Telegraph*, February 22 and March 19, 1928.
30. Quoted in Gardiner, "Nelle Reagan: Mother of Ronald Reagan," p. 6.
31. Ibid. Also see: Morris, *Dutch*, p. 12.
32. See: Swarbrick, ed., *Remembering Ronald Reagan*, pp. 3–4; Gardiner, "Nelle Reagan: Mother of Ronald Reagan," p. 6; and Morris, *Dutch*, p. 12.
33. Anne Edwards, *Early Reagan*, pp. 59 and 105.
34. See: Reagan and Hubler, *Where's the Rest of Me?* p. 10; Noonan, *When Character Was King*, p. 153; Anne Edwards, *Early Reagan*, pp. 59–60; and Swarbrick, ed., *Remembering Ronald Reagan*, pp. 4–5 and 17.
35. This information was relayed by a number of Dixon residents interviewed in June 2001.
36. Quoted in Swarbrick, ed., *Remembering Ronald Reagan*, pp. 2–5. This account was also told to me by a number of Dixon residents during conversations in the summer of 2001.
37. Anne Edwards, *Early Reagan*, pp. 59–60.
38. Interview with Olive and Savilla Palmer and Marion Foster Emmert in Dixon, IL, June 22, 2001.

39. Interview with the Palmers and Emmert. Also, the incident is recounted by Cenie Straw in Swarbrick, ed., *Remembering Ronald Reagan*, p. 10.
40. Source: "True Blue Class," *Dixon Telegraph*, March 10, 1921.
41. Source: "Christian Church Notes," *Dixon Telegraph*, June 9, 1924.
42. Source: "Fellows Home Scene of Happy Meeting," *Dixon Telegraph*, April 9, 1927.
43. The ladies agreed that non-Christian nations had their own gifts "to bring to the kingdom." These nations, too, said one speaker, desire friendship and love—wants that should be given to them in the way Christ would. According to the local paper, Mrs. Reagan joined a group of six worldly Dixonite women in answering "questions regarding the newspapers, moving pictures, radio, steamship and aeroplane, in how they tie the world together." Source: "Mrs. J. E. Reagan Is Hostess to Society," *Dixon Telegraph*, September 9, 1927.

CHAPTER 2

1. Morris, *Dutch*, p. 42; and Morris speaking during interview on "Reagan," *The American Experience*.
2. Source: Dixon church records and literature. Reviewed by author at Dixon First Christian Church, June 22, 2001.
3. Ibid. Reagan was baptized by Rev. David Franklin Seyster, who temporarily filled the pulpit following the untimely death of Rev. Harvey Garland Waggoner and before the arrival of Rev. Ben Cleaver. There is conflicting information as to whether Reagan was 11 or 12. Reagan himself once said he was 12. (See: Reagan, *An American Life*, p. 32.) Church records, however, confirm that he was 11.
4. Jerry Griswold, " 'I'm a sucker for hero worship,' " *The New York Times Book Review*, August 30, 1981, p. 11. Also see: Reagan, "Remarks at the Annual National Prayer Breakfast," February 3, 1983; and a 1967 Reagan letter published in Skinner, Anderson, and Anderson, *Reagan: A Life in Letters*, p. 276.
5. Reagan said this in 1977. Griswold, " 'I'm a sucker for hero worship,' " p. 11.
6. Harold Bell Wright, *That Printer of Udell's* (New York: A. L. Burt Company Publishers, 1903).
7. Reagan, *An American Life*, p. 32.
8. A copy of the March 13, 1984, letter is on file at the Dixon Public Library.
9. Wright, *That Printer of Udell's*, pp. 29–33.
10. New International Version of New Testament.
11. Reagan said this in the earlier referenced March 13, 1984 letter.
12. Morris, *Dutch*, p. 40.
13. Wright, *That Printer of Udell's*, pp. 118–19.
14. Ibid., pp. 44–46 and 140. Reagan said that the Soviet leadership had "openly and publicly declared that the only morality they recognize is what will further their cause, meaning they reserve unto themselves the right to commit any crime, to lie, to cheat. . . ." Reagan, "The President's News Conference," January 29, 1981.
15. Griswold, " 'I'm a sucker for hero worship,' " p. 11.
16. See Wright, *That Printer of Udell's*, pp. 118–19 and 206.
17. Ibid., pp. 122–23.
18. Ibid., pp. 115–16.
19. Ibid., p. 116.
20. Ibid., p. 73.

21. Ibid., pp. 70–71.

22. Ibid., pp. 77–78.

23. Ibid., pp. 122–23. This rings of the social gospel rhetoric of the late nineteenth, early twentieth centuries. See: Gary S. Smith, *The Search for Social Salvation: Social Christianity and America* (Lanham, MD: Lexington Books, 2000).

24. Ibid., p. 122.

25. There are a number of consistent accounts of this moment. Edmund Morris has probably said or written more about it than any other source, See: Morris, *Dutch*, p. 42; and Morris on "Reagan," *The American Experience*.

CHAPTER 3

1. This January 4, 1973, letter is published in Skinner, Anderson, and Anderson, *Reagan: A Life in Letters*, pp. 278–79.

2. Dixon First Christian Church historian Ron Marlow documents baptisms in the river between September 1, 1895, and October 12, 1895.

3. While baptized with Dutch in the Disciples church in 1922, Neil, two years older than his brother, eventually found a home in the Catholic Church. Among other things, he was attracted by the majesty of the Church and remained a devout Catholic until his death in San Diego in 1996.

4. Source: Records and Literature of Dixon First Christian Church. Reviewed by author, June 22, 2001. Also see: Swarbrick, ed., *Remembering Ronald Reagan*, pp. 25–26; and Anne Edwards, *Early Reagan*, p. 59.

5. Garry Wills, *Reagan's America: Innocents at Home* (Garden City, NY: Doubleday, 1987), p. 27.

6. "Cantatas Sung by Dixon Choirs Sunday Evening," *Dixon Telegraph*, December 22, 1924.

7. "Annual Meeting and Supper for Christian Church Last Eve," *Dixon Telegraph*, January 15, 1925.

8. "Program in Tampico Most Enjoyable," *Dixon Telegraph*, August 1, 1925.

9. Interview with Savila Palmer, June 22, 2001.

10. See: Swarbrick, ed., *Remembering Ronald Reagan*, p. 12.

11. Wymbs quotes and names these sources. Wymbs, *Ronald Reagan's Crusade*, pp. 154–55 and 164–65.

12. Reagan taught his last class on September 30, 1928. Source: Records of the First Christian Church in Dixon, including the church's *Standard Sunday-School Register and Record* for the 1926–28 period. Also: *Dixon Telegraph*, September 13, 1928; and author consultation with church historian and archivist, Ron Marlow, in Dixon, Illinois at First Christian Church, June 22, 2001.

13. Records and Literature of Dixon First Christian Church. Reviewed by author, June 22, 2001. Also see: Anne Edwards, *Early Reagan*, pp. 58–59. For Reagan himself on his Sunday schooling, see: Reagan and Hubler, *Where's the Rest of Me?* p. 14.

14. Source: Church bulletin, "Easter Week Services, Dixon Christian Church, March 30–April 4, 1926." The bulletin is located at the Dixon First Christian Church.

15. Sources: "Christian Church" notes, *Dixon Telegraph*, September 23, 1927, and January 20, 1928; and "Program of C.E. Convention Here Sunday Complete," *Dixon Telegraph*, November 30, 1926.

16. Wymbs, *Ronald Reagan's Crusade*, p. 155. All of the Dixon sources I spoke to agreed with this. They confirm that Reagan was perceived as much more mature than his age.

17. Wymbs, *Ronald Reagan's Crusade*, p. 158.

18. Interview with Ron Marlow, July 3, 2002.

19. Source: "Christian Church Notes," *Dixon Telegraph*, April 16, 1928.

20. Anne Edwards, *Early Reagan*, p. 75.

21. See: Stephen Vaughn, *Ronald Reagan in Hollywood: Movies and Politics* (New York: Cambridge University Press, 1994), p. 9.

22. See: Wills, *Reagan's America*, p. 22. Also see: Anne Edwards, *Early Reagan*, pp. 68, 75, 192–93. Also see: Garry Wills, "Nelle's Boy: Ronald Reagan and the Disciples of Christ," *The Christian Century*, November 12, 1986, p. 1003; and Wymbs, *Ronald Reagan's Crusade*, p. 158.

23. Reverend Ben H. Cleaver, "Annual Minister's Report," First Christian Church, December 31, 1925.

24. Conversation with Lynn Bond, pastor, Dixon First Christian Church, February 28, 2003.

25. Vaughn did some of the best research on Ben Cleaver. See: Stephen Vaughn, "The Moral Inheritance of a President: Reagan and the Dixon Disciples of Christ," *Presidential Studies Quarterly*, Vol. 25, Winter 1995, pp. 109–27.

26. "American Legion Auxiliary Meeting," *Dixon Telegraph*, February 17, 1927.

27. David Harrell, *A Social History of the Disciples of Christ* (Nashville: Disciples of Christ Historical Society, 1966), pp. 46–47 and 65.

28. Following what Campbell and Barton W. Stone and later Disciples had established, by the time of their 1909 Centennial Convention, the Disciples had begun work in China, the (Belgian) Congo, the "Argentine," Cuba, Hawaii, India, Jamaica, Japan, Mexico, the Philippines, Puerto Rico, and Tibet. As a testimony to their success, there are now 161 countries with Disciples congregations. See: "Our Story: A brief history of the Global family of Christian Churches, Churches of Christ, and Disciples of Christ," prepared by the World Convention of Churches of Christ (brochure); and Harrell, *A Social History of the Disciples of Christ*, pp. 45–47.

29. Dixon resident John L. Porter not only read Campbell but saw him speak. I was unable to confirm if Porter spoke to Cleaver (or Nelle) about Campbell. Source: John L. Porter, "Memory of Garfield a Reminiscence," *Dixon Telegraph*, February 10, 1927.

30. Rev. Ben H. Cleaver, "Annual Minister's Report," December 31, 1924. I'm deeply grateful to Ron Marlow for his hard work transcribing these notes and sharing them with me.

31. Rev. Ben H. Cleaver, "Annual Minister's Report," December 31, 1925.

32. The church archivist/historian Ron Marlow claims there was "no logical reason" for opening the only Bible on display to Matthew. "It just happened to open to that and I placed it there." Interview with Marlow at First Christian Church, June 22, 2001.

33. That first semester at college, Reagan came home at least three times, including the weekend of October 5, Thanksgiving break, and Christmas break. Source: Announcements in *Dixon Telegraph*, October 5, November 28, and December 24, 1928. Source on the Russian Jew speaker: "Russian Hebrew Will Lecture in Dixon Tomorrow," *Dixon Telegraph*, November 10, 1928.

34. Ben Hill Cleaver, *Some Memories of John Stephen Cleaver, by his son, Ben Hill Cleaver*, Cape Girardeau, Missouri, August 18, 1967, p. 3.

35. See: Vaughn, *Ronald Reagan in Hollywood*, pp. 9–16.
36. Letter is quoted in Helene Von Damm, *Sincerely, Ronald Reagan* (Ottawa, IL: Green Hill Publishers, 1976), p. 43.
37. Quoted in Vaughn, *Ronald Reagan in Hollywood*, p. 9.
38. Reagan expressed this in an interview with Stephen Vaughn on October 16, 1989. Cited by Vaughn in his "The Moral Inheritance of a President."
39. Dutch arrived in December 1920 and left for Eureka College in September 1928. Though he lived in Dixon full-time for eight years, he returned to live with his parents in the summers of 1929–32. Following the summer of 1932, he moved to Davenport, Iowa, to work at WOC.
40. "Delightful Guest Day Meeting," *Dixon Telegraph*, February 5, 1926.
41. See notes: "Mission Triangle Club Meeting," *Dixon Telegraph*, March 18, 1927.
42. Unless otherwise cited, sources for this section include: interview with Sarah DeMont (Garland's daughter), April 2, 2003; materials provided by DeMont; interview with Phyllis Waggoner (Harvey's daughter and Garland's sister), April 2, 2003; clips from the June 1, 2, and 19, 1922, *Dixon Telegraph*; Neva Waggoner, *Richly Blessed* (Phoenix, AZ: Imperial, 1989); and Mary L. Kline and Ernest R. Kline, *History of the Storrs Congregational Church* (Dalton, MA: The Studley Press, 1985).
43. Reagan and Hubler, *Where's the Rest of Me?* p. 23.
44. Waggoner, *Richly Blessed*, p. 148.
45. Garland spoke to the congregation on November 23, 1924. See: "Christian Church Notes," *Dixon Telegraph*, November 24, 1924. Also see: "Christian Church Notes," *Dixon Telegraph*, March 9, 1926.
46. Reagan and Hubler, *Where's the Rest of Me?*; Ronald Reagan, *An American Life*; and "Reagan," *The American Experience*.
47. Reagan wrote this in a January 4, 1973, letter to the Cleaver family. The letter is published in Skinner, Anderson, and Anderson, *Reagan: A Life in Letters*, pp. 278–79.

CHAPTER 4

1. Quoted by Anne Edwards, *Early Reagan*, pp. 145–46.
2. At one count, there were 18 liberal arts colleges and universities that were members of the Disciples of Christ's Board of Higher Education. Teegarden, *We Call Ourselves Disciples*, p. 109. On the founding of Eureka by the Disciples, see: Garrison and DeGroot, *The Disciples of Christ*, pp. 252, 304, 413, and 497.
3. Quoted by Anne Edwards, *Early Reagan*, p. 82.
4. See: "Christian Church Notes," *Dixon Telegraph*, October 2, 24, 30, and December 4, 1922, editions and the Annual Report records of the First Christian Church of Dixon, December 31, 1924.
5. Reagan said this during a Eureka visit on October 17, 1980. Quoted by Skinner, Anderson, and Anderson, *Reagan: A Life in Letters*, p. 1.
6. Reagan wrote this in a 1980 (month and day not listed) letter to his brother Neil and in a July 11, 1983, letter to William Opal Stephens. The letters are published in ibid., pp. 22–23.
7. Reagan gave his best pitch to the coach, who he convinced. Reagan and Hubler, *Where's the Rest of Me?* pp. 23–24.
8. Reagan and Hubler, *Where's the Rest of Me?* p. 55; and Reagan, *An American Life*, p. 45. It is not clear whether he gave that 10 percent once president. His tax returns did not

reveal 10 percent donations during at least some of the White House years. However, Reagan believed in tithing privately and may in fact have given 10 percent without always reporting it. For example, as president, he wrote in one letter, "Although my contributions to major charities have been made already, please accept the enclosed check as a token of my appreciation." In another letter, he explained that his tax returns did not indicate all of his contributions because some of them were not tax-deductible. He often sent checks ranging from $50 to $1,000, donated to memorial funds (including one for a soldier killed in Grenada), and even sent personal items (like a rocking chair, in one case) to those in need. See: Skinner, Anderson, and Anderson, *Reagan: A Life in Letters*, pp. 648, 653–58, and 873–74n; and Gary S. Smith, *Faith and the Presidency: Religion, Politics, and Public Policy from George Washington to George W. Bush* (unpublished manuscript).

9. Quoted by Anne Edwards, *Early Reagan*, pp. 145–46.
10. Reagan and Hubler, *Where's the Rest of Me?* pp. 58–59 and 84.
11. Ibid., p. 99; Maureen Reagan, *First Father, First Daughter* (Boston: Little, Brown and Company, 1989), p. 61; and Morris, *Dutch*, p. 12.
12. Reagan and Hubler, *Where's the Rest of Me?* pp. 189–90.
13. This November 2, 1947, letter is excerpted in Wills, *Reagan's America*, p. 29.
14. Maureen Reagan spoke of this. See: Swarbrick, ed., *Remembering Ronald Reagan*, pp. 23–24.
15. Nelle letters to Lorraine Wagner, July 31, 1957, and December (no day) 1955, YAF collection.
16. This information was told to me by Michael Reagan. Interview with Michael Reagan, September 2, 2003.
17. Nelle letter to Lorraine Wagner, July 25, 1953, YAF collection.
18. The poem was given to members of Nelle's True Blue class. It was circulated in an early 1980s pamphlet titled "Ronald Reagan's Boyhood Church" by the First Christian Church in Dixon. It was originally published in the *Dixon Telegraph* on August 17, 1928.
19. The first line of Milton's work, which bears the title of the poem, reads: "When I consider how my light is spent." Milton uses "light" rather than "life." That is the only line they share. Likewise, Milton's piece is a Christian poem on what constitutes true service to God.
20. Cited in Gardiner, "Nelle Reagan: Mother of Ronald Reagan," p. 6.
21. Reagan, "Remarks and Question-and-Answer Session With Women Leaders of Christian Religious Organizations," October 13, 1983.
22. William Rose, "The Reagans and Their Pastor," *Christian Life*, May 1968, p. 46.
23. See: Reagan weekly radio address, May 7, 1983, published in Fred Israel, editor, *Ronald Reagan's Weekly Radio Addresses, Vol. 1* (Wilmington, DE: Scholarly Resources Inc., 1987), p. 101.
24. Reagan wrote this in a January 9, 1985, letter to Mrs. Hugh Harris of Sierra Madre, California. The letter is published in Skinner, Anderson, and Anderson, *Reagan: A Life in Letters*, p. 47.
25. Reagan's Christianity was not wedded to a particular, formal denomination. This insight was shared by both Richard V. Allen and William P. Clark, each of whom knew Reagan well. Sources: Interview with Richard V. Allen, November 12, 2001; and interview with William P. Clark, July 17, 2003.
26. This was reported in July 1980. Marjorie Hyer, "Reagan, Carter, Anderson: Three 'Born Again' Christians Who Differ on Meaning," *Washington Post*, July 25, 1980, p. A28.

27. Information provided by Beverly Church administrator Glen Gray, October 25, 2002.
28. Private correspondence of Joan Sieffert, shared with the author in Pittsburgh, PA, in 2001.
29. Ronald Reagan, "My Faith," *Modern Screen*, June 1950, pp. 37 and 88.
30. Interview with Michael Reagan, September 2, 2003.
31. Ibid.
32. On this, see: Reagan, *An American Life*, pp. 106–7.
33. On Reverend Kleihauer, I thank Glen Gray, administrator at the Hollywood Beverly Christian Church, for his assistance in providing information.
34. Reagan, *An American Life*, p. 134.
35. There are a number of sources for this: One is Stalin's daughter, Svetlana Alliluyeva, on pages 5–11 of her *Twenty Letters to a Friend* (New York: Harper & Row, 1967). She was a witness to this scene. Another account is provided by Ravi Zacharias in his Harvard Veritas Forum. Zacharias received the account personally from Malcolm Muggeridge, who documented the scenario amid his three weeks of conversation with Stalin's daughter. Muggeridge was in the process of preparing a three-part series for the BBC.
36. From an actor's view, see Robert Stack in Doug McClelland, editor, *Hollywood on Ronald Reagan: Friends and Enemies Discuss Our President, the Actor* (Winchester, MA: Faber and Faber, 1983), p. 169. For a contemporaneous account, see: Hedda Hopper, "Mr. Reagan Airs His Views," *Chicago Tribune*, May 18, 1947.
37. Lyn Nofziger, *Nofziger* (Washington, D.C.: Regnery Gateway, 1992), pp. 43–44; Reagan and Hubler, *Where's the Rest of Me?* pp. 174–75; and John Meroney, "Rehearsals for a Lead Role," *Washington Post*, February 4, 2001, p. G9.
38. Reagan and Hubler, *Where's the Rest of Me?* p. 271. Also see: Reagan, "Interview with the President," December 27, 1981.
39. Meroney, "Rehearsals for a Lead Role," p. G9.
40. The letter was sent to Hugh Hefner, dated July 4, 1960. For a full transcript, see: Ibid.
41. Reagan letter to Lorraine and Elwood Wagner, June 3, 1962, YAF collection.

CHAPTER 5

1. Quoted in James Thrower, *God's Commissar: Marxism-Leninism as the Civil Religion of Soviet Society* (Lewiston, NY: Edwin Mellen Press, 1992), p. 39.
2. Interview with Olena Doviskaya, Grove City, PA, October 2, 2000. Doviskaya now travels with the Kiev symphony orchestra.
3. James Billington, "Christianity and History," presentation, 125th anniversary lecture series, Grove City College, Grove City, PA, September 27, 2001.
4. Malachi Martin, *The Keys of This Blood* (New York: Simon & Schuster, 1990), p. 401.
5. Eduard Radzinsky speaking in an interview for A&E Biography of Joseph Stalin, "The Red Terror."
6. Mikhail Gorbachev, *Memoirs* (New York: Doubleday, 1996), p. 328.
7. Mikhail Gorbachev, *On My Country and the World* (New York: Columbia University Press, 2000), pp. 20–21.
8. Interview with Alexander Donskiy, Grove City, PA, October 2, 2000. Donskiy now travels with the Kiev symphony orchestra. Christians argue that a person who chooses to follow Christ gives up a certain degree of "freedom" (or at least what a mere imperfect person thinks is freedom) in exchange for a greater, better freedom—a freedom

from sin, evil, and eternal damnation. A non-Christian, it is argued, is not as free as he or she thinks; rather, that person is a "slave to sin," as Paul put it. The Christian faith, it is asserted, also offers security and courage. Martin Luther wrote flatly: "faith gives a man courage." New Testament verses on this liberating feature of Christ include: John 8 and Galatians 5:13–24. John 8 reads: "If the Son shall make you free, you shall be free indeed." Also see Martin Luther's classic 1520 work, *A Treatise on Christian Liberty*, from which the aforementioned quote is taken. The Luther treatise is published in: Vergilius Ferm, ed., *Classics of Protestantism* (New York: Philosophical Library, 1959), p. 40.

9. Natan Sharansky, *Fear No Evil* (New York: Public Affairs, 1998), pp. 154–55.
10. Quoted by Thomas M. Magstadt and Peter M. Schotten, *Understanding Politics: Ideas, Institutions, and Issues* (New York: St. Martin's Press, 1993), p. 39.
11. Quoted in Dmitri Volkogonov, *Lenin: A New Biography* (New York: The Free Press, 1994), p. 373.
12. See: Daniel Peris, *Storming the Heavens: The Soviet League of the Militant Godless* (Ithaca, NY: Cornell University Press, 1998).
13. Quoted in Thrower, *God's Commissar*, p. 39. Another translation of this quote comes from Robert Conquest, in his "The Historical Failings of CNN," in Arnold Beichman, ed., *CNN's Cold War Documentary* (Stanford, CA: Hoover Institution Press, 2000), p. 57.
14. Lenin wrote this in a November 13 or 14, 1913, letter to Maxim Gorky. See: Thrower, *God's Commissar*, p. 39.
15. See: J. M. Bochenski, "Marxism-Leninism and Religion," in B. R. Bociurkiw et al., eds., *Religion and Atheism in the USSR and Eastern Europe* (London: MacMillan, 1975), p. 11.
16. Quoted by Beilenson, *The Treaty Trap*, p. 163. (Full citation in Whittaker Chambers chapter.)
17. Dmitri Volkogonov, *Lenin*, p. 384. On Lenin's views on, and treatment of, religion, also see pp. 372–83.
18. Quoted in Barry Lee Woolley, *Adherents of Permanent Revolution: A History of the Fourth (Trotskyist) International* (Lanham, MD: University Press of America, 1999), pp. 4–5.
19. Soviet officials instead substituted secular civil ceremonies infused with communist ideology, known as "red weddings," "red baptisms," and "red funerals." In red baptisms, infants were given social "god-parents" who undertook to ensure the child was brought up to become a worthy "builder of communism." The parents of newborn children promised to raise their children "not as slaves for the bourgeoisie, but as fighters against it." Young mothers would declare: "The child belongs to me only physically. For his spiritual upbringing, I entrust him to society." See: Thrower, *God's Commissar*, p. 64; Jennifer McDowell, "Soviet Civil Ceremonies," *Journal for the Scientific Study of Religion*, Vol. 13, No. 3, 1974, pp. 265–79; and Powell, "Rearing the New Soviet Man," in Bociurkiw and Strong, *Religion and Atheism in the USSR and Eastern Europe*, pp. 160–65.
20. W. Bruce Lincoln, *Red Victory: A History of the Russian Civil War* (New York: Simon & Schuster, 1989), pp. 476–77.
21. On the anti-religious museums, see: "A Restored Look for the Long-Ignored Churches of Russia," Associated Press, July 23, 1976, p. B3.
22. Ibid.
23. Ibid.
24. Lincoln, *Red Victory*, p. 474.

25. On this, see Aleksandr Solzhenitsyn, *The Gulag Archipelago, 1918–1956* (New York: Harper & Row, 1974), pp. 29, 37–38, 325–27, 345–51.
26. Gerhard Simon, "The Catholic Church and the Communist State in the Soviet Union and Eastern Europe," in Bociurkiw and Strong, *Religion and Atheism in the USSR and Eastern Europe*, pp. 212–13.
27. Solzhenitsyn, *The Gulag Archipelago*, p. 37.
28. Ibid.
29. Michael Bordeaux and Kathleen Matchett, "The Russian Orthodox Church in Council 1945–1971," in Bociurkiw and Strong, eds., *Religion and Atheism in the USSR and Eastern Europe*. pp. 40–41.
30. Richard Wurmbrand, *Tortured for Christ* (Bartlesville, OK: Living Sacrifice Book Company, 1998), p. 65.
31. Lincoln, *Red Victory*, pp. 476–77.
32. Janis Johnson, "Movement Grows in Congress for Soviet Christian Support," *Washington Post*, July 31, 1976, p. A3.
33. Ibid.
34. For examples not cited, see David E. Powell in Powell, "Rearing the New Soviet Man," in Bociurkiw and Strong, *Religion and Atheism in the USSR and Eastern Europe*, pp. 151–57.
35. Interview with Olena Doviskaya.
36. Reagan, "Remarks and a Question-and-Answer Session With Area High School Seniors," Jacksonville, Florida, December 1, 1987.
37. This paragraph is a synopsis of the excellent material assembled by David E. Powell in Powell, "Rearing the New Soviet Man," in Bociurkiw and Strong, *Religion and Atheism in the USSR and Eastern Europe*, pp. 156–57.
38. The most religiously repressive nations in the Soviet empire were the USSR, Romania, and Albania. The church survived best in Poland. Still, none of the communist bloc countries enjoyed religious freedom, certainly by Western standards. The regimes in these nations were nearly all intolerant of religion. On Albania, see: Peter Prifti, "Albania—Towards an Atheist Society," in Bociurkiw and Strong, eds., *Religion and Atheism in the USSR and Eastern Europe*, pp. 388–404.
39. There was no copy of Wurmbrand's work on the bookshelves at the Reagan Ranch. Reagan reportedly had a larger set of bookshelves in his Bel Air home. I did not have access to those shelves. I contacted the office of Nancy Reagan to try to get an answer, but did not get one.
40. Wurmbrand died at the age of 91 in February 2001, before I was able to interview him. This information was relayed to me by his son, Michael, in an October 22, 2001, interview. Two of the letters he wrote were answered by Fred Ryan and Anne Higgins. Ryan, who was Director of Presidential Appointments and Scheduling, replied to Wurmbrand on October 17, 1983: "The President very much appreciates your willingness to meet and talk with him and would like to have the opportunity to meet. He would be happy to meet with you, if circumstances allowed, but the heavy demands on his time just will not allow him to do so." The reaction was similar in a February 27, 1984, letter from Higgins, who was Special Assistant to the President and Director of Correspondence. I filed a FOIA request to view this classified correspondence. It was released, and I viewed all twenty-seven pages at the Reagan Library in July 2003.
41. Reagan, "Religious Freedom," radio broadcast, July 31, 1978. All radio broadcasts referenced are on file at the Reagan Library or have been published by: Kiron Skinner, Martin Anderson, Annelise Anderson, editors, *Reagan, In His Own Hand* (New York:

The Free Press, 2000); and Skinner, Anderson, and Anderson, editors, *Stories in His Own Hand* (New York: Free Press, 2001). More such volumes from the Skinner-Andersons team are being published. This book cites only those Reagan radio broadcasts in which he wrote the text.

42. One of the best authorities on Marxism as a religion was Max Eastman, the product of parents who were extremely liberal Congregationalist ministers. Eastman became an ardent atheist-Marxist. Though he left communism by mid-life, he remained an inveterate atheist. One barometer of his attitude was his resignation from the newly launched *National Review* on the grounds that the conservative publication was too religious. On this, see: Buckley, *Odyssey of a Friend*, p. 220n. (Full citation in Whittaker Chambers chapter.)

Eastman's 1941 classic, *Marxism: Is It Science?* is a seminal early work on the religious aspects of Marxism. He wrote of the ideology as a "religion" and "faith" not only to its "adherents" but also to Marx himself. The book contains chapters with titles like "Religion in *Das Kapital*" and "Trotsky Defends the Faith." See: Max Eastman, *Marxism: Is It Science* (London: George Allen and Unwin, 1941), pp. 15, 22, 124–33, and 275–98. I'm indebted to Barry Woolley for his expertise on Eastman.

43. See: Jean Jacques Rousseau, *The Social Contract*, translated by G. D. H. Cole (Buffalo, NY: Prometheus Books, 1988), pp. 130–35.

44. Robert N. Bellah, *Beyond Belief: Essays on Religion in a Post-Traditional World* (New York: Harper & Row, 1970), pp. 175–86.

45. Christel Lane, *The Rites of Rulers: Ritual in Industrial Society—the Soviet Case* (Cambridge: Cambridge University Press, 1981), pp. 40–2.

46. Quoted in Thrower, *God's Commissar*, p. 28.

47. Joseph Schumpeter, *Capitalism, Socialism, and Democracy* (London, G. Allen & Unwin, 1943), p. 5.

48. Quoted in Thrower, *God's Commissar*, p. 38. Thrower provides a large number of such quotes from a wide range of authorities on pp. 27–42.

49. Lowe provides a nice overview of Soviet civil religion. See: Brian M. Lowe, "Soviet and American Civil Religion: A Comparison," *Journal of Interdisciplinary Studies*, Vol. 13, No. 1–2, 2001, pp. 73–96. In addition to Lowe, for an in-depth recent treatment, see: Arthur Jay Klinghoffer, *Red Apocalypse: The Religious Evolution of Soviet Communism* (Lanham, MD: University Press of America, 1996).

50. Thrower refers to this as part of the "cult of Lenin." See Thrower, *God's Commissar*, pp. 77–92.

51. Thrower, *God's Commissar*, p. 88.

52. This is common knowledge. For more, see: Thrower, *God's Commissar*, pp. 79–82.

53. Interview with Olena Doviskaya.

54. Volkogonov, *Lenin*, pp. 437, 441, and 446–47.

55. Quoted in Vaughn, *Ronald Reagan in Hollywood*, p. 209.

56. Reagan, "Freedom Has No 'S,' " address at Patriotic Education Week, August 1965, p. 1. On file at Reagan Library. "RWR-Speeches and Articles (1965–6)," folder, RRL, vertical files.

57. Ibid. There are also religious references or quotes from Scripture in these speeches he wrote himself. Among others, see: Reagan, " 'Salute to Ray Page' Dinner," McCormick Place, Chicago, IL, May 15, 1965; and Reagan, "Remarks by Ronald Reagan," New Haven Arena, New Haven, CT, September 28, 1965. These speeches are all on file at Reagan Library, "RWR-Speeches and Articles (1965–6)," folder, vertical files.

CHAPTER 6

1. Whittaker Chambers, *Witness* (New York: Random House, 1952), pp. 8 and 79.
2. Ibid., p. 9.
3. On Reagan and Muggeridge, see: "Remarks at the Annual Convention of the National Religious Broadcasters," January 31, 1983. On Roepke, see: Wilhelm Roepke, "The Economic Necessity of Freedom," *Modern Age*, Summer 1959; and Edwin J. Feulner, Jr., editor, *The March of Freedom* (Dallas, TX: Spence Publishing, 1998), pp. 295–99 and 316. On Meyer, also see Reagan speech text in collection by James C. Roberts, editor, *A City Upon a Hill: Speeches by Ronald Reagan Before the Conservative Political Action Conference* (Washington, D.C.: The American Studies Center, 1989), pp. 54 and 57.
4. Laurence W. Beilenson, *The Treaty Trap: A History of the Performance of Political Treaties by the United States & European Nations* (Washington, D.C.: Public Affairs Press, 1969). Among the sections on Soviet atheism, see pp. 161–63.
5. This lasted throughout the White House years. Among all the many people with whom Reagan exchanged letters as president, Beilenson was among the most frequent.
6. He would award Chambers the Presidential Medal of Freedom posthumously on February 21, 1984. The index to Reagan's *Presidential Papers* lists eight pages that feature references to Chambers in Reagan remarks between 1981 and 1989.
7. Author made observations inside ranch on July 26, 2001. I paged through Reagan's copy of Chambers' *Witness* at the Reagan Ranch. William F. Buckley, Jr., editor, *Odyssey of a Friend: Whittaker Chambers' Letters to William F. Buckley, Jr., 1954–1961* (New York: G. P. Putnam's Sons, 1969).
8. Chambers, *Witness* (New York: Random House, 1952).
9. I have personally observed these speech copies from the presidency. On his memory: Reagan's brother, Neil, remarked on Reagan's memory a number of times. His apparent photographic memory has been noted by Michael Deaver, Ed Meese, Bill Clark, Martin Anderson, and others. Reagan staff faced an unusual problem: His memory was so good, that if staff fed Reagan incorrect statistics or information, they had a big problem ever purging them from his memory banks. Meese says Reagan had "pretty much" a photographic memory "for things he read, but not faces." Interview with Ed Meese, November 23, 2001. Also see: Edwin Meese, *With Reagan* (Washington, D.C.: Regnery, 1992), p. 26.
10. Arthur Schlesinger, Jr., "The Truest Believer," *New York Times Book Review*, March 9, 1997.
11. Sam Tanenhaus, *Whittaker Chambers: A Biography* (New York: Random House, 1997).
12. Ibid.
13. Among these, see: Tanenhaus, *Whittaker Chambers*; and Allen Weinstein, *Perjury: The Hiss-Chambers Case* (New York: Knopf, 1978). While it probably took these two books from two liberals to convince many on the left of Hiss's guilt, the case was actually closed 35 years before Tanenhaus' work in Richard Nixon's first memoirs, *Six Crises* (New York: Doubleday, 1962)—specifically the chapter, "Hiss."
14. Noted in Edward Kosner, Karl Fleming, and William Cook, "Ronald Reagan: Rising Star in the West?" *Newsweek*, May 15, 1967, p. 27. These reporters were in Reagan's office and noted this and other books.
15. Quoted in Tanenhaus, *Whittaker Chambers*.
16. Reagan letter to Lorraine Wagner, November 20, 1962, YAF collection.
17. Quoted in Schlesinger, "The Truest Believer."

18. He acknowledged this in an April 6, 1954, letter to William F. Buckley, Jr. An acquaintance who read *Witness* asked Chambers, "Do you know that witness in Greek means martyr?" Chambers said to Buckley: "Of course, he knew that I knew." Source: Letter published in Buckley, *Odyssey of a Friend*, p. 62.

19. Chambers, *Witness*, p. 85.

20. See, for example, Fuelner, *The March of Freedom*.

21. Chambers, *Witness*, p. 7.

22. Reagan, "Remarks at a Conservative Political Action Conference Dinner," February 26, 1982.

23. Chambers, *Witness*, p. 8.

24. We see this word used throughout *Witness*. See pp. 81–85 especially, and p. 461, among others.

25. Chambers, *Witness*, p. 79.

26. Ibid., pp. 80 and 83.

27. Quoted in Tanenhaus, *Whittaker Chambers*, p. 212.

28. Schlesinger, "The Truest Believer."

29. Chambers, *Witness*, p. 712.

30. Chambers, *Witness*, p. 83.

31. Ibid., p. 9.

32. Reagan, "Remarks at a Conservative Political Action Conference Dinner," March 20, 1981. Also see: Reagan, "Remarks at the Annual Convention of the National Association of Evangelicals," Columbus, Ohio, March 6, 1984.

33. Chambers, *Witness*, pp. 10–13.

34. Ibid., p. 15.

35. Ibid., pp. 22 and 25.

36. Ibid., p. 25.

37. Ibid., p. 84.

38. Quoted in Rowland Evans and Robert Novak, *The Reagan Revolution* (New York: Dutton, 1981), pp. 208–9.

39. Chambers, *Witness*, p. 85.

40. Quoted in Evans and Novak, *The Reagan Revolution*, pp. 208–9.

41. Among other examples, see: Reagan, "Remarks at the Annual Convention of the National Association of Evangelicals," Columbus, Ohio, March 6, 1984.

42. Chambers, *Witness*, p. 15

43. Reagan, "Remarks at Eureka College," Eureka, Illinois, February 6, 1984.

44. See p. 17 of draft located in PHF, PS, RRL, Box 3, Folder 57. Final text copy, which matches Reagan's handwritten changes, is: Reagan, "Remarks at a Conservative Political Action Conference Dinner," February 26, 1982.

45. Quoted in Feulner, *The March of Freedom*, p. 216.

46. Chambers, *Witness*, pp. 16–7.

47. Ibid.

48. Reagan, "Remarks at Eureka College," February 6, 1984.

49. Reagan, "Remarks at a Conservative Political Action Conference Dinner," March 20, 1981.

50. Chambers, *Witness*, p. 25.

51. The letter was written to William F. Buckley, Jr.; it is published in Buckley, *Odyssey of a Friend*, p. 60.

CHAPTER 7

1. Reagan, "America the Beautiful," commencement address, William Woods College, June 1952. This address is discussed later.
2. "Remarks at a Spirit of America Rally," Atlanta, GA, January 26, 1984.
3. The number of times Reagan used this phrase is simply too numerous to count. Two books on Reagan have been titled with derivations of the phrase. One of these is called simply *Shining City* and the other is *A City Upon a Hill*, which is a collection of his CPAC speeches, where he gave twelve addresses between 1974 and 1988, often talking about the Shining City in each.
4. Reagan speaking before CPAC, January 25, 1974, Washington, D.C. The text appears in Roberts, ed., *A City Upon a Hill*, p. 10.
5. John Winthrop, "A Modell of Christian Charity," written by Winthrop for the Massachusetts Bay Colony, 1630.
6. For an early example not cited elsewhere, see: Reagan, "Commencement to the Orme School," June 1970. Speech filed at Reagan Library, "RWR—Speeches and Articles (1968)," vertical files. Also see: Reagan, "Remarks at a Dinner Honoring Representative Jack F. Kemp of New York," December 1, 1988; Reagan, "Remarks at the Republican National Convention," New Orleans, LA, August 15, 1988; and Reagan, "Farewell Address to the Nation," January 11, 1989.
7. Reagan, "Remarks at Kansas State University at the Alfred M. Landon Lecture Series on Public Issues," September 9, 1982.
8. Matthew 5:14–16. Translation is New International Version (NIV).
9. I'm indebted to Rev. Robert McCreight for helping to bring this together one Sunday morning, March 25, 2001, in Grove City, PA, at Tower Presbyterian Church.
10. Cited in Wills, *Reagan's America*, p. 28.
11. Reagan speaking before CPAC, February 6, 1977, Washington, D.C. The text appears in Roberts, ed., *A City Upon a Hill*, p. 33.
12. Nikolay Turkatenko, commentary for Soviet news agency *TASS*, July 8, 1985, printed as "Reagan's Remarks to U.S. Bar Association Viewed," in *FBIS*, July 9, 1985, pp. A1–2.
13. Interview with Raymond McCallister, Jr., September 18, 2003.
14. The two men never lost touch. Mac would visit Reagan a number of times during the White House years. Mac died on February 8, 1993. Interview with Raymond McCallister, Jr.
15. Kate Link, "When Reagan Came to Fulton," *Kingdom Daily News*, March 22, 1981.
16. Interview with Raymond McCallister, Jr.
17. Ibid. McCallister, Jr. to this day resides in Fulton, Missouri. His father is among Eureka College's most prominent graduates; a hall on campus today bears his name.
18. Link, "When Reagan Came to Fulton."
19. Reagan, "America the Beautiful," commencement address, William Woods College, June 1952. Text provided by William Woods University.
20. On July 4, 1968, he said: "Call it mysticism if you will," he conceded. "I have always believed there was some divine plan that placed this nation between the oceans to be sought out and found by those with a special kind of courage and an overabundant love of freedom." Source: Quoted in Lou Cannon, *Ronnie and Jesse: A Political Odyssey* (Garden City, NY: Doubleday, 1969), p. 259. On January 25, 1974, speaking before CPAC in Washington, D.C., he said: "I have always believed that there was some di-

vine plan that placed this great continent between two oceans." Text in Roberts, ed., *A City Upon a Hill*, p. 3.

For other examples, see: Reagan, "Freedom Has No 'S,' " address at Patriotic Education Week, August 1965, p. 2, text on file at the Reagan Library; Reagan, "Remarks at the Opening Ceremonies for the Knoxville International Energy Exposition (World's Fair)," Knoxville, TN, May 1, 1982; "Remarks at Kansas State University," September 9, 1982; "RWR-Speeches and Articles (1965–6)," vertical files; Reagan, "Remarks at a Spirit of America Rally," Atlanta, GA, January 26, 1984; Reagan, "Remarks and a Question-and-Answer Session With Area High School Seniors," Jacksonville, FL, December 1, 1987; and Reagan, "Remarks at the Republican National Convention," New Orleans, LA, August 15, 1988. This is not a complete list.

21. Reagan, "Remarks at the Annual Convention of the National Religious Broadcasters," January 31, 1983.
22. Remarks by Reagan to the Heritage Foundation annual board meeting in Carmel, CA, June 22, 1990, published in Frederick J. Ryan Jr., editor, *Ronald Reagan: The Wisdom and Humor of the Great Communicator* (San Francisco: Collins Publishers, 1995), p. 32.
23. America the Beautiful speech, June 1952.
24. Link, "When Reagan Came to Fulton."
25. Reagan, "Commencement at Eureka College," June 7, 1957. The text to this speech is available. It is on file at the Reagan Library and has also been circulated among a number of collections, including a CPAC electronic collection titled, "Reagan Documents on Disk."
26. A 1994 book, *Many Are Chosen*, co-edited by William R. Hutchison of Harvard Divinity School and published by Harvard Theological Studies, contains case studies of such views by people in the United States, Great Britain, France, Germany, South Africa, Sweden, Switzerland, and others. Russel B. Nye asserted in 1966 that "all nations . . . have long agreed that they are chosen peoples; the idea of special destiny is as old as nationalism itself." William R. Hutchison and Hartmut Lehmann, eds., *Many Are Chosen: Divine Election and Western Nationalism* (Cambridge, MA: Harvard Theological Studies, 1994). Also see: Russel B. Nye, *This Almost Chosen People: Essays in the History of American Ideas* (East Lansing: Michigan State University Press, 1966), p. 164.
27. James H. Moorhead, "The American Israel: Protestant Tribalism and Universal Mission," in Hutchison and Lehmann, *Many Are Chosen*, pp. 145–66.
28. A number of civil leaders and theologians in the nineteenth century argued that it was part of the divine plan that America was preordained to expand to the West. This became known as America's "Manifest Destiny." Among the writers who stand out was Herman Melville, who wrote in his *White Jacket* that America was "the Israel of our time" and Americans the "chosen people." "God has predestined . . . great things from our race," wrote Melville, "and great things we feel in our souls. . . . We are the pioneers of the world." This passage is quoted in Maureen Henry, *The Intoxication of Power: An Analysis of Civil Religion in Relation to Ideology* (Dordrect, Holland: D. Reidel, 1979), p. 104.
29. Quoted in Conrad Cherry, *God's New Israel: Religious Interpretations of American Destiny* (Englewood Cliffs, NJ: Prentice-Hall, 1972), p. 288.
30. Reagan, "Proclamation 5296–National Day of Prayer, 1985," January 29, 1985.
31. Allan Nevins, ed., *John F. Kennedy, the Burden and the Glory* (New York: Harper & Row, 1964). Ironically, Reagan cited that JFK quote in closing a September 1980

speech in Philadelphia. Those Kennedy words, he said, "are appropriate today." In his speech, Reagan claimed those JFK words were never actually spoken, being intended for a speech in late November 1963. Source: Reagan, "Remarks on 'Super Senior Day,' " Philadelphia, September 7, 1980. Speech text located at Reagan Library, "Reagan 1980 Campaign Speeches, September 1980," vertical files.

32. John F. Kennedy, "Inaugural Address," January 20, 1961.

CHAPTER 8

1. Reagan, "Commencement at Eureka College," June 7, 1957.
2. Reagan, "Freedom Has No 'S,' " August 1965.
3. Ronald Reagan, "Encroaching Government Controls," *Human Events*, July 21, 1961, p. 457.
4. Hugh Heclo maintains that Reagan was a "man of ideas" in the estimable company of Jackson, Madison, and Jefferson. See: Heclo, "Ronald Reagan and the American Public Philosophy," in W. Elliot Brownlee, ed., *The Reagan Presidency* (Lawrence, KS: University Press of Kansas, 2003).
5. Reagan, "Commencement at Eureka College," June 7, 1957.
6. Ibid.
7. Ibid.
8. Among these, see, for example: "Reagan Spreads Warning About Reds in Hollywood," *The Independent* (Wilkes-Barre, PA), July 23, 1961. This was a UPI syndicated article.
9. Reagan was quoted as saying this in a UPI article that ran in the *New York Times*, May 9, 1961, titled, "Red Threat Is Cited."
10. Matthew Dallek, *The Right Moment* (New York: Free Press, 2000), p. 27.
11. Ronald Reagan, "Encroaching Government Controls," July 21, 1961, p. 457.
12. Reagan speech given to Fargo Chamber of Commerce, January 26, 1962. Quoted in Dallek, *The Right Moment*, p. 27.
13. Reagan, "Freedom Has No 'S,' " August 1965.
14. Reagan, "Remarks at the Annual Convention of the National Association of Evangelicals," Orlando, Florida, March 8, 1983. He told this story again 10 months later to the annual convention of National Religious Broadcasters. See: Reagan, "Remarks at the Annual Convention of the National Religious Broadcasters," January 30, 1984.
15. There is variation in this thinking among Christian denominations. But this, nonetheless, was Reagan's view, and it is a conventional view among Fundamentalists, Evangelicals, and most to all Protestants. That aside, Reagan himself publicly recited the covenant as president, saying in January 1984: "For God so loved the world that He gave His only begotten Son, that whosoever believeth in Him should not perish but have everlasting life." Reagan, "Remarks at the Annual Convention of the National Religious Broadcasters," January 30, 1984.
16. He also said that 2nd Chronicles 7:14 was his favorite. He usually cited one of those two.
17. Herbert E. Ellingwood, "Ronald Reagan: 'God, Home and Country,' " *Christian Life*, November 1980, p. 50.
18. I will not address the degree to which this squares with Christian theology. It is by no means unconventional. However, many Christians would counter that if an individual never hears the Gospel of Christ, that person is not eternally accountable and not damned in the afterlife. Of course, many Russian atheists heard the Gospel from un-

derground Christians but rejected it anyway, in part because of the atheistic arguments they learned through anti-Christian education subsidized by the Soviet state.

19. Reagan frequently quoted C. S. Lewis. Among others, see: Reagan, "Speech at Wheaton College," Wheaton, Illinois, October 8, 1980. Speech text located at Reagan Library, "Reagan 1980 Campaign Speeches, October 1980," vertical files.

20. C. S. Lewis, *Mere Christianity* (New York: Simon & Schuster, First Touchstone edition, 1996), p. 73.

21. In the words of Reagan's friend and later national security adviser Richard V. Allen: "He [Reagan] believed the Russian people were deeply religious. He knew these people were being deterred from expressing their faith by the communist government. This is another reason why he so hated communism." Interview with Richard V. Allen, November 12, 2001.

22. Maria Anne Hirschmann, *Hansi: The Girl Who Left the Swastika* (Hansi Ministries, 2000).

23. Ronald Reagan, "Losing Freedom by Installments," presented to the Fargo, ND, Chamber of Commerce, 78th Annual Meeting, January 26, 1962. Also see: Reagan, "America the Beautiful," commencement address, William Woods College, June 1952.

24. The Phoenix speech was given March 30, 1961, and is on file at Reagan Library. The New Jersey speech was also given in 1961.

25. Reagan, "Encroaching Government Controls," *Human Events*, July 21, 1961, pp. 457–60. Also see: March 30, 1961 Phoenix speech; Anne Edwards, *Early Reagan*, pp. 539–57; and Reagan and Hubler, *Where's the Rest of Me?* pp. 302–12.

26. Ibid.

27. This information was relayed to me by reporter Charles Wiley, who received the account directly from Knott in a lengthy conversation he had with Knott.

28. My account is drawn from Wiley's conversation with Knott. It seems consistent with a detailed account provided by Rick Perlstein in his *Before the Storm* (New York: Hill and Wang, 2001), pp. 440–41, 492, and 500–501. On Reagan, Knott, and other key California conservatives, also see: Lisa McGirr, *Suburban Warriors: The Origins of the New American Right* (Princeton, NJ: Princeton University Press, 2001).

29. Reagan said this in a November 4, 1962, speech on behalf of Richard Nixon's California gubernatorial campaign. The speech text is printed in Davis Houck and Amos Kiewe, *Actor, Ideologue, Politician: The Public Speeches of Ronald Reagan* (Westport, CT: Greenwood Press, 1993), pp. 27–35.

30. Lawrence E. Davies, "Reagan Assesses Political Future," *New York Times*, July 25, 1965, p. 52.

CHAPTER 9

1. Herbert E. Ellingwood, "Ronald Reagan: 'God, Home and Country,'" *Christian Life*, November 1980, p. 25; William Rose, "The Reagans and Their Pastor," *Christian Life*, May 1968, p. 44; and Nancy Reagan with Bill Libby, *Nancy* (New York: William Morrow, 1980), p. 168.

2. Rose, "The Reagans and Their Pastor," pp. 43–44.

3. This address is known as "The Creative Society" speech. For a transcript, see: Ronald Reagan, *The Creative Society* (New York: Devin Adair, 1968), pp. 1–14.

4. Ellingwood, "Ronald Reagan: 'God, Home and Country,'" p. 25; Rose, "The Reagans and Their Pastor," p. 44; and Nancy Reagan, *Nancy*, p. 168.

5. Quoted in Cannon, *Ronnie and Jesse*, pp. 130–1. Also see: Joseph Lewis, *What Makes Reagan Run? A Political Profile* (New York: McGraw-Hill Book Co., 1968), pp. 159–60; and Reagan, "First Inaugural Message as Governor of California," January 1967, published in *Ronald Reagan Talks to America*, p. 20.

6. His use of the term "Prince of Peace" was a favored synonym for Jesus Christ.

7. Nancy Reagan, *Nancy*, p. 168.

8. Ellingwood, "Ronald Reagan: 'God, Home and Country,' " p. 25. That realization likely struck Californians also at a prayer breakfast during inauguration week, where the governor-elect affirmed: "Belief in dependence on God is essential to our state and nation."

9. Ron Reagan interviewed on *Ronald Reagan: A Legacy Remembered*, History Channel production, 2002.

10. This took place in 1984. Interview with Michael Reagan.

11. This took place during the first Reagan-Gorbachev one-on-one meeting in Moscow on May 29, 1988. The source is: "1988 US-Soviet Summit Memcons," May 26–June 3, 1988, RRL, Box 92084, Folder 2.

12. Patti Davis, *Angels Don't Die: My Father's Gift of Faith* (New York: HarperCollins, 1995), p. 5. Among other sections, see: pp. 1–2, 9, 13, 16, 22–23, 25–27, 32–33, 35–38, 42–43, 48–51, 64, 99–102, 105–9, 117, and 120.

13. Bob Slosser, *Reagan Inside Out* (Waco, TX: Word Books, 1984), pp. 48–51.

14. Ibid.

15. Rose, "The Reagans and Their Pastor," pp. 38 and 44.

16. Slosser, *Reagan Inside Out*, pp. 48–51.

17. Rose, "The Reagans and Their Pastor," pp. 38 and 44.

18. Reagan said this during a 1968 interview with Frost. Cited by Cannon, *Role of a Lifetime*, p. 247.

19. Reagan, "The Value of Understanding Our Past," speech at Eureka College, September 28, 1967, published in *A Time for Choosing, The Speeches of Ronald Reagan, 1961–1982*, Regnery Press, 1983, p. 83.

20. Ellingwood, "Ronald Reagan: 'God, Home and Country,' " p. 50.

21. Reagan said this in 1973. Remarks published in Ryan, ed., *Ronald Reagan: The Wisdom and Humor of the Great Communicator* (San Francisco: Collins Publishers, 1995), p. 115.

22. Bookshelves at Reagan Ranch. Author made observations inside ranch on July 26, 2001. Lamar T. Berman, *Capital Punishment* (NY: H.W. Wilson, 1925).

23. Moomaw interviewed on "Ronald Reagan: A Legacy Remembered," History Channel production, 2002. Also see: Morris, *Dutch*, p. 351; Lou Cannon, *Reagan* (New York: Putnam, 1982), p. 167n; Cannon, *Role of a Lifetime*, p. 444; Skinner, Anderson, and Anderson, *Reagan: A Life in Letters*, pp. 199–200; and Lynn Nofziger interviewed in oral-history series by the University of Virginia. Published in Kenneth W. Thompson, ed., *Leadership in the Reagan Presidency* (Lanham, MD: Madison Books, 1992), p. 74.

24. Cannon, *Role of a Lifetime*, pp. 504 and 803.

25. Rose, "The Reagans and Their Pastor," p. 39.

26. Letter is quoted in Von Damm, *Sincerely, Ronald Reagan*, p. 82.

27. Nancy was interviewed and quoted by Peggy Noonan in her *When Character Was King*, p. 98.

28. Interview with William P. Clark, August 24, 2001; and William P. Clark, "President Reagan and the Wall," Address to the Council of National Policy, San Francisco, CA, March 2000, p. 11.

29. Clark was Reagan's second NSA, replacing Allen. He was NSA from January 1982 until October 1983.

30. Edmund Morris interviewed by *American Enterprise* magazine, November/December 1999 issue.

31. An example not featured is when Reagan learned of the shoot down of KAL 007 in September 1983. When Clark informed Reagan, the president's first reaction was: "Bill, let's pray it's not true." According to Clark, this was not a mere generic saying by Reagan but an actual prayer request. Interview with William P. Clark, August 24, 2001; and William P. Clark, "President Reagan and the Wall," Address to the Council of National Policy, San Francisco, California, March 2000, p. 11.

32. Interview with Clark, August 24, 2001.

33. Reagan, *An American Life*, pp. 167–68.

34. Ibid., pp. 167–68. The story is backed by Mike Deaver, who spoke to Reagan about the problem at the time in 1968, and was told by Reagan that he found the answer to his problem simply by "looking up" rather than looking to Maalox. Michael Deaver, *A Different Drummer: My Thirty Years with Ronald Reagan* (New York: HarperCollins, 2001), p. 96.

35. Rose, "The Reagans and Their Pastor," p. 39.

36. More will be said later on Reagan and Clark. Interview with Clark, August 24, 2001.

37. Sources: January 4, 1973 Reagan letter to the Cleaver family, published in Skinner, Anderson, and Anderson, *Reagan: A Life in Letters*, pp. 278–79; and May 1971 letter quoted in Von Damm, *Sincerely, Ronald Reagan*, pp. 43 and 83. On him saying the same between his governorship and presidency, see: David Nyhan, " 'Born-again' run the race for President," *Boston Globe*, May 26, 1980, pp. A10–11.

38. Quoted in Ellingwood, "Ronald Reagan: 'God, Home and Country,' " p. 50; and Slosser, *Reagan Inside Out*, p. 154.

39. See: "Reagan on God and Morality," *Christianity Today*, July 2, 1976, pp. 39–40.

40. See letters quoted by Von Damm, *Sincerely, Ronald Reagan*, pp. 22–23, 84, and 91.

41. Ellingwood, "Ronald Reagan: 'God, Home and Country,' " p. 50.

42. Quoted in ibid.

43. Once before he was governor, still traveling the mashed-potato circuit, he was invited to speak to a three-day national meeting of military chaplains. Afterward, one of the attendees came up and thanked him for being the only person in the three days who had mentioned Christ by name. Reagan, "Interview with Knight Ridder News Service," February 13, 1984.

44. See selections from letters published by Von Damm, *Sincerely, Ronald Reagan*, pp. 82–86 and 155–7.

45. "Reagan on God and Morality," *Christianity Today*, p. 39.

46. Reagan wrote this in a March 1, 1978 letter to Reverend Thomas H. Griffith of Shell Beach, California, published in Skinner, Anderson, and Anderson, *Reagan: A Life in Letters*, pp. 276–77 and 856n. Also quoted in Evans and Novak, *The Reagan Revolution*, pp. 208–9.

47. Reagan's secretary, Helene Von Damm, published this excerpt from a Reagan letter to a private citizen in the early 1970s: "It has always seemed to me that Christ in His own words gave us reason to accept literally the miracle of His birth and resurrection. He said, 'I am the Son of God.' Indeed, He said so many things that we have a very simple choice: either we believe Him, or we must assume He was the greatest liar who ever lived. If we believe the latter, then we have to ask, could such a charlatan have had the impact on the world for two thousand years that this man has had? We have known

other great fakers down through the centuries. Some are even a paragraph in history. None had a lasting effect." Quoted in Von Damm, *Sincerely, Ronald Reagan*, p. 83. Also see: Reagan, "Christmas," radio broadcast, January 9, 1978.

48. Among the few knowledgeable enough of Lewis to recognize the passage was Dinesh D'Souza. See: Dinesh D'Souza, *Ronald Reagan: How an Ordinary Man Became an Extraordinary Leader* (New York: Free Press, 1997), p. 214.

49. Lewis, *Mere Christianity*, p. 56.

50. The argument attacks the popular assertion by some non-Christians that Christ should be recognized as a "great person" or "great teacher" or "great philosopher" but not as God or the Son of God. The argument is often advanced by skeptics or non-believers to try to assuage believers during heated debate. Lewis maintained that to assert that Christ was not the Son of God but still a great man is contradictory—the two points cannot be advanced simultaneously. Such a great man, said Lewis, would also be the greatest and most successful liar in human history, providing endless millions, even billions, with a completely false security and phony sense of eternal salvation. Such a charlatan, said Lewis, who would thus have been a self-delusional lunatic, is far from a great person; likewise for the apostles, disciples, bishops, popes, theologians, nuns, and saints who subsequently would be complicit in history's most successful, devastating, and tragic conspiracy.

51. The Lewis argument became so popular that Reagan may well have picked it up somewhere else, without knowing it was from Lewis. We don't know for sure if he did or didn't read it himself—though, again, he quoted Lewis frequently and hailed his writings. See: Reagan, "Remarks at the Annual Convention of the National Association of Evangelicals," Orlando, Florida, March 8, 1983.

52. See: Reagan, *An American Life*, pp. 49, 57, 70, 123.

53. Reagan performed at the Last Frontier in February 1954. Later in 1954, he began the GE job. Information on Reagan at the Last Frontier was provided by the same hotel, which is now called the New Frontier; the name has been changed a number of times.

54. Nancy Reagan speaking in interview on "Reagan," *The American Experience*. She gives a number of other examples in her 1980 autobiography. See: Nancy Reagan, *Nancy*, p. 143.

55. See: Morris, *Dutch*, p. 304.

56. Rose, "The Reagans and Their Pastor," pp. 43–44.

57. Ibid.

58. Kosner, Fleming, and Cook, "Ronald Reagan: Rising Star in the West?" p. 36.

59. George S. Smith, *Who Is Ronald Reagan?* (New York: Pyramid Books, 1968), p. 87.

60. The Broder piece is cited and quoted in Cannon, *Ronnie and Jesse*, p. 266.

61. A strong testimony of Nelle's belief in God's will is a January 17, 1955, letter she wrote to Lorraine Wagner. Nelle letter to Lorraine Wagner, January 17, 1955, YAF collection.

62. Rose, "The Reagans and Their Pastor," p. 46.

63. Reagan, *An American Life*, pp. 20–21.

64. Anne Edwards, *Early Reagan*, p. 350.

65. Patti Davis, *Angels Don't Die*, pp. 48–49.

66. Von Damm, *Sincerely, Ronald Reagan*, p. 26.

67. Letter is quoted in Von Damm, *Sincerely, Ronald Reagan*, p. 86.

68. Ibid.

69. Letter is quoted in Von Damm, *Sincerely, Ronald Reagan*, pp. 123–25.

70. For other examples as governor, see: Von Damm, *Sincerely, Ronald Reagan*, pp. 123–26.

71. See: Reagan, "Life and Death," radio broadcast, February 20, 1978. Located in "Ronald Reagan: Pre-Presidential Papers: Selected Radio Broadcasts, 1975–1979," October 1977 to October 10, 1978, Box 3, RRL. Also published in Skinner, Anderson, and Anderson, *Stories In His Own Hand*, pp. 3–5.

72. Examples are letters he wrote to the widow of actor Ray Milland (March 13, 1986) and a moving correspondence with Mrs. Ellen Bejcek and her son Andy over the death of her husband, a secret service agent. Letters located in PHF, PR, RRL, Boxes 15 and 6, Folders 233 and 78, respectively.

73. The incident is told in line-by-line detail by Bob Slosser, a *New York Times* reporter who wrote the book *Reagan Inside Out*. Slosser, *Reagan Inside Out*, pp. 13–20.

74. Reagan said this in an April 1, 1987, letter he wrote to John T. Kehoe of Sacramento, California. Letter is located in PHF, PR, RRL, Box 18, Folder 285.

75. Interview with Rev. Louis P. Sheldon, February 6, 2003.

CHAPTER 10

1. Quoted by Ronnie Dugger, *On Reagan: The Man & His Presidency* (New York: McGraw Hill, 1983), p. 439.

2. Reagan speaking before CPAC, January 25, 1974, Washington, D.C., text appears in Roberts, ed., *A City Upon a Hill*, p. 11.

3. Reagan, *An American Life*, p. 266.

4. From the pre-presidential period, see among others: Reagan, "Speech to Members of Platform Committee," Republican National Convention, July 31, 1968, filed in "RWR—Speeches and Articles (1968)," folder, vertical files, RRL; Reagan speaking before CPAC, January 25, 1974, Washington, D.C., text appears in Roberts, ed., *A City Upon a Hill*, pp. 11–12; and Reagan, "Commencement Remarks at Marlborough College Prep School for Girls," Los Angeles, June 6, 1974, filed in, "RWR—Speeches and Articles (1974–76)," folder, vertical files, RRL. Also see: Reagan, "Letters to the Editor," radio broadcast, June 1975, located in "Ronald Reagan: Pre-Presidential Papers: Selected Radio Broadcasts, 1975–1979," January 1975 to March 1977, Box 1, RRL; and Skinner, Anderson, and Anderson, *Reagan, In His Own Hand*, pp. 15–16.

5. Reagan, "Nationally Televised Address," ABC-TV, July 6, 1976. Speech filed in, "RWR—Speeches and Articles (1974–76)," folder, vertical files, RRL.

6. Reagan speaking before CPAC, March 1, 1975, Washington, D.C., text appears in Roberts, ed., *A City Upon a Hill*, p. 25.

7. In the draft, the word "GODLESS" was inserted later. The credit for finding this speech goes to Kurt Ritter of Texas A&M University, who generously shared the two pages with me. They were given to Ritter by Reagan presidential speechwriter C. Landon Parvin. Ritter knows of no complete text of the speech.

8. Again, these transcripts are available at the Reagan Library, and have been published by Skinner, Anderson, and Anderson.

9. Quoted by Bociurkiw, "Religious Dissent and the Soviet State," in Bociurkiw and Strong, eds., *Religion and Atheism in the USSR and Eastern Europe*. pp. 81–82.

10. Johnson, "Movement Grows," p. A3.

11. In May 1988, TASS attacked Reagan on this exact point with this exact defense. TASS cited Article 52 of the Soviet constitution, which stated: "The citizens of the USSR are guaranteed freedom of conscience, that is, the right to profess any religion or not to profess any religion." Source: Statement by TASS in English, printed as

"Reagan Remarks on Human Rights, Religion Reviewed: Speaks to Churchmen," in *FBIS*, FBIS-SOV-88-087, May 4, 1988, p. 11.

12. Johnson, "Movement Grows," p. A3. Also see: "Seven Soviet Christians Appeal to World for Aid," *Religious News Services* (published in the *Washington Post*), August 13, 1980, p. C6.

13. Janis Johnson, "Congress Decries Soviet Christian Persecution," *Washington Post*, October 8, 1976, p. B18; and Johnson, "Movement Grows," p. A3.

14. "Soviets Still Repress Believers, Report Says," *Religious News Services* (published in the *Washington Post*), August 13, 1980, p. C6.

15. This particular quote, which is merely one such example, is quoted by Dugger, *On Reagan*, p. 430.

16. Located in "Ronald Reagan: Pre-Presidential Papers: Selected Radio Broadcasts, 1975–1979," January 1975 to March 1977, Box 1, RRL. Also see: Skinner, Anderson, and Anderson, *Reagan, In His Own Hand*, p. 30.

17. Reagan speaking before CPAC, February 6, 1977, Washington, D.C., text appears in Roberts, *A City Upon a Hill*, p. 33.

18. Located in "Ronald Reagan: Pre-Presidential Papers: Selected Radio Broadcasts, 1975–1979," October 1977 to October 10, 1978, Box 3, RRL. Also see: Skinner, Anderson, and Anderson, *Reagan, In His Own Hand*, p. 136.

19. Located in "Ronald Reagan: Pre-Presidential Papers: Selected Radio Broadcasts, 1975–1979," October 31, 1978 to October 1979, Box 4, RRL. Also see: Dugger, *On Reagan*, p. 516; and Skinner, Anderson, and Anderson, *Reagan, In His Own Hand*, pp. 174–75.

20. Reagan, "Address to the Roundtable National Affairs Briefing," Dallas, TX, August 22, 1980, filed in, "Reagan 1980 Campaign Speeches, August 1980," folder, vertical files, RRL.

21. Reagan, "Religious Freedom," radio broadcast, July 31, 1978. Located in "Ronald Reagan: Pre-Presidential Papers: Selected Radio Broadcasts, 1975–1979," October 1977 to October 10, 1978, Box 3, RRL. Also see: Skinner, Anderson, and Anderson, *Reagan, In His Own Hand*, p. 26.

22. He said this in radio broadcasts. Located in "Ronald Reagan: Pre-Presidential Papers: Selected Radio Broadcasts, 1975–1979," Boxes 3 and 4, RRL. Also see: Dugger, *On Reagan*, p. 516; and Skinner, Anderson, and Anderson, *Reagan, In His Own Hand*, pp. 174–75.

23. Reagan, "Religious Freedom," radio broadcast, July 31, 1978.

24. Reagan said this and much more in a 1975 interview with Charles D. Hobbs. Source: Charles D. Hobbs, *Ronald Reagan's Call to Action* (Nashville and New York: Thomas Nelson, 1976), pp. 22–23.

25. Reagan, "Religious Freedom," radio broadcast, July 31, 1978.

26. In fact, the red star did replace the traditional star atop the Christmas tree, which was renamed the New Year Tree. This was part of the secular Great Winter Festival that replaced the traditional Christmas season, celebrating merely the advent of the New Year. See: Thrower, *God's Commissar*, p. 61. On Soviet secular holidays which replaced religious holidays like Christmas and Easter, see: Powell, "Rearing the New Soviet Man," in Bociurkiw and Strong, *Religion and Atheism in the USSR and Eastern Europe*, pp. 157–65.

27. A handwritten draft of the text is on file at the Reagan Library. Located in "Ronald Reagan: Pre-Presidential Papers: Selected Radio Broadcasts, 1975–1979," April 1977 to September 1977, Box 2, RRL.

28. Quoted by Ernest Conine, "President Reagan: How Does *That* Sound?" *Los Angeles Times*, March 17, 1980, p. 5.

29. George Leggett, *The Cheka: Lenin's Political Police* (New York: Oxford University Press, 1981), p. 103.

30. Stephane Courtois et al, *The Black Book of Communism* (Cambridge: Harvard University Press, 1999), pp. 3–4.

31. Malia in Courtois, *Black Book*, pp. xvii–xviii.

32. Ibid, p. x.

33. Lee Edwards, editor, *The Collapse of Communism* (Stanford, CA: Hoover Institution Press, 1999), p. xiii.

34. Aside from WWII deaths attributed to Hitler, most estimates are that he killed 6–10 million Jews, Slavs, gypsies, and various others he dubbed "misfits."

35. Typically accepted numbers for people killed in WWI is 8.5 million and for WWII is 40–50 million.

36. Alexander Solzhenitsyn cites a lower figure of ten per month for the Inquisition. My source for forty-two per month comes from the earliest authoritative work on the subject: J. A. Llorente, *A Critical History of the Inquisition of Spain* (Williamstown, MA: J. Lilburne, 1823), pp. 575–83. Solzhenitsyn's figures are published in his *Alexander Solzhenitsyn Speaks to the West*, p. 17.

37. Located in "Ronald Reagan: Pre-Presidential Papers: Selected Radio Broadcasts, 1975–1979," January 1975 to March 1977, Box 1, RRL. Also see: Skinner, Anderson, and Anderson, *Reagan, In His Own Hand*, pp. 10–12.

38. On this, see: Gina Kolata, *Flu: The Story of the Great Influenza Pandemic of 1918 and the Search for the Virus That Caused It* (New York: Touchstone, 2001).

39. Quoted by Dugger, *On Reagan*, p. 439.

40. This passage is from a May 25, 1977, radio broadcast he wrote. Located in "Ronald Reagan: Pre-Presidential Papers: Selected Radio Broadcasts, 1975–1979," April 1977 to September 1977, Box 2, RRL. Also see: Skinner, Anderson, and Anderson, *Reagan, In His Own Hand*, pp. 33–35.

41. Speech is cited by Kiron Skinner, "Reagan's Plan," *National Interest*, Summer 1999, p. 139.

42. This is taken from two Reagan radio broadcasts titled "Strategy I" and "Strategy II." They were both recorded May 4, 1977. Located in "Ronald Reagan: Pre-Presidential Papers: Selected Radio Broadcasts, 1975–1979," April 1977 to September 1977, Box 2, RRL; and Skinner, Anderson, and Anderson, *Reagan, In His Own Hand*, pp. 109–13.

43. Marx's quote is on page 44 of the *Manifesto*. See: Courtois and Panne in Courtois, *Black Book*, pp. 271–75; and Magstadt and Schotten, *Understanding Politics*, p. 39.

44. Quoted in Woolley, *Adherents of Permanent Revolution*, pp. 12–13.

45. Volkogonov, *Lenin*, p. 390. On Lenin, world revolution, and the Comintern, also see pp. 387–407.

46. Quoted by Leon Trotsky, *The History of the Russian Revolution*, translated by Max Eastman (Ann Arbor: University of Michigan Press, 1932), p. 395. On Trotsky and global communism, see Woolley, *Adherents of Permanent Revolution*, pp. 13 and 35; and the works of Richard Pipes in particular.

47. Quoted by Trotsky, *The History of the Russian Revolution*, p. 395.

48. Citing this Lenin quote, Arthur M. Schlesinger, Jr., noted that Lenin and his followers, including Stalin and his associates, were bound to regard the United States as the enemy not because of a particular deed but because of the "primordial fact" that

America was the leading capitalist power and thus, by "Leninist syllogism," unappeasably hostile. It was assumed that America would seek to oppose, encircle, and destroy Soviet Russia. Later, the legacy of this Leninist logic would prevail, wrote Schlesinger, regardless of what FDR or Truman did or failed to do. According to Schlesinger, nothing the United States could have done in 1944–45 in particular "would have abolished this mistrust, required and sanctified as it was by Marxist gospel—nothing short of the conversion of the United States into a Stalinist despotism." Arthur M. Schlesinger, Jr., "The Origins of the Cold War," *Foreign Affairs*, Vol. 46, No. 1, October 1967, pp. 22–52.

49. An excellent, widely read, early source on the American effort was written by Arthur M. Schlesinger, Jr. See: Schlesinger's "The U.S. Communist Party," *Life*, July 29, 1946, Vol. 21, pp. 84–96.

50. Quoted by Trotsky, *The History of the Russian Revolution*, p. 395.

51. Courtois and Panne in Courtois, *Black Book*, pp. 271–75.

52. The full quotes from this program are published by Crozier, *The Rise and Fall of the Soviet Empire*, pp. 38–40.

53. Richard Pipes, "The Cold War: CNN's Version," in Beichman, ed., *CNN's Cold War Documentary*, pp. 45–46. These guidelines are consistent with the goals of Leninism, outlined in Lenin's 1920 work, *Left-Wing Communism: An Infantile Disorder*.

54. Slosser, *Reagan Inside Out*, pp. 48–51; Rose, "The Reagans and Their Pastor," p. 46; and Hyer, "Reagan, Carter, Anderson," p. A28. Other 1970s and 1980s sources are cited later.

One among a number of sources (cited later) who could've vouched for this was a Reagan colleague and friend from his gubernatorial days, Herbert Ellingwood. "Ronald Reagan is a born again Christian," wrote Ellingwood in 1980. "We've discussed it personally many times." Ellingwood, "Ronald Reagan: 'God, Home and Country,' " p. 50.

55. Frank van der Linden, *The Real Reagan* (New York: William Morrow, 1981), pp. 26–27.

56. Quoted in Evans and Novak, *The Reagan Revolution*, pp. 208–9.

57. Ibid.

58. Maureen Reagan, "A president and a father," *Washington Times*, June 16, 2000, p. A23.

59. Von Damm, *At Reagan's Side*, p. 83.

60. Waggoner, *Richly Blessed*, p. 149.

61. Speech is excerpted in Peter Hannaford, *The Reagans: A Political Portrait* (New York: Coward-McCann, 1983), pp. 214–9. The remarks at Kansas City came on August 20, 1976, the day after the big night at the Republican Convention, where Ford was awarded a slight majority of delegates and Reagan delivered an impromptu speech after being beckoned by Ford.

62. On the eve of the election, on November 3, 1980, he said these things again in a televised address. Reagan, "A Vision for America," televised address, November 3, 1980. Speech transcript located in "Reagan 1980 Campaign Speeches, November 1980," folder, vertical files, RRL.

63. Among available transcript copies, see: Houck and Kiewe, *Actor, Ideologue, Politician*, p. 166.

64. Ironically, that crew member was future Reagan speechwriter Peggy Noonan, then a lonely conservative working for CBS, who tells this story in Noonan, *When Character Was King*, pp. 130–31.

CHAPTER 11

1. Slosser, *Reagan Inside Out*, p. 166.
2. Information provided by the Reagan Library, document titled, "Residences of Ronald Reagan."
3. As Reagan put it to Noonan, "And then I came here to Washington to live in this house, and I haven't had the dream since. Not once." Noonan, *What I Saw at the Revolution*, pp. 329–30. Also see: Deaver, *A Different Drummer* (New York: HarperCollins, 2001), p. 144.
4. Sources: Slosser, *Reagan Inside Out*, p. 155; and Doug and Bill Wead, *Reagan in Pursuit of the Presidency* (Plainfield, NJ: Haven Books, 1980), p. 174.
5. For instance, to cite just one example, in one interview he recited Psalm 106, verses 2–6. See: "Reagan on God and Morality," *Christianity Today*, pp. 39–40. It was the only verse he read in his official proclamation for the National Day of Prayer in 1984. See: Reagan, "Proclamation 5138—National Day of Prayer, 1984," December 14, 1984. Here is a sample of Reagan quoting the verse in 1983 alone: Reagan, "Remarks at Annual National Prayer Breakfast," February 3, 1983; Reagan, "Remarks at a Dinner Honoring Senator Jesse Helms," June 16, 1983. Also, not citing the verse by name but in spirit, he told an audience in August 1980 that, "We have God's promise that if we turn to Him and ask His help, we shall have it. With His help, we can still become that 'shining city upon a hill.' " Reagan, "Address to the Roundtable National Affairs Briefing," Dallas, TX, August 22, 1980.
6. Photographs of Bible were provided to me by YAF. Nancy also owned a personal Bible with a special engraving. The verse engraved on hers is Lamentations 3:23–24.
7. A copy of the Bible and page is available at the Reagan Library and Museum.
8. Waggoner, *Richly Blessed*, pp. 150–51.
9. The full handwritten draft of the First Inaugural is on file at the Reagan Library: located in PHF, PS, RRL, Box 1, Folder 1.
10. Moomaw interviewed on *Ronald Reagan: A Legacy Remembered*, History Channel production, 2002.
11. Van der Linden, *The Real Reagan*, p. 26.
12. V. Soldatov, "Preelection America," *Izvestia*, May 8, 1984, p. 5, reprinted as "Soldatov Studies Reagan Election Campaign," in *FBIS*, FBIS-SOV-10-MAY-84, May 10, 1984, p. A3.
13. Ronald Reagan, "The Role Bel Air Presbyterian Church Has Played in Our Lives," *Images* (a publication of Bel Air Presbyterian Church), Summer 1990, Vol. 12, No. 1, p. 3.
14. Morris, *Dutch*, p. 427. Also see: Edmund Morris in his 1999 interview with *The American Enterprise*.
15. Interview with William P. Clark, December 11, 2001.
16. There are numerous letters between Reagan and Billy Graham on file at the Reagan Library, not to mention other ministers. Among the ministers who visited him in the White House was his old Eureka College pal "Mac" McCallister.
17. "Debate Between Reagan and Mondale," October 7, 1984.
18. Ibid.
19. Reagan, *An American Life*, p. 396.
20. A comprehensive collection of Reagan religious quotes was published by David Shepherd, *Ronald Reagan: In God I Trust* (Wheaton, IL: Tyndale, 1984). This quote is cited on p. 6 of Shepherd.

21. Letter to Lorraine and E. H. Wagner, February 13, 1984, YAF collection.
22. Interview with William P. Clark, July 17, 2003, in Paso Robles, CA.
23. Discussion with staff member (church secretary) of the Santa Ynez Presbyterian Church, August 27, 2003.
24. One reviewer of this book speculated that perhaps the Reagans feared the embarrassment of being lectured from the pulpit by liberal pastors, similar to what LBJ experienced during Vietnam. This is not difficult to imagine, particular on issues like poverty and social programs, nuclear freeze, Central America, and others. While an interesting hypothesis, Reagan staff and friends didn't back it. "I don't think that was a factor with him at all," said Ed Meese. Interview with Ed Meese, November 23, 2001.
25. Reagan, An American Life, p. 396.
26. Reynolds shared this information with me at WWOR-AM studios in New York City on February 6, 2004 and again on August 18, 2004. I was unable to reach Donn Moomaw for comment.
27. Interview with Michael Reagan.
28. Source: Interview with Ed Meese, November 23, 2001.
29. Anatoly Krasikov, commentary for Soviet news agency TASS, November 22, 1986, printed as "TASS Examines Reagan's Remarks on Religion," in FBIS, November 24, 1986, p. A11.
30. I have personally viewed these speeches. There are numerous examples. Some are cited in this book in the pages ahead.
31. Robinson remembers the phrase to be, "I will be their God, and they will be my people." The phrase occurs a number of times in the Old Testament, including in Jeremiah 31:33. Interview with Peter Robinson, September 18, 2001.
32. This is seen among the thousand-plus letters in the Presidential Handwriting File at the Reagan Library. Among the many not cited in this book is an October 29, 1983, private letter to the Dean of Faculty at St. George's University School of Medicine, who thanked Reagan (in a totally secular manner) for the Grenada mission. Reagan concluded to this person, "we're grateful to God for His help in making our mission a success." Letter is located in PHF, PR, RRL, Box 8, Folder 106.
33. Von Damm, Sincerely, Ronald Reagan, p. 23.
34. In one letter to a private citizen—provided to me by Reagan's secretary of energy Don Hodel—Reagan said he wanted to use his position as president as "an opportunity to serve Him." In an October 25, 1982 letter to an individual named Greg Brezina, Reagan wrote, "My daily prayer is that God will help me to use this position so as to serve Him." The letter to Brezina is published in Skinner, Anderson, and Anderson, Reagan: A Life in Letters, p. 654.
35. This March 11, 1987 letter is located in PHF, PR, RRL, Box 18, Folder 282.
36. Bob Slosser, a religion reporter who wrote on Reagan's faith as president, rightly noted that Reagan had hoped for such a revival for years, including during the gubernatorial period: "For years Reagan has been saying that the United States needs a spiritual revival if it is to overcome its problems." Slosser cited over half a dozen instances, dating back to 1972, where Reagan had called for such a revival. Slosser cited these in his 1984 book, Reagan Inside Out.
37. This interview with Reagan (by Slosser) took place on October 14, 1983. See: Slosser, Reagan Inside Out, p. 166.
38. Among other sources, see: Reagan, "Meeting with Editors and Publishers of Trade Magazines," September 24, 1982. Also his remarks on April 13, 1982, published in

Ryan, ed., *Ronald Reagan: The Wisdom and Humor of the Great Communicator*, p. 108.

39. Reagan, "Remarks at Kansas State University," September 9, 1982.

40. Reagan, "Remarks at the Annual Convention of the National Religious Broadcasters," January 31, 1983.

41. Reagan, "Interview with the Knight Ridder News Service," February 13, 1984. Similarly, Reagan stated, "Teddy Roosevelt once called the presidency a bully pulpit. I intend to use it to the best of my ability to serve the Lord." He wrote this in an October 25, 1982, letter to Greg Brezina of Fayetteville, GA, published in Skinner, Anderson, and Anderson, *Reagan: A Life in Letters*, p. 654.

42. Interview with Ben Elliott, September 20, 2001.

43. One of these letters was sent to Blake Steele of Portland, OR in April 1983; it is located in PHF, PR, RRL, Box 6, Folder 77. The other letter was sent to Greg Brezina of Fayetteville, GA on October 25, 1982; it is published in Skinner, Anderson, and Anderson, *Reagan: A Life in Letters*, p. 654.

44. Paul H. Boase, "Moving the Mercy Seat into the White House: An Exegesis of the Carter/Reagan Religious Rhetoric," *Journal of Communication and Religion*, September 1989, p. 1.

45. For an example of this, see Reagan, "Christmas," radio broadcast, January 9, 1978. Located in "Ronald Reagan: Pre-Presidential Papers: Selected Radio Broadcasts, 1975–1979," October 1977 to October 10, 1978, Box 3, RRL. A transcript is published by Skinner, Anderson, and Anderson, *Reagan, In His Own Hand*, pp. 17–18.

46. Interview with Ben Elliott, September 20, 2001. Reagan invoked God generally in numerous secular situations, such as inaugurals, radio addresses, or during remarks to the national Chamber of Commerce, the Boy Scouts, in Red Square, or to any university. He quoted Scripture not merely before the National Conference on Christians and Jews or the Student Congress of Evangelism but also before the U.S. League of Savings Associations, Air and Space Bicentennial Year Ceremony, and the American Bar Association. His innumerable religious reflections were made in varied contexts, most to nonreligious audiences and often in venues secularists would deem inappropriate. To cite just one example, his 1984 State of the Union contained 10 references to God. If one tallied President Reagan's multiple remarks on "God," "Creator," "Almighty," "The Lord," "Him," "Jesus," or other, the references would fall well over a thousand.

47. Draft copy is located in PHF, PS, RRL, Box 17, Folder 322.

48. Interview with Ben Elliott, September 20, 2001.

49. This speech was heavily edited by Reagan, particularly his addition of religious content. Draft is located in PHF, PS, RRL, Box 6, Folder 104. Reagan, "Remarks at Kansas State University," September 9, 1982.

50. For a few examples, see: Reagan, "Remarks at the Annual Convention of the National Religious Broadcasters," January 31, 1983; "Remarks at the Annual National Prayer Breakfast," February 3, 1983; "Remarks at the Annual Convention of the National Religious Broadcasters," January 30, 1984; "Remarks at Annual National Prayer Breakfast," February 2, 1984; and "Remarks at the Annual Convention of the National Religious Broadcasters," January 31, 1985.

51. Reagan, "Remarks at the Annual Convention of the National Religious Broadcasters," January 30, 1984.

52. Editorial, "Sermon on the Stump," *New York Times*, February 3, 1984.

53. Reagan, "Interview with the Knight Ridder News Service," February 13, 1984. 1983 in *Ronald Reagan's Weekly Radio Addresses: Vol 1*, pp. 57, 88–90, and 171–73.

54. Edmund Morris also makes note of this. See: Morris, *Dutch*, p. 427. On swearing in general, one of the conspicuous things about Reagan's private diary is his constant abbreviation of words like "d——n" and "h——l." One can find these same abbreviations for such words in Ben Cleaver's writings. See: Ben Hill Cleaver, *Some Memories of John Stephen Cleaver, by his son, Ben Hill Cleaver*, Cape Girardeau, MO, August 18, 1967, pp. 4 and 7.
55. Interview with Ben Elliott, September 20, 2001.

CHAPTER 12

1. Reagan, "Address to the Roundtable National Affairs Briefing," Dallas, TX, August 22, 1980.
2. For the original Washington quote, see: W. B. Allen, ed., *George Washington: A Collection* (Indianapolis: Liberty Fund, 1988), p. 521. For examples of Reagan invoking the quote, see: Reagan, "Remarks at Kansas State University," September 9, 1982. Among the many examples of him quoting this, here's a sample from merely 1982 and 1984: Reagan, "Remarks at the Centennial Meeting of the Supreme Council of the Knights of Columbus in Hartford, Connecticut," August 3, 1982; Reagan, "Remarks at a Spirit of America Rally," Atlanta, GA, January 26, 1984; Reagan, "Remarks at the Annual Convention of the National Association of Evangelicals," Columbus, OH, March 6, 1984; Reagan, "Remarks at an Ecumenical Prayer Breakfast," Dallas, TX, August 23, 1984; and Reagan, "Written Responses to Questions Submitted by France Soir Magazine," November 3, 1984.
3. Reagan, "Remarks at Annual Convention of NRB," January 31, 1983. For an example to a secular audience: "President's News Conference," February 21, 1985.
4. Interviews with Ben Elliot, September 20, 2001 and June 18, 2004.
5. Quote is from Reagan's May 12, 1984, weekly radio broadcast, titled "Education." *Ronald Reagan's Weekly Radio Addresses: Vol 1*, p. 211.
6. Reagan, "Remarks at the National Forum on Excellence in Education," Indianapolis, IN, December 8, 1983.
7. In the 1960s, he said this as governor, specifying Jesus as part of the equation: "[T]he answer to each and every problem is to be found in the simple words of Jesus of Nazareth." See: Ellingwood, "Ronald Reagan: 'God, Home and Country,' " p. 50. Among other 1980s examples, see: Reagan, "Remarks at the Annual National Prayer Breakfast," February 4, 1982; Reagan, "Remarks at the Annual Convention of the National Religious Broadcasters," January 30, 1984.
8. Reagan, "Remarks at Georgetown University's Bicentennial Convocation," October 1, 1988.
9. Ibid.
10. Reagan, "Address to the Roundtable National Affairs Briefing," Dallas, TX, August 22, 1980.
11. In Reagan's presidential memoir, *An American Life*, he makes constant references to prayer. This starts small, with a prayer before a football game. Then we read about him praying his first night in the White House. Then follow prayers for Anwar Sadat, for the Philippines and Marcos, before his summits at Geneva and Reykjavik, in the note he left for George Bush in handing over the White House keys. We read diary entries where he writes of his desire to help his agnostic father-in-law "turn to God" on his deathbed. We see him regularly thanking God in his memoir, such as for the release of

the fifty-two Iranian hostages and the successful completion of the Grenada mission. On the latter, his diary entry reads: "Success seems to shine on us and I thank the Lord for it. He has really held me in the hollow of His hand." He ends his 721-page memoir by asserting, "It truly is America the Beautiful, and God has, indeed, 'shed His grace on thee.'" See: Reagan, *An American Life*, pp. 56, 229, 236, 252, 261–63, 292, 307, 319, 321, 365, 379, 455, 459, 721–22. (In regard to praying for Geneva, in a nationwide address, Reagan asked his fellow Americans to "pray for God's grace and His guidance for all of us at Geneva." Reagan, "Address to the Nation," November 14, 1985.)

Reagan's memoirs alone seem to make it obvious that religious faith was a part of his life. On separate occasions, individuals have commented to me about their surprise over these unending references to God. "I bet a lot of people were really surprised by that," said one observer. "I'm sure many were a bit shocked and uncomfortable with it." Even in his co-authored first autobiography, *Where's the Rest of Me?*, published in 1965, by the third page of text the reader is hitting phrases such as "God rest his soul" and "bless her." See: Reagan and Hubler, *Where's the Rest of Me?* p. 5.

12. Reagan, "Debate Between Reagan and Mondale," October 7, 1984; and Reagan, "Written Responses to Questions Submitted by France Soir Magazine," November 3, 1984.

13. Among these many letters, see: May 31, 1985, letter to Rev. Paul T. Butler of Ozark Bible College, Joplin, MO, located in PHF, PR, RRL, Box 13, Folder 187; August 19, 1985, letter to Bernard Cardinal Law, Archbishop of Boston, PHF, PR, RRL, Box 13, Folder 198; December 22, 1986, letter to Brother Gary Gerke, Pecos, NM, PHF, PR, RRL, Box 17, Folder 271; and January 17, 1989, letter to Rev. Billy Graham, PHF, PR, RRL, Box 21, Folder 346.

In a slightly different sentiment, Reagan sent many presidential letters in which he said he needed prayer or thanked others for praying for him. Among these, see: March 18, 1981, letter to Pat Boone, located in PHF, PR, RRL, Box 1, Folder 1; July 15, 1982 letter to Rev. William D. Brown of Ithaca, NY, PHF, PR, RRL, Box 3, Folder 44; March 15, 1983, letter to Rev. Robert C. Savage of St. Croix, Virgin Islands, PHF, PR, RRL, Box 5, Folder 73; and January 6, 1988, letter to Rev. Dana C. Jones, Jr. of West Alexander, PA, PHF, PR, RRL, Box 19, Folder 316.

14. This was a December 1, 1987 letter. Correspondence located in PHF, PR, RRL, Box 19, Folder 312.

15. Interview with Don Hodel, August 28, 2003.

16. This was a February 3, 1983 speech. Draft is located in PHF, PR, RRL, Box 8, Folder 142.

17. Reagan, "White House Ceremony in Observance of National Day of Prayer," May 6, 1982. Reagan often invoked this image. Among many other instances, see: Reagan, "Proclamation 5017–National Day of Prayer, 1983," January 27, 1983.

18. Reagan weekly radio address, December 24, 1983, published in Israel, *Ronald Reagan's Weekly Radio Addresses*, Vol. 1, p. 171–2.

19. This story was told to me by William P. Clark on July 17, 2003, in Paso Robles, CA.

20. See: "Remarks at the Annual National Prayer Breakfast," February 3, 1983. In signing his proclamation for the National Day of Prayer in 1983, the president called prayer the "mainspring of the American spirit" and spoke of the country's "national dependence" on God. See: Reagan, "Proclamation 5017–National Day of Prayer, 1983," January 27, 1983.

21. This strategy is laid out at length in my forthcoming book on Reagan.

22. Reagan, Republican convention speech, August 17, 1992. As governor, he wrote a letter to Billy Graham noting his "own optimism based on faith." Letter is quoted in Von Damm, *Sincerely, Ronald Reagan*, p. 82.

23. Reagan remarks during the dedication of the Ronald Reagan Presidential Library, California, November 4, 1991, published in Ryan, ed., *Ronald Reagan: The Wisdom and Humor of the Great Communicator*, p. 123.

24. Reagan's father was also a good storyteller, and he may have acquired the gift there as well.

25. Rose, "The Reagans and Their Pastor," p. 45.

26. *Washington Post* columnist Haynes Johnson dismissed Reagan's effort in this way: "Why would God, being all-powerful, permit Himself to be expelled from public classrooms?" Haynes Johnson, *Sleepwalking Through History: America in the Reagan Years* (New York: Norton, 1991), pp. 193–214.

27. Quoted in Smith, *Who Is Ronald Reagan?* p. 86; and Bill Adler and Bill Adler Jr., editors, *The Reagan Wit: The Humor of the American President* (New York: William Morrow, 1998), p. 31. The Adler and Adler citation is taken from 1966. Also see: "Governor Reagan: 'God Is Not Dead on Your Campuses'," *CACS Quarterly Report*, April–June 1969; and Reagan letter to Lorraine and Elwood Wagner, June 16, 1964, YAF collection.

28. This quote is taken from a February 25, 1984, Reagan radio address titled simply, "Prayer in Public Schools." See: *Ronald Reagan's Weekly Radio Addresses: Vol 1*, pp. 188–89. A similar radio address from September 18, 1982, carried the same title. See: *Ronald Reagan's Weekly Radio Addresses: Vol 1*, pp. 27–29.

29. There are numerous such examples. Also from his first presidential term, see: January 22, 1983, and March 5, 1983, addresses in *Ronald Reagan's Weekly Radio Addresses: Vol 1*, pp. 67 and 81–83.

30. Among the examples, see: Reagan, "Remarks and a Question-and-Answer Session With Area High School Seniors," Jacksonville, FL, December 1, 1987.

31. See: Reagan, "Remarks at the National Association of Secondary School Principals," February 7, 1984; and Reagan, "State of the Union Address," January 25, 1984.

32. Here are merely two significant examples, showing, via back-to-back years, how he persisted: Reagan, "Message to the Congress Transmitting the Proposed Constitutional Amendment on Prayer in Schools, May 17, 1982; and Reagan, "Message to the Congress Transmitting the Proposed Constitutional Amendment on Prayer in Schools," March 8, 1983. Also see: Noonan, *What I Saw at the Revolution*, pp. 241–2.

33. Reagan wrote this in a March 5, 1987, letter to William A. Wilson. Letter is located in PHF, PR, RRL, Box 18, Folder 282.

34. Reagan actually authored and published a book about abortion during his presidency, titled, *Abortion and the Conscience of the Nation*, with an afterword from Malcolm Muggeridge (New York, Thomas Nelson Publishers: 1984.) It was the only such published work he did as president. Among many references that tie his religious convictions to his pro-life stance, see his: "Remarks at Kansas State University," September 9, 1982; "Remarks at the Annual Convention of the National Religious Broadcasters," January 31, 1983; "Remarks at the Annual Convention of the National Religious Broadcasters," January 30, 1984; "Remarks to the Student Congress on Evangelism," July 28, 1988; and "Remarks to the Students and Faculty of Archbishop Carroll and All Saints High Schools," October 17, 1988.

35. Reagan, "Remarks to the National Religious Broadcasters Annual Convention," January 30, 1984.

36. Ibid. The quote is Christ's words. See: Matthew 19:14, Mark 10:14, and Luke 18:16.

37. In an editorial, the *New York Times* blasted him for this analogy, insisting that the real modern "bondage" was "the law's refusal to let women decide whether or not to bear a child—until the Supreme Court read this basic liberty into the Constitution." Editorial, "Sermon on the Stump," *New York Times*, February 3, 1984.

38. Reagan, "State of the Union Address," February 4, 1986.

39. Edmund Morris called Reagan "the best friend Israel ever had" in the White House. On his confronting anti-Semitism, see, among other sources: Reagan and Hubler, *Where's the Rest of Me?* p. 9; Smith, *Who Is Ronald Reagan?* p. 38; Reagan, *An American Life*, p. 20; and Anne Edwards, *Early Reagan*, pp. 203–4. On his celebrating America's embrace of both Jews and Christians, see his speech, "America the Beautiful," William Woods College, commencement address, Missouri, June 1952.

   One of Reagan's first exposures to injustice toward blacks was his father's revulsion at how blacks were portrayed in the film *The Birth of a Nation*, which his father boycotted. This made an indelible impression on Reagan. He frequently referred to the incident. Among others, see Reagan's *Where's the Rest of Me?* p. 8; and Smith, *Who Is Ronald Reagan?* p. 38. Also, key religious figures in his early life, such as Ben Cleaver, detested bigotry, not to mention his mother. See: William Pemberton, *Exit with Honor: The Life and Presidency of Ronald Reagan* (Armonk, NY: M.E. Sharpe, 1997), pp. 9–10; and Vaughn, *Ronald Reagan in Hollywood*, p. 11. It has been rarely noticed that Reagan, along with Ginger Rogers and Doris Day, in 1951 made an anti-KKK film through Warner Bros., called *Storm Warning*. In addition, he was involved in a number of Hollywood efforts against the KKK and on behalf of Black Americans. For a solid treatment, see: Vaughn, *Ronald Reagan in Hollywood*, pp. 171–87.

40. Reagan wrote this in a March 5, 1987, letter to William A. Wilson. Letter is located in PHF, PR, RRL, Box 18, Folder 282.

41. Interview with William P. Clark, July 17, 2003, Paso Robles, CA. Reagan was deeply troubled by anti-Catholic bigotry he saw early in life (see Reagan and Hubler, *Where's the Rest of Me?* p. 9). He harbored no intolerance whatsoever toward Catholics, who were represented in large numbers in his inner circle. He greatly admired, and closely collaborated, with Pope John Paul II. He received spiritual guidance from occasional Catholic priests in the White House, especially after he was shot. A young Reagan wanted to marry an attractive young woman, Mary Frances, who was a dedicated Catholic. Their different denominations were a problem for her but not for him. He had no problem with her Catholicism, though she did not approve of his Protestantism. (Anne Edwards, *Early Reagan*, pp. 133–35.) Also see Smith, *Who Is Ronald Reagan?* p. 38. Anne Edwards reports a sharp Reagan disagreement with Catholic doctrine as a young man. See Anne Edwards, *Early Reagan*, p. 242.

42. Among many pre-presidential sources on Reagan's lack of prejudice, see: Van der Linden, *The Real Reagan*, pp. 39–40, 46, 80–1, and 256.

43. Reagan, "Remarks at the Annual Convention of the National Association of Evangelicals," Orlando, FL, March 8, 1983. Also see: Reagan private letter to Rev. Kenneth Bowling, January 29, 1985, located in PHF, PR, RRL, Box 11, Folder 164.

44. See: Hobbs, *Ronald Reagan's Call to Action*, p. 150.

45. On this social gospel, see McAllister and Tucker, *Journey in Faith*, pp. 286–86, 390, and 403–4; and Garrison and DeGroot, *The Disciples of Christ*, pp. 403, 420–24, and 546.

46. McAllister and Tucker, *Journey in Faith*, p. 286.

47. The evangelical was Thomas McDill, then-president of the Evangelical Free Church. Interview with Thomas McDill, January 31, 2003.

48. Reagan, "Remarks at a White House Luncheon with Black Clergymen," March 26, 1982.

49. Reagan said this in a November 4, 1962, speech on behalf of Richard Nixon's California gubernatorial campaign. Printed in Houcke and Kiewe, *Actor, Ideologue, Politician*, pp. 27–36.

50. Reagan's letter is dated December 18, 1984. Located in PHF, PR, RRL, Box 11, Folder 154.

51. Reagan, "Address to the Nation on the Soviet-United States Summit Meeting," December 10, 1987.

CHAPTER 13

1. Nancy Reagan with William Novak, *My Turn* (Thorndike, ME: Thorndike Press, 1989), pp. 88–91.

2. This information is provided by Michael Deaver in *A Different Drummer.* Deaver was there that day.

3. Quote is taken from Morris, *Dutch*, p. 429. Also see: Reagan, *An American Life*, pp. 261–62.

4. The letter exchange is published in Von Damm, *Sincerely, Ronald Reagan*, p. 118.

5. Moomaw interviewed on *Ronald Reagan: A Legacy Remembered*, History Channel production, 2002.

6. Patti Davis, *Angels Don't Die*, pp. 26–27.

7. Nancy Reagan, *My Turn*, p. 90. Ed Meese confirms this as well. Interview with Ed Meese, November 23, 2001.

8. Nancy Reagan, *My Turn*, pp. 88–89.

9. Nancy Reagan, *My Turn*, pp. 90, 92, 97, and 101; and Nancy Reagan interviewed on *Ronald Reagan: A Legacy Remembered*, History Channel production, 2002.

10. Quoted in George Hackett and Eleanor Clift, "Of Planets and the Presidency," *Newsweek*, May 16, 1988, p. 20.

11. The Reagans sent Sieffert many photos as well, including first-copy originals never reproduced. This was also true for the relationship with Reagan's fan club president in Philadelphia, Lorraine Wagner.

12. Interview with Mary Joan Roll-Sieffert, February 3, 2001, Pittsburgh, PA.

13. Nancy Reagan, *My Turn*, p. 95.

14. Michiko Kakutani, "Memoirs of a 'Chamberlain' in the White House," *New York Times*, May 9, 1988, p. C15.

15. A videotape of the episode is located at the Reagan Library. Dixon called Reagan "a man of destiny" and "a natural" for his country and politics. Asked if she thought he would one day win the presidency, she predicted he would rise to the top of the water, above all the other "ducks."

16. Quoted by Patti Davis, *Angels Don't Die*, p. x. While Nancy has no record in making the sort of countless religious statements her husband did, she did state in her 1980 autobiography that she and her husband "both have faith in God and believe He has a plan for each of us." She emphasized that the American people "need God in our lives," including via the classroom. See: Nancy Reagan, *Nancy*, pp. 143–44.

17. Nancy Reagan, *My Turn*, p. 91.

18. Ibid., p. 94.

19. Donald Regan, *For the Record* (San Diego, CA: Harcourt Brace Jovanovich, 1988), pp. 3–4 and 28.

20. Deaver interviewed on *Ronald Reagan: A Legacy Remembered*, History Channel production, 2002.
21. Nancy Reagan, *My Turn*, pp. 98–99.
22. Boyarsky, *The Rise of Ronald Reagan*, p. 14.
23. See: Joan Quigley, *"What Does Joan Say?"* (New York: Carol Publishing Group, 1990), pp. 11–12 and 72–73.
24. Ibid., pp. 72–73.
25. Kitty Kelley, *Nancy Reagan: The Unauthorized Biography* (New York: Simon & Schuster, 1991). Among the references, see: Kelley, pp. 147–50, 213–16, 230, 280, 285, 351, 407–8, 431–32, 492–93 and 570n.
26. In the *Public Presidential Papers*, there are four indexed examples of Reagan personally addressing or rejecting the astrology issue. Among these, see: Reagan, "Remarks at the Presentation Ceremony for the Small Business Person of the Year Awards, May 9, 1988, *Public Presidential Papers*, 1988, p. 572; Reagan, "Remarks and a Question-and-Answer Session With Reporters," May 17, 1988, *Public Presidential Papers*, 1988, p. 604; and Reagan, "Interview with Foreign Television Journalists," May 19, 1988, *Public Presidential Papers*, 1988, p. 611.
27. Ibid. Also see: Hackett and Clift, "Of Planets and the Presidency," p. 20.
28. Interview with Ben Elliott, September 20, 2001.
29. Interview with Ed Meese, November 23, 2001.
30. Asked if Reagan read his horoscope, Allen said: "I don't know." Laughingly, he added (in a typical response): "I did. Just for kicks." Interview with Richard Allen, November 12, 2001.
31. Reagan with Hubler, *Where's the Rest of Me?* p. 283.
32. Interview with Michael Reagan, September 2, 2003.
33. Interview with Ed Meese, November 23, 2001.
34. Van der Linden, *The Real Reagan*, p. 27. For Reagan's views on evolution vs. creation, see: Von Damm, *Sincerely, Ronald Reagan*, p. 83.
35. For an example of Reagan publicly talking about Armageddon, see: Reagan, "Presidential Debate Between Reagan and Mondale," October 21, 1984. Among Soviet media archives, I found only one serious analysis of Reagan's thoughts on Armageddon. Surprisingly, the piece was actually a fair, responsible, cautious article not written with the usual Soviet hyperbole and daggers. The piece, unattributed to an author, was titled "Pushing the World Toward Catastrophe," *Izvestia*, April 19, 1984, p. 4, reprinted as "Reagan Belief in Approach of Armageddon Analyzed," in *FBIS*, FBIS-SOV-19-APR-84, April 19, 1984, pp. A2–3.
36. Morris, *Dutch*, pp. 632–33.
37. On this, one can consult Lou Cannon's *Role of a Lifetime* and Edmund Morris' *Dutch*. Also see: Kenneth L. Woodward, "Arguing Armageddon," *Newsweek*, November 5, 1984, p. 91.
38. Wills probably knew the answer to that, which is that evangelicals had much more agreement with Reagan than Carter on political issues and philosophy. See: Garry Wills, "Faith and the Hopefuls," *Sojourners*, March 1988, p. 15. Wills is much more fair to Reagan's religious thinking in his book, *Reagan's America*, than he was in this March 1988 article, which was insulting and judgmental.
39. Wills, "Faith and the Hopefuls," p. 14.
40. Quoted in Hackett and Clift, "Of Planets and the Presidency," p. 20.
41. David Neff, "Suckers for the Zodiac," *Christianity Today*, July 15, 1988, p. 15.

42. A videotape copy of the episode is located at the Reagan Library.
43. Quigley, *"What Does Joan Say?"* p. 14. Her claim is rejected by orthodox Christians, who insist that the Bible condemns astrology.
44. Ibid., p. 112.

CHAPTER 14

1. See: Reagan, *An American Life*, p. 263; Deaver, *A Different Drummer*, pp. 145–47; and Morris, *Dutch*, p. 432.
2. Quoted in Laurence I. Barrett, *Gambling with History: Ronald Reagan in the White House* (Garden City, NY: Doubleday, 1983), p. 124.
3. Reagan, "Remarks on Proclamation for the National Day of Prayer," March 19, 1981.
4. Source: Von Damm, *At Reagan's Side*, p. 192.
5. Maureen Reagan, *First Father, First Daughter*, p. 279. Ronald Reagan's conclusion that he was spared for a special purpose has been expressed by staff and family. Among many others, including his family, see: Michael Reagan with Joe Hyams, *On the Outside Looking In* (New York: Kensington Publishing, 1988), p. 198; Davis, *Angels Don't Die*, p. 38; Slosser, *Reagan Inside Out*; and Ken Duberstein interviewed for CNN documentary, *The Reagan Years: Inside the White House*, Pt. II of series, CNN, aired February 18, 2001.
6. Reagan, *An American Life*, p. 263; and Morris, *Dutch*, p. 432.
7. Reagan, *An American Life*, p. 269.
8. Deaver interviewed for CNN documentary, *The Reagan Years: Inside the White House*, Pt. II of series, CNN, aired February 18, 2001. Also see: Deaver, *A Different Drummer*, pp. 151–53.
9. The letter was sent on April 24, 1981. Many Reagan letters followed after this, including more than one to each of the subsequent Soviet general secretaries.
10. There are slight variations on the exact quote, though all are near identical in language and clear in precise meaning. This is the more common quote cited, including by Edmund Morris. The only witness was apparently Mike Deaver, who arranged for Cooke to meet with the president. He remembered Reagan saying: "I have decided that whatever time I may have left is for Him." Deaver, *A Different Drummer*, pp. 145–47.
11. Edmund Morris, *Dutch*, pp. 434–35.
12. Reagan, "Remarks to the Annual National Prayer Breakfast," February 4, 1982.
13. Reagan, "Remarks at the First Annual Commemoration of the Days of Remembrance of Victims of the Holocaust," April 30, 1981; and Reagan, "Address at Commencement Exercises at the United States Military Academy," May 27, 1981.
14. See: Reagan, "Remarks at Eureka College," February 6, 1984. He also quoted the remark in his private correspondence with people during his presidency, such as in a December 19, 1984 letter to Rev. Edward Davis of Spokane, WA, located in PHF, PR, RRL, Box 11, Folder 155.
15. Viktor Levin speaking on weekly Moscow TV news program, "International Observers Roundtable," carried by the Moscow Domestic Service, June 3, 1984, transcript printed in *FBIS*, FBIS-4-JUN-84, June 4, 1984, pp. CC8.
16. The speech was written by Reagan speechwriter Tony Dolan, with few edits from the president. Draft is located in PHF, PS, RRL, Box 1, Folder 7.
17. Reagan, "Address at Commencement Exercises at the University of Notre Dame," May 17, 1981.

18. Ibid.
19. Ibid.
20. Ibid.
21. Reagan, "America the Beautiful," William Woods College, June 1952.
22. Reagan, "Remarks at Notre Dame," May 17, 1981.
23. The Catholic connection here is ironic. The speech is at Notre Dame, not long after Reagan's meeting with Cardinal Cooke. In the speech, Reagan asked prayer for Pope John Paul II, who had also just been shot, and commended him for his recent encyclical attacking communism.
24. Ibid.
25. Reagan, "Remarks at the Unveiling of the Knute Rockne Commemorative Stamp at the University of Notre Dame in Indiana," March 9, 1988.
26. Ibid.
27. Ibid.
28. Reagan, "Remarks at the Bicentennial Observance of the Battle of Yorktown in Virginia," October 19, 1981.
29. Quote taken from March 20, 1981, speech by Reagan to CPAC. Text is published in Roberts, A City Upon a Hill, p. 57
30. Reagan, "Remarks at the Bicentennial Observance of the Battle of Yorktown in Virginia," October 19, 1981.
31. Mother Teresa visited the White House on June 4, 1981. See: Barrett, Gambling With History, p. 124. Also, Deaver, A Different Drummer, p. 114.
32. Reagan extended recognition to the Vatican in 1984.
33. The Pope preached a "theology of hope." This is evident in the title of his biographer George Weigel's book, Witness to Hope. On John Paul II's theology of hope, I thank Michael Coulter for sharing his unpublished paper, "John Paul II and the Hope for this World and the World to Come."
34. Address of John Paul II to the 50th General Assembly of the United Nations Organization, October 5, 1995.
35. Carl Bernstein, "The Holy Alliance," Time, February 24, 1992, pp. 28 and 30. Reagan expressed his shock on the assassination attempt—and offered his prayers—in a May 13, 1981, cable to the Pope. The cable is filed in ES, NSC, HSF: Records, Vatican: Pope John Paul II, RRL, Box 41, Folder "Cables 1 of 2."
36. Bernstein, "The Holy Alliance," pp. 28 and 30.
37. "The Pope and the President: A key adviser reflects on the Reagan Administration," interview with William P. Clark, Catholic World Reporter, November 1999.
38. This is seen in a number of sources. Among them, William P. Clark confirmed this fact with the author. We can also view Reagan's early understanding of the importance of the Pope to communism in Poland in a June 29, 1979, radio broadcast. Located in "Ronald Reagan: Pre-Presidential Papers: Selected Radio Broadcasts, 1975–1979," October 31, 1978, to October 1979, Box 4, RRL; and Skinner, Anderson, and Anderson, Reagan, In His Own Hand, p. 176. Also: Reagan, An American Life, pp. 301–3; and Reagan, "Address at Commencement Exercises at Eureka College," Eureka, Illinois, May 9, 1982.
39. This is covered at length in a chapter in my next book on Reagan.
40. Gorbachev discusses this in his memoirs. In one spot, he writes of how, to the Soviet leadership, the mere emergence of Solidarity threatened not only "chaos in Poland" but the "ensuing break-up of the entire Socialist camp." Gorbachev, Memoirs, pp. 478–79. In a 1993 conference at Princeton University, Sergei Tarasenko spoke of

how the national elections in Poland in June 1989—in which Solidarity emerged the big winner—convinced him and the Soviet leadership, particularly the foreign ministry, that the Soviet system would break up. Tarasenko transcript is published in William C. Wohlforth, ed., *Witnesses to the End of the Cold War* (Baltimore and London: Johns Hopkins University, 1996), pp. 112–3.

41. Bernstein, "The Holy Alliance," p. 35.
42. Examples of the secrecy are seen in fully redacted documents at the Reagan Library, located in ES, NSC, HSF: Records, Vatican: Pope John Paul II, RRL, Box 41, Folders "Cables 1 of 2" and "Cables 2 of 2."
43. Carl Bernstein and Marco Politi, *His Holiness: John Paul II and the Hidden History of Our Time* (New York: Doubleday, 1996), pp. 362, 364, 366, 369, 461, and 474.
44. Reagan wrote the January 11, 1982, letter in response to a study by the Pontifical Academy. He was advised in this instance by NSA William Clark and staffer James Nance in memoranda from January 8, 1982, and December 4, 1981, respectively. Memoranda and letter are located at Reagan Library in ES, NSC, HSF: Records, Vatican: Pope John Paul II, RRL, Box 41, Folder 8100301-8106715.
45. Bernstein and Politi, *His Holiness*, p. 474.
46. On Reagan speaking in this way in the 1970s about the possibility of him becoming president, see him quoted in Evans and Novak, *The Reagan Revolution*, pp. 208–9.
47. Interview with Allen, November 12, 2001; and Richard Allen, "An Extraordinary Man in Extraordinary Times: Ronald Reagan's Leadership and the Decision to End the Cold War," Address to the Hoover Institution and the William J. Casey Institute of the Center for Security Policy, Washington, D.C., February 22, 1999, p. 6.
48. Interview with Richard V. Allen, November 12, 2001.
49. Ibid.
50. Interview with Clark.
51. William P. Clark, "President Reagan and the Wall," Address to the Council of National Policy, San Francisco, CA, March 2000, p. 2.
52. Interview with Clark.
53. Interview with Clark.
54. Clark shared this during a February 22, 1999 presentation in Washington, D.C. For a transcript, see: Clark in Peter Schweizer, ed., *Fall of the Berlin Wall* (Stanford, CA: Hoover Institution Press, 2000), p. 75.
55. Interview with Ed Meese, November 23, 2001.
56. Interview with Caspar Weinberger, October 10, 2002.
57. Interview with Ed Meese, November 23, 2001.
58. I'm in the process of writing a separate book that lays out precisely this effort.
59. Reagan often spoke of himself as part of a team, of his personal actions as "we," and of the necessity of sharing credit.

CHAPTER 15

1. He said this often as president. This quote was offered at least three times. See: Reagan, "State of the Union Address," February 6, 1985; Reagan, "Remarks at a Ceremony Marking the Annual Observance of Captive Nations Week," July 19, 1983; and Reagan, "First Inaugural Address," January 20, 1981.
2. Reagan, "The President's News Conference," January 29, 1981.
3. "On Soviet Morality," *Time*, February 16, 1981, p. 17.

4. Reagan, "Excerpts From an Interview With Walter Cronkite of CBS News," March 3, 1981.
5. As quoted in March 20, 1981, speech before CPAC. See collection by Roberts, *A City Upon a Hill*, p. 58.
6. "On Soviet Morality," *Time*, p. 17.
7. See: V. I. Lenin, *Collected Works, Vol. 31: April-December 1920* (Moscow: Progress Publishers, 1977), p. 291. This version of the quote doesn't match *Time's* to the exact letter, but is basically nearly identical.
8. Cannon, *Role of a Lifetime*, pp. 241–42.
9. Reagan, "Remarks at the National Conference of the National Federation of Independent Business," June 22, 1983.
10. Reagan, "Remarks at the Annual Convention of the United States Hispanic Chamber of Commerce," Tampa, FL, August 12, 1983.
11. Reagan, "Remarks at a Conference on Religious Liberty," April 16, 1985.
12. Ibid.
13. Statement by TASS in English, printed as "Reagan Remarks on Human Rights, Religion Reviewed: Speaks to Churchmen," in *FBIS*, FBIS-SOV-88-087, May 4, 1988, p. 11.
14. Reagan, "Remarks in an Interview with Representatives of Excelsior of Mexico," August 19, 1986.
15. Reagan, "Remarks at the Young Leadership Conference of the United Jewish Appeal," March 13, 1984.
16. See: Reagan, "Address to the Nation on the Situation in Nicaragua," March 16, 1986; and Reagan, "Remarks at the Annual Convention of the National Religious Broadcasters," February 1, 1988.
17. Shea's piece was published on May 22, 1987. Reagan's letter to Moomaw was December 21, 1987. This correspondence is located in PHF, PR, RRL, Box 19, Folder 314.
18. Reagan, "Remarks at the St. Ann's Festival," Hoboken, NJ, July 26, 1984.
19. For text of speech, see: Skinner, Anderson, and Anderson, *Reagan, In His Own Hand*, p. 479.
20. Reagan, "Remarks at the Centennial Meeting of the Supreme Council of the Knights of Columbus," Hartford, CT, August 3, 1982.
21. Reagan, "Remarks to American Troops," Camp Liberty Bell, Republic of Korea, November 13, 1983.
22. Reagan, "Remarks at a Conference on Religious Liberty," April 16, 1985.
23. Among examples of Reagan using this line, see: Reagan, "Remarks at the Centennial Meeting of the Supreme Council of the Knights of Columbus," Hartford, CT, August 3, 1982; and Reagan, "Address Before a Joint Session of the Irish National Parliament," June 4, 1984.
24. Yuri Kornilov, "Lies, Lies, Lies—And Nothing But Lies," *TASS*, November 19, 1986, translated and printed as "Kornilov Commentary," in *FBIS*, FBIS, November 20, 1986, p. A4.
25. Quoted in William Niskanen, *Reaganomics: An Insider's Account* (New York and Oxford: Oxford University press, 1988), p. 284.
26. Reagan, "Proclamation 4826—National Day of Prayer, 1981," March 19, 1981.
27. Reagan, "Remarks at the New York City Partnership Luncheon," NY, January 14, 1982.
28. Reagan, "Farewell Address to the Nation," January 11, 1989.
29. Reagan, "Remarks Following Discussions With Pope John Paul II," Vatican City, June

6, 1987. On Reagan and free will, see the insightful comments of Peter Robinson in his *How Ronald Reagan Changed My Life* (New York: ReganBooks, HarperCollins, 2003), pp. 192 and 200–2.

30. Among others, see: Reagan, "Remarks at a White House Luncheon Marking the 40th Anniversary of the Warsaw Uprising," August 17, 1984; and Reagan, "Remarks at a Polish Festival," Doylestown, PA, September 9, 1984.

31. See: Reagan, "State of the Union Address," February 6, 1985; and Reagan, "Address to the 40th Session of the United Nations General Assembly," NY, October 24, 1985.

32. Reagan, "Remarks at a Ceremony Marking the Annual Observance of Captive Nations Week," July 19, 1983.

33. Reagan, "Radio Address to the Nation, Independence Day," July 3, 1982, published in Clark Cassell, editor, *President Reagan's Quotations: A Collection* (Washington, D.C.: Braddock, 1984), p. 104.

34. I viewed Reagan's handwritten drafts of each of these two documents at the Reagan Library.

35. Reagan, "Remarks to Citizens," Hambach, Federal Republic of Germany, May 6, 1985.

36. Reagan, "Remarks at a Ceremony Marking the Annual Observance of Captive Nations Week," July 19, 1983.

37. Van der Linden, *The Real Reagan*, p. 27.

38. Reagan, "Remarks at a Ceremony Marking the Annual Observance of Captive Nations Week," July 19, 1983.

39. Reagan, "Remarks Upon Returning from the Soviet-United States Summit Meeting in Moscow," June 3, 1988.

40. Reagan, "Proclamation 5018—Year of the Bible, 1983," February 3, 1983.

41. Reagan, "Remarks at the Annual Convention of the National Association of Evangelicals," Orlando, FL, March 8, 1983.

42. Jefferson borrowed from John Locke's notion of life, liberty, and the pursuit of property.

43. Reagan, "Remarks at the Annual Meeting of the American Bar Association," Atlanta, GA, August 1, 1983.

44. Property not in the sense that one is entitled to property per se, but instead that one is entitled to the fruits of his or her labor. For a prepresidential example, see: July 6, 1976, Reagan speech, published in: Alfred Balitzer, ed., *A Time for Choosing: The Speeches of Ronald Reagan* (Chicago: Regnery Gateway, 1983), pp. 163–80.

45. Reagan wrote this in a January 7, 1988, letter to Mr. and Mrs. Gerhard P. Reinders of Appleton, WI. The letter is published in Skinner, Anderson, and Anderson, *Reagan: A Life in Letters*, p. 385.

46. Reagan, "Remarks at a Ceremony Marking the Annual Observation of Captive Nations Week," July 19, 1983.

47. Ibid.

48. Reagan, *An American Life*, p. 265. Also in *An American Life*, see pp. 14, 110, 575.

49. Reagan, "Interview With Representatives of Western European Publications," May 21, 1982.

50. Reagan, "Remarks on Signing the Captive Nations Week Proclamation," July 19, 1982. Also see: Reagan, "Address at Commencement Exercises at Eureka College," May 9, 1982.

51. See, for example: Reagan, "Interview with Reporters from the *Los Angeles Times*," January 20, 1982; Reagan, "Interview With Morton Kondracke and Richard H. Smith of *Newsweek* Magazine," March 4, 1985; Reagan, "Interview With Representatives of

College Radio Stations," September 9, 1985; Reagan, "Question-and-Answer Session With Students at Fallston High School," Fallston, MD, December 4, 1985.

52. Reagan, "Interview With Representatives of the *Baltimore Sun*," March 12, 1986; and Reagan, "Remarks and a Question-and-Answer Session at a White House Luncheon for Regional Editors and Broadcasters," June 13, 1986.

53. He pointed out this exception many times in his remarks. Reagan, "Remarks and a Question-and-Answer Session With Area High School Seniors," Jacksonville, FL, December 1, 1987; Reagan, "Interview with Network TV Broadcasters," December 3, 1987. Reagan, *An American Life*, pp. 641 and 706–7. This would stand out to Reagan at the 1985 Geneva Summit: "Not once during our private sessions or at the plenary meetings did he [Gorbachev] express support for the old Marxist-Leninist goal of a one-world Communist state or the Brezhnev Doctrine of Soviet expansionism. He was the first Soviet leader I knew of who hadn't done that." In fact, Gorbachev told Reagan directly in the second plenary meeting at Geneva on November 19: "[W]e have no secret plans for world domination." Source: These Gorbachev remarks were made at the 2:30–3:40 P.M. session on November 19. See: "Geneva Meeting: Memcons of Plenary Sessions and Tete-A-Tete," November 19–21, 1985, declassified May 2000, RRL, Box 92137, Folder 2.

   To further gauge Gorbachev on this, in their first session at Reykjavik on October 11, 1986, eleven months after Geneva, Reagan told Gorbachev that every Soviet leader but him—"at least so far"—had expressed the view that "socialism had to be global in scope to succeed," that "the only morality was that which advanced socialism," and had "endorsed in speeches to Soviet Communist Party Congresses the objective of establishing a world communist state." Gorbachev seemed reassured. Source: "Memcons from Reykjavik Summit, October 12 meeting, 10:00 AM–1:35," Box 92140, Folder 3.

54. Reagan, *An American Life*, p. 605.

55. A transcript of the letter is printed in Reagan, *An American Life*, p. 593.

56. At least one of the two questioners was, in the words of Gorbachev's translator, an "infamous" propagandist—the Soviet television commentator and academic Valentin Zorin. Genrikh Trofimenko, the one-time director of Moscow's prestigious Institute for U.S.A. and Canada Studies of the Russian Academy of Sciences, called the notorious Zorin a "faithful follower of Lenin's dictum regarding morality." In Trofimenko's description, that meant Zorin would happily contrive "any" information necessary to discredit what Zorin termed "American warmongers" and to promote the Communist Party's "cause of picturing the United States as an implacable, vicious enemy of the Soviet Union." Trofimenko condemned Zorin's research on the United States as "slander." He said that Zorin was a man who did not speak or read English and a "mini-Goebbels" who had spent his "whole life . . . devoted to piling on the United States heap upon heap of unspeakable dirt and, pardon me, dung." Source: Genrikh Aleksandrovich (Henry) Trofimenko, presentation at 1993 Hofstra University Conference on the Reagan Presidency, published in Eric J. Schmertz et al, eds., *President Reagan and the World* (Westport, CT: Greenwood Press, 1997), p. 144.

57. Reagan, "Interview With Soviet Television Journalists Valentin Zorin and Boris Kalyagin," May 20, 1988. In general, Reagan performed extremely effectively in this interview. Anyone who believes he was a dummy who couldn't hold his own without a script or teleprompter should turn to pp. 665–70 of the 1988 *Presidential Papers* and read more from the transcript of this interview.

CHAPTER 16

1. David Remnick, "Dead Souls," *New York Review of Books*, December 19, 1991, p. 79.

2. The letter from Kmech, as well as Reagan's response, is located in PHF, PR, RRL, Box 5, Folder 68.

3. Ibid.

4. Interview with Thomas McDill, January 31, 2003.

5. See: Reagan, "Message to the Congress Transmitting the Proposed Constitutional Amendment on Prayer in Schools," March 8, 1983.

6. This is clear from Reagan's statements and the testimony of those who knew him.

7. Clark in Schweizer, *Fall of the Berlin Wall*, p. 76.

8. C. S. Lewis, *Mere Christianity* (New York: Simon & Schuster, first Touchstone edition, 1996), p. 44.

9. Reagan said this often. This 1980 quote is taken from: Lou Cannon, "A Vision of America Frozen in Time," *Washington Post*, April 24, 1980, p. A1.

10. See the *Public Presidential Papers of Woodrow Wilson*, including: "Address to Congress," delivered to Joint Session, December 4, 1917, Vol. 17, p. 8403; "Seventh Annual Message to Congress," read (not delivered because of illness) to Congress, December 2, 1919, Vol. 18, p. 8819; *Cablegrams* Vol. 17, p. 8685; "Statements on Russia," Vol. 17, pp. 8589–92; "Note of State Department on Polish Situation," by Secretary of State Bainbridge Colby, August 10, 1920, Vol. 18, pp. 8864–66; and "Note to League of Nations" (Urging International Neutrality Towards Soviet Russia), by Acting Secretary of State Norman H. Davis, January 18, 1921, Vol. 18, p. 8910.

11. FDR said this was a "nice old proverb of the Balkans" that had (he quipped) "the full sanction of the Orthodox Church." It is common knowledge that he allegedly applied it to Stalin during WWII, though I was unable to confirm that. With the help of an archivist at the FDR library, I did locate an example of FDR using it in a press conference on November 17, 1942, in which he applied it to Vichy France. It was a proverb he apparently cited frequently.

12. These remarks were made by FDR in speeches on September 11, 1941, and December 9, 1941, titled "On Maintaining Freedom of the Seas" and "On the Declaration of War with Japan," respectively. I would like to thank Gary Gregg for bringing these remarks to my attention. See: Randall E. Adkins and Gary L. Gregg II, "America Attacked: Presidential Leadership from Pearl Harbor to 9/11," paper prepared for the annual meeting of the Midwest Political Science Association, Chicago, IL, April 3–6, 2003.

13. Henrik Bering, biographer of West German leader Helmut Kohl, describes an incident where Kohl and Reagan both jotted down their favorite president of the twentieth century on separate pieces of paper. When they shared notes, both had written Truman's name. Henrik Bering, *Helmut Kohl: The Man Who Reunited Germany, Rebuilt Europe, and Thwarted the Soviet Empire* (Washington, D.C.: Regnery, 1999), p. 28.

14. Quoted in Alonzo Hamby, *Man of the People: A Life of Harry S. Truman* (New York: Oxford University Press, 1995), pp. 313–14.

15. Quoted in David McCullough, *Truman* (New York: Simon & Schuster, 1992), p. 262.

16. Adlai Stevenson speech to the American Legion Convention at New York's Madison Square Garden, August 27, 1952. Recently published in William Safire, *Lend Me Your Ears: Great Speeches in History* (New York: W.W. Norton, 1997), p. 72.

17. These words are taken from the *Public Presidential Papers* of Kennedy, specifically the volumes for the years 1961 (p. 341) and 1962 (p. 723n). Also see: Walker, Martin, *The*

Cold War and the Making of the Modern World, (London, 1993), p. 132; and Hobsbawm, Eric, *The Age of Extremes: A History of the World, 1914–1991,* (New York: Pantheon Books, 1994), p. 231n.

18. Interview with William P. Clark, August 24, 2001.

19. Interview with Edwin Meese, March 23, 1998.

20. Reagan, "Remarks Following a Meeting with Pope John Paul II in Vatican City," June 7, 1982; and Reagan, "Address Before the Bundestag," Bonn, Federal Republic of Germany, June 9, 1982. While Reagan conceded by 1988 that the USSR had changed, he never modified his pre-Gorbachev opinion. In his 1990 memoirs, he would remind—"and yes, it was an evil empire." Reagan, *An American Life,* p. 703. For another evil reference by Reagan after March 1983, see: Reagan, "Remarks on Signing the Bill of Rights Day and Human Rights Day and Week Proclamation," December 9, 1983.

21. I attempted to contact Dolan on a number of occasions, but he did not return phone calls.

22. This is based upon my personal observations of the edited version of the speech, located at the Reagan Library, PHF, PS, RRL, Box 9, Folder 150.

23. The phrase was mentioned to Dolan by Sven Kraemer, arms control director of the NSC, after Kraemer reviewed a draft of the Evil Empire speech. See: Frank Warner, "New Word Order," *The Morning Call* (Allentown, PA), March 5, 2000, p. A1. Warner's article was an excellent piece of journalism.

    For a copy of the Solzhenitsyn speech, see: Aleksandr Solzhenitsyn, *Aleksandr Solzhenitsyn Speaks to the West* (London: The Bodley Head, 1978); the phrase is used on pp. 37 and 61. He used the word "evil" and the phrase "concentration of evil" or "world evil" at least twice in different speeches in the summer of 1975.

24. Reagan did two radio broadcasts in June 1978 that he titled simply, "Alex. Solzhenitsyn" and "Alex. Solzhenitsyn II." Source: Reagan Library files; and Skinner, Anderson, and Anderson, *Reagan, In His Own Hand,* p. 519.

25. Reagan, "Address to the Roundtable National Affairs Briefing," Dallas, TX, August 22, 1980.

26. Morris, *Dutch,* p. 472.

27. Warner, "New Word Order," p. A1.

28. I have observed these at the Reagan Library. The June 1982 Westminster speech in London is another key example.

29. Pages 14–15 of draft located in PHF, PS, RRL, Box 9, Folder 150. Other observers who emphasized the importance of this change in tense are Dinesh D'Souza and Kurt Ritter in his chapter, "Ronald Reagan," in Halford Ryan, editor, *U.S. Presidents as Orators* (Westport, CT: Greenwood Press, 1995), pp. 330–31.

30. Ibid.

31. Reagan, "Remarks at the Annual Convention of the National Association of Evangelicals," Columbus, OH, March 6, 1984.

32. Dolan said that among the items that most bothered staff were passages on abortion, another issue Reagan never backed down from. See: Cannon, *Role of a Lifetime,* p. 274.

33. On this, see: Warner, "New Word Order," p. A1.

34. Ibid.

35. Ibid.

36. Interview with Ed Meese, March 23, 1998.

37. Anthony Lewis, "Onward Christian Soldiers," *New York Times,* March 10, 1983.

38. The Commager quote has been widely quoted. Among recent sources, see: Charles Krauthammer, "Reluctant Cold Warriors," *Washington Post*, November 12, 1999, p. A35; and Morris, *Dutch*, p. 475.

39. Quoted by Krauthammer, "Reluctant Cold Warriors," p. A35.

40. Editorial, "Reverend Reagan," *The New Republic*, April 4, 1983.

41. See: March 11, 1983 statement from TASS in English, "TASS Criticism," printed in *FBIS*, March 14, 1983, pp. A2–3.

42. Richard Cohen, "Convictions," *Washington Post*, May 26, 1983, p. C1.

43. Tip O'Neill, July 1984 Democratic convention. A Lexus Nexus search yielded only one reference to the quote—a June 8, 1998, column in *Jewish World Review* by columnist Don Feder of the *Boston Herald*. Source for quote: Don Phillips, "O'Neill: Mondale must attack 'cold, mean' Reagan," UPI, July 19, 1984.

44. Morris, *Dutch*, p. 475.

45. Andrew Sullivan, "A Reagan Tribute," *The Sunday Times* (London), February 4, 2001.

46. Letter is located in PHF, PR, RRL, Box 6, Folder 78.

47. William F. Buckley, Jr., "Reagan at Orlando," *National Review*, April 15, 1983.

48. "Moscow Terms Speech 'Bellicose,' " *Facts on File*, March 1983, p. 164.

49. "Rhetoric from the Cold War Era," *Pravda*, March 10, 1983, p. 5. Printed in *The Current Digest of the Soviet Press*, April 6, 1983, pp. 19–20.

50. Manki Ponomarev, "The United States: Policy with No Future," *Krasnaya Zvezda*, March 8, 1987, p. 3, reprinted as "Army Paper on Links Between Reagan, 'Truman Doctrine,' " in *FBIS*, March 13, 1987, pp. A6-8.

51. See: March 9, 1983, statement from TASS in English, "Reagan Orlando Speech Reflects U.S. 'Militarism,' " printed in *FBIS*, March 10, 1983, pp. A1-2.

52. See: March 11, 1983, statement from TASS in English, "TASS Criticism," printed in *FBIS*, March 14, 1983, pp. A2-3.

53. See: March 13, 1983, transcript from Moscow Domestic Television Service, "Gerasimov Denunciation," printed in *FBIS*, March 14, 1983, p. A2.

54. Ibid.

55. Commentary by Eduard Grigoryev, November 7, 1983. Transcript published as "U.S. 'Evil Will' Seen Wrecking Seventies Accords," in *FBIS*, FBIS-8-NOV-83, November 8, 1983, pp. A4-5.

56. G. Arbatov, "The U.S.—Will There Be Changes?" *Pravda*, March 17, 1983. Printed in "Arbatov Assails US 'Propaganda Tricks,' " *The Current Digest of the Soviet Press*, Vol. 35, No. 11, April 13, 1983, p. 4.

57. Wurmbrand wrote this in a February 1, 1984, letter. The letter is located at the Reagan Library, filed in a box marked, WHORM, Alpha File, Wf-Wz, Box 41, Location 027/08/01, Folder "Wurmbrand, Richard."

58. Reagan, "Interview with Lou Cannon, David Hoffman, and Juan Williams of the *Washington Post* on Foreign and Domestic Issues," January 16, 1984.

59. Reagan, "The President's News Conference," June 14, 1984.

60. Reagan, "Interview with Foreign Broadcasters on the Upcoming Soviet–United States Summit Meeting in Geneva," November 12, 1985.

61. Matlock interviewed for CNN documentary, *The Reagan Years: The Great Communicator*, Pt. II of series, CNN, aired February 25, 2001.

62. See: "A Message to Moscow," *Time*, February 9, 1981.

63. Here is just a sample of the many examples: "On Reagan's Address," *Pravda* and *Izvestia*, September 26, 1984, pp. 5 and 4, printed in "At UN, Gromyko Repeats Hardline

on US,' " *The Current Digest of the Soviet Press*, Vol. 36, No. 39, October 24, 1984, p. 6; T. Kolesnichenko, "In a Web of Stereotypes—Washington's Imperial Ambitions," *Pravda*, March 27, 1986, p. 4, printed in "Has Washington Lost 'Spirit of Geneva?' " *The Current Digest of the Soviet Press*, Vol. 38, No. 13, April 30, 1986, p. 1; Manki Ponomarev, "The United States: Policy With No Future," *Krasnaya Zvezda*, March 8, 1987, p. 3, reprinted as "Army Paper on Links Between Reagan, 'Truman Doctrine,' " in *FBIS*, March 13, 1987, pp. A6-8; Gennady Vasilyev, "Of 'Demons' and the President," *Pravda*, April 29, 1988, p. 6, reprinted as "Reagan Remarks, U.S. Rights Record Condemned," in *FBIS*, FBIS-SOV-88-085, May 3, 1988, pp. 5–7; Aleksandr Bovin, "International Panorama" program, *Moscow Television Service*, May 22, 1988, translated and printed as "Senate 'Dragging Its Feet,' " in *FBIS*, FBIS-SOV-88-099, May 23, 1988, pp. 27–28; Aleksandr Bovin, "After the Third, Before the Fourth," *Izvestia*, May 28, 1988, p. 6, reprinted as "Bovin on 'Political Tact,' " in *FBIS*, FBIS-SOV-88-104, May 31, 1988, pp. 21–22; Vitaliy Kobysh, "What Are the Visitors Bringing With Them?" *Izvestia*, May 29, 1988, p. 5, reprinted as "Reagan Seen as 'Insincere,' " in *FBIS*, FBIS-SOV-88-104, May 31, 1988, p. 2; and Stanislav Kondrashov, "On Ronald Reagan and Other Matters," *Izvestia*, January 19, 1989, p. 5, printed in "Did USSR and US Grow More Alike During Reagan Years?" " *The Current Digest of the Soviet Press*, Vol. 41, No. 3, February 15, 1989, p. 4. For five added examples from early June 1988 alone, see translated texts from Soviet media printed in *FBIS*, FBIS-SOV-88-110, June 8, 1988, pp. 16–19 and FBIS-SOV-88-111, June 9, 1988, pp. 20–21.

64. John Lewis Gaddis, "The Tragedy of Cold War History," *Foreign Affairs*, January/February 1994, Vol. 73, No. 1, p. 148.

65. Kozyrev on ABC News, *This Week With David Brinkley*, August 25, 1991. From ABC News, Brinkley transcript #513, p. 7.

66. Trofimenko in earlier cited Hofstra collection, p. 136.

67. Tarasenko said this during a February 25–27, 1993, conference at Princeton. See: Wohlforth, ed., *Witnesses to the End of the Cold War*, p. 20.

68. Michael Novak, "The Return of 'Good' and 'Evil,' " *Wall Street Journal*, February 7, 2002.

69. Morris interviewed by Lesley Stahl, *60 Minutes*, CBS, September 26, 1999.

70. Morris quoted in "Reagan and History," *National Review*, May 24, 1993, p. 20.

71. Morris, *Dutch*, p. 474.

72. David Remnick, "Dead Souls," *The New York Review of Books*, December 19, 1991, p. 79.

73. Interview with Alexander Donskiy.

74. Ibid.

75. Ibid.

76. Interview with Olena Doviskaya.

77. By the time of the March 1983 speech, Bukovsky had been released to the West. He was frequently consulted by Reagan speechwriters, including Dolan, Mark Palmer (State Department), and John Lenczowski (NSC). Interview with Vladimir Bukovsky, March 5, 2003.

78. Jack F. Matlock Jr., *Autopsy on an Empire* (New York: Random House, 1995), p. 589.

79. Remarks of James Billington, presentation at Grove City College, September 27, 2001; and Billington, "The Foreign Policy of President Ronald Reagan," text of address at the International Republican Institute Freedom Dinner, September 25, 1997, Washington, D.C., pp. 2 and 4.

80. Billington, "The Foreign Policy of President Ronald Reagan," p. 4.

81. George Weigel, *The Final Revolution* (New York: Oxford University Press, 1992), p. 22.

82. Jan Winiecki, "Poland Under Communism," presentation at Grove City College, March 6, 2002.

83. Sharansky is quoted in Noonan, *When Character Was King*, pp. 213–14.

84. Quoted by Lawrence F. Kaplan, "We're All Cold Warriors Now," *Wall Street Journal*, January 18, 2000; and Krauthammer, "Reluctant Cold Warriors," p. A35.

85. Alonzo Hamby, "the Liberal Tradition in American Politics," address at the Salvatori Fellowship conference, "American Politics and the Future of Constitutional Government," the Heritage Foundation, Washington, D.C., June 16, 2000.

86. Alonzo Hamby, *Liberalism and Its Challengers: FDR to Reagan* (New York: Oxford University Press, 1985), p. 372.

87. Wills, *Reagan's America: Innocents at Home*, p. xviii.

88. Ibid.

89. Ibid.

90. Reagan, "Remarks at the Annual Convention of the National Association of Evangelicals in Orlando, Florida, March 8, 1983," Presidential Papers, Vol. 1, 1983, p. 362.

91. On Reagan and the phenomenology of evil, see: Hamby, *Liberalism and Its Challengers*, p. 374.

92. Reagan, "Remarks at a Conference on Religious Liberty," April 16, 1985.

93. Reagan, *Speaking My Mind*, pp. 168–69.

94. Cannon, *Role of a Lifetime*, p. 274, based on an interview with Bud McFarlane, January 16, 1990.

95. Reagan, *Speaking My Mind*, p. 108.

96. Reagan, "Interview with Henry Brandon of the *London Sunday Times* and New Service on Domestic and Foreign Policy Issues," March 18, 1983.

97. Reagan, *An American Life*, pp. 569–70.

98. Ibid.

99. I will cover this at length in a forthcoming work.

100. Regan, *For the Record*, p. 294.

101. Anthony R. Dolan, "Premeditated Prose: Reagan's Evil Empire," *The American Enterprise*, March/April 1993, pp. 24–26.

102. Interview with William P. Clark, August 24, 2001.

103. Dolan, "Premeditated Prose: Reagan's Evil Empire," pp. 24–26.

104. Reagan, "Remarks at a Fundraising Dinner for Senator Paula Hawkins," Miami, FL, May 27, 1985.

105. For another presidential example, see: Reagan, "Remarks at a Fundraising Luncheon for Senator Don Nickles," Oklahoma City, OK, June 5, 1985.

106. Reagan, "Remarks at the Annual Convention of the National Association of Evangelicals," Orlando, FL, March 8, 1983.

107. George Will speaking on "Reagan," *The American Experience*.

108. In doing this, Meese argues, Reagan "gave hope" to some of the captive nations that "this was a president who was accurately assessing the nature of Soviet imperialism." Ed Meese, "America at the Crossroads," address to Grove City College, May 23, 1998.

109. Hamby, *Liberalism and Its Challengers*, p. 374.

110. There is another similar strand at work in Bloom's analysis, cut from much the same cloth as moral relativism and moral equivalency—cultural relativism and cultural equivalency. Allan Bloom, *The Closing of the American Mind* (New York: Simon & Schuster, 1987), pp. 141–2.

111. Steven Merritt Miner, "The Soviet Union's Endless Paper Trail of Evil Comes to Light," *Los Angeles Times*, March 15, 1992, p. M2.
112. Reagan, "Address to 1992 Republican Convention," August 17, 1992.

CHAPTER 17

1. Reagan, "Remarks on Signing the Bill of Rights Day and Human Rights Day and Week Proclamation," December 9, 1983.
2. Reagan, "Remarks at the Annual Convention of the National Religious Broadcasters," January 30, 1984.
3. Source: Interview with William P. Clark, August 24, 2001. The date was November 10, 1982.
4. Wills also added that Reagan believed that *his* "God likes all Americans except those who ever criticize America" and that the president's God "does not like all Americans equally." This God "prefers the rich, whose prosperity is a sign of his favor." This God "likes those who encourage wars." Moreover, the "most favored man of this God, during the last year, was Oliver North." Assertions demand evidence. I've read literally thousands of Reagan remarks about God. I've never read one that serves as evidence for even one of these Wills charges. Nor have I interviewed a Reagan adviser or intimate who even partly agrees with the charges. Source: Wills, "Faith and the Hopfuls," p. 15.
5. See: Reagan, "State of the Union Address," January 25, 1984. He said this again five days later at the National Religious Broadcasters Convention. See: Reagan, "Remarks at the Annual Convention of the National Religious Broadcasters," January 30, 1984.
6. Vladimir Simonov, "Political Portrait of Ronald Reagan," *Literaturnaya Gazeta*, May 25, 1988, p. 14, printed as "Weekly Presents 'Political Portrait' of Reagan," in *FBIS*, FBIS-SOV-88-102, May 26, 1988, p. 11.
7. Vitaliy Korionov, "Production Line of Crimes and Hypocrisy," *Pravda*, January 10, 1984, p. 4, printed as " 'Unprecedented Wave' of Lies Seen in U.S.," in *FBIS*, FBIS-13-JAN-84, January 13, 1984, p. A1.
8. Reagan, "Remarks at the Annual Convention of the National Religious Broadcasters," Columbus, OH, January 30, 1984.
9. Reagan, "Remarks at the Centennial Meeting of the Supreme Council of the Knights of Columbus," Hartford, CT, August 3, 1982.
10. Reagan, "Remarks on Signing the Bill of Rights Day and Human Rights Day and Week Proclamation," December 9, 1983.
11. Reagan's letter is dated December 18, 1984. Located in PHF, PR, RRL, Box 11, Folder 154.
12. Reagan, "Remarks to Chinese Community Leaders," Beijing, China, April 27, 1984.
13. Reagan, "Remarks at Fudan University," Shanghai, China, April 30, 1984.
14. Reagan, "Question-and-Answer Session With Reporters on the Trip to China," May 1, 1984.
15. Reagan, "Remarks at a Welcoming Ceremony for Pope John Paul II," Fairbanks, AK, May 2, 1984.
16. Reagan inserted this into a November 12 draft of his November 14 address. Draft located in PHF, PS, RRL, Box 21, Folders 404 and 405.
17. Reagan, "Message on the Observance of Orthodox Christmas," January 6, 1986.

18. This is discussed in chapter 2. The letter is excerpted in Wills, *Reagan's America*, p. 29.
19. Here are some other examples: Reagan, "Remarks Following Discussions with Pope John Paul II," Vatican City, June 6, 1987; and Reagan, *An American Life*, p. 709. He said the same at the National Association of Evangelicals meetings on both March 8, 1983, and March 6, 1984.
20. Reagan, "Remarks at the Annual Convention of the National Religious Broadcasters," January 31, 1985.
21. Reagan, "Remarks at the Annual National Prayer Breakfast," February 4, 1988.
22. Reagan, "Remarks to Participants in the Yale University–Moscow State University Exchange Project," October 3, 1988.
23. This Reagan point regarding the Soviet people was made to me in interviews with Allen, Clark, and Elliott. All three men mentioned this without my asking. Quotes taken from: Reagan, "Remarks Upon Returning from the Soviet–United States Summit Meeting in Moscow," June 3, 1988; and Reagan, "Remarks and a Question-and-Answer Session at a Luncheon with Radio and Television Journalists," June 8, 1988.
24. William P. Clark, "President Reagan and the Wall," Address to the Council of National Policy, San Francisco, CA, March 2000, p. 10. Clark says the prayer is called the Universal Peace Prayer of Francis.
25. Wurmbrand wrote this in a September 30, 1983, letter located at the Reagan Library, filed in a box marked, WHORM, Alpha File, Wf-Wz, Box 41, Location 027/08/01, Folder "Wurmbrand, Richard."

CHAPTER 18

1. Igor Korchilov, *Translating History: Thirty Years on the Front Lines of Diplomacy with a Top Russian Interpreter* (New York: Scribner, 1997), p. 158.
2. Morris speaking in interview on "Reagan," *The American Experience*.
3. Reagan, "Remarks at a White House Briefing on Religious Freedom in the Soviet Union," May 3, 1988.
4. Interview with Richard V. Allen, November 12, 2001.
5. Interview with George P. Shultz, July 15, 2003, in Palo Alto, CA at Stanford University.
6. Interview with Ben Elliott, September 20, 2001.
7. Morris speaking in interview on "Reagan," *The American Experience*.
8. Reagan wrote this in a July 9, 1981, letter to John O. Koehler of New York, New York. The letter is published in Skinner, Anderson, and Anderson, *Reagan: A Life in Letters*, p. 375.
9. Reagan said this in a February 15, 1984, letter to Suzanne Massie of Irvington, NY. Ibid, p. 379.
10. Some of those interviewed for this book seemed uncomfortable endorsing the use of words like "missionary" and "crusade" concerning Reagan's actions in May–June 1988. That reticence is understandable. Yet, Reagan himself often used the word "crusade" when discussing his goals or intentions with Soviet communism.

    For their part, the Soviets frequently spoke or wrote of Reagan's "crusade" against communism, often in articles focused on his religious motivations, words, or actions. I'm not exaggerating in reporting that the Soviet media used the word "crusade" hundreds of times. Some examples were seen earlier. Here are two more: Manki Ponomarev, "The United States: Policy with No Future," *Krasnaya Zvezda*, March 8, 1987, p. 3, reprinted as "Army Paper on Links Between Reagan, 'Truman Doctrine,' " in *FBIS*, March 13, 1987, pp. A6–8.

11. Reagan, "Remarks at the Annual Convention of the National Religious Broadcasters," January 31, 1983.

12. Ibid.

13. Ibid.

14. Interview with George P. Shultz, July 15, 2003.

15. Ibid.

16. Reagan, *An American Life*, p. 558.

17. Ibid; and interview with Shultz.

18. On this, see: Shultz private letter to Reagan, July 18, 1983, located in PHF, PR, RRL, Box 7, Folder 90; George P. Shultz, *Turmoil and Triumph* (New York: Scribners, 1993), pp. 164–65; Shultz speaking on "Reagan," *The American Experience*; Reagan, *An American Life*, p. 558; interview with Shultz; and Anatoly Dobrynin, *In Confidence* (New York: Random House, 1995), pp. 517–21.

19. Interview with George P. Shultz, July 15, 2003.

20. Reagan, *An American Life*, p. 572.

21. Thompson interview with Frank Carlucci, "The Reagan Presidency," *Miller Center Journal*, Vol. 2, Spring 1995, p. 43. See also: Fred Barnes, "In the Evil Empire," *The New Republic*, June 20, 1988, pp. 8–9.

22. Aleksandr Bovin, "Geneva Motifs," *Izvestia*, October 13, 1985, p. 5, printed as "Bovin on Prospects for Geneva Summit," in *FBIS*, FBIS-15-OCT-85, October 15, 1985, p. A2.

23. G. Arbatov, "Not Just for the Sake of It; On R. Reagan's Speech," *Pravda*, November 21, 1986, p. 4, printed as "Arbatov Rebuttal to 18 Nov Reagan Speech," in *FBIS*, FBIS, November 21, 1986, p. A6.

24. Reagan, "New Year's Radio Address to the People of the Soviet Union," December 31, 1986.

25. This will be seen in the May 1988 summit in Moscow.

26. Ibid.

27. Ibid.

28. Reagan would lecture Gorbachev on this matter at each summit.

29. Reagan, "Remarks at a Luncheon Hosted by the Heritage Foundation," November 30, 1987.

30. Editorial, "Fostering Committed Atheists," *Pravda*, September 28, 1986, p. 1, printed as "Pravda Editorial on 'Struggle' Against Religion," in *FBIS*, FBIS-17-OCT-86, October 17, 1986, pp. R4–5.

31. Reagan, "Remarks and a Question-and-Answer Session With Area High School Seniors," Jacksonville, FL, December 1, 1987.

32. Graham wrote other letters to Reagan on religion in the USSR, including April 29, 1988 and April 26, 1982. Letters are located in PHF, PR, RRL, Boxes 2, 19, and 20, Folders 35, 312, and 327A.

33. Reagan, "Remarks with Area High School Seniors," Jacksonville, FL, p. 1405.

34. Reagan quoted this in the first term of his presidency, but remembered it throughout. See: Reagan, "Remarks at the Annual Convention of the National Religious Broadcasters," January 31, 1983.

35. Muggeridge March 1983 letter, located in PHF, PR, RRL, Box 6, Folder 78.

36. Morris, *Dutch*, p. 519.

37. Reagan, "Remarks at a White House Briefing on Religious Freedom in the Soviet Union," May 3, 1988.

38. Ibid.

39. "1988 US-Soviet Summit Memcons," May 26–June 3, 1988, RRL, Box 92084, Folder 2.

40. TASS political observer Anatoly Krasikov, May 3, 1988 statement, printed as "U.S. Resolution on Religious Repression Viewed," in FBIS, FBIS-SOV-88-086, May 4, 1988, pp. 4–5.

41. Reagan, "Remarks and a Question-and-Answer Session With Members of the National Strategy Forum," Chicago, IL, May 4, 1988.

42. Reagan, "Remarks on Departure for the Soviet–United States Summit in Moscow," May 25, 1988.

43. Reagan, "Remarks to the Paasikivi Society and the League of Finnish-American Societies," Helsinki, Finland, May 27, 1988.

44. For examples from May 27–29, see the four articles reprinted as "Reagan Pre-Summit Activity in Helsinki Reported," in FBIS, FBIS-SOV-88-104, May 31, 1988, pp. 1–4. An added example, a very strong one, was published on the front page of Pravda on May 31. See: T. Kolesnichenko, A. Lyutyy, and N. Prozhogin, "Dialogue Continues," Pravda, May 31, 1988, pp. 1–2, printed as "Reagan 'Platitudes' on Rights Deplored," in FBIS, FBIS-SOV-88-106, June 2, 1988, pp. 50–51. A few weeks before these, there were more, including TASS statements. See: Gennady Vasilyev, "Of 'Demons' and the President," Pravda, April 29, 1988, p. 6, reprinted as "Reagan Remarks, U.S. Rights Record Condemned," in FBIS, FBIS-SOV-88-085, May 3, 1988, pp. 5–7; Statement by TASS in English, printed as "Reagan Remarks on Human Rights, Religion Reviewed: Chicago Speech Assailed," in FBIS, FBIS-SOV-88-087, May 4, 1988, pp. 10–11; Statement by TASS in English, printed as "Reagan Remarks on Human Rights, Religion Reviewed: Speaks to Churchmen," in FBIS, FBIS-SOV-88-087, May 4, 1988, p. 11; and Statement by TASS political analyst Natoliy Krasikov, printed as "U.S. Resolution on Religion in Ukraine Noted," in FBIS, FBIS-SOV-88-088, May 6, 1988, pp. 18–19

45. Vitaliy Kobysh, "What Are the Visitors Bringing with Them?" Izvestia, May 29, 1988, p. 5, reprinted as "Reagan Seen as 'Insincere,' " in FBIS, FBIS-SOV-88-104, May 31, 1988, p. 2.

46. Statement of Moscow news agency TASS in English, May 29, 1988, printed as "Patriarch Prays for 'Success' of Summit," in FBIS, FBIS-SOV-88-104, May 31, 1988, p. 20.

47. For details in this section, I'm deeply grateful to the record keeping of Igor Korchilov, who was there. See: Korchilov, Translating History, pp. 145–55.

48. The details from this section (including the paragraphs that follow) were drawn from a number of sources, from James Billington to Igor Korchilov to records at the Reagan Library, as well as reports in the New York Times and Washington Post. Among them, Korchilov's book was most helpful. Also especially helpful was: Public Papers of the Presidents of the United States: Ronald Reagan, 1988, pp. 672–715.

49. Korchilov, Translating History, p. 155.

50. Source: "1988 US-Soviet Summit Memcons," May 26–June 3, 1988, RRL, Box 92084, Folder 2. This is the memorandum of conversation (formal notes transcribed by the official note-taker) from the first Reagan-Gorbachev one-on-one meeting, May 29, 1988.

51. "1988 US-Soviet Summit Memcons," May 26–June 3, 1988, RRL, Box 92084, Folder 2.

52. Reagan, "Toast at a Dinner Hosted by Soviet General Secretary Mikhail Gorbachev," December 9, 1987.

53. Reagan, "Remarks to Religious Leaders at the Danilov Monastery in Moscow," May 30, 1988.

54. Ibid.

55. Ibid.

56. Ibid.

57. "Filaret Regrets Reagan Remarks," *Argumenty I Fakty*, June 4–10, 1988, No. 23, p. 3, translated text from Soviet media printed in FBIS, FBIS-SOV-88-108, June 6, 1988, pp. 16–19 and FBIS-SOV-88-111, June 9, 1988, pp. 23–24.

58. See: S. Dardykin, "Who Was Invited to Spaso House?" *Izvestia*, June 1, p. 5, published in the *Current Digest of the Soviet Press*, June 29, 1988, Vol. XL, No. 22, p. 1; and T. Kolesnichenko, A. Lyutyy, and N. Prozhogin, "Dialogue Continues," *Pravda*, May 31, 1988, pp. 1–2, printed as "Reagan 'Platitudes' on Rights Deplored," in FBIS, FBIS-SOV-88-106, June 2, 1988, pp. 50–51.

59. There were, however, a number of believers in the audience and among the invitees.

60. Reagan, "Remarks to Soviet Dissidents at Spaso House in Moscow," May 30, 1988.

61. "1988 US-Soviet Summit Memcons," May 26–June 3, 1988, RRL, Box 92084, Folder 2. According to the American note-taker, Gorbachev responded that the only possible answer to whether there had been a cook had to be "yes." It is not clear from the notes if this was a Gorbachev acknowledgment of a Creator.

62. Korchilov, *Translating History*, p. 162.

63. Memcon notes from Moscow Summit; and Korchilov, *Translating History*, p. 165.

64. Ibid.

65. On this, see especially: Korchilov, *Translating History*, p. 172.

66. Ibid.

67. Reagan, "Remarks and a Question-and-Answer Session With the Students and Faculty at Moscow State University," May 31, 1988.

68. This fact has been relayed to me independently by a number of missionaries to Russia.

69. Reagan later recounted this detail in a September 1990 conservation with Gorbachev. Source: Korchilov, *Translating History*, p. 355.

70. Ibid.

71. Reagan, "Toasts at a State Dinner Hosted by the President at Spaso House in Moscow," May 31, 1988.

72. These examples are provided by Billington, "The Foreign Policy of President Ronald Reagan," p. 9. Nancy Reagan's trip was briefly reported by *Pravda*. See: "Nancy Reagan Visits Moscow Art Gallery," *Pravda*, June 2, 1988, p. 5, translated text from Soviet media printed in FBIS, FBIS-SOV-88-108, June 6, 1988, p. 24.

73. See: Reagan, "Statement at Closing Ceremony for Moscow Summit," June 2, 1988.

74. For examples, see: Morris, *Dutch*, p. 519.

75. Interview with Ed Meese, November 23, 2001.

76. Dinesh D'Souza says that Gorbachev would also invoke the name of Jesus, saying things like "Only Jesus Christ knows the answer to that." D'Souza doesn't cite a source for this reference, and he is the only source I've read that claims that Gorbachev invoked the "J" word. D'Souza, *Ronald Reagan*, p. 187.

77. See: "Geneva Meeting: Memcons of Plenary Sessions and Tete-A-Tete," November 19–21, 1985, declassified May 2000, RRL, Box 92137, Folders 1 and 2; and Morris, *Dutch*, p. 561.

78. See: "Geneva Meeting: Memcons," November 19–21, 1985.

79. Reagan quoted the passage as saying, "we are all of one blood regardless of where we live on Earth." Reagan told the guests "we should never forget that." Ibid.
80. Reagan relayed this in a February 10, 1986, letter to Suzanne Massie of New York, New York. The letter is published in Skinner, Anderson, and Anderson, *Reagan: A Life in Letters*, p. 417.
81. Deaver, *A Different Drummer*, p. 118.
82. Gorbachev, *Memoirs*, p. 457.
83. The point has been raised by D'Souza, Morris, and Cannon. In particular, see: D'Souza, *Ronald Reagan*, p. 187; and Morris, *Dutch*, pp. 561 and 569.
84. Quoted by Dugger, *On Reagan*, p. 516.
85. Larry Speakes, *Speaking Out* (New York: Scribner, 1988), pp. 134–5 and "Geneva Meeting: Memcons," November 19–21, 1985.
86. This fact was relayed by the Gorbachevs themselves in a dinner conversation with the Reagans at Geneva on November 20, 1985. These details are found in "Geneva Meeting: Memcons," November 19–21, 1985.
87. Speakes, *Speaking Out*, pp. 134–35.
88. Nixon's letter was dated December 20, 1985. Filed in PHF, PR, RRL, Box 14, Folder 213.
89. Ibid. This is acknowledged in Reagan's notes; he hand-wrote on the Nixon letter that he called Nixon.
90. See: Tip O'Neill with William Novak, *Man of the House* (New York: Random House, 1987), p. 295; and D'Souza, *Ronald Reagan*, p. 187.
91. Gorbachev, *On My Country and the World*, pp. 20–21, 93, 106, 193, and 268.
92. From earlier, see: Paul Gray and David Ellis, "Gorby, the New Age Guru?" *Time*, June 18, 1990, p. 15.
93. Hedrick Smith, *The New Russians* (New York: Random House, 1990), pp. 395–6.
94. Ibid.
95. Interview with Fred Mueller, March 28, 2001.
96. Reagan, *An American Life*, pp. 705–6.
97. Ibid.
98. Gorbachev, *On My Country and the World*, p. 21.
99. Quoted by Dusko Doder and Louise Branson, *Gorbachev: Heretic in the Kremlin* (New York: Viking, 1990), p. 320.
100. On this and Gorbachev's changes, see Hedrick Smith, *The New Russians*, pp. 395–96.
101. Terry Muck, "Still the Evil Empire?" *Christianity Today*, July 15, 1988, p. 15.
102. After the collapse of the USSR, Anatoly Sharansky moved to Israel, where he became a government official. He changed his name to Natan Sharansky.
103. Sharansky, *Fear No Evil*, pp. vi–x.
104. See: Aleksandr Solzhenitsyn, *One Day in the Life of Ivan Denisovich* (New York: Farrar, Straus, Giroux, 1991 translation), pp. 6–7, 25–27, 45, 52, 102, 109–10, 135, 174–77, and 180–81.
105. Sharansky, *Fear No Evil*, p. 362.
106. Reagan, "Remarks on Signing the Captive Nations Week Proclamation," July 13, 1988.
107. Reagan, "Remarks on Presenting Congressional Gold Medals to Natan and Avital Shcharansky and an Informal Exchange With Reporters," January 11, 1989.

CHAPTER 19

1. Reverend Ben H. Cleaver, Annual Minister's Report, December 31, 1924.
2. Reagan, "Democracy's Next Battle," remarks to the Oxford Union Society, Oxford, England, December 4, 1992, published in Ryan, ed., *Ronald Reagan: The Wisdom and Humor of the Great Communicator*, p. 19.
3. Reagan, "Remarks at the Annual Convention of the National Religious Broadcasters Association," February 1, 1988.
4. Source: Reagan, "Tale of Two Cities," radio broadcast, June 1979. Located in "Ronald Reagan: Pre-Presidential Papers: Selected Radio Broadcasts, 1975–1979," October 31, 1978, to October 1979, Box 4, RRL. For full a transcript, see: Skinner, Anderson, and Anderson, *Reagan, In His Own Hand*, pp. 176–77. He said it again in an August 1980 speech, which he apparently recycled from the radio broadcast. See: Reagan, "Address to the Roundtable National Affairs Briefing," Dallas, Texas, August 22, 1980.
5. Reagan made this request to François Mitterand in a July 7, 1986, letter. The letter is published in Skinner, Anderson, and Anderson, *Reagan: A Life in Letters*, pp. 722–23.
6. Reagan, "Remarks to Royal Institute of International Affairs in London," June 3, 1988. Aside from this occasion and the Evil Empire speech, he also quoted this passage in a December 1982 speech on Poland. See: Reagan, "Remarks on Signing the Human Rights and Day of Prayer for Poland Proclamations," December 10, 1982.
7. Reverend Ben H. Cleaver, Annual Minister's Reports, 1923, 1926, and 1927.
8. Reagan, "Remarks to Royal Institute of International Affairs in London," June 3, 1988.
9. Ibid.
10. This was a point he made often, frequently citing Churchill. For an example of him saying this in 1975, see: Hobbs, *Ronald Reagan's Call to Action*, pp. 50–51. In the 1975 case, he quoted Churchill from memory.
11. Reagan, "Remarks to Royal Institute of International Affairs in London," June 3, 1988.
12. Reagan, "Acceptance Speech at Republican National Convention," July 17, 1980.
13. This was nearly a century-long struggle that ran from 1917 to 1991, the birth of the communist state in the USSR to its death.
14. Quoted by John O'Sullivan, "Friends at Court," *National Review*, May 27, 1991, p. 4.
15. Ellingwood, "Ronald Reagan: 'God, Home and Country,' " p. 25; and Rose, "The Reagans and Their Pastor," p. 44.
16. Reagan, "Speech at Indiana State Fairgrounds," Indianapolis, IN, June 13, 1968. Speech filed at Reagan Library, "RWR—Speeches and Articles (1968)," vertical files.
17. Reagan, "Second Inaugural Address," January 21, 1985.
18. Coincidentally, William Woods is located in Fulton, MO, where another fierce opponent of Bolshevism, Winston Churchill, came to tell Americans in 1945 that it was time they pick up the mantle and resist the Soviets and the "indefinite expansion of their power and doctrines."
19. Reagan, "Democracy's Next Battle," remarks to Oxford Union Society, Oxford, England.

EPILOGUE

1. Reagan, "Address at the Republican Convention," August 17, 1992.
2. These dates include September 30, 1983, October 9, 1984, November 1, 1984, November 8, 1985, November 5, 1988, among others.

3. Reagan, "Proclamation 5900– National Alzheimer's Disease Month, 1988," November 5, 1988.
4. The letter from Bessie is dated only 1960. It, too, was sent to Sieffert.
5. Interview with Michael Reagan.
6. Ibid.
7. Reagan wrote this in a November 23, 1982, letter to Victor Honig of Palm Springs, CA. The letter is published in Skinner, Anderson, and Anderson, *Reagan: A Life in Letters*, p. 105. For another example of this Reagan sentiment, see his July 17, 1984, letter to Paul F. Bollinger, Jr. in ibid, p. 279.
8. These are excerpts; the full poem is roughly twice this length. The poem was printed by *Time* magazine in its January 5, 1981 issue marking Reagan as its Man of the Year and by Norman E. Wymbs, *A Place to Go Back to, Ronald Reagan in Dixon, Illinois* (New York: Vantage Press, 1987), pp. 69–70.
9. This story was told to me in an interview with Peter Robinson, September 18, 2001. Reagan expressed the same sentiment in a February 1978 radio broadcast. See Reagan, "Life and Death," radio broadcast, February 20, 1978. Located in "Ronald Reagan: Pre-Presidential Papers: Selected Radio Broadcasts, 1975–1979," October 1977 to October 10, 1978, Box 3, RRL. A transcript is published by Skinner, Anderson, and Anderson, *Reagan, In His Own Hand*, pp. 3–5.
10. The letter from Reagan is dated November 7, 1962, and was mailed from his Pacific Palisades office. It was sent to Mary Joan Roll-Sieffert, president of the Pittsburgh chapter of Reagan's Hollywood fan club.

AFTERWORD

1. Patti Davis recorded these details in a piece for *People* magazine. Ron Reagan said his dad's eyes had not opened for three days. Source: Larry King interview with Ron Reagan, CNN, June 26, 2004.
2. Larry King interview with Ron Reagan.
3. Arthur Spiegelman, "Ex-President Reagan Dies After Alzheimer's Ordeal," Associated Press, June 5, 2004.
4. Dr. Gary Small interviewed by Paula Zahn on CNN, June 13, 2004.
5. Statement from Michael Reagan Regarding his Father's Passing, June 5, 2004.
6. Statement from Judge William Clark Regarding Ronald Reagan's Passing, June 5, 2004.
7. Curtis Lawrence, "McCarthy took bullet for Reagan," *Chicago Sun-Times*, June 6, 2004.
8. Statement from President George W. Bush on Ronald Reagan's Passing, June 5, 2004.
9. Quoted in Ted Anthony, "U.S. and the World Mourn Reagan's Death," Associated Press, June 5, 2004. Statements were also posted on the website of the Reagan Library and Foundation.
10. David E. Hoffman, "Hastening an End to the Cold War," *Washington Post*, June 6, 2004.
11. Russert interviewed by Chris Jansing, MSNBC, June 6, 2004.
12. Gorbachev letter was posted at the website of the Reagan Library and Museum.
13. Vladimir Isachenkov and Jim Heintz, "Reagan Mourned in Former 'Evil Empire,'" *Moscow Times*, June 7, 2004.
14. Statement from Dr. Billy Graham on the death of Ronald Reagan, June 5, 2004.
15. D. James Kennedy shared this account with his radio listeners and mass email recipients, June 9, 2004.

16. Christie L. Chicoine, "Remembering Reagan's presence in Philadelphia," *The Catholic Standard & Times*, June 16, 2004.

17. Natan Sharansky's tribute in the June 7, 2004 edition of the *Jerusalem Post*.

18. Henri E. Cauvin, "President Offered in '83 To Meet With Hinckley," *Washington Post*, June 12, 2004.

19. Published by FBIS as "Romanian Daily Praises Reagan Role in Ending Cold War, Rejects Anti-US Attitude."

20. Published by FBIS as "Romania's Iliescu Pays Tribute to President Reagan as 'Defender of Democracy.' "

21. Juri Estam, "Ronald Reagan: the late 'President of Eastern Europe,' " *These Tides*, July 2004.

22. Bloomberg news service, "Germany's CDU Wants Ronald Reagan Square in Berlin, Bild Says," June 8, 2004.

23. Published by FBIS as "Czech President, Predecessor Express Sadness at Death of Former US President."

24. "Where's the Rest of Him?" *Budapest Business Journal*, June 14, 2004.

25. "Thank You, President Reagan, From A Grateful Hungarian," *Budapest Business Journal*, June 14, 2004.

26. "Russian Envoy Says Reagan Played Important Part in Washington-Moscow Relations," ITAR-TASS, June 7, 2004.

27. Vladimir Isachenkov and Jim Heintz, "Reagan Mourned in Former 'Evil Empire,' " *Moscow Times*, June 7, 2004.

28. David R. Hoffman, "The Illusory Praise," *Pravda*, June 15, 2004.

29. Christopher Hitchens, "Not Even a Hedgehog: The Stupidity of Ronald Reagan," *Slate.com*, June 7, 2004.

30. Steve Miller, "Political Cartoonist Defends Anti-Reagan Web Tirade," *Washington Times*, June 9, 2004.

31. Colin Powell interviewed by Chris Wallace on Fox News Sunday, June 13, 2004.

32. Angela Green, "Heights Pays Tribute to Reagan," *Peoria Journal-Star*, June 17, 2004.

33. David Holsted, "Blagojevich, Calling Himself a Reagan Democrat, Praises Great Communicator," *Dixon Telegraph*, June 11, 2004.

34. Clark Kelly, "Leadership Credited to Faith," *Dixon Telegraph*, June 11, 2004.

35. Colleen Cason, "Small-town Boyhood Shaped," *Chicago Sun-Times*, June 6, 2004.

36. Donna Newman, "Admirers Remember Reagan's Charisma, Caring," *Dixon Telegraph*, June 11, 2004.

37. Sources: Annie Shuppy, "State Center Serviceman Carrying Reagan's Casket During Ceremonies," *Des Moines Register*, June 11, 2004; and Dori Minert, "Duo Worked Reagan Funeral," *Peoria Journal Star*, June 16, 2004.

38. Gillian Flaccus, "Immigrants from Former Soviet Union Mourn Reagan," *Associated Press*, June 9, 2004.

39. Ibid.

40. Ibid.

41. Ibid.

42. Nancy Benac, "Nancy Reagan Visits Ronald Reagan's Casket," Associated Press, June 11, 2004; and "100,000 File Past Reagan's casket," CNN.com, June 9, 2004.

43. Edward Epstein, "A Historic Tribute, a Solemn Farewell," *San Francisco Chronicle*, June 10, 2004.

44. Nancy Benac, "Nancy Reagan Visits Ronald Reagan's Casket."

45. Vice President Dick Cheney, "Remarks at the State Funeral of Ronald W. Reagan," Washington, D.C. U.S. Capitol Rotunda, June 9, 2004.
46. Nancy Benac, "Nancy Reagan Visits Ronald Reagan's Casket."
47. See: David Von Drehle, "Reagan Hailed as Leader for 'the Ages,' " *Washington Post*, June 12, 2004.
48. Ron was asked about this in his June 26 interview with Larry King. "And you're an atheist," said King. "So you don't think he's going anywhere." Ron Reagan replied: "He's returning to life itself, I suppose."

INDEX OF NAMES

BOOKS BY PAUL KENGOR

GOD AND HILLARY CLINTON
A Spiritual Life

ISBN 978-0-06-118925-8 (paperback)

For nearly three decades, political observers have sought to understand the complex relationship between Hillary Clinton's faith and her politics. Now, acclaimed historian Paul Kengor sets out to answer the elusive question: What does Hillary Clinton believe?

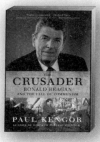

THE CRUSADER
Ronald Reagan and the Fall of Communism

ISBN 978-0-06-118924-1 (paperback)

Based on extraordinary research: a major reassessment of Ronald Reagan's lifelong crusade to dismantle the Soviet Empire—including shocking revelations about the liberal American politician who tried to collude with the USSR to counter Reagan's efforts.

GOD AND GEORGE W. BUSH
A Spiritual Life

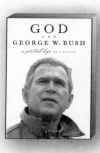

ISBN 978-0-06-077956-6 (paperback)

George W. Bush has brought the question of religion back into American political life in a way that it has not been for decades. Bush's personal faith—and his conviction about the importance of religion in our national life—have won him lasting admiration from the right, while attracting fury and scorn from the left.

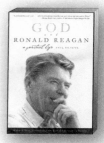

GOD AND RONALD REAGAN
A Spiritual Life

ISBN 978-0-06-057142-9 (paperback)

Reagan is hailed today for a presidency that helped bring about the fall of the Soviet Union. Until now, little attention has been paid to the role Reagan's personal spirituality played in his political career, shaping his ideas, bolstering his resolve, and ultimately compelling him to confront the brutal—and, not coincidentally, atheistic—Soviet empire.